ISAAC D'ISRAELI
ON BOOKS

Isaac D'Israeli, after John Downman, ARA (1805)
Hughenden Manor (The National Trust)

ISAAC D'ISRAELI ON BOOKS

Pre-Victorian Essays on the
History of Literature

SELECTED AND EDITED BY
MARVIN SPEVACK

THE BRITISH LIBRARY
AND
OAK KNOLL PRESS

© 2004 Marvin Spevack

First published 2004 by
The British Library
96 Euston Road
London NW1 2DB
and
Oak Knoll Press
310 Delaware Street
New Castle
DE 19720

Cataloguing-in-Publication Data
is available from both The British Library
and the Library of Congress

ISBN 0–7123–4829–8 (BL)
ISBN 1–58456–131–9 (OKP)

Printed in England by Antony Rowe Ltd

CONTENTS

IV. AUTHORS & CO.

V. PRESERVATION AND DESTRUCTION

VI. PROPERTY AND POLITICS

VII. LIBRARIES

NOTE

The text and references are based on *The Works of Isaac D'Israeli* (6 vols., 1881), the only edition available in a reprint (Georg Olms Verlag, Hildesheim, 1969). To complement my prefatory remarks I have reprinted as a general introduction to the life and works of D'Israeli the memoir by his son Benjamin. To assist the reader and to give an overview of the extraordinary scope of D'Israeli's literary pursuits, as well as a graphic illustration of the background a popular author of the time might expect of his reading public, I have added in a Directory of Personal Names (with page references) some brief information about the thousand or so persons he mentions (including household biblical and legendary ones but not the unwieldy catalogue in n. 76). D'Israeli's spellings can be idiosyncratic, however, and the indexing of Roman, French, and Italian names can be problematic. In such cases, the directory gives D'Israeli's spelling, followed by a variant or standard spelling (in parenthesis), as normally found in such leading reference works as the *Dictionary of National Biography*, the *Chambers Biographical Dictionary*, and the extensive national biographical indexes published by K. G. Saur of Munich. D'Israeli is often so casual or cryptic in his references (e.g. Miss Forrester or Father Paul) or spellings (e.g. Fust is also spelled Faust and Faustus) that identification is often difficult, as it can be when names are Latinized (Raynaudus for Ranaud) or anglicized (Don Matthews for Juan Mateos). It may also have to be speculative: D'Israeli, for example, refers to Fortunius when the context seems to require Venantius Fortunatus. For especially difficult identifications I have had to draw on the expertise of colleagues from many disciplines, whose help it is my pleasure to acknowledge: Horst-Dieter Blume, Piero Boitani, Sanford Budick, Martin Davies, Wolf Dietrich, Bernhard Fabian, Janet Ing Freeman, Heinz Grotzfeld, Philip Harris, Susanne Kramarz-Bein, Klaus Ostheeren, and Marie-Luise Spieckermann. My thanks too to Hella Appenroth and Silke Tandetzki for helping with the inputting of the data, and, again, to Peter Kollenbrandt for transforming all into the shape of a book. Finally, but not final, my debt to Helga Spevack for her engagement and patience is boundless.

PREFACE

Benjamin Disraeli was of the opinion that he was born in a library. The library was that of his father, Isaac D'Israeli. Since it is said to have consisted of some 25,000 volumes, Benjamin may well have been referring not so much to a room as to a house full of books and to the environment it reflects. Although the library began to be dispersed soon after Isaac's death in 1848, it is not difficult to reconstruct it. Less important than its size was its nature. It was not a bibliomaniacal collection, in D'Israeli's words, "an enormous heap of books without intelligent curiosity" or an ornamental one, to be viewed only and "secured from the vulgar hands of the mere reader, dazzling our eyes like eastern beauties peering through their jalousies." It was a personal library into which D'Israeli, after a morning in the library of the British Museum, disappeared daily for hours and hours. It was, above all, a working library. For all their apparent diversity, a considerable number of the 1080 lots constituting the "Considerable Portion of the Valuable Library," which Benjamin put up for sale at Sotheby's over four days from 16 March 1849, found their way through his life into his writings.

Isaac D'Israeli was a bibliophile in the fullest sense of the word. An early illness caused him to withdraw from the active life in business his father wished for him, and a benevolent maternal grandmother provided him with funds to support and pursue his love of books. He not only collected and treasured them; they became his life and his career. He was for all his long life a prolific author of essays, poems, novels, romances, reviews, and literary and historical studies. His collection of essays, *Curiosities of Literature*, first published in 1791 when he was twenty-five but undoubtedly begun in his late teens, spanned his lifetime, reaching three volumes of often revised and ever-expanding topics and a fourteenth edition a year after his death in 1848, followed by numerous popular editions thereafter. It contains 276 essays. Its range and variety are worthy of the appellation "letters." Among the telling titles of the first volume are "Amusements of the Learned" (pp. 38-41), "The Six Follies of Science" (pp. 66-67), "Cicero's Puns" (pp. 69-71), "Spanish Poetry" (pp. 100-102), "Rabbinical Stories" (pp. 120-126), "On the Custom of Saluting after Sneezing" (pp. 126-127), "Characters Described in Musical Notes" (pp. 150-151), "Dethroned Monarchs" (pp. 183-187), "Metempsychosis" (pp. 192-194), "Wax-Work" (pp. 206-208), "Jocular Preachers" (pp. 251-258), "Religious Nouvellettes" (pp. 363-370), "Ariosto and Tasso" (pp. 386-391), "A Glance into the French Academy" (pp. 413-417), "Philip and Mary" (pp. 469-471). The essays in the second and third volumes tend to be longer and stress D'Israeli's perennial interest in literature and history and an ever-widening attention to socio-political and psychological matters and popular culture, as in "Anecdotes of European Manners" (vol. 2: pp. 30-39), "The Jews of York" (2:75-79), "Popes" (2:83-84), "The Pantomimical Characters" (2:116-130), "Ancient Cookery and Cooks" (2:245-256), "Introduction of Tea, Coffee, and Chocolate" (2:317-326), "Psalm-singing" (2:472-479), "Political Nicknames" (3:80-90), "The Italian Historians" (3:177-186), "Quadrio's Account of English Poetry" (3:233-238), "Royal Proclamations" (3:371-380), "Whether Allowable to Ruin Oneself?" (3:400-408), "Secret History of Charles the First and His First Parliaments" (3:448-481). His *Literary Miscellanies*, which appeared in an enlarged and revised fifth edition in 1840, having been begun some fifty years earlier, further extends the range and variety of his literary subjects. And following such book-length collections as *Literary Character of Men of Genius* (first published in 1795), *Calamities of Authors* (1812), and *Quarrels of Authors* (1814), among other literary critical works, D'Israeli produced *Amenities of Literature*, first published in three volumes in 1841. The culmination of a bibliophilic and literary life, it is perhaps the first popular history of English letters, a chronological panorama in seventy essays, a "history of our vernacular literature [which] has occupied my studies for many years. It was my design," he continues in his preface, "not to furnish an arid narrative of books or of authors, but following the steps of the human mind through the wide track of Time, to trace from their beginnings the rise, the progress, and the decline of public opinions, and to illustrate, as the objects presented themselves, the great incidents in our national annals" (6:iii).

It is little wonder that D'Israeli should have much to say about books, about their nature, production, and dissemination, and about their socio-political and ethical character and reverberations: it was the "principle early adopted by me," he announced, "of interspersing facts with speculation." And if his historical orientation—a qualification rare among authors of literary subjects—lends a certain breadth to his observations, so his personal and independent manner furnishes them with an undeniable attractiveness and charm.

D'Israeli was a product of revolutionary times. Born in 1766, during the reign of George III, he was a passionate admirer of Alexander Pope and began writing in the shadow of Dr. Johnson and William Warburton. His early work was admired by Byron and Scott. He dedicated the fourth edition of *The Literary Character* to Robert Southey. Two years after D'Israeli's death in 1848, in the reign of Queen Victoria, Tennyson succeeded Wordsworth as poet laureate. His work reflects those times: the advent and aftermath of the French Revolution formed the nucleus of his thinking. But D'Israeli had more to offer than the experience of having had, so to speak, one foot in one century and the other in the next. His world-view was comprehensive, his curiosity unquenchable, his knowledge would admit no bounds. His works are well-nigh encyclopaedic, with cascades of names and titles drawn from centuries and civilizations. "Everything interested him," his son rightly remarked. He wrote of politicians and poetasters, of Jews and Jesuits, of coffee and Commonwealth, of scientists and servants, of bibliognosts and bibliopoles, of atlases and academies, of fables and forks. He was a Tory and yet independent and forward-looking; he was a Jew and had his children baptised. What he did not experience himself, he complemented with voracious reading. He was a man of books, firmly committed to the thesis—as expressed by Benjamin—that a "Book may be as great a thing as a battle." And he had no hesitation in giving his opinions in a forthright and honest way. Whatever the subject, his essays, long and short, are a mirror of the man and of many times and events. What gives them vitality and durability, even those which time may have proven inaccurate, is D'Israeli's absolute commitment to letters. His "constancy of purpose" and the "philosophic sweetness of his disposition" are well illustrated in the memoir "On the Life and Writings of Mr. Disraeli," written by his son for the first edition of the collected works of his father, which is reprinted below.

The essays in this volume are drawn from D'Israeli's literary works written over a period of some fifty years. Unlike those of many of his collections, which are contained only by that loose-fitting garment called "letters," they have been selected and grouped to afford a stronger focus and ultimately a more definitive statement for the edification and entertainment of a general and inquisitive public. As bibliophile, historian, author, and littérateur, D'Israeli has much to offer in the way of information, speculation, and curiosity. Despite early "decisive measures ... required to correct this evil," he remained a poet, if not always in deed then always in spirit, which accounts, according to his son Benjamin, for his popularity as a writer, one who "made belles-lettres charming to the multitude." A taste of that charm is evident in a sample of the pithy aperçus and aphorisms sprinkled throughout his works: "Authors are the creators or the creatures of opinion; the great form an epoch, the many reflect their age" (*Amenities*, 6:iii); "To impoverish the rich is not to enrich the poor" (*Amenities*, 6:331); "Whosoever in writing modern history shall follow truth too near the heels, it may haply strike out his teeth" (*Amenities*, 6:614); "Abridgers are a kind of literary men to whom the indolence of modern readers, and indeed the multiplicity of authors, give ample employment" (*Curiosities*, I:397); "It is easier to burn authors than books" (*Amenities*, 6:743); "John Donne, who closed his life as a St. Austin, had opened it as a Catullus" (*Amenities*, 6:676).

D'Israeli's "honest desire of giving useful pleasure" is evident, as well, in his employment of anecdotes. As early as 1793, in his monograph *A Dissertation on Anecdotes,* he considered them "the most agreeable parts of History—the Materials for the History of Manners"—in short, he declared them a vital ingredient of historiography. Although his most ambitious and significant work may be his five-volume *Commentaries on the Life and Reign of Charles I* (1828-1831), which earned him an honorary Doctor of Civil Law of Oxford University and was judged by Sidney Lee in the *Dictionary of National*

Biography as "mark[ing] a distinct advance in the methods of historical research," he was convinced that well-chosen anecdotes were excellent substitutes for conversation of eminent persons, similar to memoirs, and immediate revelations of character and by extension of human nature. They complement the meticulous researching of documents and sources, possessing "in some degree, the "perfection of instruction." Moreover, D'Israeli would appear to be conceiving of history as that of the actions of great men, and anecdotes, like memoirs, as a means of psychological revelation and thus inviting the reader to approach them—"In histories there is a majesty, which keeps us distant from great men." He did not restrict anecdotes to persons or biography, however. He was of the opinion that Dr. Johnson had "imperfectly defined" the word: "French for a *biographical incident*; a minute passage of *private life*" and thus limiting it "merely to *biography*." For D'Israeli *anecdote* is "more justly" defined as "a term which (now) denotes a relation of detached and interesting particulars," and thus "we give anecdotes of the art as well as the Artist; of the war as well as the General; of the nation as well as of the Monarch."

On no account, therefore, are his fondness for telling tales and smattering of pithy observations and finely chiselled phrases to be taken lightly as Disraeli's contribution to collections of old saws and sayings or as ends in themselves. Rather, they pinpoint not merely the style of the man but the extent of his perspective. A true son of the Enlightenment, his focus is always on the advance of the human intellect through time. Books are central for D'Israeli because they form the character of a civilization. Authors are precious because they tap, portray and nurture that identity. Before books and authors there could only be barbarism. Books and authors suppressed, there could only be tyranny. Whether he is declaiming against misleading titles or the vanity of critics, whether he is praising the benevolence of monarchs or the humility of scholars, D'Israeli is ever stressing the interplay of individual and society, of their personal, economic, and political interdependence. "The favourite book of every age is a certain picture of the people. The gradual depreciation of a great author marks a change in knowledge or in taste": these may be commonplaces but they do underline the flexibility and aptness of D'Israeli's assessment of books. Binding all, perhaps, and never limited is his high ideal of freedom. Restricting books and restricting authors are intolerable political and anti-social measures. "It is easier to burn authors than books": D'Israeli's axiom may appear sardonic but it surely accents his faith in the vitality of books and his commitment to freedom. D'Israeli may be amused and certainly amusing, irritated and often irritating, in dealing with the quacks and quirks of the world of letters, or outraged at the neglect and exploitation of authors or the restrictions of censorship and copyright. But he is not soft-centered about books and authors, nor ever compromising about freedom. His essays are thus pertinent and relevant.

What is even more notable is—as the present arrangement attempts to make clear—is D'Israeli's awareness of the historical and cultural process which the production and proliferation of books represents. Although the essays in this collection were written at different times and in varying contexts, Disraeli's focus is adapted to the subject matter at hand. The result is not so much a single and comprehensive picture as a series of images taken from varying angles or distances. In the opening section, Writing and Reading, D'Israeli deals globally with the basic materials of writing, the predecessors and development of paper and ink, as well as with the psycho-sociological implications of autographs or minute writing. His focus can also be historical and grammatical, as in his treatment of orthography and orthoepy, especially in England, and then very precise on the aims and influence of writing-masters on English calligraphy. Within a more or less historical orientation, evident in Printing and Publishing, are once again varying focuses: from the origins of the "mystical" or "secret" art of printing and the claims of numerous inventors and nations, to a survey of early printers and a critical biographical sketch of the first English printer, William Caxton, and, since printers tended also to be publishers, to an excursion—a demonstration of D'Israeli's wide acquaintance with fairly obscure continental literature—on those he designates as "Scribleri," voluminous authors whose "pen will still luxuriate in the forbidden page which even booksellers refuse to publish." D'Israeli's treatment of books themselves is of a somewhat different nature. Although the essays demonstrate his vast acquaintance with a wide range of books, they deal with what may be considered only the trappings—titles, dedications, and so forth. D'Israeli does, however, communicate his frothy but critical enjoyment of the absurdities of misleading titles, the "literary artifice" of dedications, the "exquisitely written" preface which is a "delicious literary morsel," and the "indispensable ... variegated forms" of notes. Still, for all their dependence on anecdote and literary gossip, they enforce the interplay of authors and the world about them, be it in their attracting a public with a tempting title, be it in their cultivating of a patron with a flattering preface, be it in their overcoming of restrictions with a cunning erratum.

Like many contemporary thinkers D'Israeli strove to delineate of the history of genius, especially the characterization of the man of genius, whether author, artist, or scientist. This pursuit was his life's work. In 1795 he published the monograph *An Essay in the Manners and Genius of the Literary Character*, which, as was his wont, he revised and enlarged in editions of 1818, 1822, and 1828, it becoming known ultimately as *Literary Character of Men of Genius*. Much the same expanding reflection—and not simply of putting old wine into new bottles—is to be found in *Miscellanies: Or, Literary Recreations* (1796), which became *Literary Miscellanies* in a second edition of 1801, and once again revised as *Miscellanies of Literature* in 1840. Whereas the *Literary Character* sought to construct a prototype of the man of genius, outlining his development from cradle to grave, as it were, his two further monographs, *Calamities of Authors; including Some Enquiries Respecting their Moral and Literary Characters* (2 vols., 1812) and *Quarrels of Authors; or, Some Memoirs of our Literary History* (3 vols., 1814) focused on the specific psychological and social situations which authors must endure, such as poverty, neglect, and critical abuse. It would be idle to attempt to compress these works into the present selection. Rather, the section Authors & Co., while including two essays from these volumes, is mainly concerned with what might be termed the constellation or cluster of which the author is the nucleus. D'Israeli's portraits, ranging from bibliomaniacs and bibliognosts, to patrons and plagiarists, to filchers and forgers, form a cabinet of characters, in the manner of the literary subgenre. Together with his continuing inflection of "character" and investigation of the psychological explanation of behavior, which he terms the "secret history," they support his conviction that biography and history are interconnected. True, they enable D'Israeli to indulge his appetite for literary gossip and draw on his well-stocked store of anecdotes. But they are without doubt lively snapshots of the time. Moreover, and most important perhaps, when seen within the context of D'Israeli's larger quest for the man of genius, they serve to isolate, and so highlight, him from the rest of his "company."

Like authors, books and, even more fragile, manuscripts, do not exist in a vacuum. They too may suffer neglect, abuse, even destruction. Their transmission—survival may be a more accurate word—is a socio-political process, often dependent not on their quality but upon the special interests, prejudices, or whims of potentates, prelates, politicians, or patrons. In the section Preservation and Destruction D'Israeli surveys many cultures and times to illustrate the ignorance, indifference, and barbarism, the "malice of Men as well as that of Time,"and of factions. D'Israeli's tone is mournful in these essays as he lists instance after instance of decay and destruction. He seems to regard books and manuscripts not simply as senseless objects but as animate organisms, referring, for example, to the discovery of manuscripts "in the last agonies of existence" or citing the Italian humanist Poggio's finding work of Quintilian "under a heap in a decayed coffer" and his "great joy" as he "drew it out of its grave." That the work was found in a monastery nourished D'Israeli's criticism of religion, especially Catholicism, as his comment on Poggio's discovery illustrates: "The monks have been complimented as the preservers of literature, but by the facts, like the present, their real affection may be doubted." But D'Israeli was not sectarian or partisan. Literature—i.e. letters—is more valuable than systems. Its "annihilation"—a word recurring like a refrain throughout—kindled his wrath: "The Romans burnt the books of the Jews, of the Christians, and the Philosophers; the Jews burnt the books of the Christians and the Pagans; and the Christians burnt the books of the Pagans and the Jews." Even D'Israeli's much-loved institution is not spared the charge of suppression: "In our national collection, the British Museum, we find a great deal against Mar-prelate [*sic*]—"that ardent conspiracy against the established hierarchy"—but not Mar-prelate himself." Not surprisingly, D'Israeli does not spare individuals, such as plagiarists, fabricators, and other "dilapidators"—he was himself involved in a public controversy for mentioning that the historian Catherine Macaulay had mutilated a Harleian manuscript in the library of the British Museum. And his dismay at the plight of certain great repositories is unmistakable in his quoting of Gibbon's description of the library of Alexandria twenty years after its destruction; "the appearance of the *empty shelves* excited the regret and indignation of every spectator."

It cannot be surprising that the liberal-minded D'Israeli should defend the literary property of the individual author against the greed of booksellers and the intrusions of the state and authority, be it in the limitation of copyright or the granting of exclusive licences to certain publishers. What he calls his history of literary property is, in the main, an unmasking of the absurd. "Is it not wonderful that even successful authors are indigent?": Milton produced what was a "five-pound epic," *Paradise Lost*, while the publisher, Jacob Tonson, "and all his family rode in their carriages on the profits." But D'Israeli, although deeply concerned about the almost endemic indigence of authors, goes farther: he strikes a chord reverberating today in such matters as the extent of copyright and the clash between copyright and the right to copy. "The verbal and tasteless lawyers," he declares, not many years past, with legal metaphysics, wrangled like the schoolmen, inquiring of each other, "whether the *style* and *ideas* of an author were tangible things; or if these were a *property*, how is *possession* to be taken, or any act of *occupancy* made on mere intellectual *ideas*." Nothing, said they, can be an object of property but which has a corporeal substance; the air and the light, to which they compared an author's ideas, are common to all; ideas in the MS. state were compared to birds in a cage; while the author confines them in his own dominion, none but he has a right to let them fly; but the moment he allows the bird to escape from his hand, it is no violation of property in any one to make it his own. And to prove that there existed no property after publication, they found an analogy in the gathering of acorns, or in seizing on a vacant piece of ground; and thus degrading that most refined piece of art formed in the highest state of society, a literary production, they brought us back to a state of nature; and seem to have concluded that literary property was purely ideal; a phantom which, as its author could neither grasp nor confine to himself, he must entirely depend on the public benevolence for his reward.

D'Israeli does not stop there, but goes beyond the economic and political aspects to what amounts to a creed:

The Ideas, that is, the work of an author, are "tangible things." "There are works," to quote the words of a near and dear relative, "which require great learning, great industry, great labour, and great capital, in their preparation. They assume a palpable form. You may fill warehouses with them, and freight ships; and the tenure by which they are held is superior to that of all other property, for it is original. It is tenure which does not exist in a doubtful title; which does not spring from any adventitious circumstances; it is not found—it is not purchased—it is not prescriptive—it is original; so it is the most natural of all titles, because it is the most simple and least artificial. It is paramount and sovereign, because it is a tenure by creation.

Consequently, it is in defense of the sovereignty of creativity that D'Israeli surveys such institutions as licensers of the press and censors of books, as well as copyright, and regards them, as the title "The War against Books" of what is perhaps his most serious and topical essay implies, as assaults on the very substance of liberal democracy. He acknowledges, however, that the freedom of the press is a "problem in the science of government [which] remains as insoluble at this days as at any former period." As historian, aware that "the noble treatise of Milton for a free press had not the slightest influence on the very parliament whose members had long suffered from its oppression," he is realistic enough to recognize that "the advocates of a free press ... become its adversaries whenever they themselves form the ruling power." If the imagery is of conflict and war, then a fortress or refuge must be sought. D'Israeli does not propose a coalition of authors and is perhaps suspicious of political support. Instead, he counts on those who, understanding the cultural value of letters, are collectors. The last three essays in this selection amount to a tribute to the growth of the "public mind of Europe" which resulted from the invention of printing, that "art of multiplying the productions of the mind," and enabled men of letters to rival royal munificence with their collections. The forming and development of libraries is his theme, his anecdotes serving to "mark either the affection, or the veneration, which civilised men have ever felt for these perennial repositories of their minds." It is in a way fitting that D'Israeli, the enlightened advocate of the advancement of the mind, should celebrate in the final essay the tireless and humanistic efforts of the first founder of a public library, Thomas Bodley, as representative of "the first marked advancement in the progress of the national understanding ... made by a new race of public benefactors, who, in their munificence, no longer endowing obsolete superstitions, and inefficient charities, erected libraries and opened academies; founders of those habitations of knowledge whose doors open to the bidding of all comers."

D'Israeli loved books not just for themselves but for what they represent in the cultural development of society. He was also keenly conscious of the special role, commitment, and responsibility of the individual author. More than everything else perhaps, D'Israeli loved his engagement with books. Although he recognized his limitations as author, and was not oblivious to errors he may have committed or fallen into,[1] he was convinced that the books he had written and collected were the "tangible depository" of his thoughts, in which "labour of love" there is a "unity" and a "secret connexion through its dependent parts." In any case there can be no denying him a lifetime of the pleasures he cites from the French naturalist George Louis Le Clerc, Comte de Buffon: "These are the most luxurious and delightful moments of life: moments which have often enticed me to pass fourteen hours at my desk in a state of transport; this gratification more than glory is my reward."

---

1. He was obliged, for example, to answer the criticism of Bolton Corney's *Curiosities of Literature Illustrated* (1837," second edition, revised and acuminated," 1838) with his own pamphlet *The Illustrator Illustrated* (1838). And, to be sure, there are errors taken over from secondhand sources, as in D'Israeli's averring that the title of Matthews's *Origin and Dignity of the Royal House* had nothing to do with its contents, hunting—the Spanish *caza* (hunt) having been mistaken for *casa* (house)—or referring to the collector Praun as the "friend" of Dürer, who died twenty years before Praun's birth, or to a Christian Latin poet as Fortunius when Venantius Fortunatus is more likely.

LIFE AND WRITINGS OF MR. DISRAELI.
BY HIS SON.

THE traditionary notion that the life of a man of letters is necessarily deficient in incident, appears to have originated in a misconception of the essential nature of human action. The life of every man is full of incidents, but the incidents are insignificant, because they do not affect his species; and in general the importance of every occurrence is to be measured by the degree with which it is recognised by mankind. An author may influence the fortunes of the world to as great an extent as a statesman or a warrior; and the deeds and performances by which this influence is created and exercised, may rank in their interest and importance with the decisions of great Congresses, or the skilful valour of a memorable field. M. de Voltaire was certainly a greater Frenchman than Cardinal Fleury, the Prime Minister of France in his time. His actions were more important; and it is certainly not too much to maintain that the exploits of Homer, Aristotle, Dante, or my Lord Bacon, were as considerable events as anything that occurred at Actium, Lepanto, or Blenheim. A Book may be as great a thing as a battle, and there are systems of philosophy that have produced as great revolutions as any that have disturbed even the social and political existence of our centuries.

The life of the author, whose character and career we are venturing to review, extended far beyond the allotted term of man: and, perhaps, no existence of equal duration ever exhibited an uniformity more sustained. The strong bent of his infancy was pursued through youth, matured in manhood, and maintained without decay to an advanced old age. In the biographic spell, no ingredient is more magical than predisposition. How pure, and native, and indigenous it was in the character of this writer, can only be properly appreciated by an acquaintance with the circumstances amid which he was born, and by being able to estimate how far they could have directed or developed his earliest inclinations.

My grandfather, who became an English Denizen in 1748, was an Italian descendant from one of those Hebrew families whom the Inquisition forced to emigrate from the Spanish Peninsula at the end of the fifteenth century, and who found a refuge in the more tolerant territories of the Venetian Republic. His ancestors had dropped their Gothic surname on their settlement in the Terra Firma, and grateful to the God of Jacob who had sustained them through unprecedented trials and guarded them through unheard-of perils, they assumed the name of DISRAELI, a name never borne before or since by any other family, in order that their race might be for ever recognised. Undisturbed and unmolested, they flourished as merchants for more than two centuries under the protection of the lion of St. Mark, which was but just, as the patron saint of the Republic was himself a child of Israel.

But towards the middle of the eighteenth century, the altered circumstances of England, favourable, as it was then supposed, to commerce and religious liberty, attracted the attention of my great-grandfather to this island, and he resolved that the youngest of his two sons, Benjamin, the "son of his right hand," should settle in a country where the dynasty seemed at length established, through the recent failure of Prince Charles Edward, and where public opinion appeared definitively adverse to persecution on matters of creed and conscience.

The Jewish families who were then settled in England were few, though, from their wealth and other circumstances, they were far from unimportant. They were all of them Sephardim, that is to say, children of Israel, who had never quitted the shores of the Midland Ocean, until Torquamada had driven them from their pleasant residences and rich estates in Arragon, and Andalusia, and Portugal, to seek greater blessings, even than a clear atmosphere and a glowing sun, amid the marshes of Holland and the fogs of Britain. Most of these families, who held themselves aloof from the Hebrews of Northern Europe, then only occasionally stealing into England, as from an inferior caste, and whose synagogue was reserved only for Sephardim, are now extinct; while the branch of the great family, which, notwithstanding their own sufferings from prejudice, they had the hardihood to look down upon, have achieved an amount of wealth and consideration which the Sephardim, even with the patronage of Mr. Pelham, never could have contemplated. Nevertheless, at the time when my grandfather settled in England, and when Mr. Pelham, who was very favourable to the Jews, was Prime Minister, there might be found, among other Jewish families flourishing in this country, the Villa Reals, who brought wealth to these shores almost as great as their name, though that is the second in Portugal, and who have twice allied themselves with the English aristocracy, the Medinas—the Laras, who were our kinsmen—and the Mendez da Costas, who, I believe, still exist.

Whether it were that my grandfather, on his arrival, was not encouraged by those to whom he had a right to look up,—which is often our hard case in the outset of life,—or whether he was alarmed at the unexpected consequences of Mr. Pelham's favourable disposition to his countrymen in the disgraceful repeal of the Jew Bill, which occurred a very few years after his arrival in this country, I know not; but certainly he appears never to have cordially or intimately mixed with his community. This tendency to alienation was, no doubt, subsequently encouraged by his marriage, which took place in 1765. My grandmother, the beautiful daughter of a family who had suffered much from persecution, had imbibed that dislike for her race which the vain are too apt to adopt when they find that they are born to public contempt. The indignant feeling that should be reserved for the persecutor, in the mortification of their disturbed sensibility, is too often visited on the victim; and the cause of annoyance is recognised not in the ignorant malevolence of the powerful, but in the conscientious conviction of the innocent sufferer. Seventeen years, however, elapsed before my grandfather entered into this union, and during that interval he had not been idle. He was only eighteen when he commenced his career, and when a great responsibility devolved upon him. He was not unequal to it. He was a man of ardent character; sanguine, courageous, speculative, and fortunate; with a temper which no disappointment could disturb, and a brain, amid reverses, full of resource. He made his fortune in the midway of life, and settled near Enfield, where he formed an Italian garden, entertained his friends, played whist with Sir Horace Mann, who was his great acquaintance, and who had known his brother at Venice as a banker, eat macaroni which was dressed by the Venetian Consul, sang canzonettas, and notwithstanding a wife who never pardoned him for his name, and a son who disappointed all his plans, and who to the last hour of his life was an enigma to him, lived till he was nearly ninety, and then died in 1817, in the full enjoyment of prolonged existence.

My grandfather retired from active business on the eve of that great financial epoch, to grapple with which his talents were well adapted; and when the wars and loans of the Revolution were about to create those families of millionaires, in which he might probably have enrolled his own. That, however, was not our destiny. My grandfather had only one child, and nature had disqualified him, from his cradle, for the busy pursuits of men.

A pale, pensive child, with large dark brown eyes, and flowing hair, such as may be beheld in one of the portraits annexed to these volumes, had grown up beneath this roof of worldly energy and enjoyment, indicating even in his infancy, by the whole carriage of his life, that he was of a different order from those among whom he lived. Timid, susceptible, lost in reverie, fond of solitude, or seeking no better company than a book, the years had stolen on, till he had arrived at that mournful period of boyhood when eccentricities excite attention and command no sympathy. In the chapter on Predisposition, in the most delightful of his works,[2] my father has drawn from his own, though his unacknowledged feelings, immortal truths. Then commenced the age of domestic criticism. His mother, not incapable of deep affections, but so mortified by her social position that she lived until eighty without indulging in a tender expression, did not recognise in her only offspring a being qualified to control or vanquish his impending fate. His existence only served to swell the aggregate of many humiliating particulars. It was not to her a source of joy, or sympathy, or solace. She foresaw for her child only a future of degradation. Having a strong, clear mind, without any imagination, she believed that she beheld an inevitable doom. The tart remark and the contemptuous comment on her part, elicited, on the other, all the irritability

---

2. "Essay on the Literary Character," Vol. I. chap. v.

of the poetic idiosyncrasy. After frantic ebullitions, for which, when the circumstances were analysed by an ordinary mind, there seemed no sufficient cause, my grandfather always interfered to soothe with good-tempered commonplaces, and promote peace. He was a man who thought that the only way to make people happy was to make them a present. He took it for granted that a boy in a passion wanted a toy or a guinea. At a later date, when my father ran away from home, and after some wanderings was brought back, found lying on a tombstone in Hackney churchyard, he embraced him, and gave him a pony.

In this state of affairs, being sent to school in the neighbourhood, was a rather agreeable incident. The school was kept by a Scotchman, one Morison, a good man, and not untinctured with scholarship, and it is possible that my father might have reaped some advantage from this change; but the school was too near home, and his mother, though she tormented his existence, was never content if he were out of her sight. His delicate health was an excuse for converting him, after a short interval, into a day scholar; then many days of attendance were omitted; finally, the solitary walk home through Mr Mellish's park was dangerous to the sensibilities that too often exploded when they encountered on the arrival at the domestic hearth a scene which did not harmonise with the fairy-land of reverie.

The crisis arrived, when, after months of unusual abstraction and irritability, my father produced a poem. For the first time, my grandfather was seriously alarmed. The loss of one of his argosies, uninsured, could not have filled him with more blank dismay. His idea of a poet was formed from one of the prints of Hogarth hanging in his room, where an unfortunate wight in a garret was inditing an ode to riches, while dunned for his milk-score. Decisive measures were required to eradicate this evil, and to prevent future disgrace—so, as seems the custom when a person is in a scrape, it was resolved that my father should be sent abroad, where a new scene and a new language might divert his mind from the ignominious pursuit which so fatally attracted him. The unhappy poet was consigned like a bale of goods to my grandfather's correspondent at Amsterdam, who had instructions to place him at some collegium of repute in that city. Here were passed some years not without profit, though his tutor was a great impostor, very neglectful of his pupils, and both unable and disinclined to guide them in severe studies. This preceptor was a man of letters, though a wretched writer, with a good library, and a spirit inflamed with all the philosophy of the eighteenth century, then (1780-1) about to bring forth and bear its long-matured fruits. The intelligence and disposition of my father attracted his attention, and rather interested him. He taught his charge little, for he was himself generally occupied in writing bad odes, but he gave him free warren in his library, and before his pupil was fifteen, he had read the works of Voltaire and had dipped into Bayle. Strange that the characteristics of a writer so born and brought up should have been so essentially English; not merely from his mastery over our language, but from his keen and profound sympathy with all that concerned the literary and political history of our country at its most important epoch.

When he was eighteen, he returned to England a disciple of Rousseau. He had exercised his imagination during the voyage in idealizing the interview with his mother, which was to be conducted on both sides with sublime pathos. His other parent had frequently visited him during his absence. He was prepared to throw himself on his mother's bosom, to bedew her hands with his tears, and to stop her own with his lips; but, when he entered, his strange appearance, his gaunt figure, his excited manners, his long hair, and his unfashionable costume, only filled her with a sentiment of tender aversion; she broke into derisive laughter, and noticing his intolerable garments, she reluctantly lent him her cheek. Whereupon Emile, of course, went into heroics, wept, sobbed, and finally, shut up in his chamber, composed an impassioned epistle. My grandfather, to soothe him, dwelt on the united solicitude of his parents for his welfare, and broke to him their intention, if it were agreeable to him, to place him in the establishment of a great merchant at Bordeaux. My father replied that he had written a poem of considerable length, which he wished to publish, against Commerce, which was the corrupter of man. In eight-and-forty hours confusion again reigned in this household, and all from a want of psychological perception in its master and mistress.

My father, who had lost the timidity of his childhood, who, by nature, was very impulsive, and indeed endowed with a degree of volatility which is only witnessed in the south of France, and which never deserted him to his last hour, was no longer to be controlled. His conduct was decisive. He enclosed his poem to Dr. Johnson, with an impassioned statement of his case, complaining, which he ever did, that he had never found a counsellor or literary friend. He left his packet himself at Bolt Court, where he was received by Mr. Francis Barber, the doctor's well-known black servant, and told to call again in a week. Be sure that he was very punctual; but the packet was returned to him unopened, with a message that the illustrious doctor was too ill to read anything. The unhappy and obscure aspirant, who received this disheartening message, accepted it, in his utter despondency, as a mechanical excuse. But, alas! the cause was too true; and, a few weeks after, on that bed, beside which the voice of Mr. Burke faltered, and the tender spirit of Benett Langton was ever vigilant, the great soul of Johnson quitted earth.

But the spirit of self-confidence, the resolution to struggle against his fate, the paramount desire to find some sympathising sage—some guide, philosopher, and friend—was so strong and rooted in my father, that I observed, a few weeks ago, in a magazine, an original letter, written by him about this time to Dr. Vicesimus Knox, full of high-flown sentiments, reading indeed like a romance of Scudery, and entreating the learned critic to receive him in his family, and give him the advantage of his wisdom, his taste, and his erudition.

With a home that ought to have been happy, surrounded with more than comfort, with the most good-natured father in the world, and an agreeable man; and with a mother whose strong intellect, under ordinary circumstances, might have been of great importance to him; my father, though himself of a very sweet disposition, was most unhappy. His parents looked upon him as moonstruck, while he himself, whatever his aspirations, was conscious that he had done nothing to justify the eccentricity of his course, or the violation of all prudential considerations in which he daily indulged. In these perplexities, the usual alternative was again had recourse to—absence; he was sent abroad, to travel in France, which the peace then permitted, visit some friends, see Paris, and then proceed to Bordeaux if he felt inclined. My father travelled in France, and then proceeded to Paris, where he remained till the eve of great events in that capital. This was a visit he recollected with satisfaction. He lived with learned men and moved in vast libraries, and returned in the earlier part of 1788, with some little knowledge of life, and with a considerable quantity of books.

At this time Peter Pindar flourished in all the wantonness of literary riot. He was at the height of his flagrant notoriety. The novelty and the boldness of his style carried the million with him. The most exalted station was not exempt from his audacious criticism, and learned institutions trembled at the sallies whose ribaldry often cloaked taste, intelligence, and good sense. His "Odes to the Academicians," which first secured him the ear of the town, were written by one who could himself guide the pencil with skill and feeling, and who, in the form of a mechanic's son, had even the felicity to discover the vigorous genius of Opie. The mock-heroic which invaded with success the sacred recesses of the palace, and which was fruitlessly menaced by Secretaries of State, proved a reckless intrepidity, which is apt to be popular with "the general." The powerful and the learned quailed beneath the lash with an affected contempt which scarcely veiled their tremor. In the meantime, as in the latter days of the Empire, the barbarian ravaged the country, while the pale-faced patricians were inactive within the walls. No one offered resistance.

There appeared about this time a satire "On the Abuse of Satire." The verses were polished and pointed; a happy echo of that style of Mr. Pope which still lingered in the spell-bound ear of the public. Peculiarly they offered a contrast to the irregular effusions of the popular assailant whom they in turn assailed, for the object of their indignant invective was the bard of the "Lousiad." The poem was anonymous, and was addressed to Dr. Warton in lines of even classic grace. Its publication was appropriate. There are moments when every one is inclined to praise, especially when the praise of a new pen may at the same time revenge the insults of an old one.

But if there could be any doubt of the success of this new hand, it was quickly removed by the conduct of Peter Pindar himself. As is not unusual with persons of his habits, Wolcot was extremely sensitive, and, brandishing a tomahawk, always himself shrank from a scratch. This was shown some years afterwards by his violent assault on Mr. Gifford, with a bludgeon, in a bookseller's shop, because the author of the "Baviad and Mæviad" had presumed to castigate the great lampooner of the age. In the present instance, the furious Wolcot leapt to the rash conclusion, that the author of the satire was no less a personage than Mr. Hayley, and he assailed the elegant author of the "Triumphs of Temper" in a virulent pasquinade. This ill-considered movement of his adversary of course achieved the complete success of the anonymous writer.

My father, who came up to town to read the newspapers at the St. James's Coffee-house, found their columns filled with extracts from the fortunate effusion of the hour, conjectures as to its writer, and much gossip respecting Wolcot and Hayley. He returned to Enfield laden with the journals, and, presenting them to his parents, broke to them the intelligence, that at length he was not only an author, but a successful one.

He was indebted to this slight effort for something almost as agreeable as the public recognition of his ability, and that was the acquaintance, and almost immediately the warm personal friendship, of Mr. Pye. Mr. Pye was the head of an ancient English family that figured in the Parliaments and struggles of the Stuarts; he was member for the County of Berkshire, where his ancestral seat of Faringdon was situate, and at a later period (1790) became Poet Laureat. In those days, when literary clubs did not exist, and when even political ones were extremely limited and exclusive in their character, the booksellers' shops were social rendezvous. Debrett's was the chief haunt of the Whigs; Hatchard's, I believe, of the Tories. It was at the latter house that my father made the acquaintance of Mr. Pye, then publishing his translation of Aristotle's Poetics, and so strong was party feeling at that period, that one day, walking together down Piccadilly, Mr. Pye, stopping at the door of Debrett, requested his companion to go in and purchase a particular pamphlet for him, adding that if he had the audacity to enter, more than one person would tread upon his toes.

My father at last had a friend. Mr. Pye, though double his age, was still a young man, and the literary sympathy between them was complete. Unfortunately, the member for Berkshire was a man rather of an elegant turn of mind, than one of that energy and vigour which a youth required for a companion at that moment. Their tastes and pursuits were perhaps a little too similar. They addressed poetical epistles to each other, and were, reciprocally, too gentle critics. But Mr. Pye was a most amiable and accomplished man, a fine classical scholar, and a master of correct versification. He paid a visit to Enfield, and by his influence hastened a conclusion at which my grandfather was just arriving, to wit, that he would no longer persist in the fruitless effort of converting a poet into a merchant, and that content with the independence he had realised, he would abandon his dreams of founding a dynasty of financiers. From this moment all disquietude ceased beneath this always well-meaning, though often perplexed, roof, while my father, enabled amply to gratify his darling passion of book-collecting, passed his days in tranquil study, and in the society of congenial spirits.

His new friend introduced him almost immediately to Mr. James Pettit Andrews, a Berkshire gentleman of literary pursuits, and whose hospitable table at Brompton was the resort of the best literary society of the day. Here my father was a frequent guest, and walking home one night together from this house, where they had both dined, he made the acquaintance of a young poet, which soon ripened into intimacy, and which throughout sixty years, notwithstanding many changes of life, never died away. This youthful poet had already gained laurels, though he was only three or four years older than my father, but I am not at this moment quite aware whether his brow was yet encircled with the amaranthine wreath of the "Pleasures of Memory."

Some years after this, great vicissitudes unhappily occurred in the family of Mr. Pye. He was obliged to retire from Parliament, and to sell his family estate of Faringdon. His Majesty had already, on the death of Thomas Warton, nominated him Poet Laureat, and after his retirement from Parliament, the government which he had supported, appointed him a Commissioner of Police. It was in these days that his friend, Mr. Penn, of Stoke Park, in Buckinghamshire, presented him with a cottage worthy of a poet on his beautiful estate; and it was thus my father became acquainted with the amiable descendant of the most successful of colonisers, and with that classic domain which the genius of Gray, as it were, now haunts, and has for ever hallowed, and from which he beheld with fond and musing eye, those

Distant spires and antique towers

that no one can now look upon without remembering him. It was amid these rambles in Stoke Park, amid the scenes of Gray's genius, the elegiac churchyard, and the picturesque fragments of the Long Story, talking over the deeds of the "Great Rebellion" with the descendants of Cavaliers and Parliament-men, that my father first imbibed that feeling for the county of Buckingham, which induced him occasionally to be a dweller in its limits, and ultimately, more than a quarter of a century afterwards, to establish his household gods in its heart. And here, perhaps, I may be permitted to mention a circumstance, which is indeed trifling, and yet, as a coincidence, not, I think, without interest. Mr. Pye was the great-grandson of Sir Robert Pye, of Bradenham, who married Anne, the eldest daughter of Mr. Hampden. How little could my father dream, sixty years ago, that he would pass the last quarter of his life in the mansion-house of Bradenham; that his name would become intimately connected with the county of Buckingham; and that his own remains would be interred in the vault of the chancel of Bradenham Church, among the coffins of the descendants of the Hampdens and the Pyes. All which should teach us that, whatever may be our natural bent, there is a power in the disposal of events greater than human will.

It was about two years after his first acquaintance with Mr. Pye, that my father, being then in his twenty-fifth year, influenced by the circle in which he then lived, gave an anonymous volume to the press, the fate of which he could little have foreseen. The taste for literary history was then of recent date in England. It was developed by Dr. Johnson and the Wartons, who were the true founders of that elegant literature in which France had so richly preceded us. The fashion for literary anecdote prevailed at the end of the last century. Mr. Pettit Andrews, assisted by Mr. Pye and Captain Grose, and shortly afterwards, his friend, Mr. Seward, in his "Anecdotes of Distinguished Persons," had both of them produced ingenious works, which had experienced public favour. But these volumes were rather entertaining than substantial, and their interest in many instances was necessarily fleeting; all which made Mr. Rogers observe, that the world was far gone in its anecdotage.

While Mr. Andrews and his friend were hunting for personal details in the recollections of their contemporaries, my father maintained one day, that the most interesting of miscellanies might be drawn up by a well-read man from the library in which he lived. It was objected, on the other hand, that such a work would be a mere compilation, and could not succeed with its dead matter in interesting the public. To test the truth of this assertion, my father occupied himself in the preparation of an octavo volume, the principal materials of which were found in the diversified collections of the French Ana; but he enriched his subjects with as much of our own literature as his reading afforded, and he conveyed the result in that lively and entertaining style which he from the first commanded. This collection of "Anecdotes, Characters, Sketches, and Observations; Literary, Critical, and Historical," as the title-page of the first edition figures, he invested with the happy baptism of "Curiosities of Literature."

He sought by this publication neither reputation nor a coarser reward, for he published his work anonymously, and avowedly as a compilation; and he not only published the work at his own expense, but in his heedlessness made a present of the copyright to the bookseller, which three or four years afterwards he was fortunate enough to purchase at a public sale. The volume was an experiment whether a taste for literature could not be infused into the multitude. Its success was so decided, that its projector was tempted to add a second volume two years afterward, with a slight attempt at more original research; l observe that there was a second edition of both volumes in 1794. For twenty years the brother volumes remained favourites of the public; when after that long interval their writer, taking advantage of a popular title, poured forth all the riches of his matured intellect, his refined taste, and accumulated knowledge into their pages, and produced what may be fairly described as the most celebrated Miscellany of Modern Literature.

The moment that the name of the youthful author of the "Abuse of Satire" had transpired, Peter Pindar, faithful to the instinct of his nature, wrote a letter of congratulation and compliment to his assailant, and desired to make his acquaintance. The invitation was responded to, and until the death of Wolcot, they were intimate. My father always described Wolcot as a warm-hearted man; coarse in his manners, and rather rough, but eager to serve those whom he liked, of which, indeed, I might appropriately mention an instance.

It so happened, that about the year 1795, when he was in his 29th year, there came over my father that mysterious illness to which the youth of men of sensibility, and especially literary men, is frequently subject—a failing of nervous energy, occasioned by study and too sedentary habits, early and habitual reverie, restless and indefinite purpose. The symptoms, physical and moral, are most distressing: lassitude and despondency. And it usually happens, as in the present, instance, that the cause of suffering is not recognised; and that medical men, misled by the superficial symptoms, and not seeking to acquaint themselves with the psychology of their patients, arrive at erroneous, often fatal, conclusions. In this case, the most eminent of the faculty gave it as their opinion, that the disease was consumption. Dr. Turton, if I recollect right, was then the most considered physician of the day. An immediate visit to a warmer climate was his specific; and as the Continent was then disturbed and foreign residence out of the question, Dr. Turton recommended that his patient should establish himself without delay in Devonshire.

When my father communicated this impending change in his life to Wolcot, the modern Skelton shook his head. He did not believe that his friend was in a consumption, but being a Devonshire man, and loving very much his native province, he highly approved of the remedy. He gave my father several letters of introduction to persons of consideration at Exeter; among others, one whom he justly described as a poet and a physician, and the best of men, the late Dr. Hugh Downman. Provincial cities very often enjoy a transient term of intellectual distinction. An eminent man often collects around him congenial spirits, and the power of association sometimes produces distant effects which even an individual, however gifted, could scarcely have anticipated. A combination of circumstances had made at this time Exeter a literary metropolis. A number of distinguished men flourished there at the same moment: some of their names are even now remembered. Jackson of Exeter still survives as a native composer of original genius. He was also an author of high æsthetical speculation. The heroic poems of Hole are forgotten, but his essay on the Arabian Nights is still a cherished volume of elegant and learned criticism. Hayter was the classic antiquary who first discovered the art of unrolling the MSS. of Herculaneum. There were many others, noisier and more bustling, who are now forgotten, though they in some degree influenced the literary opinion of their time. It was said, and I believe truly, that the two principal, if not sole, organs of periodical criticism at that time, I think the "Critical Review" and the "Monthly Review," were principally supported by Exeter contributions. No doubt this circumstance may account for a great deal of mutual praise and sympathetic opinion on literary subjects, which, by a convenient arrangement, appeared in the pages of publications otherwise professing contrary opinions on all others. Exeter had then even a learned society which published its Transactions.

With such companions, by whom he was received with a kindness and hospitality which to the last he often dwelt on, it may easily be supposed that the banishment of my father from the delights of literary London was not as productive a source of gloom as the exile of Ovid to the savage Pontus, even if it had not been his happy fortune to have been received on terms of intimate friendship by the accomplished family of Mr. Baring, who was then member for Exeter, and beneath whose roof he passed a great portion of the period of nearly three years during which he remained in Devonshire.

The illness of my father was relieved, but not removed, by this change of life. Dr. Downman was his physician, whose only remedies were port wine, horse-exercise, rowing on the neighbouring river, and the distraction of agreeable society. This wise physician recognised the temperament of his patient, and perceived that his physical derangement was an effect instead of a cause. My father instead of being in a consumption, was endowed with a frame of almost superhuman strength, and which was destined for half a century of continuous labour and sedentary life. The vital principle in him, indeed, was so strong that when he left us at eighty-two, it was only as the victim of a violent epidemic, against whose virulence he struggled with so much power, that it was clear, but for this casualty, he might have been spared to this world even for several years.

I should think that this illness of his youth, and which, though of a fitful character, was of many years' duration, arose from his inability to direct to a satisfactory end the intellectual power which he was conscious of possessing. He would mention the ten years of his life, from twenty-five to thirty-five years of age, as a period very deficient in self-contentedness. The fact is, with a poetic temperament, he had been born in an age when the poetic faith of which he was a votary had fallen into decrepitude, and had become only a form with the public, not yet gifted with sufficient fervour to discover a new creed. He was a pupil of Pope and Boileau, yet both from his native impulse and from the glowing influence of Rousseau, he felt the necessity and desire of infusing into the verse of the day more passion than might resound from the frigid lyre of Mr. Hayley. My father had fancy, sensibility, and an exquisite taste, but he had not that rare creative power, which the blended and simultaneous influence of the individual organisation and the spirit of the age, reciprocally acting upon each other, can alone, perhaps, perfectly develope; the absence of which, at periods of transition, is so universally recognised and deplored, and yet which always, when it does arrive, captivates us, as it were, by surprise. How much there was of freshness, and fancy, and natural pathos in his mind, may be discerned in his Persian romance of "The Loves of Mejnoon and Leila." We who have been accustomed to the great poets of the nineteenth century seeking their best inspiration in the climate and manners of the East; who are familiar with the land of the Sun from the isles of Ionia to the vales of Cashmere; can scarcely appreciate the literary originality of a writer who, fifty years ago, dared to devise a real Eastern story, and seeking inspiration in the pages of Oriental literature, compose it with reference to the Eastern mind, and customs, and landscape. One must have been familiar with the Almorans and Hamets, the Visions of Mirza and the kings of Ethiopia, and the other dull and monstrous masquerades of Orientalism then prevalent, to estimate such an enterprise, in which, however, one should not forget the author had the advantage of the guiding friendship of that distinguished Orientalist, Sir William Ouseley. The reception of this work by the public, and of other works of fiction which its author gave to them anonymously, was in every respect encouraging, and their success may impartially be registered as fairly proportionate to their merits; but it was not a success, or a proof of power, which, in my father's opinion, compensated for that life of literary research and study which their composition disturbed and enfeebled. It was at the ripe age of five-and-thirty that he renounced his dreams of being an author, and resolved to devote himself for the rest of his life to the acquisition of knowledge.

When my father, many years afterwards, made the acquaintance of Sir Walter Scott, the great poet saluted him by reciting a poem of half-a-dozen stanzas which my father had written in his early youth. Not altogether without agitation, surprise was expressed that these lines should have been known, still more that they should have been remembered. "Ah!" said Sir Walter, "if the writer of these lines had gone on, he would have been an English poet."[3]

It is possible; it is even probable that, if my father had devoted himself to the art, he might have become the author of some elegant and popular didactic poem, on some ordinary subject, which his fancy would have adorned with grace and his sensibility invested with sentiment; some small volume

---

3. Sir Walter was sincere, for he inserted the poem in the "English Minstrelsy." It may now be found in these volumes, Vol I. p. 230, where, in consequence of the recollection of Sir Walter, and as illustrative of manners now obsolete, it was subsequently inserted.

which might have reposed with a classic title upon our library shelves, and served as a prize volume at Ladies' Schools. This celebrity was not reserved for him: instead of this he was destined to give to his country a series of works illustrative of its literary and political history, full of new information and new views, which time and opinion has ratified as just. But the poetical temperament was not thrown away upon him; it never is on any one; it was this great gift which prevented his being a mere literary antiquary; it was this which animated his page with picture and his narrative with interesting vivacity; above all, it was this temperament, which invested him with that sympathy with his subject, which made him the most delightful biographer in our language. In a word, it was because he was a poet, that he was a popular writer, and made belles-lettres charming to the multitude.

It was during the ten years that now occurred that he mainly acquired that store of facts which were the foundation of his future speculations. His pen was never idle, but it was to note and to register, not to compose. His researches were prosecuted every morning among the MSS. of the British Museum, while his own ample collections permitted him to pursue his investigation in his own library into the night. The materials which he accumulated during this period are only partially exhausted. At the end of ten years, during which, with the exception of one anonymous work, he never indulged in composition, the irresistible desire of communicating his conclusions to the world came over him, and after all his almost childish aspirations, his youth of reverie and hesitating and imperfect effort, he arrived at the mature age of forty-five before his career as a great author, influencing opinion, really commenced.

The next ten years passed entirely in production: from 1812 to 1822 the press abounded with his works. His "Calamities of Authors," his "Memoirs of Literary Controversy," in the manner of Bayle; his "Essay on the Literary Character," the most perfect of his compositions; were all chapters in that History of English Literature which he then commenced to meditate, and which it was fated should never be completed.

It was during this period also that he published his "Inquiry into the Literary and Political Character of James the First," in which he first opened those views respecting the times and the conduct of the Stuarts, which were opposed to the long prevalent opinions of this country, but which with him were at least the result of unprejudiced research, and their promulgation, as he himself expressed it, "an affair of literary conscience."[4]

---

4. "The present inquiry originates in an affair of literary conscience. Many years ago I set off with the popular notions of the character of James the First; but in the course of study, and with a more enlarged comprehension of the age, I was frequently struck by the contrast between his real and his apparent character. *   *   *   *
*   *   *   *   It would be a cowardly silence to shrink from encountering

But what retarded his project of a History of our Literature at this time was the almost embarrassing success of his juvenile production, "The Curiosities of Literature." These two volumes had already reached five editions, and their author found himself, by the public demand, again called upon to sanction their re-appearance. Recognising in this circumstance some proof of their utility, he resolved to make the work more worthy of the favour which it enjoyed, and more calculated to produce the benefit which he desired. Without attempting materially to alter the character of the first two volumes, he revised and enriched them, while at the same time he added a third volume of a vein far more critical, and conveying the results of much original research. The success of this publication was so great, that its author, after much hesitation, resolved, as he was wont to say, to take advantage of a popular title, and pour forth the treasures of his mind in three additional volumes, which, unlike continuations in general, were at once greeted with the highest degree of popular delight and esteem. And, indeed, whether we consider the choice variety of the subjects, the critical and philosophical speculation which pervades them, the amount of new and interesting information brought to bear, and the animated style in which all is conveyed, it is difficult to conceive miscellaneous literature in a garb more stimulating and attractive. These six volumes, after many editions, are now condensed into the form at present given to the public, and in which the development of the writer's mind for a quarter of a century may be completely traced.

Although my father had on the whole little cause to complain of unfair criticism, especially considering how isolated he always remained, it is not to be supposed that a success so eminent should have been exempt in so long a course from some captious comments. It has been alleged of late years by some critics, that he was in the habit of exaggerating the importance of his researches; that he was too fond of styling every accession to our knowledge, however slight, as a discovery; that there were some inaccuracies in his early volumes (not very wonderful in so multifarious a work), and that the foundation of his "secret history" was often only a single letter, or a passage in a solitary diary.

The sources of secret history at the present day are so rich and various; there is such an eagerness among their possessors to publish family papers, even sometimes in shares, and at dates so recent, as scarcely to justify their appearance; that modern critics, in their embarrassment of manuscript wealth, are apt to view with too depreciating an eye the more limited resources of men of letters at the commencement of the century. Not five-and-twenty

---

all that popular prejudice and party feeling may oppose; this would be incompatible with that constant search after truth, which at least may be expected from the retired student."—*Preface to the Inquiry.*

years ago, when preparing his work on King Charles the First, the application of my father to make some researches in the State Paper Office was refused by the Secretary of State of the day. Now, foreign potentates and ministers of State, and public corporations and the heads of great houses, feel honoured by such appeals, and respond to them with cordiality. It is not only the State Paper Office of England, but the Archives of France, that are open to the historical investigator. But what has produced this general and expanding taste for literary research in the world, and especially in England? The labours of our elder authors, whose taste and acuteness taught us the value of the materials which we in our ignorance neglected. When my father first frequented the reading-room of the British Museum at the end of the last century, his companions never numbered half-a-dozen; among them, if I remember rightly, were Mr. Pinkerton and Mr. Douce. Now these daily pilgrims of research may be counted by as many hundreds. Few writers have more contributed to form and diffuse this delightful and profitable taste for research than the author of the "Curiosities of Literature;" few writers have been more successful in inducing us to pause before we accepted without a scruple the traditionary opinion that has distorted a fact or calumniated a character; and independently of every other claim which he possesses to public respect, his literary discoveries, viewed in relation to the age and the means, were considerable. But he had other claims: a vital spirit in his page, kindred with the souls of a Bayle and a Montaigne. His innumerable imitators and their inevitable failure for half a century alone prove this, and might have made them suspect that there were some ingredients in the spell besides the accumulation of facts and a happy title. Many of their publications, perpetually appearing and constantly forgotten, were drawn up by persons of considerable acquirements, and were ludicrously mimetic of their prototype, even as to the size of the volume and the form of the page. What has become of these "Varieties of Literature," and "Delights of Literature," and "Delicacies of Literature," and "Relics of Literature,"—and the other Protean terms of uninspired compilation? Dead as they deserve to be: while the work, the idea of which occurred to its writer in his early youth, and which he lived virtually to execute in all the ripeness of his studious manhood, remains as fresh and popular as ever,—the Literary Miscellany of the English People.

I have ventured to enter into some details as to the earlier and obscurer years of my father's life, because I thought that they threw light upon human character, and that without them, indeed, a just appreciation of his career could hardly be formed. I am mistaken, if we do not recognise in his instance two very interesting qualities of life: predisposition and self-formation. There was a third, which I think is to be honoured, and that was his sympathy with his order. No one has written so much about authors, and so well. Indeed, before his time, the Literary Character had never been fairly placed before the world. He comprehended its idiosyncrasy: all its strength and all its weakness.

He could soften, because he could explain, its infirmities; in the analysis and record of its power, he vindicated the right position of authors in the social scale. They stand between the governors and the governed, he impresses on us in the closing pages of his greatest work.[5] Though he shared none of the calamities, and scarcely any of the controversies, of literature, no one has sympathised so intimately with the sorrows, or so zealously and impartially registered the instructive disputes, of literary men. He loved to celebrate the exploits of great writers, and to show that, in these ages, the pen is a weapon as puissant as the sword. He was also the first writer who vindicated the position of the great artist in the history of genius. His pages are studded with pregnant instances and graceful details, borrowed from the life of Art and its votaries, and which his intimate and curious acquaintance with Italian letters readily and happily supplied. Above all writers, he has maintained the greatness of intellect, and the immortality of thought.

He was himself a complete literary character, a man who really passed his life in his library. Even marriage produced no change in these habits; he rose to enter the chamber where he lived alone with his books, and at night his lamp was ever lit within the same walls. Nothing, indeed, was more remarkable than the isolation of this prolonged existence; and it could only be accounted for by the united influence of three causes: his birth, which brought him no relations or family acquaintance; the bent of his disposition; and the circumstance of his inheriting an independent fortune, which rendered unnecessary those exertions that would have broken up his self-reliance. He disliked business, and he never required relaxation; he was absorbed in his pursuits. In London his only amusement was to ramble among booksellers; if he entered a club, it was only to go into the library. In the country, he scarcely ever left his room but to saunter in abstraction upon a terrace; muse over a chapter, or coin a sentence. He had not a single passion or prejudice: all his convictions were the result of his own studies, and were often opposed to the impressions which he had early imbibed. He not only never entered into the politics of the day, but he could never understand them. He never was connected with any particular body or set of men; comrades of school or college, or confederates in that public life which, in England, is, perhaps, the only foundation of real friendship. In the consideration of a question, his mind was quite undisturbed by traditionary preconceptions; and it was this exemption from passion and prejudice which, although his intelligence was naturally somewhat too ingenious and fanciful for the conduct of close argument, enabled him, in investigation, often to show many of the highest attributes of the judicial mind, and particularly to sum up evidence with singular happiness and ability.

---

5. "Essay on the Literary Character," Vol. II. chap. xxv.

Although in private life he was of a timid nature, his moral courage as a writer was unimpeachable. Most certainly, throughout his long career, he never wrote a sentence which he did not believe was true. He will generally be found to be the advocate of the discomfited and the oppressed. So his conclusions are often opposed to popular impressions. This was from no love of paradox; to which he was quite superior; but because in the conduct of his researches, he too often found that the unfortunate are calumniated. His vindication of King James the First, he has himself described as "an affair of literary conscience:" his greater work on the Life and Times of the son of the first Stuart arose from the same impulse. He had deeply studied our history during the first moiety of the seventeenth century; he looked upon it as a famous age; he was familiar with the works of its great writers, and there was scarcely one of its almost innumerable pamphlets with which he was not acquainted. During the thoughtful investigations of many years, he had arrived at results which were not adapted to please the passing multitude, but which, because he held them to be authentic, he was uneasy lest he should die without recording. Yet strong as were his convictions, although, notwithstanding his education in the revolutionary philosophy of the eighteenth century, his nature and his studies had made him a votary of loyalty and reverence, his pen was always prompt to do justice to those who might be looked upon as the adversaries of his own cause: and this was because his cause was really truth. If he has upheld Laud under unjust aspersions, the last labour of his literary life was to vindicate the character of Hugh Peters. If, from the recollection of the sufferings of his race, and from profound reflection on the principles of the Institution, he was hostile to the Papacy, no writer in our literature has done more complete justice to the conduct of the English Romanists. Who can read his history of Chidiock Titchbourne unmoved? or can refuse to sympathise with his account of the painful difficulties of the English Monarchs with their loyal subjects of the old faith? If in a parliamentary country he has dared to criticise the conduct of Parliaments, it was only because an impartial judgment had taught him, as he himself expresses it, that "Parliaments have their passions as well as individuals."

He was five years in the composition of his work on the "Life and Reign of Charles the First," and the five volumes appeared at intervals between 1828 and 1831. It was feared by his publisher, that the distracted epoch at which this work was issued, and the tendency of the times, apparently so adverse to his own views, might prove very injurious to its reception. But the effect of these circumstances was the reverse. The minds of men were inclined to the grave and national considerations that were involved in these investigations. The principles of political institutions, the rival claims of the two Houses of Parliament, the authority of the Established Church, the demands of religious sects, were, after a long lapse of years, anew the theme of public discussion.

Men were attracted to a writer who traced the origin of the anti-monarchical principle in modern Europe; treated of the arts of insurgency; gave them, at the same time, a critical history of the Puritans, and a treatise on the genius of the Papacy; scrutinised the conduct of triumphant patriots, and vindicated a decapitated monarch. The success of this work was eminent; and its author appeared for the first and only time of his life in public, when amidst the cheers of under-graduates, and the applause of graver men, the solitary student received an honorary degree from the University of Oxford, a fitting homage, in the language of the great University, "OPTIMI REGIS OPTIMO VINDICI."

I cannot but recall a trait that happened on this occasion. After my father returned to his hotel from the theatre, a stranger requested an interview with him. A Swiss gentleman, travelling in England at the time, who had witnessed the scene just closed, begged to express the reason why he presumed thus personally and cordially to congratulate the new Doctor of Civil Law. He was the son of my grandfather's chief clerk, and remembered his parent's employer; whom he regretted did not survive to be aware of this honourable day. Thus, amid all the strange vicissitudes of life, we are ever, as it were, moving in a circle.

Notwithstanding he was now approaching his seventieth year, his health being unbroken and his constitution very robust, my father resolved vigorously to devote himself to the composition of the history of our vernacular Literature. He hesitated for a moment, whether he should at once address himself to this greater task, or whether he should first complete a Life of Pope, for which he had made great preparations, and which had long occupied his thoughts. His review of "Spence's Anecdotes" in the Quarterly, so far back as 1820, which gave rise to the celebrated Pope Controversy, in which Mr. Campbell, Lord Byron, Mr. Bowles, Mr. Roscoe, and others less eminent broke lances, would prove how well qualified, even at that distant date, the critic was to become the biographer of the great writer, whose literary excellency and moral conduct he, on that occasion, alike vindicated. But, unfortunately as it turned out, my father was persuaded to address himself to the weightier task. Hitherto, in his publications, he had always felt an extreme reluctance to travel over ground which others had previously visited. He liked to give new matter, and devote himself to detached points, on which he entertained different opinions from those prevalent. Thus his works are generally of a supplementary character, and assume in their readers a certain degree of preliminary knowledge. In the present instance he was induced to frame his undertaking on a different scale, and to prepare a history which should be complete in itself, and supply the reader with a perfect view of the gradual formation of our language and literature. He proposed to effect this in six volumes; though, I apprehend, he would not have succeeded in fulfilling his intentions within that limit. His treatment of the period of Queen

Anne would have been very ample, and he would also have accomplished in this general work a purpose which he had also long contemplated, and for which he had made curious and extensive collections, namely, a History of the English Freethinkers.

But all these great plans were destined to a terrible defeat. Towards the end of the year 1839, still in the full vigour of his health and intellect, he suffered a paralysis of the optic nerve; and that eye, which for so long a term had kindled with critical interest over the volumes of so many literatures and so many languages, was doomed to pursue its animated course no more. Considering the bitterness of such a calamity to one whose powers were otherwise not in the least impaired, he bore on the whole his fate with magnanimity, even with cheerfulness. Unhappily, his previous habits of study and composition rendered the habit of dictation intolerable, even impossible to him. But with the assistance of his daughter, whose intelligent solicitude he has commemorated in more than one grateful passage, he selected from his manuscripts three volumes, which he wished to have published under the becoming title of "A Fragment of a History of English Literature," but which were eventually given to the public under that of "Amenities of Literature."

He was also enabled during these last years of physical, though not of moral, gloom, to prepare a new edition of his work on the Life and Times of Charles the First, which had been for some time out of print. He contrived, though slowly, and with great labour, very carefully to revise, and improve, and enrich these volumes. He was wont to say that the best monument to an author was a good edition of his works: it is my purpose that he should possess this memorial. He has been described by a great authority as a writer sui generis; and indeed had he never written, it appears to me, that there would have been a gap in our libraries, which it would have been difficult to supply. Of him it might be added that, for an author, his end was an euthanasia, for on the day before he was seized by that fatal epidemic, of the danger of which, to the last moment, he was unconscious, he was apprised by his publishers, that all his works were out of print, and that their re-publication could no longer be delayed.

In this notice of the career of my father, I have ventured to draw attention to three circumstances which I thought would be esteemed interesting; namely, predisposition, self-formation, and sympathy with his order. There is yet another which completes and crowns the character,—constancy of purpose; and it is only in considering his course as a whole, that we see how harmonious and consistent have been that life and its labours, which, in a partial and brief view, might be supposed to have been somewhat desultory and fragmentary.

On his moral character I shall scarcely presume to dwell. The philosophic sweetness of his disposition, the serenity of his lot, and the elevating nature of his pursuits, combined to enable him to pass through life without an evil act, almost without an evil thought. As the world has always been fond of personal details respecting men who have been celebrated, I will mention that he was fair, with a Bourbon nose, and brown eyes of extraordinary beauty and lustre. He wore a small black velvet cap, but his white hair latterly touched his shoulders in curls almost as flowing as in his boyhood. His extremities were delicate and well-formed, and his leg, at his last hour, as shapely as in his youth, which showed the vigour of his frame. Latterly he had become corpulent. He did not excel in conversation, though in his domestic circle he was garrulous. Everything interested him; and blind, and eighty-two, he was still as susceptible as a child. One of his last acts was to compose some verses of gay gratitude to his daughter-in-law, who was his London correspondent, and to whose lively pen his last years were indebted for constant amusement. He had by nature a singular volatility which never deserted him. His feelings, though always amiable, were not painfully deep, and amid joy or sorrow, the philosophic vein was ever evident. He more resembled Goldsmith than any man that I can compare him to: in his conversation, his apparent confusion of ideas ending with some felicitous phrase of genius, his naïveté, his simplicity not untouched with a dash of sarcasm affecting innocence—one was often reminded of the gifted and interesting friend of Burke and Johnson. There was, however, one trait in which my father did not resemble Goldsmith: he had no vanity. Indeed, one of his few infirmities was rather a deficiency of self-esteem.

On the whole, I hope—nay I believe—that taking all into consideration—the integrity and completeness of his existence, the fact that, for sixty years, he largely contributed to form the taste, charm the leisure, and direct the studious dispositions, of the great body of the public, and that his works have extensively and curiously illustrated the literary and political history of our country, it will be conceded, that in his life and labours, he repaid England for the protection and the hospitality which this country accorded to his father a century ago.

D.

Hughenden Manor,
    Christmas, 1848.

I. WRITING AND READING

1. ORIGIN OF THE MATERIALS OF WRITING
(*Curiosities,* vol. 2, pp. 23-30)

IT is curious to observe the various substitutes for paper before its discovery.

Ere the invention of recording events by writing, trees were planted, rude altars were erected, or heaps of stone, to serve as memorials of past events. Hercules probably could not write when he fixed his famous pillars.

The most ancient mode of writing was on *bricks, tiles,* and *oyster-shells,* and on *tables of stone;* afterwards on *plates* of various materials, on *ivory,* on *barks* of trees, on *leaves* of trees.[6]

Engraving memorable events on hard substances was giving, as it were, speech to rocks and metals. In the book of Job mention is made of writing on *stone,* on *rocks,* and on sheets of *lead.* On tables of *stone* Moses received the law written by the finger of God. Hesiod's works were written on *leaden* tables: lead was used for writing, and rolled up like a cylinder, as Pliny states. Montfaucon notices a very ancient book of eight leaden leaves, which on the back had rings fastened by a small leaden rod to keep them together. They afterwards engraved on bronze: the laws of the Cretans were on bronze tables; the Romans etched their public records on brass. The speech of Claudius, engraved on plates of bronze, is yet preserved in the town-hall of Lyons, in France.[7] Several bronze tables, with Etruscan characters, have been dug up in Tuscany. The treaties among the Romans, Spartans, and the Jews, were written on brass; and estates, for better security, were made over on this enduring metal. In many cabinets may be found the discharge of soldiers, written on copper-plates. This custom has been discovered in India: a bill of

---

6. Specimens of most of these modes of writing may be seen at the British Museum. No. 3478, in the Sloanian library, is a Nabob's letter, on a piece of bark, about two yards long, and richly ornamented with gold. No. 3207 is a book of Mexican hieroglyphics, painted on bark. In the same collection are various species, many from the Malabar coast and the East. The latter writings are chiefly on leaves. There are several copies of Bibles written on palm leaves. The ancients, doubtless, wrote on any leaves they found adapted for the purpose. Hence, the *leaf* of a *book,* alluding to that of a tree, seems to be derived. At the British Museum we have also Babylonian tiles, or *broken pots,* which the people used, and made their contracts of business on; a custom mentioned in the Scriptures.

7. This speech was made by Claudius (who was born at Lyons), when censor, A.D. 48, and was of the highest importance to the men of Lyons, inasmuch as it led to the grant of the privileges of Roman citizenship to them. This important inscription was discovered in 1528, on the heights of St. Sebastian above the town.

feoffment on copper, has been dug up near Bengal, dated a century before the birth of Christ.

Among these early inventions many were singularly rude, and miserable substitutes for a better material. In the shepherd state they wrote their songs with thorns and awls on straps of leather, which they wound round their crooks. The Icelanders appear to have scratched their *runes*, a kind of hieroglyphics, on walls; and Olaf, according to one of the Sagas, built a large house, on the bulks and spars of which he had engraved the history of his own and more ancient times; while another northern hero appears to have had nothing better than his own chair and bed to perpetuate his own heroic acts on. At the town-hall, in Hanover, are kept twelve wooden boards, overlaid with bees'-wax, on which are written the names of owners of houses, but not the names of streets. These *wooden manuscripts* must have existed before 1423, when Hanover was first divided into streets. Such manuscripts may be found in public collections. These are an evidence of a rude state of *society*. The same event occurred among the ancient Arabs, who, according to the history of Mahomet, seemed to have carved on the shoulder-bones of sheep remarkable events with a knife, and tying them with a string, hung up these sheep-bone chronicles.

The laws of the twelve tables, which the Romans chiefly copied from the Grecian code, were, after they had been approved by the people, engraven on brass: they were melted by lightning, which struck the Capitol; a loss highly regretted by Augustus. This manner of writing we still retain, for inscriptions, epitaphs, and other memorials designed to reach posterity.

These early inventions led to the discovery of tables of *wood;* and as *cedar* has an antiseptic quality from its bitterness, they chose this wood for cases or chests to preserve their most important writings. This well-known expression of the ancients, when they meant to give the highest eulogium of an excellent work, *et cedro digna locuti*, that it was worthy to be written on *cedar*, alludes to the *oil of cedar*, with which valuable MSS, of parchment were anointed, to preserve them from corruption and moths. Persius illustrates this:—

> Who would not leave posterity such rhymes
> As *cedar oil* might keep to latest times!

They stained materials for writing upon, with purple, and rubbed them with exudations from the cedar. The laws of the emperors were published on *wooden tables*, painted with ceruse; to which custom Horace alludes: *Leges incidere ligno*. Such *tables*, the term now softened into *tablets*, are still used, but in general are made of other materials than wood. The same reason for which they preferred the *cedar* to other wood induced to write on *wax*, as being incorruptible. Men generally used it to write their testaments on, the better to preserve them; thus Juvenal says, *Ceras implere capaces*. This thin paste of wax was also used on tablets of wood, that it might more easily admit of erasure, for daily use.

They wrote with an iron bodkin, as they did on the other substances we have noticed. The *stylus* was made sharp at one end to write with, and blunt and broad at the other, to efface and correct easily: hence the phrase *vertere stylum*, to turn the stylus, was used to express blotting out. But the Romans forbad the use of this sharp instrument, from the circumstance of many persons having used them as daggers. A schoolmaster was killed by the Pugillares or table-books, and the styles of his own scholars.[8] They substituted a *stylus* made of the bone of a bird, or other animal; so that their writings resembled engravings. When they wrote on softer materials, they employed *reeds* and *canes* split like our *pens* at the points, which the orientalists still use to lay their colour or ink neater on the paper.

Naudé observes, that when he was in Italy, about 1642, he saw some of those waxen tablets, called Pugillares, so called because they were held in one hand; and others composed of the barks of trees, which the ancients employed in lieu of paper.

On these tablets, or table-books Mr. Astle observes, that the Greeks and Romans continued the use of waxed table-books long after the use of the papyrus, leaves and skins became common; because they were convenient for correcting extemporaneous compositions: from these table-books they transcribed their performances correctly into parchment books, if for their own private use; but if for sale, or for the library, the *Librarii*, or Scribes, performed the office. The writing on table-books is particularly recommended by Quintilian in the third chapter of the tenth book of his Institutions; because the wax is readily effaced for any corrections: he confesses weak eyes do not see so well on paper, and observes that the frequent necessity of dipping the pen in the inkstand retards the hand, and is but ill-suited to the celerity of the mind. Some of these table-books are conjectured to have been large, and perhaps heavy, for in Plautus, a school-boy is represented breaking his master's head with his table-book. The critics, according to Cicero, were accustomed in reading their wax manuscripts to notice obscure or vicious phrases by joining a piece of red wax, as we should underline such by red ink.

Table-books written upon with styles were not entirely laid aside in Chaucer's time, who describes them in his Sompner's tale:—

> His fellow had a staffe tipp'd with horne,
> *A paire of tables all of iverie;*
> And a *pointell polished* fetouslie,

---

8. The paintings discovered at Pompeii give representations of these books and implements.

And wrote alwaies the names, as he stood,
Of all folke, that gave hem any good.[9]

By the word *pen* in the translation of the Bible we must understand an iron *style*. Table-books of ivory are still used for memoranda, written with black-lead pencils. The Romans used ivory to write the edicts of the senate on, with a black colour; and the expression of *libri elephantini*, which some authors imagine alludes to books that for their *size* were called *elephantine*, were most probably composed of ivory, the tusk of the elephant: among the Romans they were undoubtedly scarce.

The *pumice stone* was writing-material of the ancients; they used it to smoothe the roughness of the parchment, or to sharpen their reeds.

In the progress of time the art of writing consisted in *painting* with different kinds of *ink*. This novel mode of writing occasioned them to invent other materials proper to receive their writing; the thin bark of certain *trees* and *plants*, or *linen;* and at length, when this was found apt to become mouldy, they prepared the *skins of animals;* on the dried skins of serpents were once written the Iliad and Odyssey. The first place where they began to dress these skins was *Pergamus*, in Asia; whence the Latin name is derived of *Pergamenæ* or *parchment*. These skins are, however, better known amongst the authors of the purest Latin under the name of *membrana;* so called from the membranes of various animals of which they were composed. The ancients had *parchments* of three different colours, white, yellow, and purple. At Rome white parchment was disliked, because it was more subject to be soiled than the others, and dazzled the eye. They generally wrote in letters of gold and silver on purple or violet parchment. This custom continued in the early ages of the church; and copies of the evangelists of this kind are preserved in the British Museum.

When the Egyptians employed for writing the *bark* of a *plant* or *reed*, called *papyrus*, or paper-rush, it superseded all former modes, for its convenience. Formerly it grew in great quantities on the sides of the Nile. This plant has given its name to our *paper*, although the latter is now composed of linen and rags, and formerly had been of cotton-wool, which was but brittle and yellow; and improved by using cotton rags, which they glazed. After the eighth century the papyrus was superseded by parchment. The *Chinese* make their *paper* with *silk*. The use of *paper* is of great antiquity. It is what the ancient

---

9. The use of the table-book was continued to the reign of James I. or later. Shakspeare frequently alludes to them—
     "And therefore will he wipe his tables clean,
     And keep no tell-tale to his memory."
They were in the form of a modern pocket-book, the leaves of asses' skin, or covered with a composition, upon which a silver or leaden style would inscribe memoranda capable of erasure.

Latinists call *charta* or *chartæ*. Before the use of *parchment* and *paper* passed to the Romans, they used the thin peel found between the wood and the bark of trees. This skinny substance they called *liber*, from whence the Latin word *liber*, a book, and *library* and *librarian* in the European languages, and the French *livre* for book; but we of northern origin derive our *book* from the Danish *bog*, the beech-tree, because that being the most plentiful in Denmark was used to engrave on. Anciently, instead of folding this bark, this parchment, or paper, as we fold ours, they rolled it according as they wrote on it; and the Latin name which they gave these rolls has passed into our language as well as the others. We say a *volume*, or volumes, although our books are composed of leaves bound together. The books of the ancients on the shelves of their libraries were rolled up on a pin and placed erect, titled on the outside in red letters, or rubrics, and appeared like a number of small pillars on the shelves.[10]

The ancients were as curious as ourselves in having their books richly conditioned. Propertius describes tablets with gold borders, and Ovid notices their red titles; but in later times, besides the tint of purple with which they tinged their vellum, and the liquid gold which they employed for their ink, they inlaid their covers with precious stones: and I have seen, in the library at Triers or Treves, a manuscript, the donation of some princess to a monastery, studded with heads wrought in fine cameos.[11] In the early ages of the church they painted on the outside commonly a dying Christ. In the curious library of Mr. Douce is a Psalter, supposed once to have appertained to Charlemagne; the vellum is purple, and the letters gold. The Eastern nations likewise tinged their MSS. with different colours and decorations. Astle possessed Arabian MSS., of which some leaves were of a deep yellow, and others of a lilac colour. Sir William Jones describes an oriental MS., in which the name of Mohammed was fancifully adorned with a garland of tulips and carnations, painted in the brightest colours. The favourite works of the Persians are written on fine silky paper, the ground of which is often powdered with gold or silver dust; the leaves are frequently illuminated, and the whole book is sometimes perfumed with essence of roses, or sandal wood. The Romans had several sorts of paper, for which they had as many different names; one was the *Charta Augusta*, in compliment to the emperor; another *Livinia*, named after the empress. There was a *Charta blanca*, which obtained its title from its beautiful whiteness, and which we appear to have retained by applying it to a blank sheet of paper which is only signed, *Charte blanche*. They had also a *Charta nigra*, painted black, and the letters were in white or other colours.

Our present paper surpasses all other materials for ease and convenience

---

10. A box containing such written rolls is represented in one of the pictures exhumed at Pompeii.

11. See note to Vol. I. p. 5 [=note 149 below].

of writing. The first paper-mill in England was erected at Dartford, by a German, in 1588, who was knighted by Elizabeth; but it was not before 1713 that one Thomas Watkins, a stationer, brought the art of paper-making to any perfection, and to the industry of this individual we owe the origin of our numerous paper-mills. France had hitherto supplied England and Holland.

The manufacture of paper was not much encouraged at home, even so late as in 1662; and the following observations by Fuller are curious, respecting the paper of his times:—"Paper participates in some sort of the characters of the country which makes it; the *Venetian*, being neat, subtile, and court-like; the *French*, light, slight, and slender; the *Dutch*, thick, corpulent, and gross, sucking up the ink with the sponginess thereof." He complains that the paper-manufactories were not then sufficiently encouraged, "considering the vast sums of money expended in our land for paper, out of Italy, France, and Germany, which might be lessened, were it made in our nation. To such who object that we can never equal the perfection of *Venice-paper*, I return, neither can we match the purity of Venice-glasses; and yet many *green ones* are blown in Sussex, profitable to the makers, and convenient for the users. Our *home-spun paper* might be found beneficial." The present German printing-paper is made so disagreeable both to printers and readers from their paper-manufacturers making many more reams of paper from one cwt. of rags than formerly. Rags are scarce, and German writers, as well as their language, are voluminous.

Mr. Astle deeply complains of the inferiority of our *inks* to those of antiquity; an inferiority productive of the most serious consequences, and which appears to originate merely in negligence. From the important benefits arising to society from the use of ink, and the injuries individuals may suffer from the frauds of designing men, he wishes the legislature would frame some new regulations respecting it. The composition of ink is simple, but we possess none equal in beauty and colour to that used by the ancients; the Saxon MSS. written in England exceed in colour anything of the kind. The rolls and records from the fifteenth century to the end of the seventeenth, compared with those of the fifth to the twelfth centuries, show the excellence of the earlier ones, which are all in the finest preservation; while the others are so much defaced, that they are scarcely legible.

The ink of the ancients had nothing in common with ours, but the colour and gum. Gall-nuts, copperas, and gum make up the composition of our ink; whereas *soot* or *ivory-black* was the chief ingredient in that of the ancients.[12]

Ink has been made of various colours; we find gold and silver ink, and red,

---

12. The ink of old manuscripts is generally a thick solid substance, and sometimes stands in relief upon the paper. The red ink is generally a body-colour of great brilliancy.

green, yellow, and blue inks; but the black is considered as the best adapted to its purpose.

2. ORTHOGRAPHY AND ORTHOEPY
(Amenities, pp. 381-392)

SOME of the first scholars of our country stepped out of the circle of their classical studies with the patriotic design of inculcating the possibility of creating a literary language. This was a generous effort in those who had already secured their supremacy by their skill and dexterity in the two languages consecrated by scholars. Many of the learned engaged in the ambitious reform of our *orthography*, then regulated by no certain laws; but while each indulged in some scheme different from his predecessors, the language seemed only to be the more disguised amid such difficult improvements and fantastic inventions.

A curious instance of the monstrous anomalies of our orthography in the infancy of our literature, when a spelling-book was yet a precious thing which had no existence, appears in this letter of the Duchess of Norfolk to Cromwell, Earl of Essex.

"My ffary gode lord—her I sand you in tokyn hoff the neweyer a glasse hoff Setyl set in, Sellfer gyld I pra you tak hit (in) wort An hy wer habel het showlde be bater I woll hit war wort a m crone."

These lines were written by one of the most accomplished ladies of the sixteenth century, "the friend of scholars and the patron of literature." Dr. Nott, who has supplied this literary curiosity, has modernized the passage word by word; and though the idiom of the times is preserved, it no longer wears any appearance of vulgarity or of illiteracy.

"My very good lord,—Here I send you, in token of the New Year, a glass of setyll set in silver gilt; I pray you take it (in) worth. An I were able, it should be better. I would it were worth a thousand crowns."

The domestic correspondence, as appears in letters of the times, seems to indicate that the writers imagined that, by conferring larger dimensions on their words by the duplication of redundant consonants, they were augmenting the force, even of a monosyllable![13]

In such disorder lay our orthography, that writers, however peculiar in

---

13. See "The Paston Letters," edited by Sir JOHN FENN; and LODGE's authentic and valuable Collection.

their mode of spelling, did not even write the same words uniformly. Elizabeth herself wrote one word, which assuredly she had constantly in her mind, seven different ways, for thus has this queen written the word *sovereign.* The royal mistress of eight languages seemed at a loss which to choose for her command. The orthography of others eminent for their learning was as remarkable, and sometimes more eruditely whimsical, either in the attempt to retrace the etymology, or to modify exotic words to a native origin; or, finally, to suit the popular pronunciation. What system or method could be hoped for at a time when there prevailed a strange discrepancy in the very names of persons, so variously written not only by their friends but by their owners? Lord Burleigh, when Secretary of State, daily signing despatches with the favourite *Leicester,* yet spelt his name *Lecester;* and Leicester himself has subscribed his own name eight different ways.[14]

At that period down to a much later, every one seems to have been at a loss to write their own names. The name of *Villers* is spelt fourteen different ways in the deeds of that family. The simple dissyllabic but illustrious name of *Percy,* the bishop found in family documents, they had contrived to write in fifteen different ways.

This unsettled state of our *orthography,* and what it often depended on, our *orthoepy,* was an inconvenience detected even at a very early period. The learned Sir JOHN CHEKE, the most accomplished Greek scholar of the age, descended from correcting the Greek pronunciation to invent a system of English orthography. Cheke was no formal pedant; with an enlarged notion of the vernacular language, he aimed to restore the English of his day to what then he deemed to be its purity. He would allow of no words but such as were true English, or of Saxon original; admitting of no adoption of any foreign word into the English language, which at this early period our scholar deemed sufficiently copious. He objected to the English translation of the Bible, for its introduction of many foreign words; and to prove them unnecessary he retranslated the Gospel of St. Matthew, written on his own system of a new orthography. His ear was nice, and his Attic taste had the singular merit of giving concision to the perplexed periods of our early style. But his orthography deterred the eyes of his readers; however the learned Cheke was right in his abstract principle, it operated wrong when put in practice, for every newly-spelt word seemed to require a peculiar vocabulary.

When Secretaries of State were also men of literature, the learned Sir THOMAS SMITH, under Elizabeth, composed his treatise on "The English Commonwealth," both in Latin and in English—the worthy companion of

---

14. George Chalmers' "Apology for the Believers in the Shakspeare Papers," 94.—See on this subject in "Curiosities of Literature," art. "Orthography of Proper Names." [Also a note on the orthography of Shakspeare's name, in an Essay on that Poet, in a future page of the present volume.]

the great work of Fortescue. Not deterred by the fate of his friend, the learned Cheke, he projected even a bolder system, to correct the writing of English words. He designed to relieve the ear from the clash of supernumerary consonants, and to liquify by a vowelly confluence. But though the scholar exposed the absurdity of the general practice, where in certain words the redundant letters became mutes, or do not comprehend the sounds which are expressed, while in other words we have no letters which can express the sounds by which they are spoken, he had only ascertained the disease, for he was not equally fortunate in the prevention. An enlargement of the alphabet, ten vowels instead of five, and a fantastical mixture of the Roman, the Greek, and the Saxon characters, required an Englishman to be a very learned man to read and write his maternal language. This project was only substituting for one difficulty another more strange.

Were we to course the wide fields which these early "rackers of orthography" have run over, we should start, at every turn, some strange "winged words;" but they would be fantastic monsters, neither birds with wings nor hares with feet. Shakspeare sarcastically describes this numerous race: "Now he is turned ORTHOGRAPHER his words are a very fantastical banquet; just so many strange dishes." Some may amuse. One affords a quaint definition of the combination of *orthoepy* with *orthography,* for he would teach "how to write or *paint the image of man's voice* like to the life or nature."[15] The most popular amender of our defective orthography was probably BULLOKAR, for his work at least was republished. He proposed a bold confusion, to fix the fugitive sounds by recasting the whole alphabet, and enlarging its number from twenty-four to more letters, giving two sounds to one letter, to some three; at present no mark or difference shows how the sounded letters should be sounded, while our speech (or orthography) so widely differed; but the fault, says old Bullokar, is in the *picture,* that is, the letters, not the speech. His scheme would have turned the language into a sort of music-book, where the notes would have taught the tones.[16] I extract from his address to his country a curious passage. "In true orthographie, both the *eye,* the *voice,* and the *eare* must consent perfectly without any let, doubt, or maze. Which want of concord in the eye, voice, and ear I did perceive almost thirtie yeares past by the very voice of children, who, guided by the eye with the letter, and giving voice according to the name thereof, as they were taught to name letters, yielded the eare of the hearer a degree contrary sound to the word looked for; hereby grewe quarrels in the teacher, and lothsomeness in

---

15. "An Orthographic, composed by J(ohn) H(art), Chester Herald," 1569. A book of extreme rarity. A copy at Horne Tooke's sale was sold for *6l. 6s.* It is in the British Museum.

16. "Bullokar's Booke at large for the Amendment of Orthographie for English Speech," &c. &c., 1580, 4to; republished in 1586.

the learner, and great payne to both, and the conclusion was that both teacher and learner must go by rote, or no rule could be followed, when of 37 parts 31 kept no square, nor true joint."

All these reformers, with many subsequent ones, only continued to disclose the uneasy state of the minds of the learned in respect to our inveterate orthography; so difficult was it, and so long did it take to teach the nation how to spell, an art in which we have never perfectly succeeded. Even the learned Mulcaster, in his zealous labour to "the right writing of the English tongue," failed, though his principle seems one of the most obvious in simplicity. This scholar, a master of St. Paul's school, freed from collegiate prejudices, maintained that "words should be written as they were spoken." But where were we to seek for the standard of our orthoepy? Who was to furnish the model of our speech, in a land where the pronunciation varied from the court, the capital, or the county, and as mutable from age to age? The same effort was made among our neighbours. In 1570 the learned Joubert attempted to introduce a new orthography, without, however, the aid of strange characters. His rule was only to give those letters which yield the proper pronunciation; thus he wrote, *œuvres,* uvres; *françoise,* fransaise: *temps,* tems.

Among the early reformers of our vernacular idiom, the name of RICHARD MULCASTER has hardly reached posterity. Our philologer has dignified a small volume ostensibly composed for "the training of children,"[17] by the elevated view he opened of far distant times from his own of our vernacular literature—and he had the glory of having made this noble discovery when our literature was yet in its infancy.

This learned master of St. Paul's school developes the historical progress of language, on the great philosophical principle that no impediment existed to prevent the modern from rivalling the more perfect ancient languages. In opposition to the many who contended that no subject can be philosophically treated in the maternal English, he maintained that no one language, naturally, is more refined than another, but is made so by the industry of "eloquent speech" in the writers themselves, and by the excellence of the matter; a native soil becomes more genial in emulating a foreign. I preserve the pleasing illustration of his argument in the purity of his own prose, and because he was the prophet of our literature.

"The people of Athens thus beautified their speech and enriched their tongue with all kinds of knowledge, both bred within Greece and borrowed from without. The people of Rome having plotted (planned) their government much like the Athenians, became enamoured of their eloquence,

---

17. "The first part of the Elementarie, which entreateth chieflie of the *right writing of our English Tong,*" 1582, 12mo.

and translated their learning wherewith they were in love. The Roman authority first planted the Latin among us here, by force of their conquest; the use thereof for matters of learning doth cause it continue, though the conquest be expired. And, therefore, the learned tongues, so termed of their store, may thank their own people both for their fining (refinement) at home and their favour abroad. But did not these tongues use even the same means to brave (adorn) themselves, ere they proved so beautiful?

"There be two special considerations which keep the Latin and other learned tongues, though chiefly the Latin, in great countenance among us; the one is the knowledge which is registered in them; the other is the conference which the learned of Europe do commonly use by them, both in speaking and writing. We seek them for profit, and keep them for that conference; but whatever else may be done in our tongue, either to serve private use, or the beautifying our speech, I do not see but it may well be admitted, *even though in the end it displaced the Latin,* as the Latin did others, and furnished itself by the Latin learning. For is it not indeed a marvellous bondage to become servants to one tongue for learning sake, the most of our time, with loss of most time, whereas we may have the very same treasure in our own tongue, with the gain of most time? Our own, bearing the joyful title of our liberty and freedom; the Latin tongue remembering us of our thraldom. I honour the Latin, but I worship the English, I wish all were in ours which they had from others; and by their own precedent, do let us understand how boldly we may venture, notwithstanding the opinion of some of our people, as desire rather to please themselves with a foreign tongue wherewith they are acquainted, than to profit their country in her natural language, where their acquaintance should be. The tongues which we study were not the first getters, though by learned travel (labour) they prove good keepers; but they are ready to return and discharge their trust when it shall be demanded, in such a sort, as it was committed for term of years, and not for inheritance."

"But it is objected," our learned Mulcaster proceeds, with his engaging simplicity, that "the English tongue is of small reach, stretching no further than this island of ours, nay not there over all. What tho' (then)? It reigneth there, though it go not beyond sea. And be not English folk finish (refined) as well as the foreign, I pray you? And why not our tongue for speaking, and our pen for writing, as well as our bodies for apparel, and our tastes for diet? But you say that we have no cunning (knowledge) proper to our soil to cause foreigners to study it, as a treasure of such store. What tho' (then)? Why raise not the English wits, if they will bend their wills either, for matter or for method, in their own tongue, TO BE IN TIME AS WELL SOUGHT TO BY FOREIGN STUDENTS FOR INCREASE OF THEIR KNOWLEDGE, AS OUR SOIL IS SOUGHT TO AT THIS TIME BY FOREIGN MERCHANTS FOR INCREASE OF THEIR

WEALTH?"[18]

We, who have lived to verify the prediction, should not less esteem the prophet; the pedagogue, MULCASTER, is a philosopher addressing men—a genius who awakens a nation. His indeed was that "prophetic eye," which, amid the rudeness of its own days, in its clear vision contemplated on the futurity of the English language; and the day has arrived, when *"in the end it displaced the Latin,"* and "FOREIGN STUDENTS" learn our language, "FOR INCREASE OF THEIR KNOWLEDGE."

The design of Mulcaster to regulate orthography by orthoepy was revived so late as in 1701, in a curious work, under the title of "Practical Phonography," by John Jones, M.D. He proposed to write words as they are "fashionably" sounded. He notices "the constant complaints which were then rife in consequence of an unsettled orthography." He proclaims. war against "the visible letters," which, not sounded, occasion a faulty pronunciation. I suspect we had not any spelling-books in 1701. I have seen Dyche's of 1710, but I do not recollect whether this was the first edition; this sage of practical orthography was compelled to submit to custom, and taught his scholars to read by the *ear,* and not by the *eye.* "Yet custom," he adds, "is not the truest way of speaking and writing, from not regarding the originals whence words are derived; hence, abundance of errors have crept both into the pronunciation and writing, and English is grown a medley in both these respects." Such was the lamentation of an honest pedagogue in 1710.

The "Phonography" of Dr. Jones was probably well received; for three years after, in 1701, he returned to his "spelling," which, he observed, "however mean, concerned the benefit of millions of persons." He had a notion to "invent a universal language to excel all others, if he thought that people would be induced to use it."[19]

---

18. In this copious extract from Mulcaster's little volume, we have a specimen of the unadulterated simplicity of the English language. I have only modernised the orthography for the convenience of the reader, but I have not altered a single word.

19. The second work of our Phonographer is entitled "The New Art of Spelling, designed chiefly for Persons of Maturity, teaching them to Spell and Write Words by the Sound thereof, and to Sound and Read Words by the Sight therof,—rightly, neatly, and fashionably, &c.," by J. Jones, M.D., 1704.

I give a specimen of his words as they are written and as they are pronounced—

VISIBLE LETTERS.	CUSTOMARY AND FASHIONABLY.
Mayor	Mair.
Worcester	Wooster
Dictionary	Dixnary
Bought	Baut.

"All words," he observes, "were originally written as sounded and all which have since altered their sounds did it for ease and pleasure's sake from

Even the learned of our own times have indulged some of these philological reveries. One would hardly have suspected that DR. FRANKLIN, whose genius was so wholly practical, contemplated to revolutionise the English alphabet: words were to be spelt by the sounds of their letters, which were to be regulated by six new characters, and certain changes in the vowels. He seems to have revived old Bullokar. PINKERTON has left us a ludicrous scheme of what he calls "an improved language." Our vowel terminations amount but to one-fourth of the language; all substantives closing in hard consonants were to have a final vowel, and the consonant was to be omitted after the vowel. We were to acquire the Italian euphony by this presumed melody for our harsh terminations. In this disfigurement of the language, a *quack* would be a *quaco,* and *that* would be *tha.* Plurals were to terminate in *a :* *pens* would be *pena;* papers, *papera.* He has very innocently printed the entire "Vision of Mirza" from the "Spectator," on his own system; the ludicrous jargon at once annihilates itself. Not many years ago, JAMES ELPHINSTONE, a scholar, and a very injudicious one, performed an extraordinary experiment. He ventured to publish some volumes of a literary correspondence, on the plan of writing the words as they are pronounced. But this editor, being a Scotchman, had two sorts of Scotticisms to encounter—in idiom and in sound. Notwithstanding the agreeable subjects of a literary correspondence, it is not probable that any one ever conquered a single perusal of pages, which tortured the eye, if they did not the understanding.

We may smile at these repeated attempts of the learned English, in their inventions of alphabets, to establish the correspondence of pronunciation with orthography, and at their vowelly conceits to melodise our orthoepy. All these, however, demonstrate that our language has never been written as it ought to have been. All our writers have experienced this inconvenience. Considerable changes in spelling were introduced at various periods, by way of experiment; this liberty was used by the Elizabethan writers, for an improvement on the orthography of Gower and Chaucer. Since the days of Anne we have further deviated, yet after all our efforts we are constrained to read words not as they are written, and to write different words with the same letters, which leaves them ambiguous. And now, no reform shall ever happen, short of one by "the omnipotence of parliament," which the great luminary of law is pleased to affirm, "can do anything except making a man a woman." Customary errors are more tolerable than the perplexing innovations of the

---

the harder to the easier
the harsher to the pleasanter   } sound."
the longer to the shorter

most perverse ingenuity.[20] The eye bewildered in such uncouth pages as are here recorded, found the most capricious orthography in popular use always less perplexing than the attempt to write words according to their pronunciation, which every one regulated by the sounds familiar to his own ear, and usually to his own county. Even the dismemberment of words, omitting or changing letters, distracts attention;[21] and modern readers have often been deterred from the study of our early writers by their unsettled orthography. Our later literary antiquaries have, therefore, with equal taste and sagacity, modernised their text, by printing the words as the writers, were they now living, would have transcribed them.

Such have been the impracticable efforts to paint the voice to the eye, or to chain by syllables airy sounds. The imperfections for which such reforms were designed in great part still perplex us. Our written language still remains to the utter confusion of the eye and the ear of the baffled foreigner, who often discovers that what is written is not spoken, and what is spoken is not written. The orthography of some words leads to their false pronunciation. Hence originated that peculiar invention of our own, that odd-looking monster in philology, "a pronouncing dictionary," which offends our eyes by this unhappy attempt to write down sounds. They whose eyes have run over Sheridan, Walker, and other orthoepists, must often have smiled at their arbitrary disfigurements of the English language. These ludicrous attempts are after all inefficient, while they compel us to recollect, if the thing indeed be possible, a polysyllabic combination as barbarous as the language of the Cherokees.

We may sympathise with the disconcerted foreigner who is a learner of the English language. All words ending in *ugh* must confound him: for instance,

---

20. The Grammar prefixed to Johnson's Dictionary, curiously illustrated by the notes and researches of modern editors, will furnish specimens of many of these abortive attempts.

21. When we began to drop the letter K in such words as *physic, music, public,* a literary antiquary, who wrote about 1790, observed on this new fashion, that "forty years ago no schoolboy had dared to have done this with impunity." These words in older English had even another superfluous letter, being spelt *physicke, musicke, publicke.* The modern mode, notwithstanding its prevalence, must be considered anomalous; for other words ending with the consonants *ck* have not been shorn of their final *k.* We do not write *attac, ransac, bedec,* nor *bulloc,* nor *duc,* nor good *luc.*

The appearance of words deprived of their final letter, though identically the same in point of sound, produces a painful effect on the reader. Pegge furnishes a ludicrous instance. It consists of monosyllables in which the final and redundant *k* is not written,—"*Dic* gave *Jac* a *kic* when *Jac* gave *Dic* a *knoc* on the *bac* with a *thic stic.*" If even such familiar words and simple monosyllables can distract our attention, though they have only lost a single and mute letter, how greatly more in words compounded, disguised *by* the mutilation of several letters.

though, through, und *enough,* alike written, are each differently pronounced; and should he give us *bough* rightly, he may be forgiven should he blunder at *cough;* if he escape in safety from *though,* the same wind will blow him out of *thought.* What can the foreigner hope when he discovers that good judges of their language pronounce words differently? A mere English scholar who holds little intercourse with society, however familiar in his closet be his acquaintance with the words, and even their derivations, might fail in a material point, when using them in conversation or in a public speech. A list of names of places and of persons might be given, in which not a single syllable is pronounced of those that stand written.

That a language should be written as it is spoken we see has been considered desirable by the most intelligent scholars. Some have laudably persevered in writing the past tense *red,* as a distinction from the present *read,* and anciently I have found it printed *redde.* Lord Byron has even retained the ancient mode in his Diary. By not distinguishing the tenses, an audible reader has often unwarily confused the times. *G* before *I* ungrammatical orthoepists declare is sounded hard, but so numerous are the exceptions, that the exceptions might equally be adopted for the rule. It is true that the pedantry of scholarship has put its sovereign veto against the practice of writing words as they are spoken, even could the orthoepy ever have been settled by an unquestioned standard. When it was proposed to omit the mute *b* in *doubt* and *debt,* it was objected that by this castration of a superfluous letter in the pronunciation, we should lose sight of their Latin original. The same circumstance occurred in the reform of the French orthography: it was objected to the innovators, that when they wrote *tems,* rejecting the *p* in *temps,* they wholly lost sight of the Latin original, *tempus.* Milton seems to have laid down certain principles of orthography, anxiously observed in his own editions printed when the poet was blind. An orthography which would be more natural to an unlearned reader is rejected by the etymologist, whose pride and pomp exult in tracing the legitimacy of words to their primitives, and delight to write them as near as may be according to the analogy of languages.

3. AUTOGRAPHS[22]
(*Curiosities,* vol. 3, pp. 163-167)

---

22. A small volume which I met with at Paris, entitled "L'Art de jugerdu Caractère des Hommes sur leurs Ecritures," is curious for its illustrations, consisting of *twenty-four plates, exhibiting fac-similes of the writing of eminent and other persons,* correctly taken from the original autographs. Since this period both France and Germany have produced many books devoted to the use of the curious in autographs. In our own country J. T. Smith published a curious collection of fac-similes of letters, chiefly from literary characters.

THE art of judging of the characters of persons by their handwriting can only have any reality when the pen, acting without restraint, becomes an instrument guided by, and indicative of, the natural dispositions. But regulated as the pen is now too often by a mechanical process, which the present race of writing-masters seem to have contrived for their own convenience, a whole school exhibits a similar handwriting; the pupils are forced in their automatic motions, as if acted on by the pressure of a steam-engine; a bevy of beauties will now write such fac-similes of each other, that in a heap of letters presented to the most sharp-sighted lover to select that of his mistress—though, like Bassanio among the caskets, his happiness should be risked on the choice—he would despair of fixing on the right one, all appearing to have come from the same rolling-press. Even brothers of different tempers have been taught by the same master to give the same form to their letters, the same regularity to their line, and have made our handwritings as monotonous as are our characters in the present habits of society. The true physiognomy of writing will be lost among our rising generation: it is no longer a face that we are looking on, but a beautiful mask of a single pattern; and the fashionable handwriting of our young ladies is like the former tight-lacing of their mothers' youthful days, when every one alike had what was supposed to be a fine shape!

Assuredly nature would prompt every individual to have a distinct sort of writing, as she has given a peculiar countenance—a voice—and a manner. The flexibility of the muscles differs with every individual, and the hand will follow the direction of the thoughts and the emotions and the habits of the writers. The phlegmatic will portray his words, while the playful haste of the volatile will scarcely sketch them; the slovenly will blot and efface and scrawl, while the neat and orderly-minded will view themselves in the paper before their eyes. The merchant's clerk will not write like the lawyer or the poet. Even nations are distinguished by their writing; the vivacity and variableness of the Frenchman, and the delicacy and suppleness of the Italian, are perceptibly distinct from the slowness and strength of pen discoverable in the phlegmatic German, Dane, and Swede. When we are in grief, we do not write as we should in joy. The elegant and correct mind, which has acquired the fortunate habit of a fixity of attention, will write with scarcely an erasure on the page, as Fenelon, and Gray, and Gibbon; while we find in Pope's manuscripts the perpetual struggles of correction, and the eager and rapid interlineations struck off in heat. Lavater's notion of handwriting is by no means chimerical; nor was General Paoli fanciful, when he told Mr. Northcote that he had decided on the character and dispositions of a man from his letters, and the handwriting.

Long before the days of Lavater, Shenstone in one of his letters said, "I want to see Mrs. Jago's handwriting, that I may judge of her temper." One great truth must however be conceded to the opponents of *the physiognomy of writing;* general rules only can be laid down. Yet the vital principle must be true that the handwriting bears an analogy to the character of the writer, as all voluntary actions are characteristic of the individual. But many causes operate to counteract or obstruct this result. I am intimately acquainted with the handwritings of five of our great poets. The first in early life acquired among Scottish advocates a handwriting which cannot be distinguished from that of his ordinary brothers; the second, educated in public schools, where writing is shamefully neglected, composes his sublime or sportive verses in a school-boy's ragged scrawl, as if he had never finished his tasks with the writing-master; the third writes his highly-wrought poetry in the common hand of a merchant's clerk, from early commercial avocations; the fourth has all that finished neatness which polishes his verses; while the fifth is a specimen of a full mind, not in the habit of correction or alteration; so that he appears to be printing down his thoughts, without a solitary erasure. The handwriting of the *first* and *third* poets, not indicative of their character, we have accounted for; the others are admirable specimens of characteristic autographs.[23]

Oldys, in one of his curious notes, was struck by the distinctness of character in the handwritings of several of our kings. He observed nothing further than the mere fact, and did not extend his idea to the art of judging of the natural character by the writing. Oldys has described these handwritings with the utmost correctness, as I have often verified. I shall add a few comments.

"Henry the Eighth wrote a strong hand, but as if he had seldom a good pen."—The vehemence of his character conveyed itself into his writing; bold, hasty, and commanding, I have no doubt the assertor of the Pope's supremacy and its triumphant destroyer split many a good quill.

"Edward the Sixth wrote a fair legible hand."—We have this promising young prince's diary, written by his own hand; in all respects he was an assiduous pupil, and he had scarcely learnt to write and to reign when we lost him.

"Queen Elizabeth writ an upright hand, like the bastard Italian." She was indeed a most elegant caligrapher, whom Roger Ascham[24] had taught all the elegancies of the pen. The French editor of the little autographical work I have noticed has given the autograph of her name, which she usually wrote in a very large tall character, and painfully elaborate. He accompanies it with one of the Scottish Mary, who at times wrote elegantly, though usually in uneven lines; when in haste and distress of mind, in several letters during her

---

23. It will be of interest to the reader to note the names of these poets in the consecutive order they are alluded to. They are Scott, Byron, Rogers, Moore, and Campbell.

24. He was also the tutor of Lady Jane Grey, and the author of one of our earliest and best works on education.

imprisonment which I have read, much the contrary. The French editor makes this observation: "Who could believe that these writings are of the same epoch? The first denotes asperity and ostentation; the second indicates simplicity, softness, and nobleness. The one is that of Elizabeth, queen of England; the other that of her cousin, Mary Stuart. The difference of these two handwritings answers most evidently to that of their characters."

"James the First writ a poor ungainly character, all awry, and not in a straight line." James certainly wrote a slovenly scrawl, strongly indicative of that personal negligence which he carried into all the little things of life; and Buchanan, who had made him an excellent scholar, may receive the disgrace of his pupil's ugly scribble, which sprawls about his careless and inelegant letters.

"Charles the First wrote a fair open Italian hand, and more correctly perhaps than any prince we ever had." Charles was the first of our monarchs who intended to have domiciliated taste in the kingdom, and it might have been conjectured from this unfortunate prince, who so finely discriminated the manners of the different painters, which are in fact their handwritings, that he would not have been insensible to the elegancies of the pen.

"Charles the Second wrote a little fair running hand, as if wrote in haste, or uneasy till he had done." Such was the writing to have been expected from this illustrious vagabond, who had much to write, often in odd situations, and could never get rid of his natural restlessness and vivacity.

"James the Second writ a large fair hand." It is characterised by his phlegmatic temper, as an exact detailer of occurrences, and the matter-of-business genius of the writer.

"Queen Anne wrote a fair round hand;" that is the writing she had been taught by her master, probably without any alteration of manner naturally suggested by herself; the copying hand of a common character.[25]

The subject of autographs associates itself with what has been dignified by its professors as caligraphy, or the art of beautiful writing. As I have something curious to communicate on that subject considered professionally, it shall form our ... article [The History of Writing-Masters].

---

25. Since this article was written, Nichols has published a cleverly-executed series of autographs of royal, noble, and illustrious persons of Great Britain, in which the reader may study the accuracy of the criticism above given.

4. MINUTE WRITING
(*Curiosities*, vol. 1, pp. 275-276)

THE Iliad of Homer in a nutshell, which Pliny says that Cicero once saw, it is pretended might have been a fact, however to some it may appear impossible. Ælian notices an artist who wrote a distich in letters of gold, which he enclosed in the rind of a grain of corn.

Antiquity and modern times record many such penmen, whose glory consisted in writing in so small a hand that the writing could not be legible to the naked eye. Menage mentions, he saw whole sentences which were not perceptible to the eye without the microscope; pictures and portraits which appeared at first to be lines and scratches thrown down at random; one formed the face of the Dauphiness with the most correct resemblance. He read an Italian poem, in praise of this princess, containing some thousand verses, written by an officer, in a space of a foot and a half. This species of curious idleness has not been lost in our own country, where this minute writing has equalled any on record. Peter Bales, a celebrated caligrapher in the reign of Elizabeth, astonished the eyes of beholders by showing them what they could not see; for in the Harleian MSS. 530, we have a narrative of "a rare piece of work brought to pass by Peter Bales, an Englishman, and a clerk of the chancery;" it seems by the description to have been the whole Bible "in an English walnut no bigger than a hen's egg. The nut holdeth the book: there are as many leaves in his little book as the great Bible, and he hath written as much in one of his little leaves as a great leaf of the Bible." We are told that this wonderfully unreadable copy of the Bible was "seen by many thousands." There is a drawing of the head of Charles I. in the library of St. John's College, at Oxford, wholly composed of minute written characters, which, at a small distance, resemble the lines of an engraving. The lines of the head, and the ruff, are said to contain the book of Psalms, the Creed, and the Lord's Prayer. In the British Museum we find a drawing representing the portrait of Queen Anne, not much above the size of the hand. On this drawing appears a number of lines and scratches, which the librarian assures the marvelling spectator includes the entire contents of a thin *folio*, which on this occasion is carried in the hand.

The learned Huet asserts that, like the rest of the world, he considered as a fiction the story of that indefatigable trifler who is said to have enclosed the Iliad in a nutshell. Examining the matter more closely, he thought it possible. One day this learned man trifled half an hour in demonstrating it. A piece of vellum, about ten inches in length and eight in width, pliant and firm, can be folded up, and enclosed in the shell of a large walnut. It can hold in its breadth one line, which can contain 30 verses, and in its length 250 lines. With a crow-quill the writing can be perfect. A page of this piece of vellum will then contain 7500 verses, and the reverse as much; the whole 15,000 verses of the Iliad. And this he proved by using a piece of paper, and with a common pen. The thing is possible to be effected; and if on any occasion paper should be most excessively rare, it may be useful to know that a volume of matter may be contained in a single leaf.

5. NUMERICAL FIGURES
(*Curiosities*, vol. 1, pp. 276-278)

THE learned, after many contests, have at length agreed that the numerical figures 1, 2, 3, 4, 5, 6, 7, 8, 9, usually called *Arabic*, are of *Indian* origin. The Arabians do not pretend to have been the inventors of them, but borrowed them from the Indian nations. The numeral characters of the Bramins, the Persians, the Arabians, and other eastern nations, are similar. They appear afterwards to have been introduced into several European nations by their respective travellers, who returned from the East. They were admitted into calendars and chronicles, but they were not introduced into charters, says Mr. Astle, before the sixteenth century. The Spaniards, no doubt, derived their use from the Moors who invaded them. In 1240, the Alphonsean astronomical tables were made by the order of Alphonsus X. by a Jew, and an Arabian; they used these numerals, from whence the Spaniards contend that they were first introduced by them.

They were not generally used in Germany until the beginning of the fourteenth century; but in general the forms of the ciphers were not permanently fixed there till after the year 1531. The Russians were strangers to them, before Peter the Great had finished his travels in the beginning of the last century.

The origin of these useful characters with the Indians and Arabians is attributed to their great skill in the arts of astronomy and of arithmetic, which required more convenient characters than alphabetic letters for the expression of numbers.

Before the introduction into Europe of these Arabic numerals, they used alphabetical characters, or *Roman numerals*. The learned authors of the Nouveau Traité Diplomatique, the most valuable work on everything concerning the arts and progress of writing, have given some curious notices on the origin of the Roman numerals. Originally men counted by their fingers; thus, to mark the first four numbers they used an I, which naturally represents them. To mark the fifth, they chose a V, which is made out by bending inwards the three middle fingers, and stretching out only the thumb and the little finger; and for the tenth they used an X, which is a double V, one placed topsy-turvy under the other. From this the progression of these numbers is always from one to five, and from five to ten. The hundred was signified by the capital letter of that word in Latin, C—centum. The other letters, D for 500, and M for a 1000, were afterwards added. They subsequently abbreviated their characters, by placing one of these figures before another; and the figure of less value before a higher number, denotes that so much may be deducted from a greater number; for instance, IV signifies five less one, that is four; IX ten less one, that is nine; but these abbreviations are not found amongst the ancient monuments.[26] These numerical letters are still continued by us in the accounts of our Exchequer.

That men counted originally by their fingers, is no improbable supposition; it is still naturally practised by the people. In semi-civilized states small stones have been used, and the etymologists derive the words *calculate* and *calculations* from *calculus*, the Latin term for a pebble-stone, and by which they denominated their counters used for arithmetical computations.

Professor Ward, in a learned dissertation on this subject in the Philosophical Transactions, concludes that it is easier to falsify the Arabic ciphers than the Roman alphabetical numerals; when 1375 is dated in Arabic ciphers, if the 3 is only changed into an 0, three centuries are taken away; if the 3 is made into a 9 and take away the 1, four hundred years are lost. Such accidents have assuredly produced much confusion among our ancient manuscripts, and still do in our printed books; which is the reason that Dr. Robertson in his histories has also preferred writing his dates in *words*, rather than confide them to the care of a negligent printer. Gibbon observes, that some remarkable mistakes have happened by the word *mil.* in MSS., which is an abbreviation for *soldiers*, or for *thousands;* and to this blunder he attributes the incredible numbers of martyrdoms, which cannot otherwise be accounted for by historical records.

6. THE HISTORY OF WRITING-MASTERS
(*Curiosities,* vol. 3, pp. 167-177)

THERE is a very apt letter from James the First to Prince Henry when very young, on the neatness and fairness of his handwriting. The royal father suspecting that the prince's tutor, Mr., afterwards Sir Adam, Newton, had helped out the young prince in the composition, and that in this specimen of caligraphy he had relied also on the pains of Mr. Peter Bales, the great writing-

---

26. A peculiar arrangement of letters was in use by the German and Flemish printers of the 16th century. Thus CIɔ denoted 1000, and Iɔ, 500. The date 1619 would therefore be thus printed:—cIɔ. IɔCIXx.

master, for touching up his letters, his majesty shows a laudable anxiety that the prince should be impressed with the higher importance of the one over the other. James shall himself speak. "I confess I long to receive a letter from you that may be wholly yours, as well matter as form; as well formed by your mind as drawn by your fingers; for ye may remember, that in my book to you I warn you to beware with (of) that kind of wit that may fly out at the end of your fingers; not that I commend not a fair handwriting; *sed hoc facito, illud non omittito:* and the other is *multo magis præcipuum.*" Prince Henry, indeed, wrote with that elegance which he borrowed from his own mind; and in an age when such minute elegance was not universal among the crowned heads of Europe. Henry IV., on receiving a letter from Prince Henry, immediately opened it, a custom not usual with him, and comparing the writing with the signature, to decide whether it were of one hand, Sir George Carew, observing the French King's hesitation, called Mr. Douglas to testify to the fact; on which Henry the Great, admiring an art in which he had little skill, and looking on the neat elegance of the writing before him, politely observed, "I see that in writing fair, as in other things, the elder must yield to the younger."

Had this anecdote of neat writing reached the professors of caligraphy, who in this country have put forth such painful panegyrics on the art, these royal names had unquestionably blazoned their pages. Not indeed that these penmen require any fresh inflation; for never has there been a race of professors in any art who have exceeded in solemnity and pretensions the practitioners in this simple and mechanical craft. I must leave to more ingenious investigators of human nature to reveal the occult cause which has operated such powerful delusions on these "Vive la Plume!" men, who have been generally observed to possess least intellectual ability in proportion to the excellence they have obtained in their own art. I suspect this maniacal vanity is peculiar to the writing-masters of England; and I can only attribute the immense importance which they have conceived of their art to the perfection to which they have carried the art of short-hand writing; an art which was always better understood, and more skilfully practised, in England than in any other country. It will surprise some when they learn that the artists in verse and colours, poets and painters, have not raised loftier pretensions to the admiration of mankind. Writing-masters, or caligraphers, have had their engraved "effigies," with a Fame in flourishes, a pen on one hand and a trumpet in the other; and fine verses inscribed, and their very lives written! They have compared

The nimbly-turning of their silver quill

to the beautiful in art and the sublime in invention; nor is this wonderful, since they discover the art of writing, like the invention of language, in a divine original; and from the tablets of stone which the Deity himself delivered, they trace their German broad text, or their fine running-hand. One, for "the bold striking of those words, *Vive la Plume,*" was so sensible of the reputation that this last piece of command of hand would give the book which he thus adorned, and which his biographer acknowledges was the product of about a minute,—(but then how many years of flourishing had that single minute cost him!)—that he claims the glory of an artist; observing,—

> We seldom find
> The *man of business* with the *artist* join'd.

Another was flattered that his *writing* could impart immortality to the most wretched compositions!—

> And any lines prove pleasing, when you write.

Sometimes the caligrapher is a sort of hero:—

> To you, you rare commander of the quill,
> Whose wit and worth, deep learning, and high skill,
> Speak you the honour of Great Tower Hill!

The last line became traditionally adopted by those who were so lucky as to live in the neighbourhood of this Parnassus. But the reader must form some notion of that charm of caligraphy which has so bewitched its professors, when,

> Soft, bold and free, your manuscripts still please.
>
> How justly bold in SNELL'S improving hand
> The pen at once joins freedom with command!
> With softness strong, with ornaments not vain,
> Loose with proportion, and with neatness plain;
> Not swell'd, not full, complete in every part,
> And artful most, when not affecting art.

And these describe those pencilled knots and flourishes, "the angels, the men, the birds, and the beasts," which, as one of them observed, he could

> Command
> Even by the *gentle motion of his hand,*

all the *speciosa miracula* of caligraphy;

Thy *tender strokes*, inimitably fine,
Crown with perfection every *flowing line;*
And to each *grand performance* add a grace,
As *curling hair* adorns a beauteous face:
In every page *new fancies* give delight,
And *sporting round the margin* charm the sight.

One Massey, a writing-master, published in 1763, "The Origin and Progress of Letters." The great singularity of this volume is "a new species of biography never attempted before in English." This consists of the lives of "English Penmen," otherwise writing-masters! If some have foolishly enough imagined that the sedentary lives of authors are void of interest from deficient incident and interesting catastrophe, what must they think of the barren labours of those who, in the degree they become eminent, to use their own style, in the art of "dish, dash, long-tail fly," the less they become interesting to the public; for what can the most skilful writing-master do but wear away his life in leaning over his pupil's copy, or sometimes snatch a pen to decorate the margin, though he cannot compose the page? Montaigne has a very original notion on writing-masters: he says that some of those caligraphers who had obtained promotion by their excellence in the art, afterwards *affected to write carelessly, lest their promotion should be suspected to have been owing to such an ordinary acquisition!*

Massey is an enthusiast, fortunately for his subject. He considers that there are *schools of writing,* as well as of painting or sculpture; and expatiates with the eye of fraternal feeling on "a natural genius, a tender stroke, a grand performance, a bold striking freedom, and a liveliness in the sprigged letters, and pencilled knots and flourishes;" while this Vasari of writing-masters relates the controversies and the libels of many a rival pen-nibber. "George Shelley, one of the most celebrated worthies who have made a shining figure in the commonwealth of English caligraphy, born I suppose of obscure parents, because brought up in Christ's Hospital, yet under the humble blue-coat he laid the foundation of his caligraphic excellence and lasting fame, for he was elected writing-master to the hospital." Shelley published his "Natural Writing;" but, alas! Snell, another blue-coat, transcended the other. He was a genius who would "bear no brother near the throne."—"I have been informed that there were jealous heart-burnings, if not bickerings, between him and Col. Ayres, another of our *great reformers* in the writing commonweal, both eminent men, yet, *like* our most celebrated poets *Pope and Addison*, or, to carry the comparison still higher, like *Cæsar and Pompey*, one could bear no superior, and the other no equal." Indeed, the great Snell practised a little stratagem against Mr. Shelley, for which, if writing-masters held courts-martial, this hero ought to have appeared before his brothers. In one of his works he procured a number of friends to write letters, in which Massey confesses "are some satyrical strokes upon Shelley," as if he had arrogated too much to himself in his book of "Natural Writing." They find great fault with pencilled knots and sprigged letters. Shelley, who was an advocate for ornaments in fine penmanship, which Snell utterly rejected, had parodied a well-known line of Herbert's in favour of his favourite decorations:—

> A *Knot* may take him who from *letters* flies,
> And turn *delight* into an *exercise*.

These reflections created ill-blood, and even an open difference amongst several of the *superior artists in writing*. The commanding genius of Snell had a more terrific contest when he published his "Standard Rules," pretending to have *demonstrated* them as Euclid would. "This proved a bone of contention, and occasioned a terrific quarrel between Mr. Snell and Mr. Clark. This quarrel about 'Standard Rules' ran so high between them, that they could scarce forbear *scurrilous language* therein, and a treatment of each other unbecoming *gentlemen!* Both sides in this dispute had their abettors; and to say which had the most truth and reason, *non nostrum est tantas componere lites;* perhaps *both parties might be too fond of their own schemes*. They should have left them to people to choose which they liked best." A candid politician is our Massey, and a philosophical historian too; for he winds up the whole story of this civil war by describing its result, which happened as all such great controversies have ever closed. "Who now-a-days takes those *Standard Rules*, either one or the other, for their *guide* in writing?" This is the finest lesson ever offered to the furious heads of parties, and to all their men; let them meditate on the nothingness of their "Standard Rules," by the fate of Mr. Snell.

It was to be expected, when once these writing-masters imagined that they were artists, that they would be infected with those plague-spots of genius—envy, detraction, and all the *jalousie du métier*. And such to this hour we find them! An extraordinary scene of this nature has long been exhibited in my neighbourhood, where two doughty champions of the quill have been posting up libels in their windows respecting the inventor of *a new art of writing*, the Carstairian, or the Lewisian? When the great German philosopher asserted that he had discovered the method of fluxions before Sir Isaac, and when the dispute grew so violent that even the calm Newton sent a formal defiance in set terms, and got even George the Second to try to arbitrate (who would rather have undertaken a campaign), the method of fluxions was no more cleared up than the present affair between our two heroes of the quill.

A recent instance of one of these egregious caligraphers may be told of the late Tomkins. This vainest of writing-masters dreamed through life that penmanship was one of the fine arts, and that a writing-master should be seated with his peers in the Academy! He bequeathed to the British Museum his *opus magnum*—a copy of Macklin's Bible, profusely embellished with the most beautiful and varied decorations of his pen; and as he conceived that both the workman and the work would alike be darling objects with posterity, he left something immortal with the legacy, his fine bust, by Chantrey, unaccompanied by which they were not to receive the unparalleled gift! When Tomkins applied to have his bust, our great sculptor abated the usual price, and, courteously kind to the feelings of the man, said that he considered Tomkins as an artist! It was the proudest day of the life of our writing-master!

But an eminent artist and wit now living, once looking on this fine bust of Tomkins, declared, that "this man had died for want of a dinner!"—a fate, however, not so lamentable as it appeared! Our penman had long felt that he stood degraded in the scale of genius by not being received at the Academy, at least among the class of *engravers;* the next approach to academic honour he conceived would be that of appearing as a *guest* at their annual dinner. These invitations are as limited as they are select, and all the Academy persisted in considering Tomkins *as a writing-master!* Many a year passed, every intrigue was practised, every remonstrance was urged, every stratagem of courtesy was tried; but never ceasing to deplore the failure of his hopes, it preyed on his spirits, and the luckless caligrapher went down to his grave—without dining at the Academy! This authentic anecdote has been considered as "satire improperly directed"—by some friend of Mr. Tomkins—but the criticism is much too grave! The foible of Mr. Tomkins as a writing-master presents a striking illustration of the class of men here delineated. I am a mere historian—and am only responsible for the veracity of this fact. That "Mr. Tomkins lived in familiar intercourse with the Royal Academicians of his day, and was a frequent guest at their private tables," and moreover was a most worthy man, I believe—but is it less true that he was ridiculously mortified by being never invited to the Academic dinner, on account of his caligraphy? He had some reason to consider that his art was of the exalted class to which he aspired to raise it, when this friend concludes his eulogy of this writing-master thus—"Mr. Tomkins, as an artist, stood foremost in his own profession, and his name will be handed down to posterity with the *Heroes* and *Statesmen,* whose excellences his *penmanship* has contributed to illustrate and to commemorate." I always give the *Pour* and the *Contre!*

Such men about such things have produced public contests, *combats a l'outrance,* where much ink was spilled by the knights in a joust of goose-quills; these solemn trials have often occurred in the history of writing-masters, which is enlivened by public defiances, proclamations, and judicial trials by umpires! The prize was usually a golden pen of some value. One as late as in the reign of Anne took place between Mr. German and Mr. More. German having courteously insisted that Mr. More should set the copy, he thus set it, ingeniously quaint!

As more, and MORE, our understanding clears,
So more and more our ignorance appears.

The result of this pen-combat was really lamentable; they displayed such an equality of excellence that the umpires refused to decide, till one of them espied that Mr. German had omitted the tittle of an i! But Mr. More was evidently a man of genius, not only by his couplet, but in his "Essay on the Invention of Writing," where occurs this noble passage: "Art with me is of no party. A noble emulation I would cherish, while it proceeded neither from, nor to malevolence. Bales had his Johnson, Norman his Mason, Ayres his Matlock and his Shelley; yet Art the while was no sufferer. The busybody who officiously employs himself in creating misunderstandings between artists, may be compared to a turnstile, which stands in every man's way, yet hinders nobody; and he is the slanderer who gives ear to the slander."[27]

Among the knights of the "Plume volante," whose chivalric exploits astounded the beholders, must be distinguished Peter Bales in his joust with David Johnson. In this tilting-match the guerdon of caligraphy was won by the greatest of caligraphers; its *arms* were assumed by the victor, *azure, a pen or;* while the "golden pen," carried away in triumph, was painted with a hand over the door of the caligrapher. The history of this renowned encounter was only traditionally known, till with my own eyes I pondered on this whole trial of skill in the precious manuscript of the champion himself; who, like Cæsar, not only knew how to win victories, but also to record them. Peter Bales was a hero of such transcendent eminence, that his name has entered into our history. Holinshed chronicles one of his curiosities of microscopic writing at a time when the taste prevailed for admiring writing which no eye could read! In the compass of a silver penny this caligrapher put more things than would fill several of these pages. He presented Queen Elizabeth with the manuscript set in a ring of gold covered with a crystal; he had also contrived a magnifying glass of such power, that, to her delight and wonder, her majesty read the whole volume, which she held on her thumb-nail, and "commended the same to the lords of the council and the ambassadors;" and frequently, as Peter often heard, did her majesty vouchsafe to wear the caligraphic ring.[28]

----

27. I have not met with More's book, and am obliged to transcribe this from the Biog. Brit.

28. Howes, in his Chronicle under date 1576, has thus narrated the story:—"A strange piece of work, and almost incredible, was brought to pass by an Englishman from within the city of London, and a clerk of the Chancery, named Peter Bales, who by his industry and practice of his pen contrived and writ, within the compass of a penny, the Lord's Prayer, the Creed, the Ten Commandments, a prayer to God, a prayer for the queen, his posy, his name, the day of the month, the year of our Lord, and the reign of the queen: and at Hampton Court he presented the same to the

"Some will think I labour on a cobweb"—modestly exclaimed Bales in his narrative, and his present historian much fears for himself! The reader's gratitude will not be proportioned to my pains, in condensing such copious pages into the size of a "silver penny," but without its worth!

For a whole year had David Johnson affixed a challenge "To any one who should take exceptions to this my writing and teaching." He was a young friend of Bales, daring and longing for an encounter; yet Bales was magnanimously silent, till he discovered that he was "doing much less in writing and teaching" since this public challenge was proclaimed! He then set up his counter-challenge, and in one hour afterwards Johnson arrogantly accepted it, "in a most despiteful and disgraceful manner." Bales's challenge was delivered "in good terms." "To all Englishmen and strangers." It was to write for a gold pen of twenty pounds value in all kinds of hands, "best, straightest, and fastest," and most kind of ways; "a full, a mean, a small, with line, and without line; in a slow set hand, a mean facile hand, and a fast running hand;" and further, "to write truest and speediest, most secretary and clerk-like, from a man's mouth, reading or pronouncing, either English or Latin."

Young Johnson had the hardihood now of turning the tables on his great antagonist, accusing the veteran Bales of arrogance. Such an absolute challenge, says he, was never witnessed by man, "without exception of any in the world!" And a few days after meeting Bales, "of set purpose to affront and disgrace him what he could, showed Bales a piece of writing of secretary's hand, which he had very much laboured in fine abortive parchment,"[29] uttering to the challenger these words: "Mr. Bales, give me one shilling out of your purse, and if within six months you better, or equal this piece of writing, I will give you forty pounds for it." This legal deposit of the shilling was made, and the challenger, or appellant, was thereby bound by law to the performance.

The day before the trial a printed declaration was affixed throughout the city, taunting Bales's "proud poverty," and his pecuniary motives, as "a thing ungentle, base, and mercenary, and not answerable to the dignity of the golden pen!" Johnson declares he would maintain his challenge for a thousand pounds more, but for the respondent's inability to perform a thousand groats. Bales retorts on the libel; declares it as a sign of his rival's weakness, "yet who so bold as blind Bayard, that hath not a word of Latin to cast at a dog, or say Bo! to goose!"

On Michaelmas day, 1595, the trial opened before five judges: the

---

queen's majesty."

29. This was written in the reign of Elizabeth. Holyoke notices "virgin-perchment made of an *abortive skin; membrana virgo.*" Peacham, on "Drawing," calls parchment simply *an abortive.*

appellant and the respondent appeared at the appointed place, and an ancient gentleman was intrusted with "the golden pen." In the first trial, for the manner of teaching scholars, after Johnson had taught his pupil a fortnight, he would not bring him forward! This was awarded in favour of Bales.

The second, for secretary and clerk-like writing, dictating to them both in English and in Latin, Bales performed best, being first done; written straightest without line, with true orthography: the challenger himself confessing that he wanted the Latin tongue, and was no clerk!

The third and last trial for fair writing in sundry kinds of hands, the challenger prevailed for the beauty and most "authentic proportion," and for the superior variety of the Roman hand. In the court hand the respondent exceeded the appellant, and likewise in the set text; and in bastard secretary was also somewhat perfecter.

At length Bales, perhaps perceiving an equilibrium in the judicial decision, to overwhelm his antagonist presented what he distinguishes as his "masterpiece," composed of secretary and Roman hand four ways varied, and offering the defendant to let pass all his previous advantages if he could better this specimen of caligraphy! The challenger was silent! At this moment some of the judges perceiving that the decision must go in favour of Bales, in consideration of the youth of the challenger, lest he might be disgraced to the world, requested the other judges not to pass judgment in public. Bales assures us, that he in vain remonstrated; for by these means the winning of the golden pen might not be so famously spread as otherwise it would have been. To Bales the prize was awarded. But our history has a more interesting close; the subtle Machiavelism of the first challenger!

When the great trial had closed, and Bales, carrying off the golden pen, exultingly had it painted and set up for his sign, the baffled challenger went about reporting that *he* had *won* the golden pen, but that the defendant had obtained the same by "plots and shifts, and other base and cunning practices." Bales vindicated his claim, and offered to show the world his "masterpiece" which had acquired it. Johnson issued an "Appeal to all Impartial Penmen," which he spread in great numbers through the city for ten days, a libel against the judges and the victorious defendant! He declared that there had been a subtle combination with one of the judges concerning the place of trial; which he expected to have been "before penmen," but not before a multitude like a stage-play, and shouts and tumults, with which the challenger had hitherto been unacquainted. The judges were intended to be twelve; but of the five, four were the challenger's friends, honest gentlemen, but unskilled in judging of most hands; and he offered again forty pounds to be allowed in six months to equal Bales's masterpiece. And he closes his "appeal" by declaring that Bales had lost in several parts of the trial, neither did the judges deny that Bales possessed himself of the golden pen by a trick! Before judgment was awarded, alleging the sickness of his wife to be extreme, he desired she might have *a sight of the golden pen to comfort her!* The ancient gentleman who was the holder, taking the defendant's word, allowed the golden pen to be carried to the sick wife; and Bales immediately pawned it, and afterwards, to make sure work, sold it at a great loss, so that when the judges met for their definite sentence, nor pen nor pennyworth was to be had! The judges being ashamed of their own conduct, were compelled to give such a verdict as suited the occasion.

Bales rejoins: he published to the universe the day and the hour when the judges brought the golden pen to his house, and while he checks the insolence of this Bobadil, to show himself no recreant, assumes the golden pen for his sign.

Such is the shortest history I could contrive of this chivalry of the pen; something mysteriously clouds over the fate of the defendant; Bales's history, like Cæsar's, is but an *ex-parte* evidence. Who can tell whether he has not slurred over his defeats, and only dwelt on his victories?

There is a strange phrase connected with the art of the caligrapher, which I think may be found in most, if not in all modern languages, *to write like an angel!* Ladies have been frequently compared with angels; they are *beautiful* as angels, and *sing* and *dance* like angels; but, however intelligible these are, we do not so easily connect penmanship with the other celestial accomplishments. This fanciful phrase, however, has a very human origin. Among those learned Greeks who emigrated to Italy, and afterwards into France, in the reign of Francis I., was one Angelo *Vergecio*, whose beautiful caligraphy excited the admiration of the learned. The French monarch had a Greek fount cast, modelled by his writing. The learned Henry Stephens, who, like our Porson for correctness and delicacy, was one of the most elegant writers of Greek, had learnt the practice from our *Angelo*. His name became synonymous for beautiful writing, and gave birth to the vulgar proverb or familiar phrase *to write like an angel!*

7. LITERARY COMPOSITION
(*Curiosities,* vol. 2, pp. 85-92)

TO literary composition we may apply the saying of an ancient philosopher:—"A little thing gives perfection, although perfection is not a little thing."

The great legislator of the Hebrews orders us to pull off the fruit for the first three years, and not to taste them. He was not ignorant how it weakens a young tree to bring to maturity its first fruits. Thus, on literary compositions, our green essays ought to be picked away. The word *Zamar*, by a beautiful metaphor from *pruning trees*, means in Hebrew to *compose verses*.

Blotting and correcting was so much Churchill's abhorrence, that I have heard from his publisher he once energetically expressed himself, that *it was like cutting away one's own flesh*. This strong figure sufficiently shows his repugnance to an author's duty. Churchill now lies neglected, for posterity will only respect those who

> File off the mortal part
> Of glowing thought with Attic art.
>   YOUNG.

I have heard that this careless bard, after a successful work, usually precipitated the publication of another, relying on its crudeness being passed over by the public curiosity excited by its better brother. He called this getting double pay, for thus he secured the sale of a hurried work. But Churchill was a spendthrift of fame, and enjoyed all his revenue while he lived; posterity owes him little, and pays him nothing!

Bayle, an experienced observer in literary matters, tells us that *correction* is by no means practicable by some authors, as in the case of Ovid. In exile, his compositions were nothing more than spiritless repetitions of what he had formerly written. He confesses both negligence and idleness in the corrections of his works. The vivacity which animated his first productions failing him when he revised his poems, he found correction too laborious, and he abandoned it. This, however, was only an excuse. "It is certain that *some authors cannot correct*. They compose with pleasure, and with ardour; but they exhaust all their force. They fly with but one wing when they review their works; the first fire does not return; there is in their imagination a certain calm which hinders their pen from making any progress. Their mind is like a boat, which only advances by the strength of oars."

Dr. More, the Platonist, had such an exuberance of fancy, that *correction* was a much greater labour than *composition*. He used to say, that in writing his works, he was forced to cut his way through a crowd of thoughts as through a wood, and that he threw off in his compositions as much as would make an ordinary philosopher. More was a great enthusiast, and, of course, an egotist, so that *criticism* ruffled his temper, notwithstanding all his Platonism. When accused of obscurities and extravagances, he said that, like the ostrich, he laid his eggs in the sands, which would prove vital and prolific in time; however, these ostrich-eggs have proved to be addled.

A habit of correctness in the lesser parts of composition will assist the higher. It is worth recording that the great Milton was anxious for correct punctuation, and that Addison was solicitous after the minutiæ of the press. Savage, Armstrong, and others, felt tortures on similar objects. It is said of Julius Scaliger, that he had this peculiarity in his manner of composition: he wrote with such accuracy that his MSS. and the printed copy corresponded page for page, and line for line.

Malherbe, the father of French poetry, tormented himself by a prodigious slowness; and was employed rather in perfecting than in forming works. His muse is compared to a fine woman in the pangs of delivery. He exulted in his tardiness, and, after finishing a poem of one hundred verses, or a discourse of ten pages, he used to say he ought to repose for ten years. Balzac, the first writer in French prose who gave majesty and harmony to a period, did not grudge to expend a week on a page, never satisfied with his first thoughts. Our "costive" Gray entertained the same notion: and it is hard to say if it arose from the sterility of their genius, or their sensibility of taste.

The MSS. of Tasso, still preserved, are illegible from the vast number of their corrections. I have given a fac-simile, as correct as it is possible to conceive, of one page of Pope's MS. Homer, as a specimen of his continual corrections and critical erasures. The celebrated Madame Dacier never could satisfy herself in translating Homer: continually retouching the version, even in its happiest passages. There were several parts which she translated in six or seven manners; and she frequently noted in the margin—*I have not yet done it*.

When Pascal became warm in his celebrated controversy, he applied himself with incredible labour to the composition of his "Provincial Letters." He was frequently twenty days occupied on a single letter. He recommended some above seven and eight times, and by this means obtained that perfection which has made his work, as Voltaire says, "one of the best books ever published in France."

The Quintus Curtius of Vaugelas occupied him thirty years: generally every period was translated in the margin five or six different ways. Chapelain and Conrart, who took the pains to review this work critically, were many times perplexed in their choice of passages; they generally liked best that which had been first composed. Hume had never done with corrections; every edition varies from the preceding ones. But there are more fortunate and fluid minds than these. Voltaire tells us of Fenelon's Telemachus, that the amiable author composed it in his retirement, in the short period of three months. Fenelon had, before this, formed his style, and his mind overflowed with all the spirit of the ancients. He opened a copious fountain, and there were not ten erasures in the original MS. The same facility accompanied Gibbon after the experience of his first volume; and the same copious readiness attended Adam Smith, who dictated to his amanuensis, while he walked about his study.

The ancients were as pertinacious in their corrections. Isocrates, it is said, was employed for ten years on one of his works, and to appear natural studied with the most refined art. After a labour of eleven years, Virgil pronounced his Æneid imperfect. Dio Cassius devoted twelve years to the composition of his history, and Diodorus Siculus, thirty.

There is a middle between velocity and torpidity; the Italians say, it is not necessary to be a stag, but we ought not to be a tortoise.

Many ingenious expedients are not to be contemned in literary labours. The critical advice,

> To choose an *author* as we would a *friend,*

is very useful to young writers. The finest geniuses have always affectionately attached themselves to some particular author of congenial disposition. Pope, in his version of Homer, kept a constant eye on his master Dryden; Corneille's favourite authors were the brilliant Tacitus, the heroic Livy, and the lofty Lucan: the influence of their characters may be traced in his best tragedies. The great Clarendon, when employed in writing his history, read over very carefully Tacitus and Livy, to give dignity to his style; Tacitus did not surpass him in his portraits, though Clarendon never equalled Livy in his narrative.

The mode of literary composition adopted by that admirable student Sir William Jones, is well deserving our attention. After having fixed on his subject, he always added the *model* of the composition; and thus boldly wrestled with the great authors of antiquity. On board the frigate which was carrying him to India, he projected the following works, and noted them in this manner:—

1. Elements of the laws of England.
                    Model—The Essay on Bailments. ARISTOTLE.

2. The History of the American War.
                    Model—THUCYDIDES and POLYBIUS.

3. Britain Discovered, an Epic Poem. Machinery—Hindu Gods.
                    Model—HOMER.

4. Speeches, Political and Forensic.
                    Model—DEMOSTHENES.

5. Dialogues, Philosophical and Historical.
                    Model—PLATO.

And of favourite authors there are also favourite works, which we love to be familiarised with. Bartholinus has a dissertation on reading books, in which he points out the superior performances of different writers. Of St. Austin, his City of God; of Hippocrates, *Coacæ Prænotiones;* of Cicero, *De Officiis;* of Aristotle, *De Animalibus;* of Catullus, *Coma Berenices;* of Virgil, the sixth book of the Æneid, &c. Such judgments are indeed not to be our guides; but such a mode of reading is useful, by condensing our studies.

Evelyn, who has written treatises on several subjects, was occupied for years on them. His manner of arranging his materials, and his mode of composition, appear excellent. Having chosen a subject, he analysed it into its various parts, under certain heads, or titles, to be filled up at leisure. Under these heads he set down his own thoughts as they occurred, occasionally inserting whatever was useful from his reading. When his collections were thus formed, he digested his own thoughts regularly, and strengthened them by authorities from ancient and modern authors, or alleged his reasons for dissenting from them. His collections in time became voluminous, but he then exercised that judgment which the formers of such collections are usually deficient in. With Hesiod he knew that "half is better than the whole," and it was his aim to express the quintessence of his reading, but not to give it in a crude state to the world, and when his *treatises* were sent to the press, they were not half the size of his collections.

Thus also Winkelmann, in his "History of Art," an extensive work, was long lost in settling on a plan; like artists, who make random sketches of their first conceptions, he threw on paper ideas, hints, and observations which occurred in his readings—many of them, indeed, were not connected with his history, but were afterwards inserted in some of his other works.

Even Gibbon tells us of his Roman History, "at the outset all was dark and doubtful; even the title of the work, the true æra of the decline and fall of the empire, the limits of the introduction, the division of the chapters, and the order of the narration; and I was often tempted to cast away the labour of seven years." Akenside has exquisitely described the progress and the pains of genius in its delightful reveries: Pleasures of Imagination, b. iii. v. 373. The pleasures of composition in an ardent genius were never so finely described as by Buffon. Speaking of the hours of composition he said, "These are the most luxurious and delightful moments of life: moments which have often enticed me to pass fourteen hours at my desk in a state of transport, this *gratification* more than *glory* is my reward."

The publication of Gibbon's Memoirs conveyed to the world a faithful picture of the most fervid industry; it is in *youth* the foundations of such a sublime edifice as his history must be laid. The world can now trace how this Colossus of erudition, day by day, and year by year, prepared himself for some vast work.

Gibbon has furnished a new idea in the art of reading! We ought, says he, not to attend to the *order of our books, so much as of our thoughts*. "The perusal of a particular work gives birth perhaps to ideas unconnected with the subject it treats; I pursue these ideas, and quit my proposed plan of reading." Thus in the midst of Homer he read Longinus; a chapter of Longinus led to an epistle of Pliny; and having finished Longinus, he followed the train of his ideas of the sublime and beautiful in the Inquiry of Burke, and concluded with comparing the ancient with the modern Longinus. Of all our popular writers the most experienced reader was Gibbon, and he offers an important advice to an author engaged on a particular subject: "I suspended my perusal of any new book on the subject till I had reviewed all that I knew, or believed, or had thought on it, that I might be qualified to discern how much the authors added to my original stock."

These are valuable hints to students, and such have been practised by others.[30] Ancillon was a very ingenious student; he seldom read a book throughout without reading in his progress many others; his library-table was always covered with a number of books for the most part open: this variety of authors bred no confusion; they all assisted to throw light on the same topic; he was not disgusted by frequently seeing the same thing in different writers; their opinions were so many new strokes, which completed the ideas which he had conceived. The celebrated Father Paul studied in the same manner. He never passed over an interesting subject till he had confronted a variety of authors. In historical researches he never would advance, till he had fixed, once for all, the places, time, and opinions—a mode of study which appears very dilatory, but in the end will make a great saving of time, and labour of mind: those who have not pursued this method are all their lives at a loss to settle their opinions and their belief, from the want of having once brought them to such a test.

I shall now offer a plan of Historical Study, and a calculation of the necessary time it will occupy, without specifying the authors; as I only propose to animate a young student, who feels he has not to number the days of a patriarch, that he should not be alarmed at the vast labyrinth historical researches present to his eye. If we look into public libraries, more than thirty thousand volumes of history may be found.

Lenglet du Fresnoy, one of the greatest readers, calculated that he could not read, with satisfaction, more than ten hours a day, and ten pages in folio an hour; which makes one hundred pages every day. Supposing each volume to contain one thousand pages, every month would amount to three volumes, which make thirty-six volumes in folio in the year. In fifty years a student could only read eighteen hundred volumes in folio. All this, too, supposing uninterrupted health, and an intelligence as rapid as the eyes of the laborious researcher. A man can hardly study to advantage till past twenty, and at fifty his eyes will be dimmed, and his head stuffed with much reading that should never be read. His fifty years for eighteen hundred volumes are reduced to thirty years, and one thousand volumes! And, after all, the universal historian must resolutely face thirty thousand volumes!

---

30. Edgar Poe's account of the regular mode by which he designed and executed his best and most renowned poem, "The Raven," is an instance of the use of methodical rule successfully applied to what appears to be one of the most fanciful of mental works.

But to cheer the historiographer, he shows, that a public library is only necessary to be consulted; it is in our private closet where should be found those few writers who direct us to their rivals, without jealousy, and mark, in the vast career of time, those who are worthy to instruct posterity. His calculation proceeds on this plan, that *six hours* a day, and the term of *ten years*, are sufficient to pass over, with utility, the immense field of history.

He calculates an alarming extent of historical ground.

For a knowledge of Sacred History he gives .	3 months
Ancient Egypt, Babylon, and Assyria, modern Assyria or Persia	
. . . .	1 do.
Greek History	6 do.
Roman History by the moderns . . .	7 do.
Roman History by the original writers : . .	6 do.
Ecclesiastical History, general and particular : :	30 do.
Modern History : . : . .	24 do.
To this may be added for recurrences and re-perusals .	48 do

The total will amount to 10½ years.

Thus, in *ten years and a half*, a student in history has obtained an universal knowledge, and this on a plan which permits as much leisure as every student would choose to indulge.

As a specimen of Du Fresnoy's calculations, take that of Sacred History.

For reading Père Calmet's learned dissertations in the order he points out	
. . . .	12 days
For Père Calmet's History, in 2 vols. 4to (now in 4). .	12
For Prideaux's History	10
For Josephus	12
For Basnage's History of the Jews . . .	20

In all 66 days.

He allows, however, ninety days for obtaining a sufficient knowledge of Sacred History.

In reading this sketch, we are scarcely surprised at the erudition of a Gibbon; but having admired that erudition, we perceive the necessity of such a plan, if we would not learn what we have afterwards to unlearn.

A plan like the present, even in a mind which should feel itself incapable of the exertion, will not be regarded without that reverence we feel for genius animating such industry. This scheme of study, though it may never be rigidly pursued, will be found excellent. Ten years' labour of happy diligence may render a student capable of consigning to posterity a history as universal in its topics, as that of the historian who led to this investigation.

8. ON READING
(*Literary Miscellanies.*, vol. 4, pp. 298-302)

WRITING is justly denominated an art; I think that reading claims the same distinction. To adorn ideas with elegance is an act of the mind superior to that of receiving them; but to receive them with a happy discrimination is the effect of a practised taste.

Yet it will be found that taste alone is not sufficient to obtain the proper end of reading. Two persons of equal taste rise from the perusal of the same book with very different notions: the one will have the ideas of the author at command, and find a new train of sentiment awakened; while the other quits his author in a pleasing distraction, but of the pleasures of reading nothing remains but tumultuous sensations.

To account for these different effects, we must have recourse to a logical distinction, which appears to reveal one of the great mysteries in the art of reading. Logicians distinguish between perceptions and ideas. Perception is that faculty of the mind which notices the simple impression of objects: but when these objects exist in the mind, and are there treasured and arranged as materials for reflection, then they are called ideas. A perception is like a transient sunbeam, which just shows the object, but leaves neither light nor warmth; while an idea is like the fervid beam of noon, which throws a settled and powerful light.

Many ingenious readers complain that their memory is defective, and their studies unfruitful. This defect arises from their indulging the facile pleasures of perceptions, in preference to the laborious habit of forming them into ideas. Perceptions require only the sensibility of taste, and their pleasures are continuous, easy, and exquisite. Ideas are an art of combination, and an exertion of the reasoning powers. Ideas are therefore labours; and for whose who will not labour, it is unjust to complain, if they come from the harvest with scarcely a sheaf in their hands.

There are secrets in the art of reading which tend to facilitate its purposes, by assisting the memory, and augmenting intellectual opulence. Some our own ingenuity must form, and perhaps every student has peculiar habits of study, as, in short-hand, almost every writer has a system of his own.

It is an observation of the elder Pliny (who, having been a voluminous compiler, must have had great experience in the art of reading), that there was no book so bad but which contained something good. To read every book would, however, be fatal to the interest of most readers; but it is not always necessary, in the pursuits of learning, to read every book entire. Of many books it is sufficient to seize the plan, and to examine some of their portions. Of the little supplement at the close of a volume, few readers conceive the utility; but some of the most eminent writers in Europe have been great adepts in the art of index reading. I, for my part, venerate the inventor of indexes; and I know not to whom to yield the preference, either to Hippocrates, who was the first great anatomiser of the human body, or to that unknown labourer in literature, who first laid open the nerves and arteries of a book. Watts advises the perusal of the prefaces and the index of a book, as they both give light on its contents.

The ravenous appetite of Johnson for reading is expressed in a strong metaphor by Mrs. Knowles, who said, "he knows how to read better than any one; he gets at the substance of a book directly: he tears out the heart of it." Gibbon has a new idea in the "Art of Reading;" he says "we ought not to attend to the order of our books so much as of our thoughts. The perusal of a particular work gives birth perhaps to ideas unconnected with the subject it treats; I pursue these ideas, and quit my proposed plan of reading." Thus in the midst of Homer he read Longinus; a chapter of Longinus led to an epistle of Pliny; and having finished Longinus, he followed the train of his ideas of the sublime and beautiful in the "Enquiry" of Burke, and concluded by comparing the ancient with the modern Longinus.

There are some mechanical aids in reading which may prove of great utility, and form a kind of rejuvenescence of our early studies. Montaigne placed at the end of a book which he intended not to reperuse, the time he had read it, with a concise decision on its merits; "that," says he, "it may thus represent to me the air and general idea I had conceived of the author, in reading the work." We have several of these annotations. Of Young the poet it is noticed, that whenever he came to a striking passage he folded the leaf; and that at his death, books have been found in his library which had long resisted the power of closing: a mode more easy than useful; for after a length of time they must be again read to know why they were folded. This difficulty is obviated by those who note in a blank leaf the pages to be referred to, with a word of criticism. Nor let us consider these minute directions as unworthy the most enlarged minds: by these petty exertions, at the most distant periods, may learning obtain its authorities, and fancy combine its ideas. Seneca, in sending some volumes to his friend Lucilius, accompanies them with notes of particular passages, "that," he observes, "you who only aim at the useful may be spared the trouble of examining them entire." I have seen books noted by Voltaire with a word of censure or approbation on the page itself, which was his usual practice; and these volumes are precious to every man of taste.

Formey complained that the books he lent Voltaire were returned always disfigured by his remarks; but he was a writer of the old school.

A professional student should divide his readings into a *uniform* reading which is useful, and into a *diversified* reading which is pleasant. Guy Patin, an eminent physician and man of letters, had a just notion of this manner. He says, "I daily read Hippocrates, Galen, Fernel, and other illustrious masters of my profession; this I call my profitable readings. I frequently read Ovid, Juvenal, Horace, Seneca, Tacitus, and others, and these are my recreations." We must observe these distinctions; for it frequently happens that a lawyer or a physician, with great industry and love of study, by giving too much into his diversified readings, may utterly neglect what should be his uniform studies.

A reader is too often a prisoner attached to the triumphal car of an author of great celebrity; and when he ventures not to judge for himself, conceives, while he is reading the indifferent works of great authors, that the languor which he experiences arises from his own defective taste. But the best writers, when they are voluminous, have a great deal of mediocrity.

On the other side, readers must not imagine that all the pleasures of composition depend on the author, for there is something which a reader himself must bring to the book that the book may please. There is a literary appetite, which the author can no more impart than the most skilful cook can give an appetency to the guests. When Cardinal Richelieu said to Godeau, that he did not understand his verses, the honest poet replied that it was not his fault. The temporary tone of the mind may be unfavourable to taste a work properly, and we have had many erroneous criticisms from great men, which may often be attributed to this circumstance. The mind communicates its infirm dispositions to the book, and an author has not only his own defects to account for, but also those of his reader. There is something in composition like the game of shuttlecock, where if the reader do not quickly rebound the feathered cock to the author, the game is destroyed, and the whole spirit of the work falls extinct.

A frequent impediment in reading is a disinclination in the mind to settle on the subject; agitated by incongruous and dissimilar ideas, it is with pain that we admit those of the author. But on applying ourselves with a gentle violence to the perusal of an interesting work, the mind soon assimilates to the subject; the ancient rabbins advised their young students to apply themselves to their readings, whether they felt an inclination or not, because, as they proceeded, they would find their disposition restored and their curiosity awakened.

Readers may be classed into an infinite number of divisions; but an author is a solitary being, who, for the same reason he pleases one, must consequently displease another. To have too exalted a genius is more prejudicial to his celebrity than to have a moderate one; for we shall find that the most popular works are not the most profound, but such as instruct those who require instruction, and charm those who are not too learned to taste their novelty. Lucilius, the satirist, said, that he did not write for Persius, for Scipio, and for Rutilius, persons eminent for their science, but for the Tarentines, the Consentines, and the Sicilians. Montaigne has complained that he found his readers too learned, or too ignorant, and that he could only please a middle class, who have just learning enough to comprehend him. Congreve says, "there is in true beauty something which vulgar souls cannot admire." Balzac complains bitterly of readers,—"A period," he cries, "shall have cost us the labour of a day; we shall have distilled into an essay the essence of our mind, it may be a finished piece of art; and they think they are indulgent when they pronounce it to contain some pretty things, and that the style is not bad!" There is something in exquisite composition which ordinary readers can never understand.

Authors are vain, but readers are capricious. Some will only read old books, as if there were no valuable truths to be discovered in modern publications; while others will only read new books, as if some valuable truths are not among the old. Some will not read a book, because they are acquainted with the author; by which the reader may be more injured than the author: others not only read the book, but would also read the man; by which the most ingenious author may be injured by the most impertinent reader.

II. PRINTING AND PUBLISHING

1. THE INVENTION OF PRINTING
(*Amenities,* pp. 203-213)

PRINTING remained, as long as its first artificers could keep it, a secret and occult art; and it is the only one that ceaselessly operates all the miracles which the others had vainly promised.

Who first thought to carve the wooden immoveable letters on blocks?—to stamp the first sheet which ever was imprinted? Or who, second in invention, but first in utility, imagined to cast the metal with fusile types, separate from each other?—to fix this scattered alphabet in a form, and thus by one stroke write a thousand manuscripts, and, with the identical letters, multiply not a single work, but all sorts of works hereafter? Was it fortunate chance, or deliberate meditation, or both in gradual discovery, which produced this invention? In truth, we can neither detect the rude beginnings, nor hardly dare to fix on the beginners. The *Origines Typographicæ* are, even at this late hour, provoking a fierce controversy, not only among those who live in the shades of their libraries, but with honest burghers; for the glory of patriotism has connected itself with the invention of an art which came to us like a divine revelation in the history of man. But the place, the mode, and the person—the invention and the inventor—are the subject of volumes! Votaries of Fust, of Schöffer, of Gutenberg, of Costar! A sullen silence or a deadly feud is your only response. Ye jealous cities of Mentz [Mainz], of Strasbourg, and of Haarlem, each of ye have your armed champion at your gates![31]

The mystical eulogist of the art of printing, who declared that "the invention came from Heaven," was not more at a loss to detect the origin than those who have sought for it among the earliest printers.[32] Learned but

---

31. The city of Haarlem designs to erect a statue of COSTAR [since this was written the statue has been placed in the great square]; thus publicly, in the eyes of Europe, to vindicate the priority of this inventor of typography. But a statue is not the final argument which, like the cannon of monarchs (that *ultima ratio regum),* will carry conviction on the spot it is placed. Mentz has already erected a statue of GUTENBERG. I have no doubt that, in the present state of agitation, both these statues will have much to say to one another, as the mystical Pasquin and Marforio of typography.

32. "Some Observations on the Use and Original of the noble Art and Mystery of Printing," by F. Burges. Norwich, 1701. This is declared to be the first book printed at Norwich; where it appears that the establishment of a printing-office, so late as in 1701, encountered a stern opposition from its sage citizens. The writer did not know that as far back as 1570 a Dutch printer had exercised the novel art by printing religious books for a community of Dutch emigrants who had taken refuge at

angry disputants on the origin of printing, what if the art can boast of no single inventor, and was not the product of a single act? Consider the varieties of its practice, the change of wood to metal, the fixed to the moveable type; view the complexity of its machinery; repeated attempts must often have preceded so many inventions ere they terminated in the great one. From the imperfect and contradictory notices of the early essays—and of the very earliest we may have no record—we must infer that the art, though secret, was progressive, and that many imperfect beginnings were going on at the same time in different places.

Struck by the magnitude and the magnificence of the famous Bible of Fust, some have decided on the invention of the art by one of its most splendid results; this, however, is not in the usual course of human affairs, nor in the nature of things. "The Art of Printing," observes Dr. Cotton, in his introduction, "was brought almost to perfection in its infancy; so that, like Minerva, it may be said to have sprung to life, mature, vigorous, and armed for war." But in the article "Moguntia, or Mentz," this acute researcher states that "after all that has been written with such angry feelings upon the long-contested question of the *origin of the Art of Printing*, Mentz appears still to preserve the best-founded claim to the honour of being the *birth-place of the Typographic Art*; because," he adds, "the specimens adduced in favour of Haarlem and Strasbourg, even if we should allow their genuineness, are confessedly of *a rude and imperfect execution*." We require no other evidence of the important fact, that the art, in its early stages, had to pass through many transitions—from the small school-books, or Donatuses, of Costar, to the splendid Bible of Fust. Had the art been borrowed or stolen from a single source, according to the popular tradition, the works would have borne a more fraternal resemblance, and have evinced less inferiority of execution; but if several persons at the same time were working in secrecy, each by his own method, their differences and their inferiority would produce "the rude and imperfect specimens." Mr. Hallam has suffered his strong emotion on the greatness of the invention to reflect itself back on the humble discoverers themselves; and, unusual with his searching inquiries, calls once more on Dr. Cotton's Minerva, but with a more celestial panoply. "The *high-minded inventors* of this great art tried, at *the very outset*, so bold a flight as the printing *an entire Bible*. It was Minerva leaping on Earth, in her divine strength, and radiant armour, ready at the moment of her nativity to subdue and destroy her enemies."[33] The Bible called the Mazarine Bible, thus distinguished from having been found in the Cardinal's library, remains still a miracle of

---

Norwich, according to the recent discovery of Dr. Cotton, in his "Typographical Gazetteer"—a volume abounding with the most vigorous researches.

33. Hallam's "Introduction to the Literature of Europe," i. 211.

typography, not only for its type, but for the quality of the paper and the sparkling blackness of its ink.[34] The success of the art was established by this Bible; but the goldsmith Fust, who himself was no printer, was no otherwise "high-minded," than by the usurious prices he speculated on for this innocent imposture of vending what was now a printed book for a manuscript copy!

No refined considerations of the nature and the universal consequences of their discovery seem to have instigated the earliest printers; this is evident by the perpetual jealousy and the mystifying style by which they long attempted to hide that secret monopoly which they had now obtained.

The first notions of printing might have reached Europe from China. Our first block-printing seems imitated from the Chinese, who print with blocks of wood on one side of the paper, as was done in the earliest essays of printing; and the Chinese seem also to have suggested the use of thick black ink. European traders might have imported some fugitive leaves; their route has even been indicated, from Tartary, by the way of Russia; and from China and Japan, through the Indies and the Arabian Gulf. The great antiquity of printing in China has been ascertained. Du Halde and the missionary Jesuits assert that this art was practised by the Chinese half a century before the Christian era! At all events, it is evident that they exercised it many centuries before it was attempted in Europe. The history of gunpowder would illustrate the possibility of the same extraordinary invention occurring at distinct periods. Roger Bacon indicated the terrible ingredients a hundred years before the monk Schwartz, about 1330, actually struck out the fiery explosion, and had the glory of its invention. Machines to convey to a distance the thunder and the lightning described by their discoverers were not long after produced. But it would have astonished these inventors to have learnt that guns had been used as early as the year 85 A.D., and that the fatal powder had been invented previously by the Chinese. Well might the philosophical Langles be struck by "the singular coincidence of the invention in Europe of the compass, of gunpowder, and of printing, about the same period, within a century." These three mighty agents in human affairs have been traced to that wary and literary nation, who though they prohibit all intercourse with "any barbarian eye," might have suffered these sublime inventions to steal away over "their great wall."

What has happened to the art of printing also occurred to the sister-art of engraving on copper. Tradition had ascribed the invention as the accidental discovery of the goldsmith Maso Finiguerra. But the Germans insist that they possess engravings before the days of the Italian artist; and it is not doubtful that several of the compatriots of Finiguerra were equally practising the art

---

34. Twenty copies of this famous Bible exist; one is preserved in our Royal Library.

with himself. Heinecken would arbitrate between the jealous patriots; he concedes that Vasari might ascribe the invention of the art in Italy to Finiguerra, yet that engraving might have been practised in Germany, though unknown in Italy. Buonarotti, the great judge of all art, was sensible that in this sort of invention every artist makes his own discoveries. Alluding to the art of engraving, he says, "It would be sufficient to occasion our astonishment, that the ancients did not discover the art of chalcography, were it not known that DISCOVERIES OF THIS SORT generally occur ACCIDENTALLY to the mechanics in the exercise of their calling."[35] On this principle we may confidently rest. All the early printers, like the rivals of Finiguerra at home, and his unknown concurrents in Germany, were proceeding with the same art, and might urge their distinct claims.

The natural magic of concave and convex lenses, those miracles of optical science, one of which searches Nature when she eludes the eye, and the other approximates the remotest star—the microscope and the telescope; who were their inventors, and how have those inventions happened? These instruments appeared about the same time. The Germans ascribe the invention of the microscope to a Dutchman, one Drebell; while the Neapolitan Fontana claims the anterior invention; but which Viviani, the scholar of Galileo, asserts, from his own knowledge, was presented to the King of Poland by that father of modern philosophy long anterior to the date fixed on by the Germans. The history of the telescope offers a similar result. Fracastorious may have accidentally combined two lenses; but he neither specified the form nor the quality; and in these consisted the real discovery, which we find in Baptista Porta, and which subsequently was perfected by Galileo. The invention of the art of printing seems a parallel one. It appeared in various quarters about the same time; and in the process of successive attempts, by intimation, by conjecture, and by experiment, each artificer insensibly advanced into a more perfect invention; till some fortunate claimant for the discovery puts aside all preceding essayists, who, not without some claims to the invention, leave their advocates in another generation to dispute about their rights, which are buried in oblivion, or falsified by traditional legends.

Thus it has happened that obscure traditions envelope the origin of some of the most interesting inventions. Had these ingenious discoveries been as simple and as positive as their historians oppositely maintain, these origins had not admitted of such interminable disputes. We may therefore reasonably suspect that the practitioners in every art which has reached to almost a perfect state, such as that of printing, have silently borrowed from one another; that there has often existed a secret connexion in things, and a

---

35. Ottley's "Inquiry into the Early History of Engraving." See also note in "Curiosities of Literature," vol. i. p. 43.

reciprocal observation in the intercourse of men alike intent on the same object; that countries have insensibly transferred a portion of their knowledge to their neighbours; that travellers in every era have imparted their novelties, hints however crude, descriptions however imperfect; all such slight notices escape the detection of an historian; nothing can reach him but the excellence of some successful artist. In vain rival concurrents dispute the invention; the patriotic historian of the art clings to his people and his city, to fix the inventor and the invention, and promulgates fairy tales to authenticate the most uncertain evidence.[36]

The history of printing illustrates this view of its origin. The invention has been long ascribed to GUTENBERG, yet some have made it doubtful whether this presumed father of the art ever succeeded in printing a book, for we are assured that no colophon has revealed his name. We hear of his attempts and of his disappointments, his bickerings and his lawsuits. He seems to have been a speculative bungler in a new-found art, which he mysteriously hinted was to make a man's fortune. The goldsmith, Fust, advanced a capital in search of the novel alchymy—the project ends in a lawsuit, the goldsmith gains his cause, and the projector is discharged. Gutenberg lures another simple soul, and the same golden dream vanishes in the dreaming. These copartners, evidently tired of an art which had not yet found an artist, a young man, probably improving on Gutenberg's blunders, one happy day displayed to the eyes of his master, Fust, a proof pulled from his own press. In rapture, the master confers on this Peter Schœffer a share of his future fortunes; and to bind the apprentice by the safest ties of consanguinity, led the swart youth, glorious with printer's ink, to the fair hand of his young daughter. The new partnership produced their famed Psalter of 1457; and shortly followed their magnificent Bible.

While these events were occurring, COSTAR, of Haarlem, was plodding on with the same "noble mystery," but only printing on one side of a leaf, not having yet discovered that a leaf might be contrived to contain two pages. The partisans of Costar assert that it was proved he substituted moveable for fixed

---

36. Dr. WETTER, of Mentz, has lately shown that, contrary to the common opinion, Gutenberg himself printed long with *wooden blocks;* and that, instead of the invention of moveable types having been the result of long study, *it arose out of a "sudden fancy."*

How the Doctor has authenticated "the sudden fancy," I know not, but the apotheosis has passed. In three successive days, in the month of August, 1837, all Mentz congregated to worship the statue, by Thorwaldsen, of their ancient citizen in the square that henceforward bears his name. A chorus of 700 voices resounded the laud of the German printer; the flags in the regatta waved to his honour; and the festival rejoiced the city: and when the figure of Gutenberg was unveiled, the artillery, the music, and the people's voices, blending together, seemed to echo in the skies.

letters, which was a giant's footstep in this new path. A faithless servant ran off with the secret. The history of printing abounds with such tales. Every step in the progress of the newly-invented art indicates its gradual accessions. The numbering of the pages was not thought of for a considerable time; the leaves were long only distinguished by letters or signatures—a custom still preserved, though apparently superfluous.

There is something attractive for rational curiosity in the earliest beginnings of every art; every slight improvement, even though trivial, has its motive, and supplies some want. On this principle the history of punctuation enters into the history of literature. Caxton had the merit of introducing the Roman pointing as used in Italy; and his successor, Pynson, triumphed by domiciliating the Roman letter. The dash, or perpendicular line, thus, | was the only punctuation they used. It was, however, discovered that "the craft of poynting well used makes the sentence very light." The more elegant comma supplanted the long uncouth | ; the colon was a refinement, "showing that there is more to come." But the semicolon was a Latin delicacy which the obtuse English typographer resisted. So late as 1580 and 1590 treatises on orthography do not recognise any such innovator; the Bible of 1592. though printed with appropriate accuracy, is without a semicolon; but in 1633 its full rights are established by Charles Butler's "English Grammar." In this chronology of the four points of punctuation it is evident that Shakespeare could never have used the semicolon—a circumstance which the profound George Chalmers mourns over, opining that semicolons would often have saved the poet from his commentators.

Fust had bound his workmen to secrecy by the solemnity of an oath; but at the siege of Mentz that freemasonry was lost. These early printers dispersed, some were bribed away. Two Germans set up their press in the monastery of Subiaco, in the vicinity of Naples, whose confraternity consisted of German monks. These very printers finally retreated to Rome for that patronage they had still to seek; and at Rome they improved the art by adopting the Roman character. Not only the invention of the art was progressive, but the art itself was much more so.

We have other narratives of printers romantically spirited away from the parent-presses; one of the most extraordinary is the history of printing set up at Oxford, ten years before the art was practised in Europe, except at Haarlem and Mentz. Henry VI., by advice of the Archbishop of Canterbury, despatched a confidential agent in disguise, under the guidance of Caxton, in his trading journeys to Flanders. The Haarlemites were so jealous of idling strangers who had come on the same insidious design, that foreigners had frequently been imprisoned.

The royal agent never ventured to enter the city, but by heavy bribes in secret intercourse with the workmen, one dark night he smuggled a printer aboard a vessel, and carried away Frederick Corsellis. That printer, on landing in England, was attended by a guard to Oxford. There he was constantly watched till he had revealed the mysterious craft. The evidence of this unheard-of history hinged on a record at Lambeth-palace authenticating the whole narrative, and on a monument of Corsellis's art, which any one might inspect at the Bodleian, being a book bearing a date six years prior to any printing by Caxton. The record at Lambeth, however, was never found, and never heard of, and the date of the book might have been accidentally or designedly falsified. An x dropped in the date of the impression would account for the singularity of a book printed before our Caxton had acquired the art. The tale long excited a sharp controversy, when Corsellis at Oxford was considered as the first printer in England. The possibility of the existence of this person at Oxford, and even the book he printed, appears by a lively investigation of Dr. Cotton;[37] and I have been assured of a circumstance which, if true, would render the story of Corsellis probable; it is that a family of this name may still be found in Oxfordshire. The whole history has, however, by some been considered as supposititious, standing on the single evidence of a Sir Richard Atkyns, a servile lawyer and royalist of no great character in the days of Charles the Second.[38] Grafting his tale on the accident of the date of this book, he had a covert design—to maintain a theory or a right that printing was "a flower of the crown," constituting the sovereign the printer of England! all others being his servants. This enormous prevention of the abuses of the press was not deemed to extravagant for those desperate times.

The only certainty in the history of printing, after all the fables of its origin, is its native place. It is a German romance enlivened by some mysterious adventures, wanting only the opening pages, which no one can supply.[39] Even the most philosophic of bibliographers, Daunou, utters a cry of despair, and moreover, at this late day, seems at a loss to decide on the nature of the influence of the art of printing! "We live too near the epoch of the discovery of printing to judge accurately of its influence, and too far from

---

37. Dr. Cotton's curious "Typographical Gazetteer," art. OXONIA. Of a class of the earliest printed books, having no printer's name, he observes, "These may have been printed by Corsellis, or any one else."

38. Atkyns on the "Original and Growth of Printing." This quarto pamphlet is highly valued among collectors for Loggan's beautiful print of Charles the Second, Archbishop Shelden, and General Monk. Dr. Middleton refuted this ridiculous tale of an ideal printer, one Corsellis, in his "Dissertation on the Origin of Printing in England," first published 1735, and which now may be seen in his works.

39. The fourth day of the "Bibliographical Decameron" of Dr. Dibdin exhibits an ample view of the pending controversies on the "Origines Typographicæ." Every bibliographer has his favourite hero. The reader will observe that I have none! And yet possibly my tale may be the truest.

it to know the circumstances which gave birth to it." Our sage seems to think that another cycle of at least a thousand years must pass away ere we can decide on the real influence of printing over the destinies of man: this new tree of knowledge bears other fruit than that of its own sweetness, source of good and evil, of sense and of nonsense! whence we pluck the windy fruitage of opinions, crude and changeable!

How has it happened that such a plain story as that of the art of printing should have sunk into a romance? Solely because the monopolisers dreaded discovery. It originated in deception, and could only flourish for their commercial spirit in mysterious obscurity. Among the first artisans of printing every one sought to hide his work, and even to blind the workmen. After their operations, they cautiously unscrewed the four sides of their forms, and threw the scattered type beneath, for, as one craftily observed to his partner, "When the component parts of the press are in pieces, no one will understand what they mean." One of the early printers of the fifteenth century at Mutina, or Modena, professes his press to have been *in ædibus subterraneis*—doubtless, if possible, still further to darken the occult mystery. They delivered themselves in a mystical style when they alluded to their unnamed art, and impressed on the marvelling reader that the volume he held in his hand was the work of some supernatural agency. They announced that the volumes in this newly-found art were "neither drawn, nor written with a pen and ink, as all books before had been." In the "Recuyel of the Historyes of Troye," our honest printer, plain Caxton, caught the hyperbolical style of the dark monopolising spirit of the confraternity. I give his words, having first spelt them. "I have practised and learned at my great charge, and dispense to ordain (put in order) this said book in print after the manner and form as ye may here see, and it is not written with pen and ink as other books be, to the end that *every man may have them* AT ONCE; for all the books of this story, thus imprinted as ye see, were *begun in one day, and also finished in one day*." A volume of more than seven hundred folio pages, "begun and finished in one day," was not the less marvellous for being impossible. But for the times was the style! Caxton would keep up the wonder and the mystery of an art which men did not yet comprehend; and because a whole sheet might have been printed in one day, and was *all at once* pulled off, and not line by line, our venerable printer mystified the world. And all this was said at a time when so slow was the process of transcription, that one hundred Bibles could not be procured under the expense of seven thousand days, or of nearly twenty years' labour. Honest men, too eager in their zeal, particularly when their personal interests are at stake, sometimes strain truth on the tenter-hooks of fiction. The false miracle which our primeval printer professed he had performed we seem to have realized: it is amusing to conceive the wonderment of Caxton, were he now among us, to view the steam working that cylindrical machine which disperses the words of a speaker throughout the whole nation, when the voice which uttered them is still lingering on our ear!

2. EARLY PRINTING
(*Curiosities*, vol. 1, pp. 73-78)

THERE is some probability that this art originated in China, where it was practised long before it was known in Europe. Some European traveller might have imported the hint.[40] That the Romans did not practise the art of printing cannot but excite our astonishment, since they actually used it, unconscious of their rich possession. I have seen Roman stereotypes, or immoveable printing types, with which they stamped their pottery.[41] How in daily practising the art, though confined to this object, it did not occur to so ingenious a people to print their literary works, is not easily to be accounted for. Did the wise and grave senate dread those inconveniences which attend its indiscriminate use? Or perhaps they did not care to deprive so large a body of scribes of their business. Not a hint of the art itself appears in their writings.

When first the art of printing was discovered, they only made use of one side of a leaf; they had not yet found out the expedient of impressing the other. Afterwards they thought of pasting the blank sides, which made them appear like one leaf. Their blocks were made of soft woods, and their letters were carved; but frequently breaking, the expense and trouble of carving and gluing new letters suggested our moveable types, which have produced an almost miraculous celerity in this art. The modern stereotype, consisting of entire pages in solid blocks of metal, and, not being liable to break like the soft wood at first used, has been profitably employed for works which require to be frequently reprinted. Printing in carved blocks of wood must have greatly retarded the progress of universal knowledge: for one set of types could only have produced one work, whereas it now serves for hundreds.

When their editions were intended to be curious, they omitted to print the

---

40. China is the stronghold where antiquarian controversy rests. Beaten in affixing the origin of any art elsewhere, the controversialist enshrines himself within the Great Wall, and is allowed to repose in peace. Opponents, like Arabs, give up the chase when these gates close, though possibly with as little reason as the children of the desert evince when they quietly succumb to any slight defence.

41. They are small square blocks of metal, with the name in raised letters within a border, precisely similar to those used by the modern printer. Sometimes the stamp was round, or in the shape of a foot or hand, with the potter's name in the centre. They were in constant use for impressing the clay-works which supplied the wants of a Roman household. The list of potters' marks found upon fragments discovered in London alone amounts to several hundreds.

initial letter of a chapter: they left that blank space to be painted or illuminated, to the fancy of the purchaser. Several ancient volumes of these early times have been found where these letters are wanting, as they neglected to have them painted.

The initial carved letter, which is generally a fine wood-cut, among our printed books, is evidently a remains or imitation of these ornaments.[42] Among the very earliest books printed, which were religious, the Poor Man's Bible has wooden cuts in a coarse style, without the least shadowing or crossing of strokes, and these they inelegantly daubed over with broad colours, which they termed illuminating, and sold at a cheap rate to those who could not afford to purchase costly missals elegantly written and painted on vellum. Specimens of these rude efforts of illuminated prints may be seen in Strutt's Dictionary of Engravers. The Bodleian library possesses the originals.[43]

In the productions of early printing may be distinguished the various splendid editions of *Primers*, or *Prayer-books*. These were embellished with cuts finished in a most elegant taste: many of them were grotesque or obscene. In one of them an angel is represented crowning the Virgin Mary, and God the Father himself assisting at the ceremony. Sometimes St. Michael is

---

42. Another reason for the omission of a great initial is given. There was difficulty in obtaining such enriched letters by engraving as were used in manuscripts; and there was at this time a large number of professional scribes, whose interests were in some degree considered by the printer. Hence we find in early books a large space left to be filled in by the hand of the scribe with the proper letter indicated by a small type letter placed in the midst. The famous *Psalter* printed by Faust and Scheffer, at Mentz, in 1497, is the first book having large initial letters printed in red and blue inks, in imitation of the handwork of the old caligraphers.

43. The British Museum now possesses a remarkably fine series of these early works. They originated in the large sheet woodcuts, or "broadsides," representing saints, or scenes from saintly legends, used by the clergy as presents to the peasantry or pilgrims to certain shrines—a custom retained upon the Continent to the present time; such cuts exhibiting little advance in art since the days of their origin, being almost as rude, and daubed in a similar way with coarse colour. One ancient cut of this kind in the British Museum, representing the Saviour brought before Pilate, resembles in style the pen-drawings in manuscripts of the fourteenth century. Another exhibits the seven stages of human life, with the wheel of fortune in the centre. Another is an emblematic representation of the Tower of Sapience, each stone formed of some mental qualification. When books were formed, a large series of such cuts included pictures and type in each page, and in one piece. The so-called Poor Man's Bible (an evidently erroneous term for it, the invention of a bibliographer of the last century) was one of these, and consists of a series of pictures from Scripture history, with brief explanations. It was most probably preceded by the block books known as the *Apocalypse of St. John*, the *Cantico Canticorum,* and the *Ars Memorandi.*

overcoming Satan; and sometimes St. Anthony is attacked by various devils of most clumsy forms—not of the grotesque and limber family of Callot!

Printing was gradually practised throughout Europe from the year 1440 to 1500. Caxton and his successor Wynkyn de Worde were our own earliest printers. Caxton was a wealthy merchant, who, in 1464, being sent by Edward IV. to negotiate a commercial treaty with the Duke of Burgundy, returned to his country with this invaluable art. Notwithstanding his mercantile habits, he possessed a literary taste, and his first work was a translation from a French historical miscellany.[44]

The tradition of the Devil and Dr. Faustus was said to have been derived from the odd circumstance in which the Bibles of the first printer, Fust, appeared to the world; but if Dr. Faustus and Faustus the printer are two different persons, the tradition becomes suspicious, though, in some respects, it has a foundation in truth. When Fust had discovered this new art, and printed off a considerable number of copies of the Bible to imitate those which were commonly sold as MSS., he undertook the sale of them at Paris. It was his interest to conceal this discovery, and to pass off his printed copies for MSS. But, enabled to sell his Bibles at sixty crowns, while the other scribes demanded five hundred, this raised universal astonishment; and still more when he produced copies as fast as they were wanted, and even lowered his price. The uniformity of the copies increased the wonder. Informations were given in to the magistrates against him as a magician; and in searching his lodgings a great number of copies were found. The red ink, and Fust's red ink is peculiarly brilliant, which embellished his copies, was said to be his blood; and it was solemnly adjudged that he was in league with the Infernals. Fust at length was obliged, to save himself from a bonfire, to reveal his art to the Parliament of Paris, who discharged him from all prosecution in consideration of the wonderful invention.

When the art of printing was established, it became the glory of the learned to be correctors of the press to eminent printers. Physicians, lawyers, and bishops themselves occupied this department. The printers then added frequently to their names those of the correctors of the press; and editions were then valued according to the abilities of the corrector.

The *prices* of books in these times were considered as an object worthy of the animadversions of the highest power. This anxiety in favour of the studious appears from a privilege of Pope Leo X. to Aldus Manutius for

---

44. This was Raoul le Fevre's *Recueil des Histoires de Troye,* a fanciful compilation of adventures, in which the heroes of antiquity perform the parts of the *preux chevaliers* of the middle ages. It was "ended in the Holy City of Colen," in September, 1471. The first book printed by him in England was *The Game and Playe of the Chesse,* in March, 1474. It is a fanciful moralization of the game, abounding with quaint old legends and stories

printing Varro, dated 1553, signed Cardinal Bembo. Aldus is exhorted to put a moderate price on the work, lest the Pope should withdraw his privilege, and accord it to others.

Robert Stephens, one of the early printers, surpassed in correctness those who exercised the same profession.[45]

To render his editions immaculate, he hung up the proofs in public places, and generously recompensed those who were so fortunate as to detect any errata.

Plantin, though a learned man, is more famous as a printer. His printing-office was one of the wonders of Europe. This grand building was the chief ornament of the city of Antwerp. Magnificent in its structure, it presented to the spectator a countless number of presses, characters of all figures and all sizes, matrixes to cast letters, and all other printing materials; which Baillet assures us amounted to immense sums.[46]

In Italy, the three Manutii were more solicitous of correctness and

------

45. Robert Stephens was the most celebrated of a family renowned through several generations in the history of printing. The first of the dynasty, Henry Estienne, who, in the spirit of the age, latinized his name, was born in Paris, in 1470, and commenced printing there at the beginning of the sixteenth century. His three sons—Francis, Robert, and Charles—were all renowned printers and scholars; Robert the most celebrated for the correctness and beauty of his work. His Latin Bible of 1532 made for him a great reputation; and he was appointed printer to Francis I. A new edition of his Bible, in 1545, brought him into trouble with the formidable doctors of the Sorbonne, and he ultimately left Paris for Geneva, where he set up a printing-office, which soon became famous. He died in 1559. He was the author of some learned works, and a printer whose labours in the "noble art" have never been excelled. He left two sons—Henry and Robert—also remarkable as learned printers; and they both had sons who followed the same pursuits. There is not one of this large family without honourable recognition for labour and knowledge, and in their wives and daughters they found learned assistants. Chalmers says—"They were at once the ornament and reproach of the age in which they lived. They were all men of great learning, all extensive benefactors to literature, and all persecuted or unfortunate."

46. Plantin's office is still existing in Antwerp, and is one of the most interesting places in that interesting city. It is so carefully preserved, that its quadrangle was assigned to the soldiery in the last great revolution, to prevent any hostile incursion and damage. It is a lonely building, in which the old office, with its presses and printing material, still remains as when deserted by the last workman. The sheets of the last books printed there are still lying on the tables; and in the presses and drawers are hundreds of the woodcuts and copperplates used by Plantin for the books that made his office renowned throughout Europe. In the quadrangle are busts of himself and his successors, the Morels, and the scholars who were connected with them. Plantin's own room seems to want only his presence to perfect the scene. The furniture and fittings, the quaint decoration, leads the imagination insensibly back to the days of Charles V.

illustrations than of the beauty of their printing. They were ambitious of the character of the scholar, not of the printer.

It is much to be regretted that our publishers are not literary men, able to form their own critical decisions. Among the learned printers formerly, a book was valued because it came from the presses of an Aldus or a Stephens; and even in our own time the names of Bowyer and Dodsley sanctioned a work. Pelisson, in his history of the French Academy, mentions that Camusat was selected as their bookseller, from his reputation for publishing only valuable works. "He was a man of some literature and good sense, and rarely printed an indifferent work; and when we were young I recollect that we always made it a rule to purchase his publications. His name was a test of the goodness of the work." A publisher of this character would be of the greatest utility to the literary world: at home he would induce a number of ingenious men to become authors, for it would be honourable to be inscribed in his catalogue; and it would be a direction for the continental reader.

So valuable a union of learning and printing did not, unfortunately, last. The printers of the seventeenth century became less charmed with glory than with gain. Their correctors and their letters evinced as little delicacy of choice.

The invention of what is now called the *Italic* letter in printing was made by Aldus Manutius, to whom learning owes much. He observed the many inconveniences resulting from the vast number of *abbreviations*, which were then so frequent among the printers, that a book was difficult to understand; a treatise was actually written on the art of reading a printed book, and this addressed to the learned! He contrived an expedient, by which these abbreviations might be entirely got rid of, and yet books suffer little increase in bulk, This he effected by introducing what is now called the *Italic* letter, though it formerly was distinguished by the name of the inventor, and called the *Aldine*.

3. THE FIRST ENGLISH PRINTER
(*Amenities*, pp. 214-220)

THE ambitious wars of a potent aristocracy inflicted on this country half a century of public misery. Our fields were a soil of blood; and maternal England long mourned for victories she obtained over her own children—lord against lord, brother against brother, and the son against the father. Rival administrations alternately dispossess each other by sanguinary conflict; a new monarch attaints the friends of his predecessor; conspiracy rises against conspiracy—scaffold against scaffold; the king is re-enthroned—the king perishes in the Tower; York is triumphant—and York is annihilated.

Few great families there were who had not immolated their martyrs or their victims; and it frequently occurred that the same family had fallen equally on both sides, for it was a war of the aristocracy with the aristocracy: "Save the commons and kill the captains," was the general war-cry. The distracted people were perhaps indifferent to the varying fortunes of the parties, accustomed as they were to behold after each battle the heads of lords and knights raised on every bridge and gate.

During this dread interval, all things about us were thrown back into a state of the rudest infancy; the illiterature of the age approached to barbarism; the evidences of history were destroyed; there was such a paucity of readers, that no writers were found to commemorate contemporary events. Indeed, had there been any, who could have ventured to arbitrate between such contradictory accounts, where every party had to tell their own tale? Oblivion, not history, seemed to be the consolation of those miserable times.

It was at such an unhappy era that the new-found art of printing was introduced into England by an English trader, who for thirty years had passed his life in Flanders, conversant with no other languages than were used in those countries.

Our literature was interested in the intellectual character of our first English printer. A powerful mind might, by the novel and mighty instrument of thought, have created a national taste, or have sown that seed of curiosity without which no knowledge can be reared. Such a genius might have anticipated by a whole century that general passion for sound literature which was afterwards to distinguish our country. But neither the times nor the man were equal to such a glorious advancement.

The first printed book in the English language was not printed in England. It is a translation of Ráoul le Fevre's "Recuyel of the Historyes of Troye," famed in its own day as the most romantic history, and in ours, for the honour of bibliography, romantically valued at the cost of a thousand guineas. This first monument of English printing issued from the infant press at Cologne in 1471, where Caxton first became initiated in "the noble mystery and craft" of printing, when printing was yet truly "a mystery," and Caxton himself did not import the art which was to effect such an intellectual revolution till a year or two afterwards, on his return home. The first printer, it is evident, had no other conception of the machine he was about to give the nation than as an ingenious contrivance, or a cheap substitute for costly manuscripts—possibly he might, in his calculating prudence, even be doubtful of its success!

At the announcement of the first printed book in our vernacular idiom, the mind involuntarily pauses: looking on the humble origin of our bibliography, and on the obscure commencement of the newly-found art of printing itself, we are startled at the vast and complicated results.

The contemporaries of our first printer were not struck by their novel and precious possession, of which they participated in the first fruits in the circulation and multiplication of their volumes. The introduction of the art into England is wholly unnoticed by the chroniclers of the age, so unconscious they were of this new implement of the human mind. We find Fabian, who must have known Caxton personally—both being members of the Mercers' Company—passing unnoticed his friend; and instead of any account of the printing-press, we have only such things as "a new weathercock placed on the cross of St. Paul's steeple." Hall, so copious in curious matters, discovered no curiosity to memorialize in the printing-press; Grafton was too heedless; and Holinshed, the most complete of our chroniclers, seems to have had an intention of saying something by his insertion of a single line, noticing the name of "Caxton as the first practiser of the art of printing;" but he was more seriously intent in the same paragraph to give a narrative of "a bloody rain, the red drops falling on the sheets which had been hanged to dry." The history of printing in England has been vainly sought for among English historians; so little sensible were they to those expansive views and elevated conceptions, which are now too commonplace eulogies to repeat.

By what subdolous practices among the first inventors of this secret art Caxton obtained its mastery, we are not told, except that he learnt the new art "at his own great cost and expense;" and on his final return home, he was accompanied by foreigners who lived in his house, and after his death became his successors. Wynkyn de Worde, Pynson, Machlinia and others, by their names betray their German origin. We have recently discovered that we had even a French printer who printed English books. Francis Regnault (or Reynold, anglicised) was a Frenchman who fell under the displeasure of the Inquisition for printing the Bible in English. He resided in England, and had in hand a number of primers in English and other similar books, which at length excited the jealousy of *the Company of Booksellers in London*—in the reign of Henry the Eighth. To allay this bibliopolic storm, the affrighted French printer, with all his stock in hand, procured Coverdale and Grafton to intercede with Cromwell to grant him licence to sell what he had already printed, engaging hereafter "to print no more in the *English tongue* unless he have an *Englishman* that is learned to be his corrector;" and further, he offers to cancel and reprint any faulty leaf again.[47]

Caxton did not extend his views beyond those of a mercantile printer and an indifferent translator. As a writer, Caxton had reason to speak with humility of the style of his vernacular versions. His patroness, the Lady Margaret, sister to our Edward the Fourth, and Duchess of Burgundy, after inspecting some quires of his translation of the "Recuyel of the Historyes of

---

47. "State Papers of Henry the Eighth," vol. i. 589.

Troye," returned them, finding, as Caxton ingenuously acknowledges, "some defaut in his English which she commanded him to amend." Tyrwhit sarcastically observes, that the duchess might have been a purist. As we are not told what were these "defauts," we cannot decide on the good taste or the fastidiousness of the sister of Edward the Fourth. But the duchess was not the only critic whom Caxton had to encounter, for we learn by his preface to his "Boke of Æneydos compiled by Virgil," now metamorphosed into a barbarous French prose romance, and the French translation translated, that there were "gentlemen who of late have blamed me that in my translations I had over-curious terms which could not be understood by common people. I fain would satisfy every man." He apologises for his own style by alleging the unsettled state of the English language, of which he tells us that "the language now used varieth far from that which was used and spoken when I was born." An absence of thirty years from his native land did not improve a diction which originally had been none of the purest. We find in his translations an abundance of pure French words, and it is remarkable that the printer of the third edition of the Troy history, in 1607, altered whole sentences "into plainer English," alleging, "the translator, William Caxton, being, *as it seemeth*, no Englishman!"

The "curious" prices now given among the connoisseurs of our earliest typography for their "Caxtons," as his Gothic works are thus honourably distinguished, have induced some, conforming to traditional prejudice, to appreciate by the same fanciful value "the Caxtonian style." But though we are not acquainted with the "defauts" which offended the Lady Margaret, nor with the "terms which were not easily understood," as alleged by "the gentlemen," nor with "the sentences improperly Englished," as the later printer declared, we shall not, I suspect, fall short of the mark if we conclude that the style of a writer destitute of a literary education, a prolix genius with a lax verbosity, and almost a foreigner in his native idiom, could not attain to any skill or felicity in the maternal tongue.

As a printer, without erudition, Caxton would naturally accommodate himself to the tastes of his age, and it was therefore a consequence that no great author appears among "the Caxtons." The most glorious issues of his press were a Chaucer and a Gower, wherein he was simply a printer. The rest of his works are translations of fabulous histories, and those spurious writings of the monkish ages ascribed by ignorant transcribers to some ancient sage. He appears frequently to have been at a loss what book to print, and to have accidentally chosen the work in hand; so he tells us—"Having no work in hand, I sitting in my study, where as lay many diverse paunflettes and bookys, happened that to my hand came a lytel boke in French, which late was translated out of Latin by some noble clerk of France, which book is named Æneydos." And this was the origin of his puerile romance! He exercised no discrimination in his selection of authors, and the simplicity of our first printer far exceeded his learning. One of his greater works is "The noble History of King Arthur and of certain of his Knights." Caxton, who had charmed himself and his ignorant readers with his authentic "Æneydos," hesitated to print "this history," for there were different opinions that "there was no such Arthur, and that all such books as be made of him be but feigned and fables." It would be difficult to account for the scepticism of one who always found the marvellous more delectable than the natural, and who had published so many "feigned" histories—as "The veray trew History of the valiant Knight Jason," or the "Life of Hercules," and all "The Merveilles of Virgil's Necromancy," solemnly vouching for their verity! His sudden scruples were, however, relieved, when "a gentleman" assured our printer that "it was great folly and blindness in the disbelievers of this true history."

In the early stage of civilization men want knowledge to feel any curiosity; like children, they are only affected through the medium of their imagination. But it is a phenomenon in the history of the human mind, that at a period of refinement we may approximate to one of barbarism. This happens when the ruling passion wholly returns to fiction, and thus terminates in a reckless disregard for all other studies. Whenever history, severe and lofty, displaying men as they are, is degraded among the revels and the masques of romance; and the slow inductions of reasoning, and the minute discoveries of research, and the nice affinities of analogy, are impatiently rejected, while fiction in her exaggerated style swells every object into a colossal size, and raises every passion into hyperbolical violence; a distaste for knowledge, and a coldness for truth, which must follow, are fatal to the sanity of the intellect. And thus in the day of our refinement we may be reverting to our barbarous infancy.

Caxton, mindful of his commercial interests and the taste of his readers, left the glory of restoring the classical writers of antiquity, which he could not read, to the learned printers of Italy.[48] The Orator of Cicero, the histories of Herodotus and Polybius, the ethics of Seneca, and the elaborate volumes of St. Austin, were some of the rich fruits of the early typography of the German printers who had conveyed their new art to the Neapolitan monastery of Subiaco. Our English printer, indeed, might have heard of their ill-fortune, when, in a petition to the Pope, they sent forth this cry—"Our house is full of proof-sheets, but we have nothing to eat!" The trivial productions from Caxton's press, romantic or religious legends, and treatises on hunting and

---

48. We have Caxton's own confession in his preface to "The Book of Æneydos," or the Æneid of Virgil, where, in soliciting the late-created. poet-laureat in the University of Oxford, John Skelton, to oversee his prose translation of the French translation, he notices the translations of Skelton of "The Epistles of Tully," and the "History of Diodorus Siculus," *out of Latin into English,* and as "one that had read Virgil, Ovid, Tully, and all the other noble poets and orators to *me unknown.*"

hawking, and the moralities of the game of chess, with Reynard the Fox, were more amusing to the ignorant readers of his country; but the national genius was little advanced by a succession of "merveillous workes;" nor would the crude, unformed tastes of the readers be matured by stimulating their inordinate appetites. The first printing-press in England did not serve to raise the national taste out of its barbarous infancy. Caxton was not a genius to soar beyond his age, but he had the industry to keep pace with it, and with little judgment and less learning he found no impediment in his selection of authors or his progress in translation.

Our earliest printed works consist of these translations of French translations; and the historian of our poetry considered that this very circumstance, which originated in the general illiteracy of the times, was more favourable to our vernacular literature than would have been the publication of Roman writers in their original language. Had it not been for these French versions, Caxton could not have furnished any of his own. The multiplication of English copies multiplied English readers, and when at length there was a generation of readers, an English press induced many to turn authors who were only qualified to write in their native tongue.

Venerable shade of Caxton! the award of the tribunal of posterity is a severe decision, but an imprescriptible law! Men who appear at certain eras of society, however they be lauded for what they have done, are still liable to be censured for not doing what they ought to have done. Patriarch of the printing-press! who to thy last and dying day withdrew not thy hand from thy work, it is hard that thou shouldst be amenable to a law which thy faculties were not adequate to comprehend; surely thou mayst triumph, thou simple man! amid the echoes of thy "Caxtonians" rejoicing over thy Gothic leaves—but the historian of the human mind is not the historian of typography.

4. MANUSCRIPTS AND BOOKS
(*Curiosities*, vol. 1, pp. 375-377)

It would be no uninteresting literary speculation to describe the difficulties which some of our most favourite works encountered in their manuscript state, and even after they had passed through the press. Sterne, when he had finished his first and second volumes of Tristram Shandy, offered them to a bookseller at York for fifty pounds; but was refused: he came to town with his MSS.; and he and Robert Dodsley agreed in a manner of which neither repented.

The Rosciad, with all its merit, lay for a considerable time in a dormant state, till Churchill and his publisher became impatient, and almost hopeless of success.—Burn's Justice was disposed of by its author, who was weary of soliciting booksellers to purchase the MS., for a trifle, and it now yields an annual income. Collins burnt his odes after indemnifying his publisher. The publication of Dr. Blair's Sermons was refused by Strahan, and the "Essay on the Immutability of Truth," by Dr. Beattie, could find no publisher, and was printed by two friends of the author, at their joint expense.

"The sermon in Tristram Shandy" (says Sterne, in his preface to his Sermons) "was printed by itself, some years ago, but could find neither purchasers nor readers." When it was inserted in his eccentric work, it met with a most favourable reception, and occasioned the others to be collected.

Joseph Warton writes, "When Gray published his exquisite Ode on Eton College, his first publication, little notice was taken of it." The Polyeucte of Corneille, which is now accounted to be his masterpiece, when he read it to the literary assembly held at the Hotel de Rambouillet, was not approved. Voiture came the next day, and in gentle terms acquainted him with the unfavourable opinion of the critics. Such ill judges were then the most fashionable wits of France!

It was with great difficulty that Mrs. Centlivre could get her "Busy Body" performed. Wilks threw down his part with an oath of detestation—our comic authoress fell on her knees and wept.—Her tears, and not her wit, prevailed.

A pamphlet published in the year 1738, entitled "A Letter to the Society of Booksellers, on the Method of forming a true Judgment of the Manuscripts of Authors," contains some curious literary intelligence.

"We have known books, that in the MS. have been damned, as well as others which seem to be so, since, after their appearance in the world, they have often lain by neglected. Witness the 'Paradise Lost' of the famous Milton, and the Optics of Sir Isaac Newton, which last, 'tis said, had no character or credit here till noticed in France. 'The Historical Connection of the Old and the New Testament,' by Shuckford, is also reported to have been seldom inquired after for about a twelvemonth's time; however, it made a shift, though not without some difficulty, to creep up to a second edition, and afterwards even to a third. And which is another remarkable instance, the manuscript of Dr. Prideaux's 'Connection' is well known to have been bandied about from hand to hand among several, at least five or six, of the most eminent booksellers, during the space of at least two years, to no purpose, none of them undertaking to print that excellent work. It lay in obscurity, till Archdeacon Echard, the author's friend, strongly recommended it to Tonson. It was purchased, and the publication was very successful. Robinson Crusoe in manuscript also ran through the whole trade, nor would any one print it, though the writer, De Foe, was in good repute as an author. One bookseller at last, not remarkable for his discernment, but for his speculative turn, engaged in this publication. *This* bookseller got above a thousand guineas by it; and the booksellers are accumulating money every hour by editions of this work in all shapes. The undertaker of the translation of Rapin, after a very considerable part of the work had been published, was not a little dubious of its success, and was strongly inclined to drop the design. It proved at last to be a most profitable literary adventure." It is, perhaps, useful to record, that while the fine compositions of genius and the elaborate labours of erudition are doomed to encounter these obstacles to fame, and never are but slightly remunerated, works of another description are rewarded in the most princely manner; at the recent sale of a bookseller, the copyright of "Vyse's Spelling-book" was sold at the enormous price of £2200, with an annuity of 50 guineas to the author!

5. SECRET HISTORY OF AUTHORS WHO HAVE RUINED THEIR BOOKSELLERS
(*Curiosities*, vol. 2, pp. 532-546)

Aulus Gellius desired to live no longer than he was able to exercise the faculty of writing; he might have decently added—and of finding readers! This would be a fatal wish for that writer who should spread the infection of weariness, without himself partaking of the epidemia. The mere act and habit of writing, without probably even a remote view of publication, has produced an agreeable delirium; and perhaps some have escaped from a gentle confinement by having cautiously concealed those voluminous reveries which remained to startle their heirs; while others again have left a whole library of manuscripts, out of the mere ardour of transcription, collecting and copying with peculiar rapture. I discovered that one of these inscribed this distich on his manuscript collection:

> Plura voluminibus jungenda volumina nostris,
> Nec mihi scribendi terminus ullus erit:

which, not to compose better verses than our original, may be translated,

> More volumes with our volumes still shall blend;
> And to our writing there shall be no end!

But even great authors have sometimes so much indulged in the seduction of the pen, that they appear to have found no substitute for the flow of their ink, and the delight of stamping blank paper with their hints, sketches, ideas, the shadows of their mind! Petrarch exhibits no solitary instance of this passion of the pen. "I read and I write night and day; it is my only consolation. My eyes are heavy with watching, my hand is weary with writing. On the table where I dine, and by the side of my bed, I have all the materials for writing; and when I awake in the dark, I write, although I am unable to read the next morning what I have written." Petrarch was not always in his perfect senses.

The copiousness and the multiplicity of the writings of many authors have shown that too many find a pleasure in the act of composition which they do not communicate to others. Great erudition and every-day application is the calamity of that voluminous author, who, without good sense, and, what is more rare, without that exquisite judgment, which we call good taste, is always prepared to write on any subject, but at the same time on no one reasonably. At the early period of printing, two of the most eminent printers were ruined by the volumes of one author; we have their petition to the pope to be saved from bankruptcy. Nicholas de Lyra had inveigled them to print his interminable commentary on the Bible. Their luckless star prevailed, and their warehouse groaned with eleven hundred ponderous folios, as immovable as the shelves on which they for ever reposed! We are astonished at the fertility and the size of our own writers of the seventeenth century, when the theological war of words raged, spoiling so many pages and brains. They produced folio after folio, like almanacs; and Dr. Owen and Baxter wrote more than sixty to seventy volumes, most of them of the most formidable size. The truth is, however, that it was then easier to write up to a folio, than in our days to write down to an octavo; for correction, selection, and rejection were arts as yet unpractised. They went on with their work, sharply or bluntly, like witless mowers, without stopping to whet their scythes. They were inspired by the scribbling demon of that rabbin, who, in his oriental style and mania of volume, exclaimed that were "the heavens formed of paper, and were the trees of the earth pens, and if the entire sea run ink, these only could suffice" for the monstrous genius he was about to discharge on the world. The Spanish Tostatus wrote three times as many leaves as the number of days he had lived; and of Lope de Vega it is said this calculation came rather short. We hear of another who was unhappy that his lady had produced twins, from the circumstance that hitherto he had contrived to pair his labours with her own, but that now he was a book behindhand.

I fix on four celebrated Scribleri to give their secret history; our Prynne, Gaspar Barthius, the Abbé de Marolles, and the Jesuit Theophilus Ranaud, who will all show that a book might be written on "authors whose works have ruined their booksellers."

Prynne seldom dined: every three or four hours he munched a manchet, and refreshed his exhausted spirits with ale brought to him by his servant; and when "he was put into this road of writings," as crabbed Anthony telleth, he fixed on "a long quilted cap, which came an inch over his eyes, serving as an umbrella to defend them from too much light;" and then hunger nor thirst did he experience, save that of his voluminous pages. Prynne has written a library amounting, I think, to nearly two hundred books. Our unlucky author, whose life was involved in authorship, and his happiness, no doubt, in the habitual exuberance of his pen, seems to have considered the being debarred from pen, ink, and books, during his imprisonment, as an act more barbarous than the loss of his ears.[49] The extraordinary perseverance of Prynne in this fever of the pen appears in the following title of one of his extraordinary volumes. "Comfortable Cordials against discomfortable Fears of Imprisonment; containing some Latin Verses, Sentences, and Texts of Scripture, written by Mr. Wm. Prynne, on his Chamber Walls, in the Tower of London, during his imprisonment there; translated by him into English Verse, 1641." Prynne literally verified Pope's description:

> Is there, who locked from ink and paper, scrawls
> With desperate charcoal round his darkened walls.

We have also a catalogue of printed books, written by Wm. Prynne, Esq., of Lincoln's Inn, in these classes,

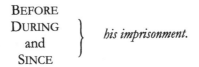

BEFORE
DURING
and   *his imprisonment.*
SINCE

with this motto, "Jucundi acti labores," 1643. The secret history of this voluminous author concludes with a characteristic event: a contemporary who saw Prynne in the pillory at Cheapside, informs us that while he stood there they "burnt his huge volumes under his nose, which had almost suffocated him." Yet such was the spirit of party, that a puritanic sister bequeathed a legacy to purchase all the works of Prynne for Sion College, where many still repose; for, by an odd fatality, in the fire which happened in that library these volumes were saved, from the idea that folios were the most valuable![50]

---

49. Prynne was condemned for his "Histriomastix," a book against actors and acting, in which he had indulged in severe remarks on female performers; and Henrietta Maria having frequently personated parts in Court Masques, the offensive words were declared to have been levelled at her. He was condemned to fine and imprisonment, was pilloried at Westminster and Cheapside, and had an ear cut off at each place.

50. Prynne, who ultimately quarrelled with the Puritans, was made Keeper of the Records of the Tower by Charles the Second, who was advised thereto by men who did not know how else to keep "busy Mr. Prynne" out of political pamphleteering. He went to the work of investigation with avidity, and it was while so employed that he

The pleasure which authors of this stamp experience is of a nature which, whenever certain unlucky circumstances combine, positively debarring them from publication, will not abate their ardour one jot; and their pen will still luxuriate in the forbidden page which even booksellers refuse to publish. Many instances might be recorded, but a very striking one is the case of Gaspar Barthius, whose "Adversaria," in two volumes folio, are in the collections of the curious.

Barthius was born to literature, for Baillet has placed him among his "Enfans Célèbres." At nine years of age he recited by heart all the comedies of Terence, without missing a line. The learned admired the puerile prodigy, while the prodigy was writing books before he had a beard. He became, unquestionably, a student of very extensive literature, modern as well as ancient. Such was his devotion to a literary life, that he retreated from the busy world. It appears that his early productions were composed more carefully and judiciously than his latter ones, when the passion for voluminous writing broke out, which showed itself by the usual prognostic of this dangerous disease—extreme facility of composition, and a pride and exultation in this unhappy faculty. He studied without using collections or references, trusting to his memory, which was probably an extraordinary one, though it necessarily led him into many errors in that delicate task of animadverting on other authors. Writing a very neat hand, his first copy required no transcript; and he boasts that he rarely made a correction: everything was sent to the press in its first state. He laughs at Statius, who congratulated himself that he employed only two days in composing the epithalamium upon Stella, containing two hundred and seventy-eight hexameters. "This," says Barthius, "did not quite lay him open to Horace's censure of the man who made two hundred verses in an hour," 'stans pede in uno.' Not," adds Barthius, "but that I think the censure of Horace too hyperbolical, for I am not ignorant what it is to make a great number of verses in a short time, and in three days I translated into Latin the three first books of the Iliad, which amount to above two thousand verses." Thus rapidity and volume were the great enjoyments of this learned man's pen, and now we must look to the fruits.

Barthius, on the system he had adopted, seems to have written a whole library; a circumstance which we discover by the continual references he makes in his printed works to his manuscript productions. In the Index Authorum to his Statius, he inserts his own name, to which is appended a long list of unprinted works, which Bayle thinks, by their titles and extracts, conveys a very advantageous notion of them. All these, and many such as these, he generously offered the world, would any bookseller be intrepid or

---

followed the mode of life narrated in the preceding page.

courteous enough to usher them from his press; but their cowardice or incivility was intractable. The truth is now to be revealed, and seems not to have been known to Bayle; the booksellers had been formerly so cajoled and complimented by our learned author, and had heard so much of the celebrated Barthius, that they had caught at the bait, and that the two folio volumes of the much referred-to "Adversaria" of Barthius had thus been published—but from that day no bookseller ever offered himself to publish again!

The "Adversaria" is a collection of critical notes and quotations from ancient authors, with illustrations of their manners, customs, laws, and ceremonies; all these were to be classed into one hundred and eighty books; sixty of which we possess in two volumes folio, with eleven indexes. The plan is vast, as the rapidity with which it was pursued: Bayle finely characterises it by a single stroke—"Its immensity tires even the imagination." But the truth is, this mighty labour turned out to be a complete failure: there was neither order nor judgment in these masses of learning; crude, obscure, and contradictory; such as we might expect from a man who trusted to his memory, and would not throw away his time on any correction. His contradictions are flagrant; but one of his friends would apologise for these by telling us that "He wrote everything which offered itself to his imagination; to-day one thing, to-morrow another, in order that when he should revise it again, this contrariety of opinion might induce him to examine the subject more accurately." The notions of the friends of authors are as extravagant as those of their enemies. Barthius evidently wrote so much that often he forgot what he had written, as happened to another great book-man, one Didymus, of whom Quintilian records, that on hearing a certain history, he treated it as utterly unworthy of credit; on which the teller called for one of Didymus's own books, and showed where he might read it at full length! That the work failed, we have the evidence of Clement in his "Bibliothèque curieuse de Livres difficiles à trouver," under the article Barthius, where we discover the winding up of the history of this book. Clement mentions more than one edition of the Adversaria; but on a more careful inspection he detected that the old title-pages had been removed for others of a fresher date; the booksellers not being able to sell the book practised this deception. It availed little; they remained with their unsold edition of the two first volumes of the Adversaria, and the author with three thousand folio sheets in manuscript—while both parties complained together, and their heirs could acquire nothing from the works of an author, of whom Bayle says that "his writings rise to such a prodigious bulk, that one can scarce conceive a single man could be capable of executing so great a variety; perhaps no copying clerk, who lived to grow old amidst the dust of an office, ever transcribed as much as this author has written." This was the memorable fate of one of that race of writers who imagine that their capacity extends with their volume.

Their land seems covered with fertility, but in shaking their wheat no ears fall.

Another memorable brother of this family of the Scribleri is the Abbé de Marolles, who with great ardour as a man of letters, and in the enjoyment of the leisure and opulence so necessary to carry on his pursuits, from an entire absence of judgment, closed his life with the bitter regrets of a voluminous author; and yet it cannot be denied that he has contributed one precious volume to the public stock of literature; a compliment which cannot be paid to some who have enjoyed a higher reputation than our author. He has left us his very curious "Memoirs." A poor writer indeed, but the frankness and intrepidity of his character enable him, while he is painting himself, to paint man. Gibbon was struck by the honesty of his pen, for he says in his life, "The dulness of Michael de Marolles and Anthony Wood[51] acquires some value from the faithful representation of men and manners."

I have elsewhere shortly noticed the Abbé de Marolles in the character of a "literary sinner;" but the extent of his sins never struck me so forcibly as when I observed his delinquencies counted up in chronological order in Niceron's "Hommes Illustres." It is extremely amusing to detect the swarming fecundity of his pen; from year to year, with author after author, was this translator wearying others, but remained himself unwearied. Sometimes two or three classical victims in a season were dragged into his slaughter-house. Of about seventy works, fifty were versions of the classical writers of antiquity, accompanied with notes. But some odd circumstances happened to our extraordinary translator in the course of his life. De l'Etang, a critic of that day, in his "Règles de bien traduire," drew all his examples of bad translation from our abbé, who was more angry than usual, and among his circle the cries of our Marsyas resounded. De l'Etang, who had done this not out of malice, but from urgent necessity to illustrate his principles, seemed very sorry, and was desirous of appeasing the angried translator. One day in Easter, finding the abbé in church at prayers, the critic fell on his knees by the side of the translator: it was an extraordinary moment, and a singular situation to terminate a literary quarrel. "You are angry with me," said De l'Etang, "and I think you have reason; but this is a season of mercy, and I now ask your pardon."—"In the manner," replied the abbé, "which you have chosen, I can no longer defend myself. Go, sir! I pardon you." Some days after, the abbé again meeting De l'Etang, reproached him with duping him out of a pardon, which he had no desire to have bestowed on him. The last reply of the critic was caustic: "Do not be so difficult; when one stands in need of a general

---

51. "I cannot subscribe to the opinion that Anthony Wood was a dull man, although he had no particular liking for works of imagination; and used ordinary poets scurvily! An author's personal character is often confounded with the nature of his work. Anthony has sallies at times to which a dull man could not be subject; without the ardour of this hermit of literature where would be our literary history?

pardon, one ought surely to grant a particular one." De Marolles was subject to encounter critics who were never so kind as to kneel by him on an Easter Sunday. Besides these fifty translations, of which the notes are often curious, and even the sense may be useful to consult, his love of writing produced many odd works. His volumes were richly bound, and freely distributed, but they found no readers! In a "Discours pour servir de Préface sur les Poëtes, traduits par Michel de Marolles," he has given an imposing list of "illustrious persons and contemporary authors who were his friends," and has preserved many singular facts concerning them. He was indeed for so long a time convinced that he had struck off the true spirit of his fine originals, that I find he at several times printed some critical treatise to back his last, or usher in his new version; giving the world reasons why the versions which had been given of that particular author, "soit en prose, soit en vers, ont été si peu approuvées jusqu'ici." Among these numerous translations he was the first who ventured on the Deipnosophists of Athenæus, which still bears an excessive price. He entitles his work, "Les quinze Livres de Deipnosophistes d'Athenée, Ouvrage delicieux, agréablement diversifié et rempli de Narrations, sçavantes sur toutes Sortes de Matières et de Sujets." He has prefixed various preliminary dissertations; yet, not satisfied with having performed this great labour, it was followed by a small quarto of forty pages, which might now be considered curious; "Analyse, en Déscription succincte des Choses conténues dans les quinzes Livres de Deipnosophistes." He wrote, "Quatrains sur les Personnes de la Cour et les Gens de Lettres," which the curious would now be glad to find. After having plundered the classical geniuses of antiquity by his barbarous style, when he had nothing more left to do, he committed sacrilege in translating the Bible; but, in the midst of printing, he was suddenly stopped by authority, for having inserted in his notes the reveries of the Pre-Adamite Isaac Peyrère. He had already revelled on the New Testament, to his version of which he had prefixed so sensible an introduction, that it was afterwards translated into Latin. Translation was the mania of the Abbé de Marolles. I doubt whether he ever fairly awoke out of the heavy dream of the felicity of his translations; for late in life I find him observing, "I have employed much time in study, and I have translated many books; considering this rather as an innocent amusement which I have chosen for my private life, than as things very necessary, although they are not entirely useless. Some have valued them, and others have cared little about them; but however it may be, I see nothing which obliges me to believe that they contain not at least as much good as bad, both for their own matter and the form which I have given to them." The notion he entertained of his translations was their closeness; he was not aware of his own spiritless style; and he imagined that poetry only consisted in the thoughts, not in grace and harmony of verse. He insisted that by giving the public his numerous translations, he was not vainly multiplying books, because he neither diminished nor increased their ideas in his faithful versions. He had a curious notion that some were more scrupulous than they ought to be respecting translations of authors who, living so many ages past, are rarely read from the difficulty of understanding them; and why should they imagine that a translation is injurious to them, or would occasion the utter neglect of the originals? "We do not think so highly of our own works," says the indefatigable and modest abbé; "but neither do I despair that they may be useful even to these scrupulous persons. I will not suppress the truth, while I am noticing these ungrateful labours; if they have given me much pain by my assiduity, they have repaid me by the fine things they have taught me, and by the opinion which I have conceived that posterity, more just than the present times, will award a more favourable judgment." Thus a miserable translator terminates his long labours, by drawing his bill of fame on posterity, which his contemporaries will not pay; but in these cases, as the bill is certainly lost before it reaches acceptance, why should we deprive the drawers of pleasing themselves with the ideal capital?

Let us not, however, imagine that the Abbé de Marolles was nothing but the man he appears in the character of a voluminous translator; though occupied all his life on these miserable labours, he was evidently an ingenious and nobly-minded man, whose days were consecrated to literary pursuits, and who was among the primitive collectors in Europe of fine and curious prints. One of his works is a "Catalogue des Livres d'Estampes et de Figures en Taille-douce." Paris, 1666, in 8vo. In the preface our author declares, that he had collected one hundred and twenty-three thousand four hundred prints, of six thousand masters, in four hundred large volumes, and one hundred and twenty small ones. This magnificent collection, formed by so much care and skill, he presented to the king; whether gratuitously given or otherwise, it was an acquisition which a monarch might have thankfully accepted. Such was the habitual ardour of our author, that afterwards he set about forming another collection, of which he has also given a catalogue in 1672, in 12mo. Both these catalogues of prints are of extreme rarity, and are yet so highly valued by the connoisseurs, that when in France I could never obtain a copy. A long life may be passed without even a sight of the "Catalogue des Livres d'Estampes" of the Abbé de Marolles.[52]

Such are the lessons drawn from this secret history of voluminous writers. We see one venting his mania in scrawling on his prison walls; another persisting in writing folios, while the booksellers, who were once caught, like

---

52. These two catalogues have always been of extreme rarity and price. Dr. Lister, when at Paris, 1668, notices this circumstance. I have since met with them in the very curious collections of my friend, Mr. Douce, who has uniques, as well as rarities. The monograms of our old masters in one of these catalogues are more correct than in some later publications; and the whole plan and arrangement of these catalogues of prints are peculiar and interesting.

Reynard who had lost his tail, and whom no arts could any longer practise on, turn away from the new trap; and a third, who can acquire no readers but by giving his books away, growing grey in scourging the sacred genius of antiquity by his meagre versions, and dying without having made up his mind, whether he were as woful a translator as some of his contemporaries had assured him.

Among these worthies of the Scribleri we may rank the Jesuit, Theophilus Raynaud, once a celebrated name, eulogised by Bayle and Patin. His collected works fill twenty folios; an edition, indeed, which finally sent the bookseller to the poor-house. This enterprising bibliopolist had heard much of the prodigious erudition of the writer; but he had not the sagacity to discover that other literary qualities were also required to make twenty folios at all saleable. Of these "Opera omnia" perhaps not a single copy can be found in England; but they may be a pennyworth on the continent. Raynaud's works are theological; but a system of grace maintained by one work and pulled down by another, has ceased to interest mankind: the literature of the divine is of a less perishable nature. Reading and writing through a life of eighty years, and giving only a quarter of an hour to his dinner, with a vigorous memory, and a whimsical taste for some singular subjects, he could not fail to accumulate a mass of knowledge which may still be useful for the curious; and besides, Raynaud had the Ritsonian characteristic. He was one of those who, exemplary in their own conduct, with a bitter zeal condemn whatever does not agree with their own notions; and, however gentle in their nature, yet will set no limits to the ferocity of their pen. Raynaud was often in trouble with the censors of his books, and much more with his adversaries; so that he frequently had recourse to publishing under a fictitious name. A remarkable evidence of this is the entire twentieth volume of his works. It consists of the numerous writings published anonymously, or to which were prefixed noms de guerre. This volume is described by the whimsical title of Apopompæus; explained to us as the name given by the Jews to the scape-goat, which when loaded with all their maledictions on its head, was driven away into the desert. These contain all Raynaud's numerous diatribes; for whenever he was refuted, he was always refuting; he did not spare his best friends. The title of a work against Arnauld will show how he treated his adversaries. "Arnauldus redivivus natus Brixiæ seculo xii. renatus in Galliæ ætate nostra." He dexterously applies the name of Arnauld by comparing him with one of the same name in the twelfth century, a scholar of Abelard's, and a turbulent enthusiast, say the Romish writers, who was burnt alive for having written against the luxury and the power of the priesthood, and for having raised a rebellion against the pope. When the learned De Launoi had successfully attacked the legends of saints, and was called the Denicheur de Saints,—the "Unnicher of Saints," every parish priest trembled for his favourite. Raynaud entitled a libel on this new iconoclast, "Hercules Commodianus Joannes

Launoius repulsus," &c.; he compares Launoi to the Emperor Commodus, who, though the most cowardly of men, conceived himself formidable when he dressed himself as Hercules. Another of these maledictions is a tract against Calvinism, described as a "religio bestiarum," a religion of beasts, because the Calvinists deny free will; but as he always fired with a double-barrelled gun, under the cloak of attacking Calvinism, he aimed a deadly shot at the Thomists, and particularly at a Dominican friar, whom he considered as bad as Calvin. Raynaud exults that he had driven one of his adversaries to take flight into Scotland, ad pultes Scoticas transgressus—to a Scotch pottage; an expression which Saint Jerome used in speaking of Pelagius. He always rendered an adversary odious by coupling him with some odious name. On one of these controversial books where Casalas refuted Raynaud, Monnoye wrote, "Raynaudus et Casalas inepti; Raynaudo tamen Casalas ineptior." The usual termination of what then passed for sense, and now is the reverse!

I will not quit Raynaud without pointing out some of his more remarkable treatises, as so many curiosities of literature.

In a treatise on the attributes of Christ, he entitles a chapter, Christus, bonus, bona, bonum: in another on the seven-branched candlestick in the Jewish temple, by an allegorical interpretation, he explains the eucharist; and adds an alphabetical list of names and epithets which have been given to this mystery.

The seventh volume bears the title of Mariolia: all the treatises have for their theme the perfections and the worship of the Virgin. Many extraordinary things are here. One is a dictionary of names given to the Virgin, with observations on these names. Another on the devotion of the scapulary, and its wonderful effects, written against De Launoi, and for which the order of the Carmes, when he died, bestowed a solemn service and obsequies on him. Another of these "Mariolia" is mentioned by Gallois in the Journal des Sçavans, 1667, as a proof of his fertility; having to preach on the seven solemn anthems which the Church sings before Christmas, and which begin by an O! he made this letter only the subject of his sermons, and barren as the letter appears, he has struck out "a multitude of beautiful particulars." This literary folly invites our curiosity.

In the eighth volume is a table of saints, classed by their station, condition, employment, and trades: a list of titles and prerogatives, which the councils and the fathers have attributed to the sovereign pontiff.

The thirteenth volume has a subject which seems much in the taste of the sermons on the letter O! it is entitled Laus Brevitatis! in praise of brevity. The maxims are brief, but the commentary long. One of the natural subjects treated on is that of Noses: he reviews a great number of noses, and, as usual, does not forget the Holy Virgin's. According to Raynaud, the nose of the Virgin Mary was long and aquiline, the mark of goodness and dignity; and as

Jesus perfectly resembled his mother, he infers that he must have had such a nose.

A treatise entitled Heteroclita spiritualia et anomala Pietatis Cælestium, Terrestrium, et Infernorum, contains many singular practices introduced into devotion, which superstition, ignorance, and remissness, have made a part of religion.

A treatise directed against the new custom of hiring chairs in churches, and being seated during the sacrifice of the mass. Another on the Cæsarean operation, which he stigmatises as an act against nature. Another on eunuchs. Another entitled Hipparchus de Religioso Negotiatore, is an attack on those of his own company; the monk turned merchant; the Jesuits were then accused of commercial traffic with the revenues of their establishment. The rector of a college at Avignon, who thought he was portrayed in this honest work, confined Raynaud in prison for five months.

The most curious work of Raynaud connected with literature, I possess; it is entitled Erotemata de malis ac bonis Libris, deque justa aut injusta eorundem confixione. Lugduni, 1653, 4to, with necessary indexes. One of his works having been condemned at Rome, he drew up these inquiries concerning good and bad books, addressed to the grand inquisitor. He divides his treatise into "bad and nocent books; bad books but not nocent; books not bad, but nocent; books neither bad nor nocent." His immense reading appears here to advantage, and his Ritsonian feature is prominent; for he asserts, that when writing against heretics all mordacity is innoxious; and an alphabetical list of abusive names, which the fathers have given to the heterodox is entitled Alphabetum bestialitatis Hæretici, ex Patrum Symbolis.

After all, Raynaud was a man of vast acquirement, with a great flow of ideas, but tasteless, and void of all judgment. An anecdote may be recorded of him, which puts in a clear light the state of these literary men. Raynaud was one day pressing hard a reluctant bookseller to publish one of his works, who replied—"Write a book like Father Barri's, and I shall be glad to print it." It happened that the work of Barri was pillaged from Raynaud, and was much liked, while the original lay on the shelf. However, this only served to provoke a fresh attack from our redoubtable hero, who vindicated his rights, and emptied his quiver on him who had been ploughing with his heifer.

Such are the writers who, enjoying all the pleasures without the pains of composition, have often apologised for their repeated productions, by declaring that they write only for their own amusement; but such private theatricals should not be brought on the public stage. One Catherinot all his life was printing a countless number of feuilles volantes in history and on antiquities, each consisting of about three or four leaves in quarto: Lenglet du Fresnoy calls him "grand auteur des petits livres." This gentleman liked to live among antiquaries and historians; but with a crooked headpiece, stuck with whims, and hard with knotty combinations, all overloaded with prodigious erudition, he could not ease it at a less rate than by an occasional dissertation of three or four quarto pages. He appears to have published about two hundred pieces of this sort, much sought after by the curious for their rarity: Brunet complains he could never discover a complete collection. But Catherinot may escape "the pains and penalties" of our voluminous writers, for De Bure thinks he generously printed them to distribute among his friends. Such endless writers, provided they do not print themselves into an alms-house, may be allowed to print themselves out; and we would accept the apology which Monsieur Catherinot has framed for himself, which I find preserved in Beyeri Memoriæ Librorum Rariorum. "I must be allowed my freedom in my studies, for I substitute my writings for a game at the tennis-court, or a club at the tavern; I never counted among my honours these opuscula of mine, but merely as harmless amusements. It is my partridge, as with St. John the Evangelist; my cat, as with Pope St. Gregory; my little dog, as with St. Dominick; my lamb, as with St. Francis; my great black mastiff, as with Cornelius Agrippa; and my tame hare, as with Justus Lipsius." I have since discovered in Niceron that this Catherinot could never get a printer, and was rather compelled to study economy in his two hundred quartos of four or eight pages: his paper was of inferior quality; and when he could not get his dissertations into his prescribed number of pages, he used to promise the end at another time, which did not always happen. But his greatest anxiety was to publish and spread his works; in despair he adopted an odd expedient. Whenever Monsieur Catherinot came to Paris, he used to haunt the quaies where books are sold, and while he appeared to be looking over them, he adroitly slided one of his own dissertations among these old books. He began this mode of publication early, and continued it to his last days. He died with a perfect conviction that he had secured his immortality; and in this manner had disposed of more than one edition of his unsaleable works. Niceron has given the titles of 118 of his things, which he had looked over.

III. BOOKS

1. TITLES OF BOOKS
(*Curiosities*, vol. 1, pp. 288-292)

WERE it inquired of an ingenious writer what page of his work had occasioned him most perplexity, he would often point to the *title-page*. The curiosity which we there would excite, is, however, most fastidious to gratify.

Among those who appear to have felt this irksome situation, are most of our periodical writers. The "Tatler" and the "Spectator," enjoying priority of conception, have adopted titles with characteristic felicity; but perhaps the invention of the authors begins to fail in the "Reader," the "Lover," and the "Theatre!" Succeeding writers were as unfortunate in their titles, as their works; such are the "Universal Spectator," and the "Lay Monastery." The copious mind of Johnson could not discover an appropriate title, and indeed in the first "Idler" acknowledged his despair. The "Rambler" was so little understood, at the time of its appearance, that a French journalist has translated it as "*Le Chevalier Errant*," and when it was corrected to *L'Errant*, a foreigner drank Johnson's health one day, by innocently addressing him by the appellation of Mr. "Vagabond!" The "Adventurer" cannot be considered as a fortunate title; it is not appropriate to those pleasing miscellanies, for any writer is an adventurer. The "Lounger," the "Mirror," and even the "Connoisseur," if examined accurately, present nothing in the titles descriptive of the works. As for the "World," it could only have been given by the fashionable egotism of its authors, who considered the world as merely a circuit round St. James's Street. When the celebrated father of reviews, *Le Journal des Sçavans*, was first published, the very title repulsed the public. The author was obliged in his succeeding volumes to soften it down, by explaining its general tendency. He there assures the curious, that not only men of learning and taste, but the humblest mechanic, may find a profitable amusement. An English novel, published with the title of "The Champion of Virtue," could find no readers; but afterwards passed through several editions under the happier invitation of "The Old English Baron." "The Concubine," a poem by Mickle, could never find purchasers, till it assumed the more delicate title of "Sir Martyn."

As a subject of literary curiosity, some amusement may be gathered from a glance at what has been doing in the world, concerning this important portion of every book.

The Jewish and many oriental authors were fond of allegorical titles, which always indicate the most puerile age of taste. The titles were usually adapted to their obscure works. It might exercise an able enigmatist to explain their allusions; for we must understand by "The Heart of Aaron," that it is a commentary on several of the prophets. "The Bones of Joseph" is an introduction to the Talmud. "The Garden of Nuts," and "The Golden Apples," are theological questions; and "The Pomegranate with its Flower," is a treatise of ceremonies, not any more practised. Jortin gives a title, which he says of all the fantastical titles he can recollect is one of the prettiest. A rabbin published a catalogue of rabbinical writers, and called it *Labia Dormientium*, from Cantic. vii. 9. "Like the best wine of my beloved that goeth down sweetly, causing *the lips of those that are asleep to speak.*" It hath a double meaning, of which he was not aware, for most of his rabbinical brethren talk very much like *men in their sleep*.

Almost all their works bear such titles as bread–gold–silver–roses–eyes, &c.; in a word, anything that signifies nothing.

Affected title-pages were not peculiar to the orientals: the Greeks and the Romans have shown a finer taste. They had their Cornucopias, or horns of abundance—Limones, or meadows—Pinakidions, or tablets—Pancarpes, or all sorts of fruits; titles not unhappily adapted for the miscellanists. The nine books of Herodotus, and the nine epistles of Æschines, were respectively honoured by the name of a Muse; and three orations of the latter, by those of the Graces.

The modern fanatics have had a most barbarous taste for titles. We could produce numbers from abroad, and at home. Some works have been called, "Matches lighted at the Divine Fire,"—and one "The Gun of Penitence:" a collection of passages from the fathers is called "The Shop of the Spiritual Apothecary:" we have "The Bank of Faith," and "The Sixpennyworth of Divine Spirit:" one of these works bears the following elaborate title: "Some fine Biscuits baked in the Oven of Charity, carefully conserved for the Chickens of the Church, the Sparrows of the Spirit, and the sweet Swallows of Salvation." Sometimes their quaintness has some humour. Sir Humphrey Lind, a zealous puritan, published a work which a Jesuit answered by another, entitled "A Pair of Spectacles for Sir Humphrey Lind." The doughty knight retorted, by "A Case for Sir Humphrey Lind's Spectacles."

Some of these obscure titles have an entertaining absurdity; as "The Three Daughters of Job," which is a treatise on the three virtues of patience, fortitude, and pain. "The Innocent Love, or the Holy Knight," is a description of the ardours of a saint for the Virgin. "The Sound of the Trumpet," is a work on the day of judgment; and "A Fan to drive away Flies," is a theological treatise on purgatory.

We must not write to the utter neglect of our title; and a fair author should have the literary piety of ever having "the fear of his title-page before his eyes." The following are improper titles. Don Matthews, chief huntsman to Philip IV. of Spain, entitled his book "The Origin and Dignity of the Royal House," but the entire work relates only to hunting. De Chantereine composed several moral essays, which being at a loss how to entitle, he called

"The Education of a Prince." He would persuade the reader in his preface, that though they were not composed with a view to this subject, they should not, however, be censured for the title, as they partly related to the education of a prince. The world was too sagacious to be duped, and the author in his second edition acknowledges the absurdity, drops "the magnificent title," and calls his work "Moral Essays." Montaigne's immortal history of his own mind, for such are his "Essays," has assumed perhaps too modest a title, and not sufficiently discriminative. Sorlin equivocally entitled a collection of essays, "The Walks of Richelieu," because they were composed at that place; "The Attic Nights" of Aulus Gellius were so called, because they were written in Attica. Mr. Tooke, in his grammatical "Diversions of Purley," must have deceived many.

A rhodomontade title-page was once a great favourite. There was a time when the republic of letters was over-built with "Palaces of Pleasure," "Palaces of Honour," and "Palaces of Eloquence;" with "Temples of Memory," and "Theatres of Human Life," and "Amphitheatres of Providence;" "Pharoses, Gardens, Pictures, Treasures." The epistles of Guevara dazzled the public eye with their splendid title, for they were called "Golden Epistles;" and the "Golden Legend" of Voragine had been more appropriately entitled leaden.

They were once so fond of novelty, that every book recommended itself by such titles as "A new Method; new Elements of Geometry; the new Letter Writer, and the new Art of Cookery."

To excite the curiosity of the pious, some writers employed artifices of a very ludicrous nature. Some made their titles rhyming echoes; as this one of a father, who has given his works under the title of *Scalæ Alæ animi;* and *Jesus esus novus Orbis*. Some have distributed them according to the measure of time, as one Father Nadasi, the greater part of whose works are *years, months, weeks, days,* and *hours*. Some have borrowed their titles from the parts of the body; and others have used quaint expressions, such as—*Think before you leap*—*We must all die*—*Compel them to enter*. Some of our pious authors appear not to have been aware that they were burlesquing religion. One Massieu having written a moral explanation of the solemn anthems sung in Advent, which begin with the letter O, published this work under the punning title of *La douce Moelle, et la Sauce friande des* OS *Savoureux de l'Avent*.[53]

---

53. Religious parody seems to have carried no sense of impropriety with it to the minds of the man of the 15th and 16th centuries. Luther was an adept in this art, and the preachers who followed him continued the practice. The sermons of divines in the following century often sought an attraction by quaint titles, such as—"Heaven ravished"—"The Blacksmith, a sermon preached at Whitehall before the King," 1606. Beloe, in his *Anecdotes of Literature,* vol. 6, has recorded many of these quaint titles, among them the following:—"*The Nail hit on the head,* and driven into the city and

The Marquis of Carraccioli assumed the ambiguous title of *La Jouissance de soi-même*. Seduced by the epicurean title of self-enjoyment, the sale of the work was continual with the libertines, who, however, found nothing but very tedious essays on religion and morality. In the sixth edition the marquis greatly exults in his successful contrivance; by which means he had punished the vicious curiosity of certain persons, and perhaps had persuaded some, whom otherwise his book might never have reached.

If a title be obscure, it raises a prejudice against the author; we are apt to suppose that an ambiguous title is the effect of an intricate or confused mind. Baillet censures the Ocean Macromicrocosmic of one Sachs. To understand this title, a grammarian would send an inquirer to a geographer, and he to a natural philosopher; neither would probably think of recurring to a physician, to inform one that his ambiguous title signifies the connexion which exists between the motion of the waters with that of the blood. He censures Leo Allatius for a title which appears to me not inelegantly conceived. This writer has entitled one of his books the *Urban Bees;* it is an account of those illustrious writers who flourished during the pontificate of one of the Barberinis. The allusion refers to the *bees* which were the arms of this family, and Urban VIII. is the Pope designed.

The false idea which a title conveys is alike prejudicial to the author and the reader. Titles are generally too prodigal of their promises, and their authors are contemned; but the works of modest authors, though they present more than they promise, may fail of attracting notice by their extreme simplicity. In either case, a collector of books is prejudiced; he is induced to collect what merits no attention, or he passes over those valuable works whose titles may not happen to be interesting. It is related of Pinelli, the celebrated collector of books, that the booksellers permitted him to remain hours, and sometimes days, in their shops to examine books before he purchased. He was desirous of not injuring his precious collection by useless acquisitions; but he confessed that he sometimes could not help being dazzled by magnificent titles, nor being mistaken by the simplicity of others, which

---

cathedral wall of Norwich. By John Carter, 1644." *"The Wheel turned* by a voice from the throne of glory. By John Carter, 1647." "*Two Sticks made one,* or the excellence of Unity. By Matthew Mead, 1691." "*Peter's Net let downe,* or the Fisher and the Fish, both prepared towards a blessed haven. By R. Matthew, 1634." In the middle of the last century two religious tracts were published, one bearing the alarming title, "Die and be Damned," the other being termed, "A sure Guide to Hell." The first was levelled against the preaching of the Methodists, and the title obtained from what the author asserts to be the words of condemnation then frequently applied by them to all who differed from their creed. The second is a satirical attack on the prevalent follies and vices of the day, which form, the surest "guide," in the opinion of the author, to the bottomless pit.

had been chosen by the modesty of their authors. After all, many authors are really neither so vain, nor so honest, as they appear; for magnificent, or simple titles, have often been given from the difficulty of forming any others.

It is too often with the Titles of Books, as with those painted representations exhibited by the keepers of wild beasts; where, in general, the picture itself is made more striking and inviting to the eye, than the inclosed animal is always found to be.

2. DEDICATIONS
(*Curiosities*, vol. 1, pp. 337-341)

SOME authors excelled in this species of literary artifice. The Italian Doni dedicated each of his letters in a book called *La Libraria*, to persons whose name began with the first letter of the epistle, and dedicated the whole collection in another epistle; so that the book, which only consisted of forty-five pages, was dedicated to above twenty persons. This is carrying literary mendicity pretty high. Politi, the editor of the *Martyrologium Romanum*, published at Rome in 1751, has improved on the idea of Doni; for to the 365 days of the year of this Martyrology he has prefixed to each an epistle dedicatory. It is fortunate to have a large circle of acquaintance, though they should not be worthy of being saints. Galland, the translator of the Arabian Nights, prefixed a dedication to each tale which he gave; had he finished the "one thousand and one," he would have surpassed even the Martyrologist.

Mademoiselle Scudery tells a remarkable expedient of an ingenious trader in this line—One Rangouze made a collection of letters which he printed without numbering them. By this means the bookbinder put that letter which the author ordered him first; so that all the persons to whom he presented this book, seeing their names at the head, considered they had received a particular compliment. An Italian physician, having written on Hippocrates's Aphorisms, dedicated each book of his Commentaries to one of his friends, and the index to another!

More than one of our own authors have dedications in the same spirit. It was an expedient to procure dedicatory fees: for publishing books by subscription was then an art undiscovered. One prefixed a different dedication to a certain number of printed copies, and addressed them to every great man he knew, who he thought relished a morsel of flattery, and would pay handsomely for a coarse luxury. Sir Balthazar Gerbier, in his "Counsel to Builders," has made up half the work with forty-two dedications, which he excuses by the example of Antonio Perez; but in these dedications Perez scatters a heap of curious things, for he was a very universal genius. Perez, once secretary of state to Philip II. of Spain, dedicates his "Obras," first to

"Nuestro sanctissimo Padre," and "Al Sacro Collegio," then follows one to "Henry IV.," and then one still more embracing, "A Todos." Fuller, in his "Church History," has with admirable contrivance introduced twelve title-pages, besides the general one, and as many particular dedications, and no less than fifty or sixty of those by inscriptions which are addressed to his benefactors; a circumstance which Heylin in his severity did not overlook; for "making his work bigger by forty sheets at the least; and he was so ambitious of the number of his patrons, that having but four leaves at the end of his History, he discovers a particular benefactress to inscribe them to!" This unlucky lady, the patroness of four leaves, Heylin compares to Roscius Regulus, who accepted the consular dignity for that part of the day on which Cecina by a decree of the senate was degraded from it, which occasioned Regulus to be ridiculed by the people all his life after, as the consul of half a day.

The price for the dedication of a play was at length fixed, from five to ten guineas from the Revolution to the time of George I., when it rose to twenty; but sometimes a bargain was to be struck when the author and the play were alike indifferent. Sometimes the party haggled about the price, or the statue while stepping into his niche would turn round on the author to assist his invention. A patron of Peter Motteux, dissatisfied with Peter's colder temperament, actually composed the superlative dedication to himself, and completed the misery of the apparent author by subscribing it with his name. This circumstance was so notorious at the time, that it occasioned a satirical dialogue between Motteux and his patron Heveningham. The patron, in his zeal to omit no possible distinction that might attach to him, had given one circumstance which no one but himself could have known.

PATRON.
I must confess I was to blame,
That one particular to name;
The rest could never have been known
I made the style so like thy own.

POET.
I beg your pardon, Sir, for that.

PATRON.
Why d——e what would you be at?
I writ below myself, you sot!
Avoiding figures, tropes, what-not;
For fear I should my fancy raise
Above the level of thy plays!

Warton notices the common practice, about the reign of Elizabeth, of an author's dedicating a work at once to a number of the nobility. Chapman's Translation of Homer has sixteen sonnets addressed to lords and ladies. Henry Lock, in a collection of two hundred religious sonnets, mingles with such heavenly works the terrestrial composition of a number of sonnets to his noble patrons; and not to multiply more instances, our great poet Spenser, in compliance with this disgraceful custom, or rather in obedience to the established tyranny of patronage, has prefixed to the Faery Queen fifteen of these adulatory pieces, which in every respect are the meanest of his compositions. At this period all men, as well as writers, looked up to the peers as if they were beings on whose smiles or frowns all sublunary good and evil depended. At a much later period, Elkanah Settle sent copies round to the chief party, for he wrote for both parties, accompanied by addresses to extort pecuniary presents in return. He had latterly one standard *Elegy*, and one *Epithalamium*, printed off with blanks, which by ingeniously filling up with the printed names of any great person who died or was married; no one who was going out of life, or was entering into it, could pass scot-free.

One of the most singular anecdotes respecting DEDICATIONS in English bibliography is that of the Polyglot Bible of Dr. Castell. Cromwell, much to his honour, patronized that great labour, and allowed the paper to be imported free of all duties, both of excise and custom. It was published under the protectorate, but many copies had not been disposed of ere Charles II. ascended the throne. Dr. Castell had dedicated the work gratefully to Oliver, by mentioning him with peculiar respect in the preface, but he wavered with Richard Cromwell. At the Restoration, he cancelled the two last leaves, and supplied their places with three others, which softened down the republican strains, and blotted Oliver's name out of the book of life! The differences in what are now called the *republican* and the *loyal* copies have amused the curious collectors; and the former being very scarce, are most sought after. I have seen the republican. In the *loyal* copies the patrons of the work are mentioned, but their *titles* are essentially changed; *Serenissimus, Illustrissimus*, and *Honoratissimus*, were epithets that dared not shew themselves under the *levelling* influence of the great fanatic republican.

It is a curious literary folly, not of an individual but of the Spanish nation, who, when the laws of Castile were reduced into a code under the reign of Alfonso X. surnamed the Wise, divided the work into *seven volumes;* that they might be dedicated to the *seven letters* which formed the name of his majesty!

Never was a gigantic baby of adulation so crammed with the soft pap of *Dedications* as Cardinal Richelieu. French flattery even exceeded itself.—Among the vast number of very extraordinary dedications to this man, in which the Divinity itself is disrobed of its attributes to bestow them on this miserable creature of vanity, I suspect that even the following one is not the most blasphemous he received. "Who has seen your face without being seized by those softened terrors which made the prophets shudder when God showed the beams of his glory! But as He whom they dared not to approach in the burning bush, and in the noise of thunders, appeared to them sometimes in the freshness of the zephyrs, so the softness of your august countenance dissipates at the same time, and changes into dew, the small vapours which cover its majesty." One of these herd of dedicators, after the death of Richelieu, suppressed in a second edition his hyperbolical panegyric, and as a punishment to himself, dedicated the work to Jesus Christ!

The same taste characterises our own dedications in the reigns of Charles II. and James II. The great Dryden has carried it to an excessive height; and nothing is more usual than to compare the *patron* with the *Divinity*—and at times a fair inference may be drawn that the former was more in the author's mind than God himself! A Welsh bishop made an *apology* to James I. for *preferring* the Deity——to his Majesty! Dryden's extravagant dedications were the vices of the time more than of the man; they were loaded with flattery, and no disgrace was annexed to such an exercise of men's talents; the contest being who should go farthest in the most graceful way, and with the best turns of expression.

An ingenious dedication was contrived by Sir Simon Degge, who dedicated "the Parson's Counsellor" to Woods, Bishop of Lichfield. Degge highly complimented the bishop on having most nobly restored the church, which had been demolished in the civil wars, and was rebuilt but left unfinished by Bishop Hacket. At the time he wrote the dedication, Woods had not turned a single stone, and it is said, that much against his will he did something, from having been so publicly reminded of it by this ironical dedication.

3. PREFACES I
(*Curiosities*, vol. 1, pp. 71-72)

A PREFACE, being the entrance to a book, should invite by its beauty. An elegant porch announces the splendour of the interior. I have observed that ordinary readers skip over these little elaborate compositions. The ladies consider them as so many pages lost, which might better be employed in the addition of a picturesque scene, or a tender letter to their novels. For my part I always gather amusement from a preface, be it awkwardly or skilfully written; for dulness, or impertinence, may raise a laugh for a page or two. A preface is frequently a superior composition to the work itself: for, long before the days of Johnson, it had been a custom for many authors to solicit for this department of their work the ornamental contribution of a man of genius. Cicero tells his friend Atticus, that he had a volume of prefaces or introductions always ready by him to be used as circumstances required. These must have been like our periodical essays. A good preface is as essential to put the reader into good humour, as a good prologue is to a play, or a fine symphony to an opera, containing something analogous to the work itself; so that we may feel its want as a desire not elsewhere to be gratified. The Italians call the preface *La salsa del libro*, the sauce of the book, and if well seasoned it creates an appetite in the reader to devour the book itself. A preface badly composed prejudices the reader against the work. Authors are not equally fortunate in these little introductions; some can compose volumes more skilfully than prefaces, and others can finish a preface who could never be capable of finishing a book.

On a very elegant preface prefixed to an ill-written book, it was observed that they ought never to have *come together;* but a sarcastic wit remarked that he considered such *marriages* were allowable, for they were *not of kin.*

In prefaces an affected haughtiness or an affected humility are alike despicable. There is a deficient dignity in Robertson's; but the haughtiness is now to our purpose. This is called by the French, "*la morgue littéraire,*" the surly pomposity of literature. It is sometimes used by writers who have succeeded in their first work, while the failure of their subsequent productions appears to have given them a literary hypochondriasm. Dr. Armstrong, after his classical poem, never shook hands cordially with the public for not relishing his barren labours. In the *preface* to his lively "Sketches" he tells us, "he could give them much bolder strokes as well as more delicate touches, but that he *dreads the danger of writing too well,* and feels the value of his own labour too sensibly to bestow it upon the *mobility.*" This is pure milk compared to the gall in the *preface* to his poems. There he tells us, "that at last he has taken the *trouble to collect them!* What he has destroyed would, probably enough, have been better received by the *great majority of readers.* But he has always *most heartily despised their opinion.*" These prefaces remind one of the *prologi galeati,* prefaces with a helmet! As St. Jerome entitles the one to his Version of the Scriptures. These *armed prefaces* were formerly very common in the age of literary controversy; for half the business of an author consisted then, either in replying, or anticipating a reply, to the attacks of his opponent.

Prefaces ought to be dated; as these become, after a series of editions, leading and useful circumstances in literary history.

Fuller with quaint humour observes on INDEXES—"An INDEX is a necessary implement, and no impediment of a book, except in the same sense wherein the carriages of an army are termed *Impedimenta.* Without this, a large author is but a labyrinth without a clue to direct the reader therein. I confess there is a lazy kind of learning which is *only Indical;* when scholars (like adders which only bite the horse's heels) nibble but at the tables, which are *calces librorum,* neglecting the body of the book. But though the idle deserve no crutches (let not a staff be used by them, but on them), pity it is the weary should be denied the benefit thereof, and industrious scholars prohibited the accommodation of an index, most used by those who most pretend to contemn it."

4. PREFACES II
(*Literary Miscellanies.*, vol. 4, pp. 286-291)

I DECLARE myself infinitely delighted by a preface. Is it exquisitely written? no literary morsel is more delicious. Is the author inveterately dull? it is kind of preparatory information, which may be very useful. It argues a deficiency in taste to turn over an elaborate preface unread; for it is the attar of the author's roses; every drop distilled at an immense cost. It is the reason of the reasoning, and the folly of the foolish.

I do not wish, however, to conceal that several writers, as well as readers, have spoken very disrespectfully of this species of literature. That fine writer Montesquieu, in closing the preface to his "Persian Letters," says, "I do not praise my 'Persians;' because it would be a very tedious thing, put in a place already very tedious of itself; I mean a preface." Spence, in the preface to his "Polymetis," informs us, that "there is not any sort of writing which he sits down to with so much unwillingness as that of prefaces; and as he believes most people are not much fonder of reading them than he is of writing them, he shall get over this as fast as he can." Pelisson warmly protested against prefatory composition; but when he published the works of Sarrasin, was wise enough to compose a very pleasing one. He, indeed, endeavoured to justify himself for acting against his own opinions, by this ingenious excuse, that, like funeral honours, it is proper to show the utmost regard for them when given to others, but to be inattentive to them for ourselves.

Notwithstanding all this evidence, I have some good reasons for admiring prefaces; and barren as the investigation may appear, some literary amusement can be gathered.

In the first place, I observe that a prefacer is generally a most accomplished liar. Is an author to be introduced to the public? the preface is as genuine a panegyric, and nearly as long a one, as that of Pliny's on the Emperor Trajan. Such a preface is ringing an alarum bell for an author. If we look closer into the characters of these masters of ceremony, who thus sport with and defy the judgment of their reader, and who, by their extravagant panegyric, do considerable injury to the cause of taste, we discover that some accidental occurrence has occasioned this vehement affection for the author, and which, like that of another kind of love, makes one commit so many extravagances.

Prefaces are indeed rarely sincere. It is justly observed by Shenstone, in his prefatory Essay to the "Elegies," that "discourses prefixed to poetry inculcate such tenets as may exhibit the performance to the greatest advantage. The fabric is first raised, and the measures by which we are to judge of it are afterwards adjusted." This observation might be exemplified by more instances than some readers might choose to read. It will be sufficient to observe with what art both Pope and Fontenelle have drawn up their Essays on the nature of Pastoral Poetry, that the rules they wished to establish might be adapted to their own pastorals. Has accident made some ingenious student apply himself to a subordinate branch of literature, or to some science which is not highly esteemed—look in the preface for its sublime panegyric. Collectors of coins, dresses, and butterflies, have astonished the world with eulogiums which would raise their particular studies into the first ranks of philosophy.

It would appear that there is no lie to which a prefacer is not tempted. I pass over the commodious prefaces of Dryden, which were ever adapted to the poem and not to poetry, to the author and not to literature.

The boldest preface-liar was Aldus Manutius, who, having printed an edition of Aristophanes, first published in the preface that Saint Chrysostom was accustomed to place this comic poet under his pillow, that he might always have his work at hand. As, in that age, a saint was supposed to possess every human talent, good taste not excepted, Aristophanes thus recommended became a general favourite. The anecdote lasted for nearly two centuries; and what was of greater consequence to Aldus, quickened the sale of his Aristophanes. This ingenious invention of the prefacer of Aristophanes at length was detected by Menage.

The insincerity of prefaces arises whenever an author would disguise his solicitude for his work, by appearing negligent, and even undesirous of its success. A writer will rarely conclude such a preface without betraying himself. I think that even Dr. Johnson forgot his sound dialectic in the admirable Preface to his Dictionary. In one part he says, "having laboured this work with so much application, I cannot but have some degree of parental fondness." But in his conclusion he tells us, "I dismiss it with frigid tranquillity, having little to fear or hope from censure or from praise." I deny the doctor's "frigidity." This polished period exhibits an affected stoicism, which no writer ever felt for the anxious labour of a great portion of life, addressed not merely to a class of readers, but to literary Europe.

But if prefaces are rarely sincere or just, they are, notwithstanding, literary opuscula in which the author is materially concerned. A work with a poor preface, like a person who comes with an indifferent recommendation, must display uncommon merit to master our prejudices, and to please us, as it were, in spite of ourselves. Works ornamented by a finished preface, such as Johnson not infrequently presented to his friends or his booksellers, inspire us with awe; we observe a veteran guard placed in the porch, and we are induced to conclude from this appearance that some person of eminence resides in the place itself.

The public are treated with contempt when an author professes to publish his puerilities. This Warburton did, in his pompous edition of Shakspeare. In the preface he informed the public, that his notes "were among his *younger amusements*, when he turned over these *sort of writers*." This ungracious compliment to Shakspeare and the public, merited that perfect scourging which our haughty commentator received from the sarcastic "Canons of Criticism." Scudery was a writer of some genius, and great variety. His prefaces are remarkable for their gasconades. In his epic poem of Alaric, he says, "I have such a facility in writing verses, and also in my invention, that a poem of double its length would have cost me little trouble. Although it contains only eleven thousand lines, I believe that longer epics do not exhibit more embellishments than mine." And to conclude with one more student of this class, Amelot de la Houssaie, in the preface to his translation of "The Prince" of Machiavel, instructs us, that "he considers his copy as superior to the original, because it is everywhere intelligible, and Machiavel is frequently obscure." I have seen in the playbills of strollers, a very pompous description of the triumphant entry of Alexander into Babylon; had they said nothing about the triumph, it might have passed without exciting ridicule; and one might not so maliciously have perceived how ill the four candle-snuffers crawled as elephants, and the triumphal car discovered its want of a lid. But having pre-excited attention, we had full leisure to sharpen our eye. To these imprudent authors and actors we may apply a Spanish proverb, which has the peculiar quaintness of that people, *Aviendo pregonado vino, venden vinagre:* "Having cried up their wine, they sell us vinegar."

A ridiculous humility in a preface is not less despicable. Many idle apologies were formerly in vogue for publication, and formed a literary cant, of which now the meanest writers perceive the futility. A literary anecdote of the Romans has been preserved, which is sufficiently curious. One Albinus, in the preface to his Roman History, intercedes for pardon for his numerous blunders of phraseology; observing that they were the more excusable, as he had composed his history in the Greek language, with which he was not so familiar as his maternal tongue. Cato severely rallies him on this; and justly observes, that our Albinus had merited the pardon he solicits, if a decree of the senate had compelled him thus to have composed it, and he could not have obtained a dispensation. The avowal of our ignorance of the language we employ is like that excuse which some writers make for composing on topics in which they are little conversant. A reader's heart is not so easily mollified; and it is a melancholy truth for literary men that the pleasure of abusing an author is generally superior to that of admiring him. One appears to display more critical acumen than the other, by showing that though we do not choose to take the trouble of writing, we have infinitely more genius than the author. These suppliant prefaces are described by Boileau.

> Un auteur à genoux dans une humble préface
> Au lecteur qu'il ennuie a beau demander grace;
> Il ne gagnera rien sur ce juge irrité,
> Qui lui fait son procès de pleine autorité.
>
> Low in a humble preface authors kneel;
> In vain, the wearied reader's heart is steel.
> Callous, that irritated judge with awe,
> Inflicts the penalties and arms the law.

The most entertaining prefaces in our language are those of Dryden; and though it is ill-naturedly said, by Swift that they were merely formed

> To raise the volume's price a shilling,

yet these were the earliest commencements of English criticism, and the first attempt to restrain the capriciousness of readers, and to form a national taste. Dryden has had the candour to acquaint us with his secret of prefatory composition; for in that one to his Tales he says, "the nature of preface-writing is rambling; never wholly out of the way, nor in it. This I have learnt from the practice of honest Montaigne." There is no great risk in establishing this observation as an axiom in literature; for should a prefacer loiter, it is never difficult to get rid of lame persons, by escaping from them; and the reader may make a preface as concise as he chooses.

It is possible for an author to paint himself in amiable colours, in this useful page, without incurring the contempt of egotism. After a writer has rendered himself conspicuous by his industry or his genius, his admirers are not displeased to hear something relative to him from himself. Hayley, in the preface to his poems, has conveyed an amiable feature in his personal character, by giving the cause of his devotion to literature as the only mode by which he could render himself of some utility to his country. There is a modesty in the prefaces of Pope, even when this great poet collected his immortal works; and in several other writers of the most elevated genius, in a Hume and a Robertson, which becomes their happy successors to imitate, and inferior writers to contemplate with awe.

There is in prefaces a due respect to be shown to the public and to ourselves. He that has no sense of self-dignity, will not inspire any reverence in others; and the ebriety of vanity will be sobered by the alacrity we all feel in disturbing the dreams of self-love. If we dare not attempt the rambling prefaces of a Dryden, we may still entertain the reader, and soothe him into good-humour, for our own interest. This, perhaps, will be best obtained by making the preface (like the symphony to an opera) to contain something analogous to the work itself, to attune the mind into harmony of tone.[54]

5. QUOTATION
(*Curiosities*, vol. 2, pp. 416-420)

IT is generally supposed that where there is no QUOTATION, there will be found most originality. Our writers usually furnish their pages rapidly with the productions of their own soil: they run up a quickset hedge, or plant a poplar, and get trees and hedges of this fashion much faster than the former landlords procured their timber. The greater part of our writers, in consequence, have become so original, that no one cares to imitate them; and those who never quote, in return are seldom quoted!

This is one of the results of that adventurous spirit which is now stalking forth and raging for its own innovations. We have not only rejected AUTHORITY, but have also cast away EXPERIENCE; and often the unburthened vessel is driving to all parts of the compass, and the passengers no longer know whither they are going. The wisdom of the wise, and the experience of ages, may be preserved by QUOTATION.

It seems, however, agreed, that no one would quote if he could think; and it is not imagined that the well-read may quote from the delicacy of their taste, and the fulness of their knowledge. Whatever is felicitously expressed risks being worse expressed; it is a wretched taste to be gratified with mediocrity when the excellent lies before us. We quote to save proving what has been demonstrated, referring to where the proofs may be found. We quote to screen ourselves from the odium of doubtful opinions, which the world would not willingly accept from ourselves; and we may quote from the curiosity which only a quotation itself can give, when in our own words it would be divested of that tint of ancient phrase, that detail of narrative, and that *naïveté* which we have for ever lost, and which we like to recollect once had an existence.

The ancients, who in these matters were not, perhaps, such blockheads as some may conceive, considered poetical quotation as one of the requisite ornaments of oratory. Cicero, even in his philosophical works, is as little sparing of quotations as Plutarch. Old Montaigne is so stuffed with them, that he owns, if they were taken out of him little of himself would remain; and yet this never injured that original turn which the old Gascon has given to his

---

54. See "Curiosities of Literature," vol. i., for an article on Prefaces [i.e. the previous essay].

thoughts. I suspect that Addison hardly ever composed a Spectator which was not founded on some quotation, noted in those three folio manuscript volumes which he previously collected; and Addison lasts, while Steele, who always wrote from first impressions and to the times, with perhaps no inferior genius, has passed away, insomuch that Dr. Beattie once considered that he was obliging the world by collecting Addison's papers, and carefully omitting Steele's.

Quotation, like much better things, has its abuses. One may quote till one compiles. The ancient lawyers used to quote at the bar till they had stagnated their own cause. "Retournons à nos moutons," was the cry of the client. But these vagrant prowlers must be consigned to the beadles of criticism. Such do not always understand the authors whose names adorn their barren pages, and which are taken, too, from the third or the thirtieth hand. Those who trust to such false quoters will often learn how contrary this transmission is to the sense and the application of the original. Every transplantation has altered the fruit of the tree; every new channel the quality of the stream in its remove from the spring-head. Bayle, when writing on "Comets," discovered this; for having collected many things applicable to his work, as they stood quoted in some modern writers, when he came to compare them with their originals, he was surprised to find that they were nothing for his purpose! the originals conveyed a quite contrary sense to that of the pretended quoters, who often, from innocent blundering, and sometimes from purposed deception, had falsified their quotations. This is an useful story for second-hand authorities!

Selden had formed some notions on this subject of quotations in his "Table-talk," art. "*Books and Authors;*" but, as Le Clerc justly observes, proud of his immense reading, he has too often violated his own precept. "In quoting of books," says Selden, "quote such authors as are usually read; others read for your own satisfaction, but not name them." Now it happens that no writer names more authors, except Prynne,[55] than the learned Selden. La Mothe le Vayer's curious works consist of fifteen volumes; he is among the greatest quoters. Whoever turns them over will perceive that he is an original thinker, and a great wit; his style, indeed, is meagre, which, as much as his quotations, may have proved fatal to him. But in both these cases it is evident that even quoters who have abused the privilege of quotation are not necessarily writers of a mean genius.

The Quoters who deserve the title, and it ought to be an honorary one, are those who trust to no one but themselves. In borrowing a passage, they carefully observe its connexion; they collect authorities to reconcile any

---

55. It was said of Prynne, and his custom of quoting authorities by hundreds in the margins of his books to corroborate what he said in the text, that "he always had his wits beside him in the margin, to be beside his wits in the text." This jest is Milton's.

disparity in them before they furnish the one which they adopt; they advance no fact without a witness, and they are not loose and general in their references, as I have been told is our historian Henry so frequently, that it is suspected he deals much in second-hand ware. Bayle lets us into a mystery of author-craft. "Suppose an able man is to prove that an ancient author entertained certain particular opinions, which are only insinuated here and there through his works, I am sure it will take him up more days to collect the passages which he will have occasion for, than to *argue at random* on those passages. Having once found out his authorities and his quotations, which perhaps will not fill six pages, and may have cost him a month's labour, he may finish in two mornings' work twenty pages of arguments, objections, and answers to objections; and consequently, *what proceeds from our own genius sometimes costs much less time than what is requisite for collecting.* Corneille would have required more time to defend a tragedy by a great collection of authorities, than to write it; and I am supposing the same number of pages in the tragedy and in the defence. Heinsius perhaps bestowed more time in defending his *Herodes infanticida* against Balzac, than a Spanish (or a Scotch) metaphysician bestows on a large volume of controversy, where he takes all from his own stock." I am somewhat concerned in the truth of this principle. There are articles in the present work occupying but a few pages, which could never have been produced had not more time been allotted to the researches which they contain than some would allow to a small volume, which might excel in genius, and yet be likely not to be long remembered! All this is labour which never meets the eye. It is quicker work, with special pleading and poignant periods, to fill sheets with generalising principles; those bird's-eye views of philosophy for the *nonce* seem as if things were seen clearer when at a distance and *en masse*, and require little knowledge of the individual parts. Such *an art of writing* may resemble the famous Lullian method, by which the *doctor illuminatus* enabled any one to invent arguments by a machine! Two tables, one of *attributes*, and the other of *subjects*, worked about circularly in a frame, and placed correlatively to one another produced certain combinations; the number of *questions* multiplied as they were worked! So that here was a mechanical invention by which they might dispute without end, and write on without any particular knowledge of their subject!

But the painstaking gentry, when heaven sends them genius enough, are the most instructive sort, and they are those to whom we shall appeal while time and truth can meet together. A well-read writer, with good taste, is one who has the command of the wit of other men;[56] he searches where knowledge is to be found; and though he may not himself excel in invention,

---

56. Southey says—"A quotation may be likened to a text on which a sermon is preached."

his ingenuity may compose one of those agreeable books, the *deliciæ* of literature, that will outlast the fading meteors of his day. Epicurus is said to have borrowed from no writer in his three hundred inspired volumes, while Plutarch, Seneca, and the elder Pliny made such free use of their libraries; and it has happened that Epicurus, with his unsubstantial nothingness, has "melted into thin air," while the solid treasures have buoyed themselves up amidst the wrecks of nations.

On this subject of quotation, literary politics,—for the commonwealth has its policy and its cabinet-secrets,—are more concerned than the reader suspects. Authorities in matters of fact are often called for; in matters of opinion, indeed, which perhaps are of more importance, no one requires any authority. But too open and generous a revelation of the chapter and the page of the original quoted has often proved detrimental to the legitimate honours of the quoter. They are unfairly appropriated by the next comer; the quoter is never quoted, but the authority he has afforded is produced by his successor with the air of an original research. I have seen MSS. thus confidently referred to, which could never have met the eye of the writer. A learned historian declared to me of a contemporary, that the latter had appropriated his researches; he might, indeed, and he had a right to refer to the same originals; but if his predecessor had opened the sources for him, gratitude is not a silent virtue. Gilbert Stuart thus lived on Robertson; and as Professor Dugald Stewart observes, "his curiosity has seldom led him into any path where the genius and industry of his predecessor had not previously cleared the way." It is for this reason some authors, who do not care to trust to the equity and gratitude of their successors, will not furnish the means of supplanting themselves; for, by not yielding up their authorities, they themselves become one. Some authors, who are pleased at seeing their names occur in the margins of other books than their own, have practised this political management; such as Alexander ab Alexandro, and other compilers of that stamp, to whose labours of small value we are often obliged to refer, from the circumstance that they themselves have not pointed out their authorities.

One word more on this long chapter of QUOTATION. To make a happy one is a thing not easily to be done.[57] Cardinal du Perron used to say, that the happy application of a verse from Virgil was worth a talent; and Bayle, perhaps too much prepossessed in their favour, has insinuated, that there is not less invention in a just and happy application of a thought found in a book, than in being the first author of that thought. The art of quotation requires more delicacy in the practice than those conceive who can see

---

57. Hone had this faculty in a large degree, and one of his best political satires, the "Political Showman at Home," is entirely made out of quotations from older authors applicable to the real or fancied characteristics of the politicians he satirized.

nothing more in a quotation than an extract. Whenever the mind of a writer is saturated with the full inspiration of a great author, a quotation gives completeness to the whole; it seals his feelings with undisputed authority. Whenever we would prepare the mind by a forcible appeal, an opening quotation is a symphony preluding on the chords whose tones we are about to harmonise. Perhaps no writers of our times have discovered more of this delicacy of quotation than the author of the "Pursuits of Literature;" and Mr. Southey, in some of his beautiful periodical investigations, where we have often acknowledged the solemn and striking effect of a quotation from our elder writers.

6. NOTES I
(*Quarrels*, vol. 5, pp. 231-232)

I have freely enlarged in the *notes* to this work; a practice which is objectionable to many, but indispensable perhaps in this species of literary history.

The late Mr. CUMBERLAND, in a conversation I once held with him on this subject, triumphantly exclaimed, "You will not find a single note through the whole volume of my 'Life.' I never wrote a note. The ancients never wrote notes; but they introduced into their text all which was proper for the reader to know."

I agreed with that elegant writer, that a fine piece of essay-writing, such as his own "Life," required notes no more than his novels and his comedies, among which it may be classed. I observed that the ancients had no literary history; this was the result of the discovery of printing, the institution of national libraries, the general literary intercourse of Europe, and some other causes which are the growth almost of our own times. The ancients have written history without producing authorities.

Mr. CUMBERLAND was then occupied on a review of Fox's History; and of CLARENDON, which lay open before him,—he had been complaining, with all the irritable feelings of a dramatist, of the frequent suspensions, and the tedious minuteness of his story.

I observed that *notes* had not then been discovered. Had Lord CLARENDON known their use, he had preserved the unity of design in his text. His Lordship has unskilfully filled it with all that historical furniture his diligence had collected, and with those minute discussions which his anxiety for truth, and his lawyer-like mode of scrutinising into facts and substantiating evidence, amassed. Had these been cast into *notes*, and were it now possible to pass them over in the present text, how would the story of the noble historian clear up! The greatness of his genius will appear when disencumbered of its unwieldy and misplaced accompaniments.

If this observation be just, it will apply with greater force to literary history itself, which, being often the mere history of the human mind, has to record opinions as well as events—to discuss as well as to narrate—to show how accepted truths become suspicious—or to confirm what has hitherto rested in obscure uncertainty, and to balance contending opinions and opposite facts with critical nicety. The multiplied means of our knowledge now opened to us, have only rendered our curiosity more urgent in its claims, and raised up the most diversified objects. These, though accessories to the leading one of our inquiries, can never melt together in the continuity of a text. It is to prevent all this disorder, and to enjoy all the usefulness and the pleasure of this various knowledge, which has produced the invention of *notes* in literary history. All this forms a sort of knowledge peculiar to the present more enlarged state of literature. Writers who delight in curious and rare extracts, and in the discovery of new facts and new views of things, warmed by a fervour of research which brings everything nearer to our eye and close to our touch, study to throw contemporary feelings in their page. Such rare extracts and such new facts BAYLE eagerly sought, and they delighted JOHNSON; but all this luxury of literature can only be produced to the public eye in the variegated forms of *notes*.

7. NOTES II
(*Amenities*, pp. 567-570)

WHEN we observe the massive *variorum* edition of Shakespeare, we are struck by the circumstance that nothing similar has happened to any other national author. It was not to be expected that, after the invention of the art of printing, an author could arise, whose works should be disfigured by treacherous transcribers, corrupted by interpolations, and still more by a race of men whose art was unknown to the ancients, subjecting his text to the mercy of contending commentators and conjectural critics. But a singular combination of untoward circumstances attached to this poet and his works, produced this remarkable result. The scholiasts among the ancient classics had rejoiced in some rare emendation of the text, or the rhetorical commentator had flourished in the luxuriance of the latent beauties of some favourite author. But a far wider and deeper source of inquiry was now to be attempted, historical or explanatory—comments to clear up obscure allusions; to indicate unknown prototypes; to trace the vicissitudes of words as well as things; to picture forth the customs and the manners which had faded into desuetude; and to re-open for us the records of our social and domestic life, thus at once to throw us back into that age, and to familiarize us with that language of Shakespeare which had vanished. Shakespeare, it may be said,, suddenly became the favourite object of literary inquiry. Every literary man in the nation conned over and illumined "the infinite variety" of the bard. And assuredly they enriched our vernacular literature with a collection of historical, philological, and miscellaneous information, unparalleled among any other literary people. In 1785, ISAAC REED, in one of his prefaces, informs us, that "the works of Shakespeare, during the last twenty years, have been the object of public attention."

All this novel knowledge was, however, not purchased at a slight cost. It was not only to be snatched up by accidental discovery, but it was more severely tasked by what Steevens called "a course of black-letter!"—dusty volumes, and fugitive tracts, and the wide range of antiquarian research. The sources whence they drew their waters were muddy; and STEEVENS, who affected more gaiety in his chains than his brothers in the Shakespearian galley, with bitter derision reproached his great coadjutor MALONE, whom he looked on with the evil eye of rivalry for drawing his knowledge from "books too mean to be formally quoted."

The commentators have encumbered the poet, who often has been a secondary object of their lucubrations, for they not only write notes on Shakespeare, but notes, and bitter ones too, on one another. This commentary has been turned into a gymnasium for the public sports of friendly and of unfriendly wrestlers; where some have been so earnest, that it is evident that, in measuring a cast, they congratulated themselves in the language of Orlando, "If ever he goes alone again, I'll never wrestle for prize more."

THOMAS WARTON once covered with his shield some of the minor brotherhood: "If Shakespeare is worth reading, he is worth explaining; and the researches used for so valuable and elegant a purpose merit the thanks of genius and candour, not the satire of prejudice and ignorance." But this serves not as an apology for abusing the privilege of a commentator; elucidating the poet into obscurity by information equally contradictory and curious; racking us by fantastic readings which no one imagined before or since; and laying us open to the mercy of some who never ventured to sharpen their pens but on our irresistible Shakespeare. What has been the result of the petty conflicts between the arch maliciousness of Steevens and the fervent plodding of Malone, which raised up two parties among the Shakespearian commentators, till they became so personal that a Steevenite and a Malonist looked on each other suspiciously, and sometimes would drop the ordinary civilities of life? At length, strange to tell, after Steevens had laboured with zeal equal to the whole confraternity, it became a question with him, In what manner the poet COULD be read? Are we to con over each note appended to each word or passage?—but this would be perpetually to turn aside the flow of our imagination; or are we to read a large portion of the text uninterruptedly, and then return to the notes?—but this would be breaking up the unity of the poet into fragments; or, for a final decision, and the avowal must have mortified the ingenuous illustrator, according to a third class of readers, were these illustrations to be altogether rejected? must the poet or the commentator be at continual variance? Or shall we endure to see "Alcides beaten by his page?"

Might I be allowed to offer an award on a matter so involved and delicate as this union between the genius of Shakespeare and the genius of his commentators, I would concede the divorce, from the incompatibility of temper between the parties; but I would insist on a separate maintenance, to preserve the great respectability attached to the party most complained of. The true reader of Shakespeare may then accommodate himself with two editions; the one for his hand, having nothing but what the poet has written; the other for the shelf, having all the commentators have conjectured, confuted, and confounded.[58]

8. INDEXES I
(*Curiosities*, vol. 1., p. 72)

Fuller with quaint humour observes on INDEXES—"An INDEX is a necessary implement, and no impediment of a book, except in the same sense wherein the carriages of an army are termed *Impedimenta*. Without this, a large author is but a labyrinth without a clue to direct the reader therein. I confess there is a lazy kind of learning which is *only Indical;* when scholars (like adders which only bite the horse's heels) nibble but at the tables, which are *calces librorum*, neglecting the body of the book. But though the idle deserve no crutches (let not a staff be used by them, but on them), pity it is the weary should be denied the benefit thereof, and industrious scholars prohibited the accommodation of an index, most used by those who most pretend to contemn it."

---

58. Much, if not all, that is valuable in this great body of varied information, has been alphabetically arranged in "A Glossary, or Collection of Words, Phrases, Names, and Allusions to Customs, Proverbs, &c., which have required illustration in the *works of English Authors,* particularly *Shakespeare and his Contemporaries,*" by Archdeacon Nares, 4to, 1822: a compilation as amusing as it is useful, and which I suspect has not been justly appreciated. It is a substitute for all these commentators; and with this volume, at an easy rate, we are made free of the whole Shakespearian corporation.

9. INDEXES II
(Literary Miscellanies., vol. 4, p. 299)

It is an observation of the elder Pliny (who, having been a voluminous compiler, must have had great experience in the art of reading), that there was no book so bad but which contained something good. To read every book would, however, be fatal to the interest of most readers; but it is not always necessary, in the pursuits of learning, to read every book entire. Of many books it is sufficient to seize the plan, and to examine some of their portions. Of the little supplement at the close of a volume, few readers conceive the utility; but some of the most eminent writers in Europe have been great adepts in the art of index reading. I, for my part, venerate the inventor of indexes; and I know not to whom to yield the preference, either to Hippocrates, who was the first great anatomiser of the human body, or to that unknown labourer in literature, who first laid open the nerves and arteries of a book. Watts advises the perusal of the prefaces and the index of a book, as they both give light on its contents.

10. ERRATA
(Curiosities, vol. 1, pp. 78-82)

BESIDES the ordinary *errata*, which happen in printing a work, others have been purposely committed, that the *errata* may contain what is not permitted to appear in the body of the work. Wherever the Inquisition had any power, particularly at Rome, it was not allowed to employ the word *fatum*, or *fata*, in any book. An author, desirous of using the latter word, adroitly invented this scheme; he had printed in his book *facta*, and, in the *errata*, he put, "For *facta*, read *fata*."

Scarron has done the same thing on another occasion. He had composed some verses, at the head of which he placed this dedication—*A Guillemette, Chienne de ma Sœur;* but having a quarrel with his sister, he maliciously put into the *errata*, "Instead of *Chienne de ma Sœur*, read *ma Chienne de Sœur*."

Lully, at the close of a bad prologue said, the word *fin du prologue* was an *erratum*, it should have been *fi du prologue!*

In a book, there was printed, *le docte Morel.* A wag put into the *errata*, "For *le docte Morel*, read *le Docteur Morel*." This *Morel* was not the first *docteur* not *docte*.

When a fanatic published a mystical work full of unintelligible raptures, and which he entitled *Les Délices de l'Esprit*, it was proposed to print in his errata, "For *Délices* read *Délires*."

The author of an idle and imperfect book ended with the usual phrase of *cetera desiderantur,* one altered it, *Non desiderantur sed desunt;* "The rest is *wanting,* but not *wanted.*"

At the close of a silly book, the author as usual printed the word FINIS.——A wit put this among the errata, with this pointed couplet:—

> FINIS!——an error, or a lie, my friend!
> In writing foolish books——there is *no End!*

In the year 1561 was printed a work, entitled "the Anatomy of the Mass." It is a thin octavo, of 172 pages, and it is accompanied by an *Errata* of 15 pages! The editor, a pious monk, informs us that a very serious reason induced him to undertake this task: for it is, says he, to forestal the *artifices of Satan.* He supposes that the Devil, to ruin the fruit of this work, employed two very malicious frauds: the first before it was printed, by drenching the MS. in a kennel, and having reduced it to a most pitiable state, rendered several parts illegible: the second, in obliging the printers to commit such numerous blunders, never yet equalled in so small a work. To combat this double machination of Satan he was obliged carefully to re-peruse the work, and to form this singular list of the blunders of printers under the influence of Satan. All this he relates in an advertisement prefixed to the *Errata.*

A furious controversy raged between two famous scholars from a very laughable but accidental *Erratum,* and threatened serious consequences to one of the parties. Flavigny wrote two letters, criticising rather freely a polyglot Bible edited by Abraham Ecchellensis. As this learned editor had sometimes censured the labours of a friend of Flavigny, this latter applied to him the third and fifth verses of the seventh chapter of St. Matthew, which he printed in Latin. Ver 3. *Quid vides festucam in* OCULO *fratris tui, et trabem in* OCULO *tuo non vides?* Ver. 5 *Ejice primùm trabem de* OCULO *tuo, et tunc videbis ejicere festucam de* OCULO *fratris tui.* Ecchellensis opens his reply by accusing Flavigny of an *enormous crime* committed in this passage; attempting to correct the sacred text of the Evangelist, and daring to reject a word, while he supplied its place by another as *impious* as *obscene!* This crime, exaggerated with all the virulence of an angry declaimer, closes with a dreadful accusation. Flavigny's morals are attacked, and his reputation overturned by a horrid imputation. Yet all this terrible reproach is only founded on an *Erratum!* The whole arose from the printer having negligently suffered the *first letter* of the word *Oculo* to have dropped from the form when he happened to touch a line with his finger, which did not stand straight! He published another letter to do away the imputation of Ecchellensis; but thirty years afterwards his rage against the negligent printer was not extinguished; the wits were always reminding him of it.

Of all literary blunders none equalled that of the edition of the Vulgate, by Sixtus V. His Holiness carefully superintended every sheet as it passed through the press; and, to the amazement of the world, the work remained without a rival—it swarmed with errata! A multitude of scraps were printed to paste over the erroneous passages, in order to give the true text. The book makes a whimsical appearance with these patches; and the heretics exulted in this demonstration of papal infallibility! The copies were called in, and violent attempts made to suppress it; a few still remain for the raptures of the biblical collectors; not long ago the bible of Sixtus V. fetched above sixty guineas—not too much for a mere book of blunders! The world was highly amused at the bull of the editorial Pope prefixed to the first volume, which excommunicates all printers who in reprinting the work should make any *alteration* in the text!

In the version of the Epistles of St. Paul into the Ethiopic language, which proved to be full of errors, the editors allege a good-humoured reason—They who printed the work could not read, and we could not print; they helped us, and we helped them, as the blind helps the blind."

A printer's widow in Germany, while a new edition of the Bible was printing at her house, one night took an opportunity of stealing into the office, to alter that sentence of subjection to her husband, pronounced upon Eve in Genesis, chap. 3, v. 16. She took out the two first letters of the word HERR, and substituted NA in their place, thus altering the sentence from "and he shall be thy LORD" *(Herr)*, to "and he shall be thy FOOl" *(Narr)*. It is said her life paid for this intentional erratum; and that some secreted copies of this edition have been bought up at enormous prices.

We have an edition of the Bible, known by the name of *The Vinegar Bible;* from the erratum in the title to the 20th chap. of St. Luke, in which "Parable of the *Vineyard,*" is printed, "Parable of the *Vinegar.*" It was printed in 1717, at the Clarendon press.

We have had another, where "Thou shalt commit adultery" was printed, omitting the negation; which occasioned the archbishop to lay one of the heaviest penalties on the Company of Stationers that was ever recorded in the annals of literary history.[59]

Herbert Croft used to complain of the incorrectness of our English classics, as reprinted by the booksellers. It is evident some stupid printer often changes a whole text intentionally. The fine description by Akenside of the Pantheon, "SEVERELY great," not being understood by the blockhead, was printed *serenely great.* Swift's own edition of "The City Shower," has "old ACHES throb." *Aches* is two syllables, but modern printers, who had lost the right pronunciation, have *aches* as one syllable; and then, to complete the

---

59. It abounded with other errors, and was so rigidly suppressed, that a well-known collector was thirty years endeavouring ineffectually to obtain a copy. One has recently been added to the British Museum collection.

metre, have foisted in "aches *will* throb." Thus what the poet and the linguist wish to preserve is altered, and finally lost.[60]

It appears by a calculation made by the printer of Steevens's edition of Shakspeare, that every octavo page of that work, text and notes, contains 2680 distinct pieces of metal; which in a sheet amount to 42,880—the misplacing of any one of which would inevitably cause a blunder! With this curious fact before us, the accurate state of our printing, in general, is to be admired, and errata ought more freely to be pardoned than the fastidious minuteness of the insect eye of certain critics has allowed.

Whether such a miracle as an immaculate edition of a classical author does exist, I have never learnt; but an attempt has been made to obtain this glorious singularity—and was as nearly realised as is perhaps possible in the magnificent edition of *Os Lusiadas* of Camoens, by Dom Joze Souza, in 1817. This amateur spared no prodigality of cost and labour, and flattered himself, that by the assistance of Didot, not a single typographical error should be found in that splendid volume. But an error was afterwards discovered in some of the copies, occasioned by one of the letters in the word *Lusitano* having got misplaced during the working of one of the sheets. It must be confessed that this was an *accident* or *misfortune*—rather than an *Erratum!*

One of the most remarkable complaints on ERRATA is that of Edw. Leigh, appended to his curious treatise on "Religion and Learning." It consists of two folio pages, in a very minute character, and exhibits an incalculable number of printers' blunders. "We have not," he says, "Plantin nor Stephens amongst us; and it is no easy task to specify the chiefest errata; false interpunctions there are too many; here a letter wanting, there a letter too much; a syllable too much, one letter for another; words parted where they should be joined; words joined which should be severed; words misplaced;

---

60. A good example occurs in *Hudibras* (Part iii. canto 2, line 407), where persons are mentioned who

        "Can by their pangs and *aches* find
        All turns and changes of the wind."

The rhythm here demands the dissyllable *a-ches,* as used by the older writers, Shakspeare particularly, who, in his *Tempest,* makes Prospero threaten Caliban—

        "If thou neglect'st, or dost unwillingly
        What I command, I'll rack thee with old cramps;
        Fill all thy bones with aches; make thee roar
        That beasts shall tremble at thy din."

John Kemble was aware of the necessity of using this word in this instance as a dissyllable, but it was so unusual to his audiences that it excited ridicule; and during the O.P. row, a medal was struck, representing him as manager, enduring the din of cat-calls, trumpets, and rattles, and exclaiming, "Oh! my head *aitches!*"

chronological mistakes," &c. This unfortunate folio was printed in 1656. Are we to infer, by such frequent complaints of the authors of that day, that either they did not receive proofs from the printers, or that the printers never attended to the corrected proofs? Each single erratum seems to have been felt as a stab to the literary feelings of the poor author!

IV. AUTHORS & CO.

1. EARLY WRITERS, THEIR DREAD OF THE PRESS; THE TRANSITION TO AUTHORS BY PROFESSION
(*Amenities*, vol. 6, pp. 670-680)

AT the close of the reign of Elizabeth, the public, awakening at the first dawn of knowledge, with their stirring passions and their eager curiosity, found their wants supplied by a new race of "ready writers," who now teased the groaning press—a diversified race of miscellaneous writers, who had discovered the wants of the people for books which excited their sympathies and reflected their experience, and who caught on their fugitive pages the manners and the passions of their contemporaries. No subject was too mean to be treated; and had domestic encyclopædias been then invented, these would have been precisely the library the people required: but now, every book was to be separately worked. The indiscriminate curiosity of an uneducated people was gratified by immature knowledge; but it was essential to amuse as well as to inform: hence that multitude of fugitive subjects. The mart of literature opened, and with the book-manufactory, in the language of that primeval critic, WEBBE, of innumerable sorts of English books, and infinite fardles of printed pamphlets, "all shops were stuffed."

It has been attempted to fix on the name of that great patriarch, the Abraham of our Israel, who first invented our own book-craft; but it would be indiscreet to assign the honour to any particular person, or even to inquire whether the cupidity of the book-vender first set to work the ingenuity of the book-weaver. Who first dipped his silver pen into his golden ink, and who first conceived the notion of this literary alchemy, which transmutes paper into gold or lead? It was, I believe, no solitary invention; the rush of "authors by profession" was simultaneous.

Former writers had fearfully courted fame; they were the children of the pleasures of the pen; these were a hardier race, who at once seized on popularity; and a new trade was opened by the arts of authorship. In the primitive age of publication, before there existed "a reading public," literary productions were often anonymous, or, which answered the same purpose, they wore the mask of a fictitious name, and were pseudonymous, or they hid themselves under naked initials, by which means the owners have sometimes lost their own property. It seems a paradox that writers should take such great pains to defraud themselves of their claims.

This coyness of publication was prevalent among our earliest writers, when writing and publishing were not yet almost synonymous terms. Before we had "authors by profession," we had authors who wrote, and seemed to avoid every sort of publicity. To the secluded writers of that day, the press was arrayed with terrors which have ceased to haunt those who are familiar with its daily labours, and our primeval writers trembled before that halo of immortality, which seemed to hang over that ponderous machinery. Writers eagerly affixed their names to polemical tracts, or to devotional effusions, during the melancholy reigns of EDWARD the Sixth and MARY, as a record of their zeal, and sometimes as an evidence of their voluntary martyrdom; but the productions of imagination and genius were yet rare and private. The noble-minded hardly ventured out of the halcyon state of manuscript to be tossed about in open sea; it would have been compromising their dignity, or disturbing their repose, to submit themselves to the cavils of the Cynics, for even at this early period of printed books we find that the ancient family of the *Malevoli,* whom Terence has noticed, had survived the fall of Rome, and here did not find their "occupation gone." With many scholars, too, it was still doubtful whether the vernacular muses in verse and prose were not trivial and homely. In the inchoate state of our literature, some who were imbued with classical studies might have felt their misgivings, in looking over their "gorgeous inventions," or their "pretty devices," as betraying undisciplined strength, bewildering fancies, and unformed tastes. They were not aware, even at that more advanced period, when a series of "poetical collections" appeared, of what they had already done; and it has been recently discovered, that when the printer of "England's Helicon" had innocently affixed the names of some writers to their pieces, to quiet their alarms, he was driven to the clumsy expedient of pasting slips of paper over their names. This was a spell which Time only dissolved, that great revealer of secrets more deeply concealed.

When publication appeared thus terrible, an art which was not yet valued even the artists themselves would slight. "We have a striking instance of this feeling in the circumstance of a sonnet of our Maiden Queen, on the conspiracies then hatching by the party of her royal sister of Scotland. One of the ladies of her bedchamber had surreptitiously transcribed the poem from her majesty's tablet; and the innocent criminal had thereby cast herself into extreme peril. The queen affected, or at least expressed, her royal anger lest the people should imagine that she was busied in "such toys," and her majesty was fearful of being considered too lightly of, for so doing. The grave sonnet might, however, have been accepted as a state-paper. The solemn theme, the grandeur of the queenly personages, and the fortunes of two great nations at issue, communicated to these verses the profound emotions of contemplative royalty, more exquisite than the poetry. Yet Elizabeth could be checked by "the fear to be held too lightly by such toys."

The same motive had influenced some of the greater personages in our literature, who, by the suppression of their names, anxiously eluded public observation, at the very moment they were in reality courting it! *Ignoto* and *Immerito,* or bare initials, were the concealing signatures of Rawleigh, of

Sidney, and of Spenser. The works of the Earl of Surrey, then the finest poems in the language, were posthumous. "The Arcadia" of Sidney possibly was never intended for the press. The noble Sackville, who planned the grand poem of "The Mirror of Magistrates," willingly left his lofty "Induction" anonymous among the crowd. In the first poetical miscellany in our language collected by the printer Tottell, are "The Poems of *uncertain Authors;*" so careless were the writers themselves to preserve their names, and so little aware of having claims on posterity. Some years after, when those other poetical collections, "The Paradise of Dainty Devices" and "England's Helicon," were projected by their publishers, they were borrowed or stolen from manuscripts which lay neglected with their authors, and who for the most part conceal themselves under quaint signatures.

The metropolis, in the days of Elizabeth and James, bore a pretty close resemblance to those ancient cities now existing before us on the Continent, famous in their day, but which, from causes not here necessary to specify, have not grown with the growth of time, Cologne, Coblentz, and Mayence, are such cities; and the city of Rouen, in its more ancient site, exhibits a picture of the streets of London in the days of Shakspeare. Stationary in their limits and their population, the classes of society are more distinctly marked out; but the individual lives more constantly under the survey of his neighbours. Their art of living is to live in the public eye; to keep up appearances, however this pride may prove inconvenient. No one would seem to have an established household, or always care to indicate its locality; their meals are at a public table, and their familiar acquaintance are found in the same public resorts; their social life becomes contracted as their own ancient narrow streets.

Such was London, when the Strand was a suburb, with only a few scattered mansions; the present streets still retain the family names, thus separating London from its regal sister. The glory of the goldsmiths and the mercers blazed in Cheapside, "the beauty of London;" and Fleet-street was the Bond-street of fashionable loungers. In this contracted sphere, where all moved, and the observers had microscopical eyes, any trivial novelty was strangely magnified, and the great personage was an object for their scrutiny as well as the least considerable. Thus we find that the Lord Chancellor Bacon is censured by one of the gossiping pens of that day for his inordinate pride and pomp on the most ordinary occasions. He went in his state robes "to cheapen and buy silks and velvets at Sir Baptist Hicker's and Burner's shops." James the First, I think, once in Parliament alluded to the "goldsmiths at Cheap, who showed not the bravery of former days," as a mark of the decline of national prosperity. One of the popular alarms of that day was "the rising of the apprentices," whenever the city's clumsy "watch and ward" were put to the rout; the apprentices usually made an attempt on their abhorrence, Bridewell, or pulled down two or three houses on Shrove-Tuesday. Once, on the trying of some ordnance in Moorfields, the court was seized by a panic of "a rising in the city." From all this we may form some notion of the size of the metropolis, and its imbecile police. In a vast and flourishing metropolis the individual in liberty and security passes among the countless waves of this ocean of men.

A metropolis thus rising from its contracted infancy, extending in growth, and diversified by new classes of society, presented many novelties in its crowded scenes; mutable manners, humorous personages, all the affectations or the homeliness of its citizens. Many writers, among whom were some of admirable genius, devoted their pens to fugitive objects and evanescent scenes, sure of finding an immediate reception from the sympathy of their readers. New modes of life, and altered manners during a lengthened peace, brought men into closer observation of each other; the ranks in society were no longer insulated; their haunts were the same localities, the playhouse, the ordinary, and Paul's Walk. There we find the gay and the grave—the disbanded captain—the critic from the inns of court—fantastic "fashion-mongers"—the coney-catcher who watches "the warren,"—and the gull, "town or country," a term which, unlike that of "the coney-catcher," has survived the times before us, and is imbedded in the language.[61] They even touched on the verge of that last refinement in society, critical coteries. We learn from Jonson, that there was "a college of critics," where a new member, "if he could pay for their suppers," might abuse the works of any man, and purchase for himself "the terrible name of a critic;" and ladies "lived free from their husbands," held coteries, and "gave entertainments to all the wits." This was the incipient state of the new world of manners, and what we now call "society;" and society provokes satire!

It was at the close of the Elizabethan period that our first town-satirists arose, from whom we learn the complicate system of manners, in the artifices practised in society; and in looking on their phantasmagorias, we are often startled among their grotesque forms by discovering our own exact faces. Satires on manners, descriptive of the lighter follies and the more involved artifices of social life, could hitherto have had no scope. The great in station

---

61. This technical term, designating the class of youthful loungers, was a new term in 1596, when Sir John Davis wrote his "Epigrams"—

"Oft in my laughing rimes I name a GULL,
   But this *new terme* will many questions breed;
Therefore, at first, I will express at full
   Who is a true and perfect Gull indeed."

His delineation is admirable; Gifford, in his "Jonson," quotes it at length,—i.14. But whoever may be curious about these masculine "birds" will be initiated into the mysteries of "Gullery" by "The Gull's Horn-book" of DEKKER, of which we have a beautiful edition, with appropriate embellishments, by Dr. Nott.

alone constituted what may be considered as society, without any of those marking differences resulting from the inequalities of fortune. Satire then, as with Skelton, was an invective discharged at some potent individual at the risk of life; or it was an attack on a whole body, as Piers Ploughman's on the clergy of the times, while Will, or John, or Piers, whatever was his name, hid himself behind a hedge on Malvern Hills. Society, in the modern acceptation, of a miscellaneous mixture, which equalizes men even in their inequality, supplying passing objects for raillery or indignation, opened that wider stage, which a growing metropolis only could exhibit. We must become intimate with men to sound even the depths of superficial follies, and declamation may even fall short in the conception of some enormous criminal. Society must have considerably advanced before a town-satirist could appear.

The change in style was not less remarkable than that in manners. Towards the close of the reign of Elizabeth, after the wild luxuriance of fancy which had everywhere covered the fresh soil of the public mind, in the riot of our genius, a great change was occurring in the minds of our writers. Nature, in her open paths of sunshine, no longer busied them, while they stole into the bye-corners of abstract ideas, and roved after glittering conceits. Philosophy introduced itself into poetry, and wit became the substitute for passion. It was then that Sir John Davies wrote his "Immortality of the Soul," which still remains a model of didactic verse; and Donne, "The Progress of the Soul," a progress which he did not venture to conclude—a poem the most creative and eccentric in the language, but which must be reserved for the few. Donne, who closed his life as a St. Austin, had opened it as a Catullus.

The depth of sentiment was contracted into sententious epigrams, alike in prose and verse; and in the display of their ingenuity, the remotest objects were brought into collision, and the most differing things into a strange coherence, to startle by surprises, and to make us admire these wonders by their novelty. They cast about them their pointed antitheses, and often subsided into a clink of similar syllables, and the clench of an ambiguous word.

In all matters they affected curt phrases; and it has been observed that even the colloquial style was barbarously elliptical. They spoke gruff and short, affecting brevity of words, which was probably held to be epigrammatic. It became fashionable to write what they entitled books of "Epigrams" and books of "Characters." They appear to have taken their notion of an epigram from the Greek anthology, where the term was confined to any inscription for a statue or a tomb, or any object to be commemorated. Modern literature, in adopting the term, has applied it to a different purpose from its original signification. An epigram now is a short satire closing with a point of wit. Wit, in our present sense, was yet unpractised, and the modern epigram was not yet discovered, Ben Jonson has composed books of epigrams; but, though he has censured Sir John Harrington's as not being epigrams, but mere narratives, has written himself in the prevalent style of his day. They are short poems on persons, and on incidents in his own life, which he poured out to relieve his own feelings when they were outraged, and, so far, they are a reflection of the poet's state of mind—the autobiography of his potent intellect. As among these epigrammatists we never had a Martial, so among these character-writers we could hardly expect a La Bruyère for his refined causticity; but the most skilful, as Sir Thomas Overbury and Bishop Earle, are so witty as to seem grotesque, but it is human nature disguised in the fashions of the day.[62]

This infection of style must have come from a higher source than a mere fashionable affectation of the day, for it endured through half a century. The axiomatic style of Bacon in his "Essaies," which first appeared in 1597, probably set the model of the curt period for these Senecas in prose and verse, who found no difficulty in putting together short sentences, without, however, having discovered the art of short thoughts.

This change in style is considered as characteristic of the age of James, but it began before his reign. The age of this monarch has been universally condemned as the age of pedantry, and of quibbles and conceits, all which, indeed, have been liberally ascribed to his taste; but in the plentiful evidence of his wit and humour, it would be difficult to find an instance of these bastard ornaments of style.

In the history of literature the names of sovereigns usually only serve to mark its dates; and an "author-sovereign," to use Lord Shaftesbury's emphatic expression, can exercise no prerogative, and yields even his precedence. In more than one respect JAMES THE FIRST may form an exception; for the barren list of his writings alone might serve to indicate the age; their subjects were not so peculiar to this monarch's taste as they were common with higher geniuses than his majesty.

When on the throne of England, it was deemed advisable to collect his majesty's writings, the honour of the editorship was conferred on Montague, Bishop of Winton, whom Fuller has characterised as "a potent courtier;" and the courtly potency of the prelatical editor effuses itself before the "majesty of kings" in the most awful of all prefaces.

Cavillers there were, who, on distinct principles, objected to a king being a writer of books, carrying on war "by the pen instead of the pike, and spending his passion on paper instead of powder." This was a military cry from those whose "occupation had long gone." Others, more critically nice, assumed that, "since writing of books had grown into a trade, it was as discreditable for a king to become an author as it would be for him to be a

---

62. Dr. Bliss has given an excellent edition of Bishop Earle's "Microcosmography, or a Piece of the World Discovered in Essays and Characters."

practitioner in a profession." Such objectors were not difficult to put down, and the bishop has furnished an ample catalogue of "royal authors" among all great nations; and, in our own, from Alfred to Elizabeth. The royal family of James were particularly distinguished for their literary acquirements. As that was the day when no argument could be urged without standing by the side of some authority, the bishop had done well, and no scholar in an upper class could have done better; but this bishop was imprudent, his restless courtliness fatigued his pen till he found a *divine origin of king-writing!* "The majesty of kings," he asserts, "is not unsuited to a writer of books;" and proceeds—"*The first royal author* is the King of kings—God himself, who doth so many things for our imitation. It pleased his divine wisdom to be *the first in this rank,* that we read of, that did *ever write.* He wrote on the tables on both sides, which was the work of God." This was in the miserable strain of those unnatural thoughts and remote analogies which were long to disfigure the compositions even of our scholars. How James and the bishop looked on one another at their first meeting, after this preface was fairly read, one would like to learn; but here we have the age!

One work by this royal author must not pass away with the others; it is not only stamped with the idiosyncrasy of the author, but it is one of those original effusions which are precious to the history of man. "THE BASILICON DORON, or His Majesty's Instructions to His Dearest Son Henry the Prince," is a genuine composition in the vernacular idiom; not the prescribed labour of a secretary, nor the artificial composition of the salaried literary man, but warm with the personal emotions of the royal author. He writes for the Prince of Scotland, and about the Scottish people; he instructs the prince even by his own errors and misfortunes. Some might be surprised to find the king strenuously warning the prince against pedantry; exhorting his pupil to avoid what he calls any "corrupt leide, as book-language and pen-and-ink terms;" counselling him *to write in his own language,* "for it best becometh a king to purify and make famous his own tongue." To have ventured on so complete an emancipation from the prevalent prejudices, in the creation of a vernacular literature, is one evidence, among many, that this royal author was not a mere pedant; and the truth is, that his writings on popular subjects are colloquially unostentatious; abstaining from those oratorical periods and rhetorical fancies which the scholar indulged in his speeches and proclamations—the more solemn labours of his own hand.

It is due to the literary character of James the First to notice his prompt sympathies with the productions of genius. This monarch had not exceeded his twentieth year when we find him in an intercourse with men of letters and science at home and abroad. The death of Sidney called forth an elegiac poem, and the works of the astronomer Tycho Brahe are adorned by a poetical tribute from the royal hand; during the winter the king passed in Denmark he was a frequent visitor of the philosopher, on whom he conferred an honour and a privilege. That he addressed a letter to Shakspeare, grateful for the compliments received in *Macbeth,* there is little reason to doubt; for Davenant, the possessor of the letter, which was finally lost, told it to the Duke of Buckingham; few traditions are so clearly traced to their source; and indeed some mark of James's attention to Shakspeare is positively told by Ben Jonson in his Elegy on "The Swan of Avon"—

> ——What a sight it were,
> To see thee on our waters yet appear;
> And make those flights upon the banks of Thames,
> That so did take Eliza and OUR JAMES![63]

Hooker was the favourite vernacular author of James; and his earliest inquiry, on his arrival in England, was after Hooker, whose death he deeply regretted. James wrote a congratulatory letter to Lord Bacon on his great work; the king at least bowed to the genius of the man. It was by the especial command of this royal "pedant," twenty-four years after the publication of Fairfax's *Tasso,* that a second edition revived that version; and he provided Herbert the poet with a sinecure or pension, that his muse might cease to be disturbed. James the First was not only the patron of Ben Jonson, but admitted the bard to a literary intercourse; and it is probable that we owe to those conferences some of the splendour of the Masques, and in which there are many strokes of the familiar acquaintance of the poet with his royal admirer. More grave and important objects sometimes engaged his attention. It was James the First who assigned to the learned Usher the task of unfolding the antiquities of the British churches; and it was under the protection of this monarch that Father Paul composed the famous history, which, as fast as it was written, was despatched to England by our ambassador, Sir Henry Wotton; and, in this country, this great history was first published. These are not the only testimonies of his strong affection for literature and literary men; but they may surprise some who only hear of a pedant-king, who in reality was only a "learned" one.

2. AUTHORS BY PROFESSION
(Calamities, vol. 5, pp. 7-15)

A GREAT author once surprised me by inquiring what I meant by "an Author

---

63. Every atom of candour is to be grudged to this hapless monarch; it is lamentable to see such a writer as Mr. Hallam prompt instantly to confirm a mere suggestion of Mr. Collier, that James could never have written a letter to Shakespeare, incapacitated to sympathize with the genial effusions of our poet.

by Profession." He seemed offended at the supposition that I was creating an odious distinction between authors. I was only placing it among their calamities.

The title of AUTHOR is venerable; and in the ranks of national glory, authors mingle with its heroes and its patriots. It is indeed by our authors that foreigners have been taught most to esteem us; and this remarkably appears in the expression of Gemelli, the Italian traveller round the world, who wrote about the year 1700; for he told all Europe that "he could find nothing amongst us but our writings to distinguish us from the worst of barbarians." But to become an "Author by Profession," is to have no other means of subsistence than such as are extracted from the quill; and no one believes these to be so precarious as they really are, until disappointed, distressed, and thrown out of every pursuit which can maintain independence, the noblest mind is cast into the lot of a doomed labourer.

Literature abounds with instances of "Authors by Profession" accommodating themselves to this condition. By vile artifices of faction and popularity their moral sense is injured, and the literary character sits in that study which he ought to dignify, merely, as one of them sings,

To keep his mutton twirling at the fire.

Another has said, "He is a fool who is a grain honester than the times he lives in."

Let it not, therefore be conceived that I mean to degrade or vilify the literary character, when I would only separate the Author from those polluters of the press who have turned a vestal into a prostitute; a grotesque race of famished buffoons or laughing assassins; or that populace of unhappy beings, who are driven to perish in their garrets, unknown and unregarded by all, for illusions which even their calamities cannot disperse. Poverty, said an ancient, is a sacred thing—it is, indeed, so sacred, that it creates a sympathy even for those who have incurred it by their folly, or plead by it for their crimes.

The history of our Literature is instructive—let us trace the origin of characters of this sort among us: some of them have happily disappeared, and, whenever great authors obtain their due rights, the calamities of literature will be greatly diminished.

As for the phrase of "Authors by Profession," it is said to be of modern origin; and GUTHRIE, a great dealer in literature, and a political scribe, is thought to have introduced it, as descriptive of a class of writers which he wished to distinguish from the general term. I present the reader with an unpublished letter of Guthrie, in which the phrase will not only be found, but, what is more important, which exhibits the character in its degraded form. It was addressed to a minister.

"My Lord,   *June* 3, 1762.

"In the year 1745-6, Mr. Pelham, then First Lord of the Treasury, acquainted me, that it was his Majesty's pleasure I should receive, till better provided for, which never has happened, 200*l.* a-year, to be paid by him and his successors in the Treasury. I was satisfied with the august name made use of, and the appointment has been regularly and quarterly paid me ever since. I have been equally punctual in doing the government all the services that fell within my abilities or sphere of life, especially in those critical situations that call for unanimity in the service of the crown.

"Your Lordship may possibly now suspect that *I am an Author by Profession:* you are not deceived; and will be less so, if you believe that I am disposed to serve his Majesty under your Lordship's *future patronage and protection, with greater zeal, if possible, than ever.*

"I have the honour to be,

"My Lord, &c.,

"William Guthrie."

Unblushing venality! In one part he shouts like a plundering hussar who has carried off his prey; and in the other he bows with the tame suppleness of the "quarterly" Swiss chattering his halbert for his price;—"to serve his Majesty" for—"his Lordship's future patronage."

Guthrie's notion of "An Author by Profession," entirely derived from his own character, was twofold; literary taskwork, and political degradation. He was to be a gentleman convertible into an historian, at——per sheet; and, when he had not time to write histories, he chose to sell his name to those he never wrote. These are mysteries of the craft of authorship; in this sense it is only a trade, and a very bad one! But when in his other capacity, this gentleman comes to hire himself to one lord as he had to another, no one can doubt that the stipendiary would change his principles with his livery.[64]

Such have been some of the "Authors by Profession" who have worn the literary mask; for literature was not the first object of their designs. They form a race peculiar to our country. They opened their career in our first great revolution, and flourished during the eventful period of the civil wars. In the form of newspapers, their "Mercuries" and "Diurnals" were political pamphlets.[65] Of these, the Royalists, being the better educated, carried off to

---

64. It has been lately disclosed that Home, the author of "Douglas," was pensioned by Lord Bute to answer all the papers and pamphlets of the Government, and to be a vigilant defender of the measures of Government.

65. I have elsewhere portrayed the personal characters of the hireling chiefs of these paper wars: the versatile and unprincipled Marchmont Needham, the Cobbett of his day; the factious Sir Roger L'Estrange; and the bantering and profligate Sir John Birkenhead.

their side all the spirit, and only left the foam and dregs for the Parliamentarians; otherwise, in lying, they were just like one another; for "the father of lies" seems to be of no party! Were it desirable to instruct men by a system of political and moral calumny, the complete art might be drawn from these archives of political lying, during their flourishing era. We might discover principles among them which would have humbled the genius of Machiavel himself, and even have taught Mr. Sheridan's more popular scribe, Mr. Puff, a sense of his own inferiority.

It is known that, during the administration of Harley and Walpole, this class of authors swarmed and started up like mustard-seed in a hot-bed. More than fifty thousand pounds were expended among them! Faction, with mad and blind passions, can affix a value on the basest things that serve its purpose.[66] These "Authors by Profession" wrote more assiduously the better they were paid; but as attacks only produced replies and rejoinders, to remunerate them was heightening the fever and feeding the disease. They were all fighting for present pay, with a view of the promised land before them; but they at length became so numerous, and so crowded on one another, that the minister could neither satisfy promised claims nor actual dues. He had not at last the humblest office to bestow, not a commissionership of wine licences, as Tacitus Gordon had: not even a collectorship of the customs in some obscure town, as was the wretched worn-out Oldmixon's pittance;[67] not a crumb for a mouse!

The captain of this banditti in the administration of Walpole was Arnall, a young attorney, whose mature genius for scurrilous party-papers broke forth in his tender nonage. This hireling was "The Free Briton," and in "The Gazetteer" *Francis Walsingham, Esq.*, abusing the name of a profound statesman. It is said that he received above ten thousand pounds for his obscure labours; and this patriot was suffered to retire with all the dignity

---

66. An ample view of these lucubrations is exhibited in the early volumes of the *Gentleman's Magazine.*

67. It was said of this man that "he had submitted to labour at the press, like a horse in a mill, till he became as blind and as wretched." To show the extent of the conscience of this class of writers, and to what lengths mere party-writers can proceed, when duly encouraged, Oldmixon, who was a Whig historian, if a violent party-writer ought ever to be dignified by so venerable a title, unmercifully rigid to all other historians, was himself guilty of the crimes with which he so loudly accused others. He charged three eminent persons with interpolating Lord Clarendon's History; this charge was afterwards disproved by the passages being produced in his Lordship's own handwriting, which had been fortunately preserved; and yet this accuser of interpolation, when employed by Bishop Kennett to publish his collection of our historians, made no scruple of falsifying numerous passages in Daniel's Chronicle, which makes the first edition of that collection of no value.

which a pension could confer. He not only wrote for hire, but valued himself on it; proud of the pliancy of his pen and of his principles, he wrote without remorse what his patron was forced to pay for, but to disavow. It was from a knowledge of the "Authors by Profession," writers of a faction in the name of the community, as they have been well described, that our great statesman Pitt fell into an error which he lived to regret. He did not distinguish between authors; he confounded the mercenary with the men of talent and character; and with this contracted view of the political influence of genius, he must have viewed with awe, perhaps with surprise, its mighty labour in the volumes of Burke.

But these "Authors by Profession" sometimes found a retribution of their crimes even from their masters. When the ardent patron was changed into a cold minister, their pen seemed wonderfully to have lost its point, and the feather could not any more tickle. They were flung off, as Shakspeare's striking imagery expresses it, like

> An unregarded bulrush on the stream,
> To rot itself with motion.

Look on the fate and fortune of AMHURST. The life of this "Author by Profession" points a moral. He flourished about the year 1730. He passed through a youth of iniquity, and was expelled his college for his irregularities: he had exhibited no marks of regeneration when he assailed the university with the periodical paper of the *Terræ Filius;* a witty Saturnalian effusion on the manners and Toryism of Oxford, where the portraits have an extravagant kind of likeness, and are so false and so true that they were universally relished and individually understood. Amhurst, having lost his character, hastened to reform the morals and politics of the nation. For near twenty years he toiled at "The Craftsman," of which ten thousand are said to have been sold in one day. Admire this patriot! an expelled collegian becomes an outrageous zealot for popular reform, and an intrepid Whig can bend to be yoked to all the drudgery of a faction! Amhurst succeeded in writing out the minister, and writing in Bolingbroke and Pulteney. Now came the hour of gratitude and generosity. His patrons mounted into power—but—they silently dropped the instrument of their ascension. The political prostitute stood shivering at the gate of preferment, which his masters had for ever flung against him. He died broken-hearted, and owed the charity of a grave to his bookseller.

I must add one more striking example of a political author in the case of Dr. JAMES DRAKE, a man of genius, and an excellent writer. He resigned an honourable profession, that of medicine, to adopt a very contrary one, that of becoming an author by profession for a party. As a Tory writer, he dared every extremity of the law, while he evaded it by every subtlety of artifice; he sent a masked lady with his MS. to the printer, who was never discovered, and was once saved by a flaw in the indictment from the simple change of an *r* for a *t*, or *nor* for *not;*—one of those shameful evasions by which the law, to its perpetual disgrace, so often protects the criminal from punishment. Dr. Drake had the honour of hearing himself censured from the throne; of being imprisoned; of seeing his "Memorials of the Church of England" burned at London, and his "Historia Anglo-Scotica" at Edinburgh. Having enlisted himself in the pay of the booksellers, among other works, I suspect, he condescended to practise some literary impositions. For he has reprinted Father Parson's famous libel against the Earl of Leicester in Elizabeth's reign, under the title of "Secret Memoirs of Robert Dudley, Earl of Leicester, 1706," 8vo, with a preface pretending it was printed from an old MS.

Drake was a lover of literature; he left behind him a version of Herodotus, and a "System of Anatomy," once the most popular and curious of its kind. After all this turmoil of his literary life, neither his masked lady nor the flaws in his indictments availed him. Government brought a writ of error, severely prosecuted him; and, abandoned, as usual, by those for whom he had annihilated a genius which deserved a better fate, his perturbed spirit broke out into a fever, and he died raving against cruel persecutors, and patrons not much more humane.

So much for some of those who have been "Authors by Profession" in one of the twofold capacities which Guthrie designed, that of writing for a minister; the other, that of writing for the bookseller, though far more honourable, is sufficiently calamitous.

In commercial times, the hope of profit is always a stimulating, but a degrading motive; it dims the clearest intellect, it stills the proudest feelings. Habit and prejudice will soon reconcile even genius to the work of money, and to avow the motive without a blush. "An author by profession," at once ingenious and ingenuous, declared that, "till fame appears to be worth more than money, he would always prefer money to fame." JOHNSON had a notion that there existed no motive for writing but money! Yet, crowned heads have sighed with the ambition of authorship, though this great master of the human mind could suppose that on this subject men were not actuated either by the love of glory or of pleasure! FIELDING, an author of great genius and of "the profession," in one of his "Covent-garden Journals" asserts, that "An author, in a country where there is no public provision for men of genius, is not obliged to be a more disinterested patriot than any other. Why is he whose *livelihood is in his pen* a greater monster in using it to serve himself, than he who uses his tongue for the same purpose?"

But it is a very important question to ask, is this "livelihood in the pen" really such? Authors drudging on in obscurity, and enduring miseries which can never close but with their life—shall this be worth even the humble designation of a "livelihood?" I am not now combating with them whether their taskwork degrades them, but whether they are receiving an equivalent for the violation of their genius, for the weight of the fetters they are wearing, and for the entailed miseries which form an author's sole legacies to his widow and his children. Far from me is the wish to degrade literature by the inquiry; but it will be useful to many a youth of promising talent, who is impatient to abandon all professions for this one, to consider well the calamities in which he will most probably participate.

Among "Authors by Profession" who has displayed a more fruitful genius, and exercised more intense industry, with a loftier sense of his independence, than SMOLLETT? But look into his life and enter into his feelings, and you will be shocked at the disparity of his situation with the genius of the man. His life was a succession of struggles, vexations, and disappointments, yet of success in his writings. Smollett, who is a great poet, though he has written little in verse, and whose rich genius composed the most original pictures of human life, was compelled by his wants to debase his name by selling it to voyages and translations, which he never could have read. When he had worn himself down in the service of the public or the booksellers, there remained not, of all his slender remunerations, in the last stage of life, sufficient to convey him to a cheap country and a restorative air on the Continent. The father may have thought himself fortunate, that the daughter whom he loved with more than common affection was no more to share in his wants; but the husband had by his side the faithful companion of his life, left without a wreck of fortune. Smollett, gradually perishing in a foreign land, neglected by an admiring public, and without fresh resources from the booksellers, who were receiving the income of his works, threw out his injured feelings in the character of *Bramble;* the warm generosity of his temper, but not his genius, seemed fleeting with his breath. In a foreign land his widow marked by a plain monument the spot of his burial, and she perished in solitude! Yet Smollett dead—soon an ornamented column is raised at the place of his birth, while the grave of the author seemed to multiply the editions of his works. There are indeed grateful feelings in the public at large for a favourite author; but the awful testimony of those feelings, by its gradual progress, must appear beyond the grave! They visit the column consecrated by his name, and his features are most loved, most venerated, in the bust.

Smollett himself shall be the historian of his own heart; this most successful "Author by Profession," who, for his subsistence, composed masterworks of genius, and drudged in the toils of slavery, shall himself tell us what happened, and describe that state between life and death, partaking of both, which obscured the faculties and sickened his lofty spirit.

"Had some of those who were pleased to call themselves my friends been at any pains to deserve the character, and told me ingenuously what I had to expect in *the capacity of an author, when I first professed myself of that venerable fraternity*, I should in all probability have spared myself the *incredible labour and chagrin I have since undergone.*"

As a relief from literary labour, Smollett once went to revisit his family, and to embrace the mother he loved; but such was the irritation of his mind and the infirmity of his health, exhausted by the hard labours of authorship, that he never passed a more weary summer, nor ever found himself so incapable of indulging the warmest emotions of his heart. On his return, in a letter, he gave this melancholy narrative of himself:—"Between friends, I am now convinced that *my brain was in some measure affected;* for I had a kind of *Coma Vigil* upon me from April to November, without intermission. In consideration of this circumstance, I know you will forgive all my peevishness and discontent; tell Mrs. Moore that with regard to me, she has as yet seen nothing but the wrong side of the tapestry." Thus it happens in the life of authors, that they whose comic genius diffuses cheerfulness, create a pleasure which they cannot themselves participate.

The *Coma Vigil* may be described by a verse of Shakspeare:—

Still-waking sleep! That is not what it is!

Of praise and censure, says Smollett, in a letter to Dr. Moore, "Indeed I am sick of both, and wish to God my circumstances would allow me to consign my pen to oblivion." A wish, as fervently repeated by many "Authors by Profession," who are not so fully entitled as was Smollett to write when he chose, or to have lived in quiet for what he had written. An author's life is therefore too often deprived of all social comfort whether he be the writer for a minister, or a bookseller—but their case requires to be stated.

3. THE MALADIES OF AUTHORS
(*Calamities*, vol. 5, pp. 70-75)

THE practice of every art subjects the artist to some particular inconvenience, usually inflicting some malady on that member which has been over-wrought by excess: nature abused, pursues man into his most secret corners, and avenges herself. In the athletic exercises of the ancient Gymnasium, the pugilists were observed to become lean from their hips downwards, while the superior parts of their bodies, which they over-exercised, were prodigiously swollen; on the contrary, the racers were meagre upwards, while their feet acquired an unnatural dimension. The secret source of life seems to be carried forwards to those parts which are making the most continued efforts.

In all sedentary labours, some particular malady is contracted by every worker, derived from particular postures of the body and peculiar habits. Thus the weaver, the tailor, the painter, and the glass-blower, have all their respective maladies. The diamond-cutter, with a furnace before him, may be said almost to live in one; the slightest air must be shut out of the apartment, lest it scatter away the precious dust—a breath would ruin him!

The analogy is obvious;[68] and the author must participate in the common fate of all sedentary occupations. But his maladies, from the very nature of the delicate organ of thinking, intensely exercised, are more terrible than those of any other profession; they are more complicated, more hidden in their causes, and the mysterious union and secret influence of the faculties of the soul over those of the body, are visible, yet still incomprehensible; they frequently produce a perturbation in the faculties, a state of acute irritability, and many sorrows and infirmities, which are not likely to create much sympathy from those around the author, who, at a glance, could have discovered where the pugilist or the racer became meagre or monstrous: the intellectual malady eludes even the tenderness of friendship.

The more obvious maladies engendered by the life of a student arise from over-study. These have furnished a curious volume to Tissot, in his treatise "On the Health of Men of Letters;" a book, however, which chills and terrifies more than it does good.

The unnatural fixed postures, the perpetual activity of the mind, and the inaction of the body; the brain exhausted with assiduous toil deranging the nerves, vitiating the digestive powers, disordering its own machinery, and breaking the calm of sleep by that previous state of excitement which study throws us into, are some of the calamities of a studious life: for like the ocean when its swell is subsiding, the waves of the mind too still heave and beat; hence all the small feverish symptoms, and the whole train of hypochondriac affections, as well as some acute ones.[69]

---

68. Hawkesworth, in the second paper of the "Adventurer," has composed, from his own feelings, an elegant description of intellectual and corporeal labour, and the sufferings of an author, with the uncertainty of his labour and his reward.

69. Dr. Fuller's "Medicina Gymnastica, or, a treatise concerning the power of Exercise, with respect to the Animal Œconomy, fifth edition, 1718," is useful to remind the student of what he is apt to forget; for the object of this volume is to *substitute exercise for medicine.* He wrote the book before he became a physician. He considers horse-riding as the best and noblest of all exercises, it being "a mixed exercise, partly active and partly passive, while other sports, such as walking, running, stooping, or the like, require some labour and more strength for their performance." Cheyne, in his well-known treatise of "The English Malady," published about twenty years after Fuller's work, acknowledges that riding on horseback is the best of all exercises, for which he details his reasons. "Walking," he says, "though it will answer the same end, yet is it more laborious and tiresome;" but amusement ought always to be combined with the exercise of a student; the mind will receive no refreshment by a solitary walk or ride, unless it be agreeably withdrawn from all thoughtfulness and anxiety; if it continue studying in its recreations, it is the sure means of obtaining

Among the correspondents of the poets Hughes and Thomson, there is a pathetic letter from a student. Alexander Bayne, to prepare his lectures, studied fourteen hours a-day for eight months successively, and wrote 1,600 sheets. Such intense application, which, however, not greatly exceeds that of many authors, brought on the bodily complaints he has minutely described, with "all the dispiriting symptoms of a nervous illness, commonly called vapours, or lowness of spirits." Bayne, who was of an athletic temperament, imagined he had not paid attention to his diet, to the lowness of his desk, and his habit of sitting with a particular compression of the body; in future all these were to be avoided. He prolonged his life for five years, and, perhaps, was still flattering his hopes of sharing one day in the literary celebrity of his friends, when, to use his words, "the same illness made a fierce attack upon me again, and has kept me in a very bad state of inactivity and disrelish of all my ordinary amusements:" those *amusements* were his serious *studies*. There is a fascination in literary labour: the student feeds on magical drugs; to withdraw him from them requires nothing less than that greater magic which could break his own spells. A few months after this letter was written Bayne died on the way to Bath, a martyr to his studies.

The excessive labour on a voluminous work, which occupies a long life, leaves the student with a broken constitution, and his sight decayed or lost. The most admirable observer of mankind, and the truest painter of the human heart, declares, "The corruptible body presseth down the soul, and the earthy tabernacle weigheth down the *mind that museth on many things*." Of this class was old Randle Cotgrave, the curious collector of the most copious dictionary of old French and old English words and phrases. The work is the only treasury of our genuine idiom. Even this labour of the lexicographer, so copious and so elaborate, must have been projected with rapture, and pursued

---

neither of its objects—a friend, not an author, will at such a moment be the better companion.

The last chapter in Fuller's work contains much curious reading on the ancient physicians, and their gymnastic courses, which Asclepiades, the pleasantest of all the ancient physicians, greatly studied; he was most fortunate in the invention of exercises to supply the place of much physic, and (says Fuller) no man in any age ever had the happiness to obtain so general an applause; Pliny calls him the delight of mankind. Admirable physician, who had so many ways, it appears, to make physic agreeable! He invented the *lecti pensiles*, or hanging beds, that the sick might be rocked to sleep; which took so much at that time, that they became a great luxury among the Romans.

Fuller judiciously does not recommend the gymnastic course, because horse-riding, for persons of delicate constitutions, is preferable; he discovers too the reason why the ancients did not introduce this mode of exercise—it arose from the simple circumstance of their not knowing the use of stirrups, which was a later invention. Riding with the ancients was, therefore, only an exercise for the healthy and the robust; a horse without stirrups was a formidable animal for a valetudinarian.

with pleasure, till, in the progress, "the mind was musing on many things." Then came the melancholy doubt, that drops mildew from its enveloping wings over the voluminous labour of a laborious author, whether he be wisely consuming his days, and not perpetually neglecting some higher duties or some happier amusements. Still the enchanted delver sighs, and strikes on in the glimmering mine of hope. If he live to complete the great labour, it is, perhaps, reserved for the applause of the next age; for, as our great lexicographer exclaimed, "In this gloom of solitude I have protracted my work, till those whom I wished to please have sunk into the grave, and success and miscarriage are empty sounds;" but, if it be applauded in his own, that praise has come too late for him whose literary labour has stolen away his sight. Cotgrave had grown blind over his dictionary, and was doubtful whether this work of his laborious days and nightly vigils was not a superfluous labour, and nothing, after all, but a "poor bundle of words." The reader may listen to the gray-headed martyr addressing his patron, Lord Burghley:

"I present to your lordship an account of the *expense of many hours*, which, in your service, and to mine own benefit, *might have been otherwise employed*. My desires have aimed at more substantial marks; but *mine eyes* failed them, and forced me to *spend out their vigour in this bundle of words*, which may be unworthy of your lordship's great patience, and, perhaps, *ill-suited to the expectation of others*."

A great number of young authors have died of over-study. An intellectual enthusiasm, accompanied by constitutional delicacy, has swept away half the rising genius of the age. Curious calculators have affected to discover the average number of infants who die under the age of five years: had they investigated those of the children of genius who perish before their thirtieth year, we should not be less amazed at this waste of man. There are few scenes more afflicting, nor which more deeply engage our sympathy, than that of a youth, glowing with the devotion of study, and resolute to distinguish his name among his countrymen, while death is stealing on him, touching with premature age, before he strikes the last blow. The author perishes on the very pages which give a charm to his existence. The fine taste and tender melancholy of Headley, the fervid genius of Henry Kirke White, will not easily pass away; but how many youths as noble-minded have not had the fortune of Kirke White to be commemorated by genius, and have perished without their fame! Henry Wharton is a name well known to the student of English literature; he published historical criticisms of high value; and he left, as some of the fruits of his studies, sixteen volumes of MS. preserved in the Archiepiscopal Library at Lambeth. These great labours were pursued with the ardour that only could have produced them; the author had not exceeded his thirtieth year when he sank under his continued studies, and perished a martyr to literature. Our literary history abounds with instances of the sad effects of an over indulgence in study: that agreeable writer, Howel, had nearly lost his life by an excess of this nature, studying through long nights in the depth of winter. This severe study occasioned an imposthume in his head; he was eighteen days without sleep; and the illness was attended with many other afflicting symptoms. The eager diligence of Blackmore, protracting his studies through the night, broke his health, and obliged him to fly to a country retreat. Harris, the historian, died of a consumption by midnight studies, as his friend Hollis mentions. I shall add a recent instance, which I myself witnessed: it is that of John Macdiarmid. He was one of those Scotch students whom the golden fame of Hume and Robertson attracted to the metropolis. He mounted the first steps of literary adventure with credit; and passed through the probation of editor and reviewer, till he strove for more heroic adventures. He published some volumes, whose subjects display the aspirings of his genius: "An Inquiry into the Nature of Civil and Military Subordination;" another into "the System of Military Defence." It was during these labours I beheld this inquirer, of a tender frame, emaciated, and study-worn, with hollow eyes, where the mind dimly shone like a lamp in a tomb. With keen ardour he opened a new plan of biographical politics. When, by one who wished the author was in better condition, the dangers of excess in study were brought to his recollection, he smiled, and, with something of a mysterious air, talked of unalterable confidence in the powers of his mind; of the indefinite improvement in our faculties: and, with this enfeebled frame, considered himself capable of continuous labour. His whole life, indeed, was one melancholy trial. Often the day cheerfully passed without its meal, but never without its page. The new system of political biography was advancing, when our young author felt a paralytic stroke. He afterwards resumed his pen; and a second one proved fatal. He lived just to pass through the press his "Lives of British Statesmen," a splendid quarto, whose publication he owed to the generous temper of a friend, who, when the author could not readily procure a publisher, would not see the dying author's last hope disappointed. Some research and reflection are combined in this literary and civil history of the sixteenth and seventeenth centuries; but it was written with the blood of the author, for Macdiarmid died of over-study and exhaustion.

Among the maladies of poor authors, who procure a precarious existence by their pen, one, not the least considerable, is their old age; their flower and maturity of life were shed for no human comforts; and old age is the withered root. The late THOMAS MORTIMER, the compiler, among other things, of that useful work, "The Student's Pocket Dictionary," felt this severely—he himself experienced no abatement of his ardour, nor deficiency in his intellectual powers, at near the age of eighty;—but he then would complain "of the paucity of literary employment, and the preference given to young adventurers." Such is the *youth*, and such the *old age* of ordinary authors!

4. THE BIBLIOMANIA
(*Curiosities*, vol. 1, pp. 9-12)

THE [...] article ["Libraries," pp. 222-228 below] is honourable to literature, yet even a passion for collecting books is not always a passion for literature.

The BIBLIOMANIA, or the collecting an enormous heap of books without intelligent curiosity, has, since libraries have existed, infected weak minds, who imagine that they themselves acquire knowledge when they keep it on their shelves. Their motley libraries have been called the *madhouses of the human mind;* and again, *the tomb of books,* when the possessor will not communicate them, and coffins them up in the cases of his library. It was facetiously observed, these collections are not without a *Lock on the Human Understanding.*[70]

The BIBLIOMANIA never raged more violently than in our own times. It is fortunate that literature is in no ways injured by the follies of collectors, since though they preserve the worthless, they necessarily protect the good.[71]

Some collectors place all their fame on the *view* of a splendid library, where volumes, arrayed in all the pomp of lettering, silk linings, triple gold bands, and tinted leather, are locked up in wire cases, and secured from the vulgar

---

70. An allusion and pun which occasioned the French translator of the present work an unlucky blunder: puzzled, no doubt, by my *facetiously,* he translates "mettant, comme on l'a *très-judicieusement* fait observer, l'entendement humain sous la clef." The great work and the great author alluded to, having quite escaped him!

71. The earliest satire on the mere book-collector is to be found in Barclay's translation of Brandt's "Ship of Fools," first printed by Wynkyn de Worde, in 1508. He thus announces his true position :—

> I am the first fool of the whole navie
> To keepe the poupe, the helme, and eke the sayle:
> For this is my minde, this one pleasure have I,
> Of bookes to have greate plentie and apparayle.
> Still I am busy bookes assembling,
> For to have plenty it is a pleasaunt thing
> In my conceyt, and to have them aye in hande:
> But what they meane do I not understande.
> But yet I have them in great reverence
> And honoure, saving them from filth and ordure,
> By often brushing and much diligence;
> Full goodly bound in pleasaunt coverture,
> Of damas, satten, or else of velvet pure:
> I keepe them sure, fearing least they should be lost,
> For in them is the cunning wherein I me boast.

hands of the *mere reader*, dazzling our eyes like eastern beauties peering through their jalousies!

LA BRUYERE has touched on this mania with humour:—"Of such a collector, as soon as I enter his house, I am ready to faint on the staircase, from a strong smell of Morocco leather. In vain he shows me fine editions, gold leaves, Etruscan bindings, and naming them one after another, as if he were showing a gallery of pictures! a gallery, by-the-bye, which he seldom traverses when *alone*, for he rarely reads; but me he offers to conduct through it! I thank him for his politeness, and as little as himself care to visit the tan-house, which he calls his library."

LUCIAN has composed a biting invective against an ignorant possessor of a vast library, like him, who in the present day, after turning over the pages of an old book, chiefly admires the *date*. LUCIAN compares him to a pilot, who was never taught the science of navigation; to a rider who cannot keep his seat on a spirited horse; to a man who, not having the use of his feet, would conceal the defect by wearing embroidered shoes; but, alas! he cannot stand in them! He ludicrously compares him to Thersites wearing the armour of Achilles, tottering at every step; leering with his little eyes under his enormous helmet, and his hunchback raising the cuirass above his shoulders. Why do you buy so many books? You have no hair, and you purchase a comb; you are blind, and you will have a grand mirror; you are deaf, and you will have fine musical instruments! Your costly bindings are only a source of vexation, and you are continually discharging your librarians for not preserving them from the silent invasion of the worms, and the nibbling triumphs of the rats!

Such *collectors* will contemptuously smile at the *collection* of the amiable Melancthon. He possessed in his library only four authors,—Plato, Pliny, Plutarch, and Ptolemy the geographer.

Ancillon was a great collector of curious books, and dexterously defended himself when accused of the *Bibliomania*. He gave a good reason for buying the most elegant editions; which he did not consider merely as a literary luxury.[72] The less the eyes are fatigued in reading a work, the more liberty the

---

72. David Ancillon was born at Metz in 1617. From his earliest years his devotion to study was so great as to call for the interposition of his father, to prevent his health being seriously affected by it; he was described as "intemperately studious." The Jesuits of Metz gave him the free range of their college library; but his studies led him to Protestantism, and in 1633 he removed to Geneva, and devoted himself to the duties of the Reformed Church. Throughout an honourable life he retained unabated his love of books; and having a fortune by marriage, he gratified himself in constantly collecting them, so that he ultimately possessed one of the finest private libraries in France. For very many years his life passed peaceably and happily amid his books and his duties, when the revocation of the Edict of Nantes drove him from his country. His noble library was scattered at waste-paper prices, "thus in a single day was

mind feels to judge of it: and as we perceive more clearly the excellences and defects of a printed book than when in MS.; so we see them more plainly in good paper and clear type, than when the impression and paper are both bad. He always purchased *first editions*, and never waited for second ones; though it is the opinion of some that a first edition is only to be considered as an imperfect essay, which the author proposes to finish after he has tried the sentiments of the literary world. Bayle approves of Ancillon's plan. Those who wait for a book till it is reprinted, show plainly that they prefer the saving of a pistole to the acquisition of knowledge. With one of these persons, who waited for a second edition, which never appeared, a literary man argued, that it was better to have two editions of a book rather than to deprive himself of the advantage which the reading of the first might procure him. It has frequently happened, besides, that in second editions, the author omits, as well as adds, or makes alterations from prudential reasons; the displeasing truths which he *corrects*, as he might call them, are so many losses incurred by Truth itself. There is an advantage in comparing the first and subsequent editions; among other things, we feel great satisfaction in tracing the variations of a work after its revision. There are also other secrets, well known to the intelligent curious, who are versed in affairs relating to books. Many first editions are not to be purchased for the treble value of later ones. The collector we have noticed frequently said, as is related of Virgil, "I collect gold from Ennius's dung." I find, in some neglected authors, particular things, not elsewhere to be found. He read many of these, but not with equal attention—"*Sicut canis ad Nilum, bibens et fugiens;*" like a dog at the Nile, drinking and running.

Fortunate are those who only consider a book for the utility and pleasure they may derive from its possession. Students, who know much, and still thirst to know more, may require this vast sea of books; yet in that sea they may suffer many shipwrecks.

Great collections of books are subject to certain accidents besides the damp, the worms, and the rats; one not less common is that of the *borrowers*, not to say a word of the *purloiners!*

5. A BIBLIOGNOSTE
(*Curiosities*, vol. 3, pp. 340-346)

A STARTLING literary prophecy, recently sent forth from our oracular literature, threatens the annihilation of public libraries, which are one day to

---

destroyed the labour, care, and expense of forty-four years." He died seven years afterwards at Brandenburg.

moulder away!

Listen to the vaticinator! "As conservatories of mental treasures, their value in times of darkness and barbarity was incalculable; and even in these happier days, when men are incited to explore new regions of thought, they command respect as depôts of methodical and well-ordered references for the researches of the curious. But what in one state of society is invaluable, may at another be worthless; and the progress which the world has made within a very few centuries has considerably reduced the estimation which is due to such establishments. We will say more—"[73] but enough! This idea of striking into dust "the god of his idolatry," the Dagon of his devotion, is sufficient to terrify the bibliographer, who views only a blind Samson pulling down the pillars of his temple!

This future universal inundation of books, this superfluity of knowledge, in billions and trillions, overwhelms the imagination! It is now about four hundred years since the art of multiplying books has been discovered; and an arithmetician has attempted to calculate the incalculable of these four ages of typography, which he discovers have actually produced 3,641,960 works! Taking each work at three volumes, and reckoning only each impression to consist of three hundred copies, which is too little, the actual amount from the presses of Europe will give to 1816, 3,277,764,000 volumes! each of which being an inch thick, if placed on a line, would cover 6069 leagues! Leibnitz facetiously maintained that such would be the increase of literature, that future generations would find whole cities insufficient to contain their libraries. We are, however, indebted to the patriotic endeavours of our grocers and trunkmakers, alchemists of literature! they annihilate the gross bodies without injuring the finer spirits. We are still more indebted to that neglected race, the bibliographers!

The science of books, for so bibliography is sometimes dignified, may deserve the gratitude of a public, who are yet insensible of the useful zeal of those book-practitioners, the nature of whose labours is yet so imperfectly comprehended. Who is this vaticinator of the uselessness of public libraries? Is he a *bibliognoste*, or a *bibliographe*, or a *bibliomane*, or a *bibliophile*, or a *bibliotaphe*? A *bibliothecaire*, or a *bibliopole*, the prophet cannot be; for the *bibliothecaire* is too delightfully busied among his shelves, and the *bibliopole* is too profitably concerned in furnishing perpetual additions to admit of this hyperbolical terror of annihilation![74]

---

73. "Edinburgh Review," vol. xxxiv. 384.

74. Will this writer pardon me for ranking him, for a moment, among those "generalisers" of the age who excel in what a critical friend has happily discriminated as *ambitious writing?* that is, writing on any topic, and not least strikingly on that of which they know least; men otherwise of fine taste, and who excel in every charm of composition.

Unawares, we have dropped into that professional jargon which was chiefly forged by one who, though seated in the "scorner's chair," was the Thaumaturgus of books and manuscripts. The Abbé Rive had acquired a singular taste and curiosity, not without a fermenting dash of singular *charlatanerie*, in bibliography: the little volumes he occasionally put forth are things which but few hands have touched. He knew well, that for some books to be noised about, they should not be read: this was one of those recondite mysteries of his, which we may have occasion farther to reveal. This bibliographical hero was librarian to the most magnificent of book-collectors, the Duke de la Vallière. The Abbé Rive was a strong but ungovernable brute, rabid, surly, but *très-mordant.* His master, whom I have discovered to have been the partner of the cur's tricks, would often pat him; and when the *bibliognostes,* and the *bibliomanes* were in the heat of contest, let his "bull-dog" loose among them, as the duke affectionately called his librarian. The "bull-dog" of bibliography appears, too, to have had the taste and appetite of the tiger of politics, but he hardly lived to join the festival of the guillotine. I judge of this by an expression he used to one complaining of his parish priest, whom he advised to give "une messe dans son ventre!" He had tried to exhaust his genius in *La Chasse aux Bibliographes et aux Antiquaires mal avisés*, and acted Cain with his brothers! All Europe was to receive from him new ideas concerning books and manuscripts. Yet all his mighty promises fumed away in projects; and though he appeared for ever correcting the blunders of others, this French Ritson left enough of his own to afford them a choice of revenge. His style of criticism was perfectly *Ritsonian.* He describes one of his rivals as *l'insolent et très-insensé auteur de l'Almanach de Gotha,* on the simple subject of the origin of playing-cards!

The Abbé Rive was one of those men of letters, of whom there are not a few who pass all their lives in preparations. Dr. Dibdin, since the above was written, has witnessed the confusion of the mind and the gigantic industry of our *bibliognoste,* which consisted of many trunks full of *memoranda.* The description will show the reader to what hard hunting these book-hunters voluntarily doom themselves, with little hope of obtaining fame! "In one trunk were about *six thousand* notices of MSS. of all ages. In another were wedged about *twelve thousand* descriptions of books in all languages, except those of French and Italian; sometimes with critical notes. In a third trunk was a bundle of papers relating to the *History of the Troubadours.* In a fourth was a collection of memoranda and literary sketches connected with the invention of arts and sciences, with pieces exclusively bibliographical. A fifth trunk contained between *two* and *three thousand* cards, written upon each side, respecting a collection of prints. In a sixth trunk were contained his papers respecting earthquakes, volcanoes, and geographical subjects."[75] This *Ajax flagellifer* of the bibliographical tribe, who was, as Dr. Dibdin observes, "the terror of his acquaintance, and the pride of his patron," is said to have been in private a very different man from his public character; all which may be true, without altering a shade of that public character. The French Revolution showed how men, mild and even kind in domestic life, were sanguinary and ferocious in their public.

The rabid Abbé Rive gloried in terrifying, without enlightening his rivals; he exulted that he was devoting to "the rods of criticism and the laughter of Europe the *bibliopoles*," or dealers in books, who would not get by heart his "Catechism" of a thousand and one questions and answers: it broke the slumbers of honest De Bure, who had found life was already too short for his own "Bibliographie Instructive."

The Abbé Rive had contrived to catch the shades of the appellatives necessary to discriminate book amateurs; and of the first term he is acknowledged to be the inventor.

A *bibliognoste*, from the Greek, is one knowing in title-pages and colophons, and in editions; the place and year when printed; the presses whence issued; and all the *minutiæ* of a book.

A *bibliographe* is a describer of books and other literary arrangements.

A *bibliomane* is an indiscriminate accumulator, who blunders faster than he buys, cock-brained, and purse-heavy!

A *bibliophile*, the lover of books, is the only one in the class who appears to read them for his own pleasure.

A *bibliotaphe* buries his books, by keeping them under lock, or framing them in glass cases.

I shall catch our *bibliognoste* in the hour of book-rapture! It will produce a collection of bibliographical writers, and show to the second-sighted Edinburgher what human contrivances have been raised by the art of more painful writers than himself—either to postpone the day of universal annihilation, or to preserve for our posterity, three centuries hence, the knowledge which now so busily occupies us, and transmit to them something more than what Bacon calls "Inventories" of our literary treasures.

"Histories, and literary *bibliothèques* (or bibliothecas), will always present to us," says La Rive, "an immense harvest of errors, till the authors of such catalogues shall be fully impressed by the importance of their art; and, as it were, reading in the most distant ages of the future the literary good and evil

---

75. The late Wm. Upcott possessed, in a large degree, a similar taste for miscellaneous collections. He never threw an old hat away, but used it as a receptacle for certain "cuttings" from books and periodicals on some peculiar subjects. He had filled a room with hats and trunks thus crammed; but they were sacrificed at his death for want of necessary arrangement.

which they may produce, force a triumph from the pure devotion to truth, in spite of all the disgusts which their professional tasks involve; still patiently enduring the heavy chains which bind down those who give themselves up to this pursuit, with a passion which resembles heroism.

"The catalogues of *bibliothèques fixes* (or critical, historical, and classified accounts of writers) have engendered that enormous swarm of bibliographical errors, which have spread their roots, in greater or less quantities, in all our bibliographers." He has here furnished a long list, which I shall preserve in the note.[76]

The list, though curious, is by no means complete. Such are the men of whom the Abbé Rive speaks with more respect than his accustomed courtesy. "If such," says he, "cannot escape from errors, who shall? I have only marked them out to prove the importance of bibliographical history. A writer of this sort must occupy himself with more regard for his reputation than his own profit, and yield himself up entirely to the study of books."

The mere knowledge of books, which has been called an erudition of title-pages, may be sufficient to occupy the life of some; and while the wits and "the million" are ridiculing these hunters of editions, who force their passage through secluded spots, as well as course in the open fields, it will be found that this art of book-knowledge may turn out to be a very philosophical pursuit, and that men of great name have devoted themselves to labours more frequently contemned than comprehended. Apostolo Zeno, a poet, a critic, and a true man of letters, considered it as no small portion of his glory to have annotated Fontanini, who, himself an eminent prelate, had passed his life in forming his *Bibliotheca Italiana.* Zeno did not consider that to correct errors and to enrich by information this catalogue of Italian writers was a mean task. The enthusiasm of the Abbé Rive considered bibliography as a sublime pursuit, exclaiming on Zeno's commentary on Fontanini—"He chained together the knowledge of whole generations for posterity, and he read in future ages."

There are few things by which we can so well trace the history of the human mind as by a classed catalogue, with dates of the first publication of books; even the relative prices of books at different periods, their decline and then their rise, and again their fall, form a chapter in this history of the human

---

76. Gessner, Simler, Bellarmin, L'Abbé, Mabillon, Montfaucon, Moreri, Bayle, Baillet, Niceron, Dupin, Cave, Warton, Casimir Oudin, Le Long, Goujet, Wolfius, John Albert Fabricius, Argelati, Tiraboschi, Nicholas Antonio, Walchius, Struvius, Brucker, Scheuchzer, Linnæus, Seguier, Haller, Adamson, Manget, Kestner, Eloy, Douglas, Weidler, Hailbronner, Montucia, Lalande, Bailly, Quadrio, Morhoff, Stollius, Funccius, Schelhorn, Engles, Beyer, Gerdesius, Vogts, Freytag, David Clement, Chevillier, Maittaire, Orlandi, Prosper Marchand, Schoeplin, De Boze, Abbé Sallier, and de Saint Leger.

mind; we become critics even by this literary chronology, and this appraisement of auctioneers. The favourite book of every age is a certain picture of the people. The gradual depreciation of a great author marks a change in knowledge or in taste.

But it is imagined that we are not interested in the history of indifferent writers, and scarcely in that of the secondary ones. If none but great originals should claim our attention, in the course of two thousand years we should not count twenty authors! Every book, whatever be its character, may be considered as a new experiment made by the human understanding; and as a book is a sort of individual representation, not a solitary volume exists but may be personified, and described as a human being. Hints start discoveries: they are usually found in very different authors who could go no further; and the historian of obscure books is often preserving for men of genius indications of knowledge, which without his intervention we should not possess! Many secrets we discover in bibliography. Great writers, unskilled in this science of books, have frequently used defective editions, as Hume did the castrated Whitelocke; or, like Robertson, they are ignorant of even the sources of the knowledge they would give the public; or they compose on a subject which too late they discover had been anticipated. Bibliography will show what has been done, and suggest to our invention what is wanted. Many have often protracted their journey in a road which had already been worn out by the wheels which had traversed it: bibliography unrolls the whole map of the country we purpose travelling over—the post-roads and the by-paths.

Every half-century, indeed, the obstructions multiply; and the Edinburgh prediction, should it approximate to the event it has foreseen, may more reasonably terrify a far distant posterity. Mazzuchelli declared, after his laborious researches in Italian literature, that one of his more recent predecessors, who had commenced a similar work, had collected notices of forty thousand writers—and yet, he adds, my work must increase that number to ten thousand more! Mazzuchelli said this in 1753; and the amount of nearly a century must now be added, for the presses of Italy have not been inactive.

But the literature of Germany, of France, and of England has exceeded the multiplicity of the productions of Italy, and an appalling population of authors swarm before the imagination.[77] Hail then the peaceful spirit of the literary historian, which sitting amidst the night of time, by the monuments of genius, trims the sepulchral lamps of the human mind! Hail to the literary Reaumur, who by the clearness of his glasses makes even the minute interesting, and reveals to us the world of insects! These are guardian spirits who, at the close of every century standing on its ascent, trace out the old roads we had

---

77. The British Museum Library now numbers more than 500,000 volumes. The catalogue alone forms a small library.

pursued, and with a lighter line indicate the new ones which are opening, from the imperfect attempts, and even the errors of our predecessors!

6. MEN OF LETTERS
(*Literary Character*, vol. 4, pp. 226-238)

AMONG the active members of the literary republic, there is a class whom formerly we distinguished by the title of MEN OF LETTERS—a title which, with us, has nearly gone out of currency, though I do not think that the general term of "literary men" would be sufficiently appropriate.

The man of letters, whose habits and whose whole life so closely resemble those of an author, can only be distinguished by this simple circumstance, that the man of letters is not an author.

Yet he whose sole occupation through life is literature—he who is always acquiring and never producing, appears as ridiculous as the architect who never raised an edifice, or the statuary who refrains from sculpture. His pursuits are reproached with terminating in an epicurean selfishness, and amidst his incessant avocations he himself is considered as a particular sort of idler.

This race of literary characters, as we now find them, could not have appeared till the press had poured forth its affluence. In the degree that the nations of Europe became literary, was that philosophical curiosity kindled which induced some to devote their fortunes and their days, and to experience some of the purest of human enjoyments in preserving and familiarising themselves with "the monuments of vanished minds," as books are called by D'Avenant with so much sublimity. Their expansive library presents an indestructible history of the genius of every people, through all their eras—and whatever men have thought and whatever men have done, were at length discovered in books.

Men of letters occupy an intermediate station between authors and readers. They are gifted with more curiosity of knowledge, and more multiplied tastes, and by those precious collections which they are forming during their lives, are more completely furnished with the means than are possessed by the multitude who read, and the few who write.

The studies of an author are usually restricted to particular subjects. His tastes are tinctured by their colouring, his mind is always shaping itself by their form. An author's works form his solitary pride, and his secret power; while half his life wears away in the slow maturity of composition, and still the ambition of authorship torments its victim alike in disappointment or in possession.

But soothing is the solitude of the MAN OF LETTERS! View the busied inhabitant of the library surrounded by the objects of his love! He possesses them—and they possess him! These volumes—images of our mind and passions!—as he traces them from Herodotus to Gibbon, from Homer to Shakspeare—those portfolios which gather up the inventions of genius, and that selected cabinet of medals which holds so many unwritten histories;—some favourite sculptures and pictures, and some antiquities of all nations, here and there about his house—these are his furniture!

In his unceasing occupations the only repose he requires, consists not in quitting, but in changing them. Every day produces its discovery; every day in the life of a man of letters may furnish a multitude of emotions and of ideas. For him there is a silence amidst the world; and in the scene ever opening before him, all that has passed is acted over again, and all that is to come seems revealed as in a vision. Often his library is contiguous to his chamber,[78] and this domain *"parva sed apta,"* this contracted space, has often marked the boundary of the existence of the opulent owner, who lives where he will die, contracting his days into hours; and a whole life thus passed is found too short to close its designs. Such are the men who have not been unhappily described by the Hollanders as *lief-hebbers*, lovers or fanciers, and their collection as *lief-hebbery*, things of their love. The Dutch call everything for which they are impassioned *lief-hebbery;* but their feeling being much stronger than their delicacy, they apply the term to everything, from poesy and picture to tulips and tobacco. The term wants the melody of the languages of genius; but something parallel is required to correct that indiscriminate notion which most persons associate with that of *collectors*.

It was fancifully said of one of these lovers, in the style of the age, that, "His book was his bride, and his study his bride-chamber." Many have voluntarily relinquished a public station and their rank in society, neglecting even their fortune and their health, for the life of self-oblivion of the man of

---

78. The contiguity of the CHAMBER to the LIBRARY is not the solitary fancy of an individual, but marks the class. Early in life, when in France and Holland, I met with several of these *amateurs,* who had bounded their lives by the circle of their collections, and were rarely seen out of them. The late Duke of ROXBURGH once expressed his delight to a literary friend of mine, that he had only to step from his sleeping apartment into his fine library; so that he could command, at all moments, the gratification of pursuing his researches while he indulged his reveries. The Chevalier VERHULST, of Bruxelles, of whom we have a curious portrait prefixed to the catalogue of his pictures and curiosities, was one of these men of letters who experienced this strong affection for his collections, and to such a degree, that he never went out of his house for twenty years; where, however, he kept up a courteous intercourse with the lovers of art and literature. He was an enthusiastic votary of Rubens, of whom he has written a copious life in Dutch, the only work he appears to have composed.

letters. Count DE CAYLUS expended a princely income in the study and the encouragement of Art. He passed his mornings among the studios of artists, watching their progress, increasing his collections, and closing his day in the retirement of his own cabinet. His rank and his opulence were no obstructions to his settled habits. CICERO himself, in his happier moments, addressing ATTICUS, exclaimed—"I had much rather be sitting on your little bench under Aristotle's picture, than in the curule chairs of our great ones." This wish was probably sincere, and reminds us of another great politician who in his secession from public affairs retreated to a literary life, where he appears suddenly to have discovered a new-found world. Fox's favourite line, which he often repeated, was—

> How various his employments whom the world
> Calls idle!

De Sacy, one of the Port-Royalists, was fond of repeating this lively remark of a man of wit—"That all the mischief in the world comes from not being able to keep ourselves quiet in our room."

But tranquillity is essential to the existence of the man of letters—an unbroken and devotional tranquillity. For though, unlike the author, his occupations are interrupted without inconvenience, and resumed without effort; yet if the painful realities of life break into this visionary world of literature and art, there is an atmosphere of taste about him which will be dissolved, and harmonious ideas which will be chased away, as it happens when something is violently flung among the trees where the birds are singing—all instantly disperse!

Even to quit their collections for a short time is a real suffering to these lovers; everything which surrounds them becomes endeared by habit, and by some higher associations. Men of letters have died with grief from having been forcibly deprived of the use of their libraries. DE THOU, with all a brother's sympathy, in his great history, has recorded the sad fates of several who had witnessed their collections dispersed in the civil wars of France, or had otherwise been deprived of their precious volumes. SIR ROBERT COTTON fell ill, and betrayed, in the ashy paleness of his countenance, the misery which killed him on the sequestration of his collections. "They have broken my heart who have locked up my library from me," was his lament.

If this passion for acquisition and enjoyment be so strong and exquisite, what wonder that these "lovers" should regard all things as valueless in comparison with the objects of their love? There seem to be spells in their collections, and in their fascination they have often submitted to the ruin of their personal, but not of their internal enjoyments. They have scorned to balance in the scales the treasures of literature and art, though imperial magnificence once was ambitious to outweigh them.

VAN PRAUN, a friend of Albert [Albrecht] Durer's, of whom we possess a catalogue of pictures and prints, was one of these enthusiasts of taste. The Emperor of Germany, probably desirous of finding a royal road to a rare collection, sent an agent to procure the present one entire; and that some delicacy might be observed with such a man, the purchase was to be proposed in the form of a mutual exchange; the emperor had gold, pearls, and diamonds. Our *lief-hebber* having silently listened to the imperial agent, seemed astonished that such things should be considered as equivalents for a collection of works of art, which had required a long life of experience and many previous studies and practised tastes to have formed, and compared with which gold, pearls, and diamonds, afforded but a mean, an unequal, and a barbarous barter.

If the man of letters be less dependent on others for the very perception of his own existence than men of the world are, his solitude, however, is not that of a desert: for all there tends to keep alive those concentrated feelings which cannot be indulged with security, or even without ridicule in general society. Like the Lucullus of Plutarch, he would not only live among the votaries of literature, but would live for them; he throws open his library, his gallery, and his cabinet, to all the Grecians. Such men are the fathers of genius; they seem to possess an aptitude in discovering those minds which are clouded over by the obscurity of their situations; and it is they who so frequently project those benevolent institutions, where they have poured out the philanthropy of their hearts in that world which they appear to have forsaken. If Europe be literary, to whom does she owe this more than to these men of letters? Is it not to their noble passion of amassing through life those magnificent collections, which often bear the names of their founders from the gratitude of a following age? Venice, Florence, and Copenhagen, Oxford, and London, attest the existence of their labours. Our BODLEYS and our HARLEYS, our COTTONS and our SLOANES, our CRACHERODES, our TOWNLEYS, and our BANKS, were of this race! In the perpetuity of their own studies they felt as if they were extending human longevity, by throwing an unbroken light of knowledge into the next age. The private acquisitions of a solitary man of letters during half a century have become public endowments. A generous enthusiasm inspired these intrepid labours, and their voluntary privations of what the world calls its pleasures and its honours, would form an interesting history not yet written; their due, yet undischarged.

But "men of the world," as they are emphatically distinguished, imagine that a man so lifeless in "the world" must be one of the dead in it, and, with mistaken wit, would inscribe over the sepulchre of his library, "Here lies the body of our friend." If the man of letters have voluntarily quitted their "world," at least he has passed into another, where he enjoys a sense of existence through a long succession of ages, and where Time, who destroys all things for others, for him only preserves and discovers. This world is best described by one who has lingered among its inspirations. "We are wafted into other times and strange lands, connecting us by a sad but exalting relationship with the great events and great minds which have passed away. Our studies at once cherish and control the imagination, by leading it over an unbounded range of the noblest scenes in the overawing company of departed wisdom and genius."[79]

Living more with books than with men, which is often becoming better acquainted with man himself, though not always with men, the man of letters is more tolerant of opinions than opinionists are among themselves. Nor are his views of human affairs contracted to the day, like those who, in the heat and hurry of a too active life, prefer expedients to principles; men who deem themselves politicians because they are not moralists; to whom the centuries behind have conveyed no results, and who cannot see how the present time is always full of the future. "Everything," says the lively Burnet, "must be brought to the nature of tinder or gunpowder, ready for a spark to set it on fire," before they discover it. The man of letters indeed is accused of a cold indifference to the interests which divide society; he is rarely observed as the head or the "rump of a party;" he views at a distance their temporary passions—those mighty beginnings, of which he knows the miserable terminations.

Antiquity presents the character of a perfect man of letters in ATTICUS, who retreated from a political to a literary life. Had his letters accompanied those of Cicero, they would have illustrated the ideal character of his class. But the sage ATTICUS rejected a popular celebrity for a passion not less powerful, yielding up his whole soul to study. CICERO, with all his devotion to literature, was at the same time agitated by another kind of glory, and the most perfect author in Rome imagined that he was enlarging his honours by the intrigues of the consulship. He has distinctly marked the character of the man of letters in the person of his friend ATTICUS, for which he has expressed his respect, although he could not content himself with its imitation. "I know," says this man of genius and ambition, "I know the greatness and ingenuousness of your soul, nor have I found any difference between us, but in a different choice of life; a certain sort of ambition has led me earnestly to seek after honours, while other motives, by no means blameable, induced you to adopt an honourable leisure; *honestum otium.*"[80] These motives appear in the interesting memoirs of this man of letters; a contempt of political intrigues combined with a desire to escape from the splendid bustle of Rome to the learned leisure of Athens. He wished to dismiss a pompous train of slaves for

---

79. "Quarterly Review," No. xxxiii. p. 145.
80. "Ad Atticum," Lib. i. Ep. 17.

the delight of assembling under his roof a literary society of readers and transcribers. And having collected under that roof the portraits or busts of the illustrious men of his country, inspired by their spirit and influenced by their virtues or their genius, he inscribed under them, in concise verses, the characters of their mind. Valuing wealth only for its use, a dignified economy enabled him to be profuse, and a moderate expenditure allowed him to be generous.

The result of this literary life was the strong affections of the Athenians. At the first opportunity the absence of the man of letters offered, they raised a statue to him, conferring on our POMPONIUS the fond surname of ATTICUS. To have received a name from the voice of the city they inhabited has happened to more than one man of letters. PINELLI, born a Neapolitan, but residing at Venice, among other peculiar honours received from the senate, was there distinguished by the affectionate title of "the Venetian."

Yet such a character as ATTICUS could not escape censure from "men of the world." They want the heart and the imagination to conceive something better than themselves. The happy indifference, perhaps the contempt of our ATTICUS for rival factions, they have stigmatised as a cold neutrality, a timid pusillanimous hypocrisy. Yet ATTICUS could not have been a mutual friend, had not both parties alike held the man of letters as a sacred being amidst their disguised ambition; and the urbanity of ATTICUS, while it balanced the fierceness of two heroes, Pompey and Cæsar, could even temper the rivalry of genius in the orators Hortensius and Cicero. A great man of our own country widely differed from the accusers of Atticus. Sir MATTHEW HALE lived in distracted times, and took the character of our man of letters for his model, adopting two principles in the conduct of the Roman. He engaged himself with no party business, and afforded a constant relief to the unfortunate, of whatever party. He was thus preserved amidst the contests of the times.

If the personal interests of the man of letters be not deeply involved in society, his individual prosperity, however, is never contrary to public happiness. Other professions necessarily exist by the conflict and the calamities of the community: the politician becomes great by hatching an intrigue; the lawyer, in counting his briefs; the physician, his sick-list. The soldier is clamorous for war; the merchant riots on high prices. But the man of letters only calls for peace and books to unite himself with his brothers scattered over Europe; and his usefulness can only be felt at those intervals, when, after a long interchange of destruction, men, recovering their senses, discover that "knowledge is power." BURKE, whose ample mind took in every conception of the literary character, has finely touched on the distinction between this order of contemplative men, and the other active classes of society. In addressing Mr. MALONE, whose real character was that of a man of letters who first showed us the neglected state of our literary history, BURKE observed—for I shall give his own words, always too beautiful to alter—"If you are not called to exert your great talents, and employ your great acquisitions in the transitory service of your country, which is done in active life, you will continue to do it that permanent service which it receives from the labours of those who know how to make the silence of closets more beneficial to the world than all the noise and bustle of courts, senates, and camps."

A moving picture of the literary life of a man of letters who was no author, would have been lost to us, had not PEIRESC found in GASSENDI a twin spirit. So intimate was the biographer with the very thoughts, so closely united in the same pursuits, and so perpetual an observer of the remarkable man whom he has immortalised, that when employed on this elaborate resemblance of his friend, he was only painting himself with all the identifying strokes of self-love.[81]

It was in the vast library of PINELLI, the founder of the most magnificent one in Europe, that PEIRESC, then a youth, felt the remote hope of emulating the man of letters before his eyes. His life was not without preparation, nor without fortunate coincidences; but there was a grandeur of design in the execution which originated in the genius of the man himself.

The curious genius of PEIRESC was marked by its precocity, as usually are strong passions in strong minds; this intense curiosity was the germ of all those studies which seemed mature in his youth. He early resolved on a personal intercourse with the great literary characters of Europe; and his friend has thrown over these literary travels that charm of detail by which we accompany PEIRESC into the libraries of the learned; there with the historian opening new sources of history, or with the critic correcting manuscripts, and settling points of erudition; or by the opened cabinet of the antiquary, deciphering obscure inscriptions, and explaining medals. In the galleries of the curious in art, among their marbles, their pictures, and their prints, PEIRESC has often revealed to the artist some secret in his own art. In the museum of the naturalist, or the garden of the botanist, there was no rarity of nature on which he had not something to communicate. His mind toiled with that impatience of knowledge, that becomes a pain only when the mind is not on the advance. In England PEIRESC was the associate of Camden and Selden, and had more than one interview with that friend to literary men, our calumniated James the First. One may judge by these who were the men whom PEIRESC sought, and by whom he himself was ever after sought. Such, indeed, were immortal friendships! Immortal they may be justly called, from the objects in which they concerned themselves, and from the permanent

---

81. "I suppose," writes EVELYN, that most agreeable enthusiast of literature, to a travelling friend, "that you carry the life of that incomparable virtuoso always about you in your motions, not only because it is portable, but for that it is written by the pen of the great Gassendus."

results of the combined studies of such friends.

Another peculiar greatness in this literary character was PEIRESC's enlarged devotion to literature out of its purest love for itself alone. He made his own universal curiosity the source of knowledge to other men. Considering the studious as forming but one great family wherever they were, for PEIRESC the national repositories of knowledge in Europe formed but one collection for the world. This man of letters had possessed himself of their contents, that he might have manuscripts collated, unedited pieces explored, extracts supplied, and even draughtsmen employed in remote parts of the world, to furnish views and plans, and to copy antiquities for the student, who in some distant retirement often discovered that the literary treasures of the world were unfailingly opened to him by the secret devotion of this man of letters.

Carrying on the same grandeur in his views, his universal mind busied itself in every part of the habitable globe. He kept up a noble traffic with all travellers, supplying them with philosophical instruments and recent inventions, by which he facilitated their discoveries, and secured their reception even in barbarous realms. In return he claimed, at his own cost, for he was "born rather to give than to receive," says Gassendi, fresh importations of Oriental literature, curious antiquities, or botanic rarities; and it was the curiosity of PEIRESC which first embellished his own garden, and thence the gardens of Europe, with a rich variety of exotic flowers and fruits. Whenever presented with a medal, a vase, or a manuscript, he never slept over the gift till he had discovered what the donor delighted in; and a book, a picture, a plant, when money could not be offered, fed their mutual passion, and sustained the general cause of science. The correspondence of PEIRESC branched out to the farthest bounds of Ethiopia, connected both Americas, and had touched the newly-discovered extremities of the universe, when this intrepid mind closed in a premature death.

I have drawn this imperfect view of PEIRESC's character, that men of letters may be reminded of the capacities they possess. In the character of PEIRESC, however, there still remains another peculiar feature. His fortune was not great; and when he sometimes endured the reproach of those whose sordidness was startled at his prodigality of mind, and the great objects which were the result, PEIRESC replied, that "a small matter suffices for the natural wants of a literary man, whose true wealth consists in the monuments of arts, the treasures of his library, and the brotherly affections of the ingenious." PEIRESC was a French judge, but he supported his rank more by his own character than by luxury or parade. He would not wear silk, and no tapestry hangings ornamented his apartments; but the walls were covered with the portraits of his literary friends; and in the unadorned simplicity of his study, his books, his papers, and his letters were scattered about him on the tables, the seats, and the floor. There, stealing from the world, he would sometimes admit to his spare supper his friend Gassendi, "content," says that amiable philosopher, "to have me for his guest."

PEIRESC, like PINELLI, never published any work. These men of letters derived their pleasure, and perhaps their pride, from those vast strata of knowledge which their curiosity had heaped together in their mighty collections. They either were not endowed with that faculty of genius which strikes out aggregate views, or were destitute of the talent of composition which embellishes minute ones. This deficiency in the minds of such men may be attributed to a thirst of learning, which the very means to allay can only inflame. From all sides they are gathering information; and that knowledge seems never perfect to which every day brings new acquisitions. With these men, to compose is to hesitate; and to revise is to be mortified by fresh doubts and unsupplied omissions. PEIRESC was employed all his life on a history of Provence; but observes Gassendi, "He could not mature the birth of his literary offspring, or lick it into any shape of elegant form; he was therefore content to take the midwife's part, by helping the happier labours of others."

Such are the cultivators of knowledge, who are rarely authors, but who are often, however, contributing to the works of others; and without whose secret labours the public would not have possessed many valued ones. The delightful instruction which these men are constantly offering to authors and to artists, flows from their silent but uninterrupted cultivation of literature and the arts.

When Robertson, after his successful "History of Scotland," was long irresolute in his designs, and still unpractised in that curious research which habitually occupies these men of letters, his admirers had nearly lost his popular productions, had not a fortunate introduction to Dr. BIRCH enabled him to open the clasped books, and to drink of the sealed fountains. ROBERTSON has confessed his inadequate knowledge, and his overflowing gratitude, in letters which I have elsewhere printed. A suggestion by a man of letters has opened the career of many an aspirant. A hint from WALSH conveyed a new conception of English poetry to one of its masters. The celebrated treatise of GROTIUS on "Peace and War" was projected by PEIRESC. It was said of MAGLIABECHI, who knew all books, and never wrote one, that by his diffusive communications he was in some respect concerned in all the great works of his times. Sir ROBERT COTTON greatly assisted CAMDEN and SPEED; and that hermit of literature, BAKER of Cambridge, was ever supplying with his invaluable researches Burnet, Kennet, Hearne, and Middleton. The concealed aid which men of letters afford authors, may be compared to those subterraneous streams, which, flowing into spacious lakes, are, though unobserved, enlarging the waters which attract the public eye.

Count DE CAYLUS, celebrated for his collections, and for his generous patronage of artists, has given the last touches to this picture of the man of letters, with all the delicacy and warmth of a self-painter.

"His glory is confined to the mere power which he has of being one day useful to letters and to the arts; for his whole life is employed in collecting materials of which learned men and artists make no use till after the death of him who amassed them. It affords him a very sensible pleasure to labour in hopes of being useful to those who pursue the same course of studies, while there are so great a number who die without discharging the debt which they incur to society."

Such a man of letters appears to have been the late Lord WOODHOUSE-LEE. Mr. Mackenzie, returning from his lordship's literary retirement, meeting Mr. Alison, finely said, that "he hoped he was going to Woodhouselee; for no man could go there without being happier, or return from it without being better."

Shall we then hesitate to assert, that this class of literary men forms a useful, as well as a select order in society? We see that their leisure is not idleness, that their studies are not unfruitful for the public, and that their opinions, purified from passions and prejudices, are always the soundest in the nation. They are counsellors whom statesmen may consult; fathers of genius to whom authors and artists may look for aid, and friends of all nations; for we ourselves have witnessed, during a war of thirty years, that the MEN OF LETTERS in England were still united with their brothers in France. The abode of Sir JOSEPH BANKS was ever open to every literary and scientific foreigner; while a wish expressed or a communication written by this MAN OF LETTERS, was even respected by a political power which, acknowledging no other rights, paid a voluntary tribute to the claims of science and the privileges of literature.

7. PATRONS
(*Curiosities*, vol. 1, pp. 82-84)

AUTHORS have too frequently received ill treatment even from those to whom they dedicated their works.

Some who felt hurt at the shameless treatment of such mock Mæcenases have observed that no writer should dedicate his works but to his FRIENDS, as was practised by the ancients, who usually addressed those who had solicited their labours, or animated their progress. Theodosius Gaza had no other recompense for having inscribed to Sixtus IV. his translation of the book of Aristotle on the Nature of Animals, than the price of the binding, which this charitable father of the church munificently bestowed upon him.

Theocritus fills his Idylliums with loud complaints of the neglect of his patrons; and Tasso was as little successful in his dedications.

Ariosto, in presenting his Orlando Furioso to the Cardinal d'Este, was gratified with the bitter sarcasm of—*"Dove diavolo avete pigliato tante coglionerie?"* Where the devil have you found all this nonsense?

When the French historian Dupleix, whose pen was indeed fertile, presented his book to the Duke d'Epernon, this Mæcenas, turning to the Pope's Nuncio, who was present, very coarsely exclaimed—"Cadedids! ce monsieur a un flux enragé, il chie un livre toutes les lunes!"

Thomson, the ardent author of the Seasons, having extravagantly praised a person of rank, who afterwards appeared to be undeserving of eulogiums, properly employed his pen in a solemn recantation of his error. A very different conduct from that of Dupleix, who always spoke highly of Queen Margaret of France for a little place he held in her household: but after her death, when the place became extinct, spoke of her with all the freedom of satire. Such is too often the character of some of the literati, who only dare to reveal the truth when they have no interest to conceal it.

Poor Mickle, to whom we are indebted for so beautiful a version of Camoens' Lusiad, having dedicated this work, the continued labour of five years, to the Duke of Buccleugh, had the mortification to find, by the discovery of a friend, that he had kept it in his possession three weeks before he could collect sufficient intellectual desire to cut open the pages! The neglect of this nobleman reduced the poet to a state of despondency. This patron was a political economist, the pupil of Adam Smith! It is pleasing to add, in contrast with this frigid Scotch patron, that when Mickle went to Lisbon, where his translation had long preceded his visit, he found the Prince of Portugal waiting on the quay to be the first to receive the translator of his great national poem; and during a residence of six months, Mickle was warmly regarded by every Portuguese nobleman.

"Every man believes," writes Dr. Johnson to Baretti, "that mistresses are unfaithful, and patrons are capricious. But he excepts his own mistress, and his own patron."

A patron is sometimes oddly obtained. Benserade attached himself to Cardinal Mazarin; but his friendship produced nothing but civility. The poet every day indulged his easy and charming vein of amatory and panegyrical poetry, while all the world read and admired his verses. One evening the cardinal, in conversation with the king, described his mode of life when at the papal court. He loved the sciences; but his chief occupation was the belles lettres, composing little pieces of poetry; he said that he was then in the court of Rome what Benserade was now in that of France. Some hours afterwards, the friends of the poet related to him the conversation of the cardinal. He quitted them abruptly, and ran to the apartment of his eminence, knocking with all his force, that he might be certain of being heard. The cardinal had just gone to bed; but he incessantly clamoured, demanding entrance; they were compelled to open the door. He ran to his eminence, fell upon his knees, almost pulled off the sheets of the bed in rapture, imploring a thousand pardons for thus disturbing him; but such was his joy in what he had just heard, which he repeated, that he could not refrain from immediately giving vent to his gratitude and his pride, to have been compared with his eminence for his poetical talents! Had the door not been immediately opened, he should have expired; he was not rich, it was true, but he should now die contented! The cardinal was pleased with his *ardour*, and probably never suspected his *flattery;* and the next week our new actor was pensioned.

On Cardinal Richelieu, another of his patrons, he gratefully made this epitaph:—

> Cy gist, ouy gist, par la mort bleu,
> Le Cardinal de Richelieu,
> Et ce qui cause mon ennuy
> Ma PENSION avec lui.
>
> Here lies, egad, 'tis very true,
> The illustrious Cardinal Richelieu:
> My grief is genuine—void of whim!
> Alas! my pension lies with him!

Le Brun, the great French artist, painted himself holding in his hand the portrait of his earliest patron. In this accompaniment the Artist may be said to have portrayed the features of his soul. If genius has too often complained of its patrons, has it not often over-valued their protection?

8. ABRIDGERS
(*Curiosities*, vol. 1, pp. 397-400)

ABRIDGERS are a kind of literary men to whom the indolence of modern readers, and indeed the multiplicity of authors, give ample employment.

It would be difficult, observed the learned Benedictines, the authors of the Literary History of France, to relate all the unhappy consequences which ignorance introduced, and the causes which produced that ignorance. But we must not forget to place in this number the mode of reducing, by way of abridgment, what the ancients had written in bulky volumes. Examples of this practice may be observed in preceding centuries, but in the fifth century it began to be in general use. As the number of students and readers diminished, authors neglected literature, and were disgusted with composition; for to write is seldom done, but when the writer entertains the hope of finding readers. Instead of original authors, there suddenly arose numbers of Abridgers. These men, amidst the prevailing disgust for literature, imagined they should gratify the public by introducing a mode of reading works in a few hours, which otherwise could not be done in many months; and, observing that the bulky volumes of the ancients lay buried in dust, without any one condescending to examine them, necessity inspired them with an invention that might bring those works and themselves into public notice, by the care they took of renovating them. This they imagined to effect by forming abidgments of these ponderous tomes.

All these Abridgers, however, did not follow the same mode. Some contented themselves with making a mere abridgment of their authors, by employing their own expressions, or by inconsiderable alterations. Others formed abridgments in drawing them from various authors, but from whose works they only took what appeared to them most worthy of observation, and embellished them in their own style. Others again, having before them several authors who wrote on the same subject, took passages from each, united them, and thus combined a new work; they executed their design by digesting in commonplaces, and under various titles, the most valuable parts they could collect, from the best authors they read. To these last ingenious scholars we owe the rescue of many valuable fragments of antiquity. They fortunately preserved the best maxims, characters, descriptions, and curious matters which they had found interesting in their studies.

Some learned men have censured these Abridgers as the cause of our having lost so many excellent entire works of the ancients; for posterity becoming less studious was satisfied with these extracts, and neglected to preserve the originals, whose voluminous size was less attractive. Others, on the contrary, say that these Abridgers have not been so prejudicial to literature; and that had it not been for their care, which snatched many a perishable fragment from that shipwreck of letters which the barbarians occasioned, we should perhaps have had no works of the ancients remaining. Many voluminous works have been greatly improved by their Abridgers. The vast history of Trogus Pompeius was soon forgotten and finally perished, after the excellent epitome of it by Justin, who winnowed the abundant chaff from the grain.

Bayle gives very excellent advice to an Abridger, Xiphilin, in his "Abridgment of Dion," takes no notice of a circumstance very material for entering into the character of Domitian;—the recalling the empress Domitia after having turned her away for her intrigues with a player. By omitting this fact in the abridgment, and which is discovered through Suetonius, Xiphilin has evinced, he says, a deficient judgment; for Domitian's ill qualities are much better exposed, when it is known that he was mean-spirited enough to restore to the dignity of Empress the prostitute of a player.

Abridgers, Compilers, and Translators, are now slightly regarded; yet to form their works with skill requires an exertion of judgment, and frequently of taste, of which their contemners appear to have no due conception. Such literary labours it is thought the learned will not be found to want; and the unlearned cannot discern the value. But to such Abridgers as Monsieur Le Grand, in his "Tales of the Minstrels," and Mr. Ellis, in his "English Metrical Romances," we owe much; and such writers must bring to their task a congeniality of genius, and even more taste than their original possessed. I must compare such to fine etchers after great masters:—very few give the feeling touches in the right place.

It is an uncommon circumstance to quote the Scriptures on subjects of *modern literature!* but on the present topic the elegant writer of the books of the Maccabees has delivered, in a kind of preface to that history, very pleasing and useful instructions to an *Abridger.* I shall transcribe the passages, being concise, from Book ii. Chap. ii. v. 23, that the reader may have them at hand:—

"All these things, I say, being declared by Jason of Cyrene, in *five books,* we will assay to *abridge* in one volume. We will be careful that they that will read may have *delight,* and that they that are desirous to commit to memory might have *ease,* and that all into whose hands it comes might have *profit.*" How concise and Horatian! He then describes his literary labours with no insensibility:—"To us that have taken upon us this painful labour of *abridging,* it was not easy, but a matter of *sweat* and *watching.*"—And the writer employs an elegant illustration: "Even as it is no ease unto him that prepareth a banquet, and seeketh the benefit of others; yet for the pleasuring of many, we will undertake gladly this great pain; leaving to the author the exact handling of every particular, and labouring to follow the *rules of an abridgment.*" He now embellishes his critical account with a sublime metaphor to distinguish the original from the copier:—"For as the master builder of a new house must care for the whole building; but he that undertaketh to set it out, and paint it, must seek out fit things for the adorning thereof; even so I think it is with us. To stand upon *every point,* and *go over things at large,* and to be *curious* in *particulars,* belonging to the *first author* of the story; but to use *brevity,* and avoid *much labouring* of the work, is to be granted to him that will make an Abridgment."

Quintilian has not a passage more elegantly composed, nor more judiciously conceived.

9. IMITATORS
(*Curiosities,* vol. 1, pp. 67-69)

SOME writers, usually pedants, imagine that they can supply, by the labours of industry, the deficiencies of nature. Paulus Manutius frequently spent a month in writing a single letter. He affected to imitate Cicero. But although he painfully attained to something of the elegance of his style, destitute of the native graces of unaffected composition, he was one of those whom Erasmus bantered in his *Ciceronianus*, as so slavishly devoted to Cicero's style, that they ridiculously employed the utmost precautions when they were seized by a Ciceronian fit. The *Nosoponus* of Erasmus tells of his devotion to Cicero; of his three indexes to all his words, and his never writing but in the dead of night, employing months upon a few lines; and his religious veneration for *words*, with his total indifference about the *sense*.

Le Brun, a Jesuit, was a singular instance of such unhappy imitation. He was a Latin poet, and his themes were religious. He formed the extravagant project of substituting a *religious Virgil* and *Ovid* merely by adapting his works to their titles. His *Christian Virgil* consists, like the Pagan Virgil, of *Eclogues*, *Georgics*, and of an *Epic* of twelve books; with this difference, that devotional subjects are substituted for fabulous ones. His epic is the *Ignaciad*, or the pilgrimage of Saint Ignatius. His *Christian Ovid*, is in the same taste; everything wears a new face. His *Epistles* are pious ones; the *Fasti* are the six days of the Creation; the *Elegies* are the six Lamentations of Jeremiah; a poem on the *Love of God* is substituted for the *Art of Love;* and the history of some *Conversions* supplies the place of the *Metamorphoses!* This Jesuit would, no doubt, have approved of a *family Shakspeare!*

A poet of a far different character, the elegant Sannazarius, has done much the same thing in his poem *De Partu Virginis*. The same servile imitation of ancient taste appears. It professes to celebrate the birth of *Christ*, yet his name is not once mentioned in it! The *Virgin* herself is styled *spes deorum!* "The hope of the gods!" The *Incarnation* is predicted by *Proteus!* The Virgin, instead of consulting the *sacred writings*, reads the *Sibylline oracles!* Her attendants are *dryads*, *nereids*, &c. This monstrous mixture of polytheism with the mysteries of Christianity, appears in everything he had about him. In a chapel at one of his country seats he had two statues placed at his tomb, *Apollo* and *Minerva;* catholic piety found no difficulty in the present case, as well as in innumerable others of the same kind, to inscribe the statue of *Apollo* with the name of *David*, and that of *Minerva* with the female one of *Judith!*

Seneca, in his 114th Epistle, gives a curious literary anecdote of the sort of imitation by which an inferior mind becomes the monkey of an original writer. At Rome, when Sallust was the fashionable writer, short sentences, uncommon words, and an obscure brevity, were affected as so many elegances. Arruntius, who wrote the history of the Punic Wars, painfully laboured to imitate Sallust. Expressions which are rare in Sallust are frequent in Arruntius, and, of course, without the motive that induced Sallust to adopt them. What rose naturally under the pen of the great historian, the minor one must have run after with ridiculous anxiety. Seneca adds several instances of the servile affectation of Arruntius, which seem much like those we once had of Johnson, by the undiscerning herd of his apes.

One cannot but smile at these imitators; we have abounded with them. In the days of Churchill, every month produced an effusion which tolerably imitated his slovenly versification, his coarse invective, and his careless mediocrity,—but the genius remained with the English Juvenal. Sterne had his countless multitude; and in Fielding's time, Tom Jones produced more bastards in wit than the author could ever suspect,. To such literary echoes, the reply of Philip of Macedon to one who prided himself on imitating the notes of the nightingale may be applied: "I prefer the nightingale herself!" Even the most successful of this imitating tribe must be doomed to share the fate of Silius Italicus, in his cold imitation of Virgil, and Cawthorne in his empty harmony of Pope.

To all these imitators I must apply an Arabian anecdote. Ebn Saad, one of Mahomet's amanuenses, when writing what the prophet dictated, cried out by way of admiration—"Blessed be God, the best Creator!" Mahomet approved of the expression, and desired him to write those words down as part of the inspired passage.—The consequence was, that Ebn Saad began to think himself as great a prophet as his master, and took upon himself to imitate the Koran according to his fancy; but the imitator got himself into trouble, and only escaped with life by falling on his knees, and solemnly swearing he would never again imitate the Koran, for which he was sensible God had never created him.

10. PROFESSORS OF PLAGIARISM AND OBSCURITY
(*Curiosities*, vol. 1, pp. 400-402)

AMONG the most singular characters in literature may be ranked those who do not blush to profess publicly its most dishonourable practices. The first vender of printed sermons imitating manuscripts, was, I think, Dr. Trusler. He to whom the following anecdotes relate had superior ingenuity. Like the famous orator, Henley, he formed a school of his own. The present lecturer openly taught not to *imitate* the best authors, but to *steal* from them!

Richesource, a miserable declaimer, called himself "Moderator of the Academy of Philosophical Orators." He taught how a person destitute of literary talents might become eminent for literature; and published the principles of his art under the title of "The Mask of Orators; or the manner of disguising all kinds of composition; briefs, sermons, panegyrics, funeral orations, dedications, speeches, letters, passages," &c. I will give a notion of the work:—

The author very truly observes, that all who apply themselves to polite literature do not always find from their own funds a sufficient supply to insure success. For such he labours, and teaches to gather, in the gardens of others, those fruits of which their own sterile grounds are destitute; but so artfully to gather, that the public shall not perceive their depredations. He dignifies this fine art by the title of PLAGIANISM, and thus explains it:—

"The Plagianism of orators is the art, or an ingenious and easy mode, which some adroitly employ, to change, or disguise, all sorts of speeches of their own composition, or that of other authors, for their pleasure or their utility; in such a manner that it becomes impossible, even for the author himself to recognise his own work, his own genius, and his own style, so skilfully shall the whole be disguised."

Our professor proceeds to reveal the manner of managing the whole economy of the piece which is to be copied or disguised; and which consists in giving a new order to the parts, changing the phrases, the words, &c. An orator, for instance, having said that a plenipotentiary should possess three qualities,—*probity*, *capacity*, and *courage;* the plagiarist, on the contrary, may employ, *courage*, *capacity*, and *probity*. This is only for a general rule, for it is too simple to practise frequently. To render the part perfect we must make it more complex, by changing the whole of the expressions. The plagiarist in place of *courage*, will put *force*, *constancy*, or *vigour*. For *probity* he may say *religion*, *virtue*, or *sincerity*. Instead of *capacity*, he may substitute *erudition*, *ability*, or *science*. Or he may disguise the whole by saying, that the *plenipotentiary should be firm*, *virtuous*, and *able*.

The rest of this uncommon work is composed of passages extracted from celebrated writers, which are turned into the new manner of the plagiarist; their beauties, however, are never improved by their dress. Several celebrated writers when young, particularly the famous Flechier, who addressed verses to him, frequented the lectures of this professor!

Richesource became so zealous in this course of literature, that he published a volume, entitled, "The Art of Writing and Speaking; or, a Method of composing all sorts of Letters, and holding a polite Conversation." He concludes his preface by advertising his readers, that authors who may be in want of essays, sermons, letters of all kinds, written pleadings and verses, may be accommodated on application to him.

Our professor was extremely fond of copious title-pages, which I suppose to be very attractive to certain readers; for it is a custom which the Richesources of the day fail not to employ. Are there persons who value *books* by the length of their titles, as formerly the ability of a physician was judged by the dimensions of his wig?

To this article may be added an account of another singular school, where the professor taught *obscurity* in literary composition!

I do not believe that those who are unintelligible are very intelligent. Quintilian has justly observed, that the obscurity of a writer is generally in proportion to his incapacity. However, as there is hardly a defect which does not find partisans, the same author informs us of a rhetorician, who was so great an admirer of obscurity, that he always exhorted his scholars to preserve it; and made them correct, as blemishes, those passages of their works which appeared to him too intelligible. Quintilian adds, that the greatest panegyric they could give to a composition in that school was to declare, "I understand nothing of this piece." Lycophron possessed this taste, and he protested that he would hang himself if he found a person who should understand his poem, called the "Prophecy of Cassandra." He succeeded so well, that this piece has been the stumbling-block of all the grammarians, scholiasts, and commentators; and remains inexplicable to the present day. Such works Charpentier admirably compares to those subterraneous places, where the air is so thick and suffocating, that it extinguishes all torches. A most sophistical dilemma, on the subject of *obscurity*, was made by Thomas Anglus, or White, an English Catholic priest, the friend of Sir Kenelm Digby. This learned man frequently wandered in the mazes of metaphysical subtilties; and became perfectly unintelligible to his readers. When accused of this obscurity, he replied, "Either the learned understand me, or they do not. If they understand me, and find me in an error, it is easy for them to refute me; if they do not understand me, it is very unreasonable for them to exclaim against my doctrines."

This is saying all that the wit of man can suggest in favour of *obscurity!* Many, however, will agree with an observation made by Gravina on the over-refinement of modern composition, that "we do not think we have attained genius, till others must possess as much themselves to understand us." Fontenelle, in France, followed by Marivaux, Thomas, and others, first introduced that subtilised manner of writing, which tastes more natural and simple reject; one source of such bitter complaints of obscurity.

11. OF LITERARY FILCHERS
(*Curiosities*, vol. 3, pp. 316-319)

AN honest historian at times will have to inflict severe strokes on his favourites. This has fallen to my lot, for in the course of my researches, I have to record that we have both forgers and purloiners, as well as other more obvious impostors, in the republic of letters! The present article descends to relate anecdotes of some contrivances to possess our literary curiosities by other means than by purchase; and the only apology which can be alleged for the *splendida peccata*, as St. Austin calls the virtues of the heathen, of the present innocent criminals, is their excessive passion for literature, and otherwise the respectability of their names. According to Grose's "Classical Dictionary of the Vulgar Tongue," we have had celebrated *collectors*, both in the learned and vulgar idioms. But one of them, who had some reasons too to be tender on this point, distinguished this mode of completing his collections, not by *book-*

stealing, but by *book-coveting.* On some occasions, in mercy, we must allow of softening names. Were not the Spartans allowed to steal from one another, and the bunglers only punished?

It is said that Pinelli made occasional additions to his literary treasures sometimes by his skill in an art which lay much more in the hand than in the head: however, as Pinelli never stirred out of his native city but once in his lifetime, when the plague drove him from home, his field of action was so restricted, that we can hardly conclude that he could have been so great an enterpriser in this way. No one can have lost their character by this sort of exercise in a confined circle, and be allowed to prosper! A light-fingered Mercury would hardly haunt the same spot: however, this is as it may be! It is probable that we owe to this species of accumulation many precious manuscripts in the Cottonian collection. It appears by the manuscript note-book of Sir Nicholas Hyde, chief justice of the King's Bench from the second to the seventh year of Charles the First, that Sir Robert Cotton had in his library, records, evidences, ledger-books, original letters, and other state papers, belonging to the king; for the attorney-general of that time, to prove this, showed a copy of the *pardon* which Sir Robert had obtained from King James for *embezzling records,* &c.[82]

Gough has more than insinuated that Rawlinson and his friend Umfreville "lie under very strong suspicions;" and he asserts that the collector of the Wilton treasures made as free as Dr. Willis with his friend's coins.[83] But he has also put forth a declaration relating to Bishop More, the famous collector, that "the bishop collected his library by *plundering* those of the clergy in his diocese; some he paid with sermons or more modern books; others, less civilly, only with a *quid illiterati cum libris?*" This *plundering* then consisted rather of *cajoling* others out of what they knew not how to value; and this is an advantage which every skilful lover of books must enjoy over those whose apprenticeship has not expired. I have myself been plundered by a very dear friend of some such literary curiosities, in the days of my innocence and of his precocity of knowledge. However, it does appear that Bishop More did actually lay violent hands in a snug corner on some irresistible little charmer; which we gather from a precaution adopted by a friend of the bishop, who one day was found busy in *hiding his rarest books,* and locking up as many as he could. On being asked the reason of this odd occupations, the bibliopolist ingenuously replied, "The Bishop of Ely dines with me to-day." This fact is quite clear, and here is another as indisputable. Sir Robert Saville writing to Sir

---

82. Lansdowne MSS. 888, in the former printed catalogue, art. 79.

83. Coins are the most dangerous things which can be exhibited to a professed collector. One of the fraternity, who died but a few years since, absolutely kept a record of his pilferings; he succeeded in improving his collection by attending sales also, and changing his own coins for others in better preservation.

Robert Cotton, appointing an interview with the founder of the Bodleian Library, cautions Sir Robert, that "If he held any book so dear as that he would be loath to lose it, he should *not let Sir Thomas out of his sight*, but set 'the boke' aside beforehand." A surprise and detection of this nature has been revealed in a piece of secret history by Amelot de la Houssaie, which terminated in very important political consequences. He assures us that the personal dislike which Pope Innocent X. bore to the French had originated in his youth, when cardinal, from having been detected in the library of an eminent French collector, of having purloined a most rare volume. The delirium of a collector's rage overcame even French politeness; the Frenchman not only openly accused his illustrious culprit, but was resolved that he should not quit the library without replacing the precious volume—from accusation and denial both resolved to try their strength: but in this literary wrestling-match the book dropped out of the cardinal's robes!—and from that day he hated the French—at least their more curious collectors!

Even an author on his dying bed, at those awful moments, should a collector be by his side, may not be considered secure from his too curious hands. Sir William Dugdale possessed the minutes of King James's life, written by Camden, till within a fortnight of his death; as also Camden's own life, which he had from Hacket, the author of the folio life of Bishop Williams: who, adds, Aubrey, "did *filch* it from Mr. Camden, as he lay a dying!" He afterwards corrects his information, by the name of Dr. Thorndyke, which, however, equally answers our purpose, to prove that even dying authors may dread such collectors!

The medalists have, I suspect, been more predatory than these subtractors of our literary treasures; not only from the facility of their conveyance, but from a peculiar contrivance which of all those things which admit of being secretly purloined, can only be practised in this department—for they can steal and no human hand can search them with any possibility of detection; they can pick a cabinet and swallow the curious things, and transport them with perfect safety, to be digested at their leisure. An adventure of this kind happened to Baron Stosch, the famous antiquary. It was in looking over the gems of the royal cabinet of medals, that the keeper perceived the loss of one; his place, his pension, and his reputation were at stake: and he insisted that Baron Stosch should be most minutely examined; in this dilemma, forced to confession, this erudite collector assured the keeper of the royal cabinet, that the strictest search would not avail: "Alas, sir! I have it here within," he said, pointing to his breast—an emetic was suggested by the learned practitioner himself, probably from some former experiment. This was not the first time that such a natural cabinet had been invented; the antiquary Vaillant, when attacked at sea by an Algerine, zealously swallowed a whole series of Syrian kings; when he landed at Lyons, groaning with his concealed treasure, he hastened to his friend, his physician, and his brother antiquary Dufour,—who at first was only anxious to inquire of his patient, whether the medals were of the higher empire? Vaillant showed two or three, of which nature had kindly relieved him. A collection of medals was left to the city of Exeter, and the donor accompanied the bequest by a clause in his will, that should a certain antiquary, his old friend and rival, be desirous of examining the coins, he should be watched by two persons, one on each side. La Croze informs us in his life, that the learned Charles Patin, who has written a work on medals, was one of the present race of collectors: Patin offered the curators of the public library at Basle to draw up a catalogue of the cabinet of Amberback there preserved, containing a good number of medals; but they would have been more numerous, had the catalogue-writer not diminished both them and his labour, by sequestrating some of the most rare, which was not discovered till this plunderer of antiquity was far out of their reach.

When Gough touched on this odd subject in the first edition of his "British Topography," "An Academic" in the *Gentleman's Magazine* for August 1772, insinuated that this charge of literary pilfering was only a jocular one; on which Gough, in his second edition, observed that this was not the case, and that "one might point out enough *light-fingered antiquaries* in the present age, to render such a charge extremely probable against earlier ones." The most extraordinary part of this slight history is, that our public denouncer some time after proved himself to be one of these "light-fingered antiquaries:" the deed itself, however, was more singular than disgraceful. At the disinterment of the remains of Edward the First, around which thirty years ago assembled our most erudite antiquaries, Gough was observed, as Steevens used to relate, in a wrapping great-coat of unusual dimensions; that witty and malicious "Puck," so capable himself of inventing mischief, easily suspected others, and divided his glance as much on the living piece of antiquity as on the elder. In the act of closing up the relics of royalty, there was found wanting an entire fore-finger of Edward the First; and as the body was perfect when opened, a murmur of dissatisfaction was spreading, when "Puck" directed their attention to the great antiquary in the watchman's great-coat—from whence—too surely was extracted Edward the First's great fore-finger!—so that "the light-fingered antiquary" was recognised ten years after he denounced the race, when he came to "try his hand."[84]

---

84. It is probable that this story of Gough's pocketing the fore-finger of Edward the First, was one of the malicious inventions of George Steevens, after he discovered that the antiquary was among the few admitted to the untombing of the royal corpse; Steevens himself was not there! Sylvanus Urban (the late respected John Nichols), who must know much more than he cares to record of "Puck,"—has, however, given the following "secret history" of what he calls "ungentlemanly and unwarrantable attacks" on Gough by Steevens. It seems that Steevens was a collector of the works of

12. LITERARY FORGERIES
(*Curiosities*, vol. 3, pp. 303-315)

THE preceding article has reminded me of a subject by no means incurious to the lovers of literature. A large volume might be composed on literary impostors; their modes of deception, however, were frequently repetitions; particularly those at the restoration of letters, when there prevailed a *mania* for burying spurious antiquities, that they might afterwards be brought to light to confound their contemporaries. They even perplex us at the present day. More sinister forgeries have been performed by Scotchmen, of whom Archibald Bower, Lauder, and Macpherson, are well known.

Even harmless impostures by some unexpected accident have driven an unwary inquirer out of the course. George Steevens must again make his appearance for a memorable trick played on the antiquary Gough. This was the famous tombstone on which was engraved the drinking-horn of Hardyknute, to indicate his last fatal carouse; for this royal Dane died drunk! To prevent any doubt, the name, in Saxon characters, was sufficiently legible. Steeped in pickle to hasten a precocious antiquity, it was then consigned to the corner of a broker's shop, where the antiquarian eye of Gough often pored on the venerable odds and ends; it perfectly succeeded on the "Director of the Antiquarian Society." He purchased the relic for a trifle, and dissertations of a due size were preparing for the Archæologia![85] Gough never forgave himself nor Steevens for this flagrant act of ineptitude. On every occasion in the *Gentleman's Magazine*, when compelled to notice this illustrious imposition, he always struck out his own name, and muffled himself up under his titular office of "The Director!" Gough never knew that this "modern antique" was only a piece of retaliation. In reviewing Masters's Life of Baker he found two heads, one scratched down from painted glass by George

---

Hogarth, and while engaged in forming his collection, wrote an abrupt letter to Gough to obtain from him some early impressions, by purchase or exchange. Gough resented the manner of his address by a rough refusal, for it is admitted to have been "a peremptory one." Thus arose the implacable vengence of Steevens, who used to boast that all the mischievous tricks he played on the grave antiquary, who was rarely over-kind to any one, was but a pleasant kind of revenge.

85. I have since been informed that this famous invention was originally a flim-flam of a Mr. Thomas White, a noted collector and dealer in antiquities. But it was Steevens who placed it in the broker's shop, where he was certain *of catching* the antiquary. When the late Mr. Pegge, a profound brother, was preparing to write a dissertation on it, the first inventor of the flam stepped forward to save any further tragical termination; the wicked wit had already succeeded too well.

Steevens, who would have passed it off for a portrait of one of our kings. Gough, on the watch to have a fling at George Steevens, attacked his graphic performance, and reprobated a portrait which had nothing human in it! Steevens vowed, that wretched as Gough deemed his pencil to be, it should make "The Director" ashamed of his own eyes, and be fairly taken in by something scratched much worse. Such was the origin of his adoption of this fragment of a chimney-slab, which I have seen, and with a better judge wondered at the injudicious antiquary, who could have been duped by the slight and ill-formed scratches, and even with a false spelling of the name, which, however, succeeded in being passed off as a genuine Saxon inscription: but he had counted on his man.[86] The trick is not so original as it seems. One De Grassis had engraved on marble the epitaph of a mule, which he buried in his vineyard: some time after, having ordered a new plantation on the spot, the diggers could not fail of disinterring what lay ready for them. The inscription imported that one Publius Grassus had raised this monument to his mule! De Grassis gave it out as an odd coincidence of names, and a prophecy about his own mule! It was a simple joke! The marble was thrown by, and no more thought of. Several years after it rose into celebrity, for with the erudite it then passed for an ancient inscription, and the antiquary Poracchi inserted the epitaph in his work on "Burials." Thus De Grassis and his mule, equally respectable, would have come down to posterity, had not the story by some means got wind! An incident of this nature is recorded in Portuguese history, contrived with the intention to keep up the national spirit, and diffuse hopes of the new enterprise of Vasco de Gama, who had just sailed on a voyage of discovery to the Indies. Three stones were discovered near Cintra, bearing in ancient characters a Latin inscription; a sibylline oracle addressed prophetically "To the Inhabitants of the West!" stating that when

---

86. The stone may be found in the British Museum. HARDCNVT is he reading on the *Harthacnut* stone; but the true orthography of the name is HARDACNVT. It was reported to have been discovered in Kennington-lane, where the palace of the monarch was said to have been located, and the inscription carefully made in Anglo-Saxon characters, was to the effect that "Here Hardcnut drank a wine horn dry, stared about him, and died."

Sylvanus Urban, my once excellent and old friend, seems a trifle uncourteous on this grave occasion.—He tells us, however, that "The history of this wanton trick, with a *fac-simile* of Schnebbelie's drawing, may be seen in his volume Ix. p. 217." He says that this wicked contrivance of George Steevens was to entrap this famous draughtsman! Does Sylvanus then deny that "the Director" was not also "entrapped?" and that he always struck out his own *name* in the proof-sheets of the Magazine, substituting his official designation, by which the whole society itself seemed to screen "the Director!"

these three stones shall be found, the Ganges, the Indus, and the Tagus should exchange their commodities! This was the pious fraud of a Portuguese poet, sanctioned by the approbation of the king. When the stones had lain a sufficient time in the damp earth, so as to become apparently antique, our poet invited a numerous party to a dinner at his country-house; in the midst of the entertainment a peasant rushed in, announcing the sudden discovery of this treasure! The inscription was placed among the royal collections as a sacred curiosity! The prophecy was accomplished, and the oracle was long considered genuine!

In such cases no mischief resulted; the annals of mankind were not confused by spurious dynasties and fabulous chronologies; but when literary forgeries are published by those whose character hardly admits of a suspicion that they are themselves the impostors, the difficulty of assigning a motive only increases that of forming a decision; to adopt or reject them may be equally dangerous.

In this class we must place Annius of Viterbo,[87] who published a pretended collection of historians of the remotest antiquity, some of whose *names* had descended to us in the works of ancient writers, while their works themselves had been lost. Afterwards he subjoined commentaries to confirm their authority by passages from known authors. These at first were eagerly accepted by the learned; the blunders of the presumed editor, one of which was his mistaking the right name of the historian he forged, were gradually detected, till at length the imposture was apparent! The pretended originals were more remarkable for their number than their volume; for the whole collection does not exceed 171 pages, which lessened the difficulty of the forgery; while the commentaries which were afterwards published must have been manufactured at the same time as the text. In favour of Annius, the high rank he occupied at the Roman Court, his irreproachable conduct, and his declaration that he had recovered some of these fragments at Mantua, and that others had come from Armenia, induced many to credit these pseudo-historians. A literary war soon kindled; Niceron has discriminated between four parties engaged in this conflict. One party decried the whole of the collection as gross forgeries; another obstinately supported their authenticity; a third decided that they were forgeries before Annius possessed them, who was only credulous; while a fourth party considered them as partly authentic, and ascribed their blunders to the interpolations of the editor, to increase their importance. Such as they were, they scattered confusion over the whole face of history. The false Berosus opens his history before the deluge, when,

---

87. He was a Dominican monk, his real name being Giovanni Nanni, which he Latinized in conformity with the custom of his era. He was born 1432, and died 1502. His great work, *Antiquitatem Rariorum,* professes to contain the works of Manetho, Berosus, and other authors of equal antiquity.

according to him, the Chaldeans through preceding ages had faithfully preserved their historical evidences! Annius hints, in his commentary, at the archives and public libraries of the Babylonians: the days of Noah comparatively seemed modern history with this dreaming editor. Some of the fanciful writers of Italy were duped: Sansovino, to delight the Florentine nobility, accommodated them with a new title of antiquity in their ancestor Noah, *Imperatore e monarcha delle genti, visse e morì in quelle parti.* The Spaniards complained that in forging these fabulous origins of different nations, a new series of kings from the ark of Noah had been introduced by some of their rhodomontade historians to pollute the sources of their history. Bodin's otherwise valuable works are considerably injured by Annius's supposititious discoveries. One historian died of grief, for having raised his elaborate speculations on these fabulous originals; and their credit was at length so much reduced, that Pignori and Maffei both announced to their readers that they had not referred in their works to the pretended writers of Annius! Yet, to the present hour, these presumed forgeries are not always given up. The problem remains unsolved—and the silence of the respectable Annius, in regard to the forgery, as well as what he affirmed when alive, leave us in doubt whether he really intended to laugh at the world by these fairy tales of the giants of antiquity. Sanchoniathon, as preserved by Eusebius, may be classed among these ancient writings as forgeries, and has been equally rejected and defended.

Another literary forgery, supposed to have been grafted on those of Annius, involved the Inghirami family. It was by digging in their grounds that they discovered a number of Etruscan antiquities, consisting of inscriptions, and also fragments of a chronicle, pretended to have been composed sixty years before the vulgar era. The characters on the marbles were the ancient Etruscan, and the historical work tended to confirm the pretended discoveries of Annius. They were collected and enshrined in a magnificent folio by Curtius Inghirami, who, a few years after, published a quarto volume exceeding one thousand pages to support their authenticity. Notwithstanding the erudition of the forger, these monuments of antiquity betrayed their modern condiment.[88] There were uncial letters which no one knew; but these were said to be undiscovered ancient Etruscan characters; it was more difficult to defend the small italic letters, for they were not used in the age assigned to them; besides that, there were dots on the letter *i*, a custom not practised till the eleventh century. The style was copied from the Latin of the Psalms and

---

88. A forgery of a similar character has been recently effected in the *débris* of the Chapelle St. Eloi (Département de L'Eure, France), where many inscriptions connected with the early history of France were exhumed, which a deputation of antiquaries, convened to examine their authenticity, have since pronounced to be forgeries!

the Breviary; but Inghirami discovered that there had been an intercourse between the Etruscans and the Hebrews, and that David had imitated the writings of Noah and his descendants! Of Noah the chronicle details speeches and anecdotes!

The Romans, who have preserved so much of the Etruscans, had not, however, noticed a single fact recorded in these Etruscan antiquities. Inghirami replied that the manuscript was the work of the secretary of the college of the Etrurian augurs, who alone was permitted to draw his materials from the archives, and who, it would seem, was the only scribe who has favoured posterity with so much secret history. It was urged in favour of the authenticity of these Etruscan monuments, that Inghirami was so young an antiquary at the time of the discovery, that he could not even explain them; and that when fresh researches were made on the spot, other similar monuments were also disinterred, where evidently they had long lain; the whole affair, however contrived, was confined to the *Inghirami family*. One of them, half a century before, had been the librarian of the Vatican, and to him is ascribed the honour of the forgeries which he buried where he was sure they would be found. This, however, is a mere conjecture! Inghirami, who published and defended their authenticity, was not concerned in their fabrication; the design was probably merely to raise the antiquity of Volaterra, the family estate of the Inghirami; and for this purpose one of its learned branches had bequeathed his posterity a collection of spurious historical monuments, which tended to overturn all received ideas on the first ages of history.[89]

It was probably such impostures, and those of *false decretals of* Isidore, which were forged for the maintenance of the papal supremacy, and for eight hundred years formed the fundamental basis of the canon law, the discipline of the church, and even the faith of Christianity, which led to the monstrous pyrrhonism of father Hardouin, who, with immense erudition, had persuaded himself that, excepting the Bible and Homer, Herodotus, Plautus, Pliny the elder, with fragments of Cicero, Virgil, and Horace, all the remains of classical literature were forgeries of the thirteenth and fourteenth centuries! In two dissertations he imagined that he had proved that the Æneid was not written by Virgil, nor the Odes of Horace by that poet. Hardouin was one of those wrong-headed men who, once having fallen into a delusion, whatever afterwards occurs to them on their favourite subject only tends to strengthen it. He died in his own faith! He seems not to have been aware that by ascribing such prodigal inventions as Plutarch, Thucydides, Livy, Tacitus, and

---

89. The volume of these pretended Antiquities is entitled *Etruscarum Antiquitatum Fragmenta, fo. Franc.* 1637. That which Inghirami published to defend their authenticity is in Italian, *Discorso sopra l' Opposizioni fatte all' Antichita Toscane*, 4to, *Firenze*, 1645.

other historians, to the men he did, he was raising up an unparalleled age of learning and genius when monks could only write meagre chronicles, while learning and genius themselves lay in an enchanted slumber with a suspension of all their vital powers.

There are numerous instances of the forgeries of smaller documents. The Prayer-book of Columbus, presented to him by the Pope, which the great discoverer of a new world bequeathed to the Genoese republic, has a codicil in his own writing, as one of the leaves testifies, but as volumes composed against its authenticity deny. The famous description in Petrarch's Virgil, so often quoted, of his first *rencontre* with Laura in the church of St. Clair on a Good Friday, 6th April, 1327, it has been recently attempted to be shown is a forgery. By calculation, it appears that the 6th April, 1327, fell on a Monday! The Good Friday seems to have been a blunder of the manufacturer of the note. He was entrapped by reading the second sonnet, as it appears in the *printed* editions!

> Era il giorno ch' al sol *si scolorana*
> *Per la* pietà del suo fattore i rai.

"It was on the day when the rays of the sun were obscured by compassion for his Maker." The forger imagined this description alluded to Good Friday and the eclipse at the Crucifixion. But how stands the passage in the MS. in the Imperial Library of Vienna, which Abbé Costaing has found?

> Er il giorno ch' al sol *di color raro*
> *Parve* la pietà da suo fattore, *ai rai*
> Quand Io fu preso; e non mi guardai
> Che ben vostri occhi dentro mi legaro.

"It was on the day that I was captivated, devotion for its Maker appeared in the rays of a brilliant sun, and I did not well consider that it was your eyes that enchained me!"

The first meeting, according to the Abbé Costaing, was not in a *church*, but in a *meadow*—as appears by the ninety-first sonnet. The Laura of Sade was *not* the Laura of Petrarch, but Laura de Baux, unmarried, and who died young, residing in the vicinity of Vaucluse. Petrarch had often viewed her from his own window, and often enjoyed her society amidst her family.[90] If the Abbé

---

90. I draw this information from a little "new year's gift," which my learned friend, the Rev. S. Weston, presented to his friends in 1822, entitled "A Visit to Vaucluse," accompanied by a Supplement. He derives his account apparently from a curious publication of L'Abbé Costaing de Pusigner d'Avignon, which I with other inquirers have not been able to procure, but which it is absolutely necessary to examine, before

Costaing's discovery be confirmed, the good name of Petrarch is freed from the idle romantic passion for a married woman. It would be curious if the famous story of the first meeting with Laura in the church of St. Clair originated in the blunder of the forger's misconception of a passage which was incorrectly printed, as appears by existing manuscripts!

Literary forgeries have been introduced into bibliography; dates have been altered; fictitious titles affixed; and books have been reprinted, either to leave out or to interpolate whole passages! I forbear entering minutely into this part of the history of literary forgery, for this article has already grown voluminous. When we discover, however, that one of the most magnificent of *amateurs*, and one of the most critical of bibliographers, were concerned in a forgery of this nature, it may be useful to spread an alarm among collectors. The Duke de la Vallière, and the Abbé de St. Leger once concerted together to supply the eager purchaser of literary rarities with a copy of *De Tribus Impostoribus*, a book, by the date, pretended to have been printed in 1598, though probably a modern forgery of 1698. The title of such a work had long existed by rumours, but never was a copy seen by man! Works printed with this title have all been proved to be modern fabrications. A copy, however, of the *introuvable* original was sold at the Duke de la Vallière's sale! The history of this volume is curious. The Duke and the Abbé having manufactured a text, had it printed in the old Gothic character, under the title, *De Tribus Impostoribus*. They proposed to put the great bibliopolist, De Bure, in good humour, whose agency would sanction the imposture. They were afterwards to dole out copies at twenty-five louis each, which would have been a reasonable price for a book which no one ever saw! They invited De Bure to dinner, flattered and cajoled him, and, as they imagined, at the moment they had wound him up to their pitch, they exhibited their manufacture; the keen-eyed glance of the renowned cataloguer of the "Bibliographie Instructive" instantly shot like lightning over it, and, like lightning, destroyed the whole edition. He not only discovered the forgery, but reprobated it! He refused his sanction; and the forging Duke and Abbé, in confusion, suppressed the *livre introuvable;* but they owed a grudge to the honest bibliographer, and attempted to write down the work whence the De Bures derive their fame.

Among the extraordinary literary impostors of our age—if we except Lauder, who, detected by the Ithuriel pen of Bishop Douglas, lived to make his public recantation of his audacious forgeries, and Chatterton, who has buried his inexplicable story in his own grave, a tale, which seems but half told—we must place a man well known in the literary world under the assumed name of George Psalmanazar. He composed his autobiography as

---

we can decide on the very curious but unsatisfactory accounts we have hitherto possessed of the Laura of Petrarch.

the penance of contrition, not to be published till he was no more, when all human motives have ceased which might cause his veracity to be suspected. The life is tedious; but I have curiously traced the progress of the mind in an ingenious imposture, which is worth preservation. The present literary forgery consisted of personating a converted islander of Formosa: a place then little known but by the reports of the Jesuits, and constructing a language and a history of a new people and a new religion, entirely of his own invention! This man was evidently a native of the south of France; educated in some provincial college of the Jesuits, where he had heard much of their discoveries of Japan; he had looked over their maps, and listened to their comments. He forgot the manner in which the Japanese wrote; but supposed, like orientalists, they wrote from the right to the left, which he found difficult to manage. He set about excogitating an alphabet; but actually forgot to give names to his letters, which afterwards baffled him before literary men.

He fell into gross blunders; having inadvertently affirmed that the Formosans sacrificed eighteen thousand male infants annually, he persisted in not lessening the number. It was proved to be an impossibility in so small an island, without occasioning a depopulation. He had made it a principle in this imposture never to vary when he had once said a thing. All this was projected in haste, fearful of detection by those about him.

He was himself surprised at his facility of invention, and the progress of his forgery. He had formed an alphabet, a considerable portion of a new language, a grammar, a new division of the year into twenty months, and a new religion! He had accustomed himself to write his language; but being an inexpert writer with the unusual way of writing backwards, he found this so difficult, that he was compelled to change the complicated forms of some of his letters. He now finally quitted his home, assuming the character of a Formosan convert, who had been educated by the Jesuits. He was then in his fifteenth or sixteenth year. To support his new character, he practised some religious mummeries; he was seen worshipping the rising and setting sun. He made a prayer-book with rude drawings of the sun, moon, and stars, to which he added some gibberish prose and verse, written in his invented character, muttering or chanting it, as the humour took him. His custom of eating raw flesh seemed to assist his deception more than the sun and moon.[91]

In a garrison at Sluys he found a Scotch regiment in the Dutch pay; the commander had the curiosity to invite our Formosan to confer with Innes, the chaplain to his regiment. This Innes was probably the chief cause of the imposture being carried to the extent it afterwards reached. Innes was a clergyman, but a disgrace to his cloth. As soon as he fixed his eye on our

91. For some further notices of Psalmanazar and his literary labours, we may refer the reader to vol. i. p. 137, note [=note 97 below].

Formosan, he hit on a project; it was nothing less than to make Psalmanazar the ladder of his own ambition, and the stepping-place for him to climb up to a good living! Innes was a worthless character; as afterwards appeared, when by an audacious imposition Innes practised on the Bishop of London, he avowed himself to be the author of an anonymous work, entitled "A Modest Inquiry after Moral Virtue;" for this he obtained a good living in Essex: the real author, a poor Scotch clergyman, obliged him afterwards to disclaim the work in print, and to pay him the profit of the edition which Innes had made! He lost his character, and retired to the solitude of his living; if not penitent, at least mortified.

Such a character was exactly adapted to become the foster-father of imposture. Innes courted the Formosan, and easily won on the adventurer, who had hitherto in vain sought for a patron. Meanwhile no time was lost by Innes to inform the unsuspicious and generous Bishop of London of the prize he possessed—to convert the Formosan was his ostensible pretext; to procure preferment his concealed motive. It is curious enough to observe, that the ardour of conversion died away in Innes, and the most marked neglect of his convert prevailed, while the answer of the bishop was protracted or doubtful. He had at first proposed to our Formosan impostor to procure his discharge, and convey him to England; this was eagerly consented to by our pliant adventurer. A few Dutch schellings, and fair words, kept him in good humour; but no letter coming from the bishop, there were fewer words, and not a stiver! This threw a new light over the character of Innes to the inexperienced youth. Psalmanazar sagaciously now turned all his attention to some Dutch ministers; Innes grew jealous lest they should pluck the bird which he had already in his net. He resolved to baptize the impostor—which only the more convinced Psalmanazar that Innes was one himself; for before this time Innes had practised a stratagem on him which had clearly shown what sort of a man his Formosan was.

This stratagem was this: he made him translate a passage in Cicero, of some length, into his pretended language, and give it him in writing; this was easily done, by Psalmanazar's facility of inventing characters. After Innes had made him construe it, he desired to have another version of it on another paper. The proposal, and the arch manner of making it, threw our impostor into the most visible confusion. He had had but a short time to invent the first paper, less to recollect it; so that in the second transcript not above half the words were to be found which existed in the first. Innes assumed a solemn air, and Psalmanazar was on the point of throwing himself on his mercy, but Innes did not wish to unmask the impostor; he was rather desirous of fitting the mask closer to his face. Psalmanazar, in this hard trial, had given evidence of uncommon facility, combined with a singular memory. Innes cleared his brow, smiled with a friendly look, and only hinted in a distant manner that he ought to be careful to be better provided for the future! An advice which Psalmanazar afterwards bore in mind, and at length produced the forgery of an entire new language; and which, he remarkably observes, "by what I have tried since I came into England, I cannot say but I could have compassed it with less difficulty than can be conceived had I applied closely to it." When a version of the catechism was made into the pretended Formosan language, which was submitted to the judgment of the first scholars, it appeared to them grammatical, and was pronounced to be a real language, from the circumstance that it resembled no other! and they could not conceive that a stripling could be the inventor of a language. If the reader is curious to examine this extraordinary imposture, I refer him to that literary curiosity, "An Historical and Geographical Description of Formosa, with Accounts of the Religion, Customs and Manners of the Inhabitants, by George Psalmanazar, a Native of the said Isle," 1704; with numerous plates, wretched inventions! of their dress! religious ceremonies! their tabernacle and altars to the sun, the moon, and the ten stars! their architecture! the viceroy's castle! a temple! a city house! a countryman's house! and the Formosan alphabet! In his conferences before the Royal Society with a Jesuit just returned from China, the Jesuit had certain strong suspicions that our hero was an impostor. The good father remained obstinate in his own conviction, but could not satisfactorily communicate it to others; and Psalmanazar, after politely asking pardon for the expression, complains of the Jesuit that "HE *lied most impudently," mentitur impudentissime!* Dr. Mead absurdly insisted Psalmanazar was a Dutchman or a German; some thought him a Jesuit in disguise, a tool of the non-jurors; the Catholics thought him bribed by the Protestants to expose their church; the Presbyterians that he was paid to explode their doctrine, and cry up episcopacy! This fabulous history of Formosa seems to have been projected by his artful prompter Innes who put Varenius into Psalmanazar's hands to assist him; trumpeted forth in the domestic and foreign papers an account of this converted Formosan; maddened the booksellers to hurry the author, who was scarcely allowed two months to produce this extraordinary volume; and as the former accounts which the public possessed of this island were full of monstrous absurdities and contradictions, these assisted the present imposture. Our forger resolved not to describe new and surprising things as they had done, but rather studied to clash with them, probably that he might have an opportunity of pretending to correct them. The first edition was immediately sold; the world was more divided than ever in opinion; in a second edition he prefixed a vindication!—the unhappy forger got about twenty guineas for an imposture, whose delusion spread far and wide! Some years afterwards Psalmanazar was engaged in a minor imposture; one man had persuaded him to father a white composition called the *Formosan japan!* which was to be sold at a high price! It was curious for its whiteness, but it had its faults. The project failed, and

Psalmanazar considered the miscarriage of the *white Formosan japan* as a providential warning to repent of all his impostures of Formosa!

Among these literary forgeries may be classed several ingenious ones fabricated for a *political* purpose. We had certainly numerous ones during our civil wars in the reign of Charles the First. This is not the place to continue the controversy respecting the mysterious *Eikon* Basiliké, which has been ranked among them, from the ambiguous claim of Gauden.[92] A recent writer who would probably incline not to leave the monarch, were he living, not only his head but the little fame he might obtain by the "Verses" said to be written by him at Carisbrook Castle, would deprive him also of these. Henderson's death-bed recantation is also reckoned among them; and we have a large collection of "Letters of Sir Henry Martin to his Lady of Delight," which were the satirical effusions of a wit of that day, but by the price they have obtained, are probably considered as genuine ones, and exhibit an amusing picture of his loose rambling life.[93] There is a ludicrous speech of the strange Earl of Pembroke, which was forged by the inimitable Butler. Sir John Birkenhead, a great humourist and wit, had a busy pen in these spurious letters and speeches.[94]

---

92. The question has been discussed with great critical acumen by Dr. Wordsworth.

93. Since this was published I have discovered that Harry Martin's Letters are not forgeries, but I cannot immediately recover my authority.

94. One of the most amusing of these tricks was perpetrated on William Prynne, the well-known puritanic hater of the stage, by some witty cavalier. Prynne's great work, "Histriomastix, the Player's Scourge; or, Actor's Tragedy," an immense quarto, of 1100 pages, was a complete condemnation of all theatrical amusements; but in 1649 appeared a tract of four leaves, entitled "Mr. William Prynne, his Defence of Stage Playes; or, a Retractation of a former Book of his called Histriomastix." It must have astonished many readers in his own day, and would have passed for his work in more modern times, but for the accidental preservation of a single copy of a handbill Prynne published disclaiming the whole thing. His style is most amusingly imitated throughout, and his great love for quoting authorities in his margin. He is made to complain that "this wicked and tyrannical army did lately in a most inhumane, cruell, rough, and barbarous manner, take away the poor players from their houses, being met there to discharge the duty of their callings: as if this army were fully bent, and most trayterously and maliciously set, to put down and depresse all the King's friends, not only in the parliament but in the very theatres; they have no care of covenant or any thing else." And he is further made to declare, in spite of "what the malicious, clamorous, and obstreporous people" may object, that he once wrote against stage-plays,—that it was" when I had not so clear a light as now I have." We can fancy the amusement this pamphlet must have been to many readers during the great Civil War.

13. LITERARY IMPOSTURES
(Curiosities, vol. 1, pp. 132-139)

SOME authors have practised singular impositions on the public. Varillas, the French historian, enjoyed for some time a great reputation in his own country for his historical compositions; but when they became more known, the scholars of other countries destroyed the reputation which he had unjustly acquired. His continual professions of sincerity prejudiced many in his favour, and made him pass for a writer who had penetrated into the inmost recesses of the cabinet; but the public were at length undeceived, and were convinced that the historical anecdotes which Varillas put off for authentic facts had no foundation, being wholly his own inventions—though he endeavoured to make them pass for realities by affected citations of titles, instructions, letters, memoirs, and relations, all of them imaginary! He had read almost everything historical, printed and manuscript; but his fertile political imagination gave his conjectures as facts, while he quoted at random his pretended authorities. Burnet's book against Varillas is a curious little volume.[95]

Gemelli Carreri, a Neapolitan gentleman, for many years never quitted his chamber; confined by a tedious indisposition, he amused himself with writing a *Voyage round the World;* giving characters of men, and descriptions of countries, as if he had really visited them: and his volumes are still very interesting. I preserve this anecdote as it has long come down to us; but Carreri, it has been recently ascertained, met the fate of Bruce—for he had visited the places he has described; Humboldt and Clavigero have confirmed his local knowledge of Mexico and of China, and found his book useful and veracious. Du Halde, who has written so voluminous an account of China, compiled it from the Memoirs of the Missionaries, and never travelled ten leagues from Paris in his life,—though he appears, by his writings, to be familiar with Chinese scenery.

---

95. Burnet's little 12mo volume was printed at Amsterdam, "in the Warmoes-straet near the Dam," 1686, and compiled by him when living for safety in Holland during the reign of James II. He particularly attacks Varillas' ninth book, which relates to England, and its false history of the Reformation, or rather "his own imagination for true history." On the authority of Catholic students, he says "the greatest number of the pieces he cited were to be found nowhere but in his own fancy." Burnet allows full latitude to an author for giving the best colouring to his own views and that of his party—a latitude he certainly always allowed to himself; but he justly censures the falsifying, or rather inventing, of history; after Varillas' fashion. "History," says Burnet, "is a sort of trade, in which false coyn and false weights are more criminal than in other matters; because the errour may go further and run longer, though their authors colour their copper too slightly to make it keep its credit long."

Damberger's Travels some years ago made a great sensation—and the public were duped; they proved to be the ideal voyages of a member of the German Grub-street, about his own garret. Too many of our "Travels" have been manufactured to fill a certain size; and some which bear names of great authority were not written by the professed authors.

There is an excellent observation of an anonymous author:—"*Writers* who never visited foreign countries, and *travellers* who have run through immense regions with fleeting pace, have given us long accounts of various countries and people; evidently collected from the idle reports and absurd traditions of the ignorant vulgar, from whom only they could have received those relations which we see accumulated with such undiscerning credulity."

Some authors have practised the singular imposition of announcing a variety of titles of works preparing for the press, but of which nothing but the titles were ever written.

Paschal, historiographer of France, had a reason for these ingenious inventions; he continually announced such titles, that his pension for writing on the history of France might not be stopped. When he died, his historical labours did not exceed six pages!

Gregorio Leti is an historian of much the same stamp as Varillas. He wrote with great facility, and hunger generally quickened his pen. He took everything too lightly; yet his works are sometimes looked into for many anecdotes of English history not to be found elsewhere; and perhaps ought not to have been there if truth had been consulted. His great aim was always to make a book: he swells his volumes with digressions, intersperses many ridiculous stories, and applies all the repartees he collected from old novel-writers to modern characters.

Such forgeries abound; the numerous "Testaments Politiques" of Colbert, Mazarin, and other great ministers, were forgeries usually from the Dutch press, as are many pretended political "Memoirs."

Of our old translations from the Greek and Latin authors, many were taken from French versions.

The Travels, written in Hebrew, of Rabbi Benjamin of Tudela, of which we have a curious translation, are, I believe, apocryphal. He describes a journey, which, if ever he took, it must have been with his night-cap on; being a perfect dream! It is said that to inspirit and give importance to his nation, he pretended that he had travelled to all the synagogues in the East; he mentions places which he does not appear ever to have seen, and the different people he describes no one has known. He calculates that he has found near eight hundred thousand Jews, of which about half are independent, and not subjects of any Christian or Gentile sovereign. These fictitious travels have been a source of much trouble to the learned; particularly to those who in their zeal to authenticate them followed the aërial footsteps of the Hyppogriffe of Rabbi Benjamin. He affirms that the tomb of Ezekiel, with the library of the first and second temples, were to be seen in his time at a place on the banks of the river Euphrates; Wesselius of Groningen, and many other literati, travelled on purpose to Mesopotamia, to reach the tomb and examine the library; but the fairy treasures were never to be seen, nor even heard of!

The first on the list of impudent impostors is Annius of Viterbo, a Dominican, and master of the sacred palace under Alexander VI. He pretended he had discovered the entire works of Sanchoniatho, Manetho, Berosus, and others, of which only fragments are remaining. He published seventeen books of antiquities! But not having any MSS. to produce, though he declared he had found them buried in the earth, these literary fabrications occasioned great controversies; for the author died before he made up his mind to a confession. At their first publication universal joy was diffused among the learned. Suspicion soon rose, and detection followed. However, as the forger never would acknowledge himself as such, it has been ingeniously conjectured that he himself was imposed on, rather than that he was the impostor; or, as in the case of Chatterton, possibly all may not be fictitious. It has been said that a great volume in MS., anterior by two hundred years to the seventeen books of Annius, exists in the Bibliothèque Colbertine, in which these pretended histories were to be read; but as Annius would never point out the sources of his, the whole may be considered as a very wonderful imposture. I refer the reader to Tyrwhitt's Vindication of his Appendix to Rowley's or Chatterton's Poems, p. 140, for some curious observations, and some facts of literary imposture.

An extraordinary literary imposture was that of one Joseph Vella, who, in 1794, was an adventurer in Sicily, and pretended that he possessed seventeen of the lost books of Livy in Arabic: he had received this literary treasure, he said, from a Frenchman, who had purloined it from a shelf in St. Sophia's church at Constantinople. As many of the Greek and Roman classics have been translated by the Arabians, and many were first known in Europe in their Arabic dress, there was nothing improbable in one part of his story. He was urged to publish these long-desired books; and Lady Spencer, then in Italy, offered to defray the expenses. He had the effrontery, by way of specimen, to edit an Italian translation of the sixtieth book, but that book took up no more than one octavo page! A professor of Oriental literature in Prussia introduced it in his work, never suspecting the fraud; it proved to be nothing more than the epitome of Florus. He also gave out that he possessed a code which he had picked up in the abbey of St. Martin, containing the ancient history of Sicily in the Arabic period, comprehending above two hundred years; and of which ages their own historians were entirely deficient in knowledge. Vella declared he had a genuine official correspondence between the Arabian governors of Sicily and their superiors in Africa, from the first landing of the Arabians in that island. Vella was now loaded with honours and pensions! It is true he showed Arabic MSS., which, however, did not contain a syllable of what he said. He pretended he was in continual correspondence with friends at Morocco and elsewhere. The King of Naples furnished him with money to assist his researches. Four volumes in quarto were at length published! Vella had the adroitness to change the Arabic MSS. he possessed, which entirely related to Mahomet, to matters relative to Sicily; he bestowed several weeks' labour to disfigure the whole, altering page for page, line for line, and word for word, but interspersed numberless dots, strokes, and flourishes; so that when he published a fac-simile, every one admired the learning of Vella, who could translate what no one else could read. He complained he had lost an eye in this minute labour; and every one thought his pension ought to have been increased. Everything prospered about him, except his eye, which some thought was not so bad neither. It was at length discovered by his blunders, &c., that the whole was a forgery: though it had now been patronised, translated, and extracted through Europe. When this MS. was examined by an Orientalist, it was discovered to be nothing but a history of *Mahomet and his family*. Vella was condemned to imprisonment.

The Spanish antiquary, Medina Conde, in order to favour the pretensions of the church in a great lawsuit, forged deeds and inscriptions, which he buried in the ground, where he knew they would shortly be dug up. Upon their being found, he published engravings of them, and gave explanations of their unknown characters, making them out to be so many authentic proofs and evidences of the contested assumptions of the clergy.

The Morocco ambassador purchased of him a copper bracelet of Fatima, which Medina proved by the Arabic inscription and many certificates to be genuine, and found among the ruins of the Alhambra, with other treasures of its last king, who had hid them there in hope of better days. This famous bracelet turned out afterwards to be the work of Medina's own hand, made out of an old brass candlestick!

George Psalmanazar, to whose labours we owe much of the great Universal History, exceeded in powers of deception any of the great impostors of learning. His Island of Formosa was an illusion eminently bold,[96]

---

96. The volume was published in 8vo in 1704, as "An Historical and Geographical Description of Formosa, an Island subject to the Emperor of Japan." It is dedicated to the Bishop of London, who is told that "the Europeans have such obscure and various notions of Japan, and especially of our island Formosa, that they believe nothing for truth that has been said of it." He accordingly narrates the political history of the place; the manners and customs of its inhabitants; their religion, language, &c. A number of engravings illustrate the whole, and depict the dresses of the people, their houses, temples, and ceremonies. A "Formosan Alphabet" is also given, and the Lord's Prayer, Apostles' Creed, and Ten Commandments, are "translated" into this imaginary language. To keep up the imposition, he ate raw meat when dining with the Secretary to the Royal Society, and Formosa appeared in the maps as a real island, in

and maintained with as much felicity as erudition; and great must have been that erudition which could form a pretended language and its grammar, and fertile the genius which could invent the history of an unknown people: it is said that the deception was only satisfactorily ascertained by his own penitential confession; he had defied and baffled the most learned.[97] The literary impostor Lauder had much more audacity than ingenuity, and he died contemned by all the world.[98] Ireland's "Shakspeare" served to show that commentators are not blessed, necessarily, with an interior and unerring tact.[99] Genius and learning are ill directed in forming literary impositions, but at least they must be distinguished from the fabrications of ordinary impostors.

---

the spot he had described as its locality.

97. Psalmanazar would never reveal the true history of his early life, but acknowledged one of the southern provinces of France as the place of his birth, about 1679. He received a fair education, became lecturer in a Jesuit college, then a tutor at Avignon; he afterwards led a wandering life, subsisting on charity, and pretending to be an Irish student travelling to Rome for conscience sake. He soon found he would be more successful if he personated a Pagan stranger, and hence he gradually concocted his tale of *Formosa;* inventing an alphabet, and perfecting his story, which was not fully matured before he had had a few years' hard labour as a soldier in the Low Countries; where a Scotch gentleman introduced him to the notice of Dr. Compton, Bishop of London; who patronised him, and invited him to England. He came, and to oblige the booksellers compiled his *History of Formosa,* by the two editions of which he realized the noble sum of *22 l.* He ended in becoming a regular bookseller's hack, and so highly moral a character, that Dr. Johnson, who knew him well, declared he was "the best man he had ever known."

98. William Lauder first began his literary impostures in the *Gentleman's Magazine* for 1747, where he accused Milton of gross plagiarisms in his *Paradise Lost,* pretending that he had discovered the prototypes of his best thoughts in other authors. This he did by absolute invention, in one instance interpolating twenty verses of a Latin translation of Milton into the works of another author, and then producing them with great virulence as a proof that Milton was a plagiarist. The falsehood of his pretended quotations was demonstrated by Dr. Douglas, Bishop of Salisbury, in 1751, but he returned to the charge in 1754. His character and conduct became too bad to allow of his continued residence in England, and he died in Barbadoes, "in universal contempt," about 1771.

99. Ireland's famous forgeries began when, as a young man in a lawyer's office, he sought to imitate old deeds and letters in the name of Shakspeare and his friends, urged thereto by his father's great anxiety to discover some writings connected with the great bard. Such was the enthusiasm with which they were received by men of great general knowledge, that Ireland persevered in fresh forgeries until an entire play was "discovered." It was a tragedy founded on early British history, and named *Vortigern.* It was produced at Kemble's Theatre, and was damned. Ireland's downward course commenced from that night. He ultimately published confessions of his frauds, and died very poor in 1835.

A singular forgery was practised on Captain Wilford by a learned Hindu, who, to ingratiate himself and his studies with the too zealous and pious European, contrived, among other attempts, to give the history of Noah and his three sons, in his "Purana," under the designation of Satyavrata. Captain Wilford having *read* the passage, transcribed it for Sir William Jones, who translated it as a curious extract; the whole was an interpolation by the dexterous introduction of a forged sheet, discoloured and prepared for the purpose of deception, and which, having served his purpose for the moment, was afterwards withdrawn. As books in India are not bound, it is not difficult to introduce loose leaves. To confirm his various impositions, this learned forger had the patience to write two voluminous sections, in which he connected all the legends together in the style of the *Puranas*, consisting of 12,000 lines. When Captain Wilford resolved to collate the manuscript with others, the learned Hindu began to disfigure his own manuscript, the captain's, and those of the college, by erasing the name of the country and substituting that of Egypt. With as much pains, and with a more honourable direction, our Hindu Lauder might have immortalized his invention.

We have authors who sold their names to be prefixed to works they never read; or, on the contrary, have prefixed the names of others to their own writings. Sir John Hill, once when he fell sick, owned to a friend that he had overfatigued himself with writing seven works at once! one of which was on architecture, and another on cookery! This hero once contracted to translate Swammerdam's work on insects for fifty guineas. After the agreement with the bookseller, he recollected that he did not understand a word of the Dutch language! Nor did there exist a French translation! The work, however, was not the less done for this small obstacle. Sir John bargained with another translator for twenty-five guineas. The second translator was precisely in the same situation as the first—as ignorant, though not so well paid as the knight. He rebargained with a third, who perfectly understood his original, for twelve guineas! So that the translators who could not translate feasted on venison and turtle, while the modest drudge, whose name never appeared to the world, broke in patience his daily bread! The craft of authorship has many mysteries.[100] One of the great patriarchs and primeval dealers in English

---

100. Fielding, the novelist, in *The Author's Farce*, one of those slight plays which he wrote so cleverly, has used this incident, probably from his acquaintance with Hill's trick. He introduces his author trying to sell a translation of the *Æneid*, which the bookseller will not purchase; but after some conversation offers him "employ" in the house as a translator; he then is compelled to own himself "not qualified," because he "understands no language but his own." "What! and translate *Virgil!*" exclaims the astonished bookseller. The detected author answers despondingly, "Alas! sir, I translated him out of Dryden!" The bookseller joyfully exclaims, "Not qualified! If I was an Emperor, thou should'st be my Prime Minister! Thou art as well vers'd in thy

literature was Robert Green, one of the most facetious, profligate, and indefatigable of the Scribleri family. He laid the foundation of a new dynasty of literary emperors. The first act by which he proved his claim to the throne of Grub-street has served as a model to his numerous successors—it was an ambidextrous trick! Green sold his "Orlando Furioso" to two different theatres, and is among the first authors in English literary history who wrote as a *trader*;[101] or as crabbed Anthony Wood phrases it, in the language of celibacy and cynicism, "he wrote to maintain his *wife*, and that high and loose course of living which *poets generally follow*." With a drop still sweeter, old Anthony describes Gayton, another worthy; "he came up to London to live in a *shirking condition*, and wrote *trite things* merely to get bread to sustain him and his *wife*."[102] The hermit Anthony seems to have had a mortal antipathy against the Eves of literary men.

14. CRITICS
(*Curiosities*, vol. 1, pp. 406-408)

WRITERS who have been unsuccessful in original composition have their other productions immediately decried, whatever merit they might once have been allowed to possess. Yet this is very unjust; an author who has given a wrong direction to his literary powers may perceive, at length, where he can more securely point them. Experience is as excellent a mistress in the school of literature as in the school of human life. Blackmore's epics are insufferable; yet neither Addison nor Johnson erred when they considered his philosophical poem as a valuable composition. An indifferent poet may exert the art of criticism in a very high degree; and if he cannot himself produce an original work, he may yet be of great service in regulating the happier genius of another. This observation I shall illustrate by the characters of two French critics; the one is the Abbé d'Aubignac, and the other Chapelain.

Boileau opens his Art of Poetry by a precept which though it be common is always important; this critical poet declares, that "It is in vain a daring author thinks of attaining to the height of Parnassus if he does not feel the

---

trade as if thou had'st laboured in my garret these ten years!"

101. The story is told in *The Defence of Coneycatching*, 1592, where he is said to have "sold *Orlando Furioso* to the Queen's players for twenty nobles, and when they were in the country sold the same play to the Lord Admirall's men for as much more."

102. Edmund Gayton was born in 1609, was educated at Oxford, then led the life of a literary drudge in London, where the best book he produced was *Pleasant Notes upon Don Quixote*, in which are many curious and diverting stories, and among the rest the original of Prior's *Ladle*. He ultimately retired to Oxford, and died there very poor, in a subordinate place in his college.

secret influence of heaven, and if his natal star has not formed him to be a poet." This observation he founded on the character of our Abbé; who had excellently written on the economy of dramatic composition. His *Pratique du Théâtre* gained him an extensive reputation. When he produced a tragedy, the world expected a finished piece; it was acted, and reprobated. The author, however, did not acutely feel its bad reception; he everywhere boasted that he, of all the dramatists, had most scrupulously observed the *rules* of Aristotle. The Prince du Guemené, famous for his repartees, sarcastically observed, "I do not quarrel with the Abbé d'Aubignac for having so closely followed the precepts of Aristotle; but I cannot pardon the precepts of Aristotle, that occasioned the Abbé d'Aubignac to write so wretched a tragedy."

The *Pratique du Théâtre* is not, however, to be despised, because the *Tragedy* of its author is despicable.

Chapelain's unfortunate epic has rendered him notorious. He had gained, and not undeservedly, great reputation for his critical powers. After a retention of above thirty years, his *Pucelle* appeared. He immediately became the butt of every unfledged wit, and his former works were eternally condemned; insomuch that when Camusat published, after the death of our author, a little volume of extracts from his manuscript letters, it is curious to observe the awkward situation in which he finds himself. In his preface he seems afraid that the very name of Chapelain will be sufficient to repel the reader.

Camusat observes of Chapelain that "he found flatterers, who assured him his *Pucelle* ranked above the Æneid; and this Chapelain but feebly denied. However this may be, it would be difficult to make the bad taste which reigns throughout this poem agree with that sound and exact criticism with which he decided on the works of others. So true is it, that *genius* is very superior to a justness of mind which is *sufficient to judge* and to advise others." Chapelain was ordered to draw up a critical list of the chief living authors and men of letters in France, for the king. It is extremely impartial, and performed with an analytical skill of their literary characters which could not have been surpassed by an Aristotle or a Boileau.

The *talent of judging* may exist separately from the *power of execution*. An amateur may not be an artist, though an artist should be an amateur; and it is for this reason that young authors are not to contemn the precepts of such critics as even the Abbé d'Aubignac and Chapelain. It is to Walsh, a miserable versifier, that Pope stands indebted for the hint of our poetry then being deficient in correctness and polish; and it is from this fortunate hint that Pope derived his poetical excellence. Dionysius Halicarnassensis has composed a lifeless history; yet, as Gibbon observes, how admirably has *he* judged the masters, and defined the rules, of historical composition! Gravina, with great taste and spirit, has written on poetry and poets, but he composed tragedies which give him no title to be ranked among them.

V. PRESERVATION AND DESTRUCTION

1. RECOVERY OF MANUSCRIPTS
(*Curiosities*, vol. 1, pp. 17-24)

OUR ancient classics had a very narrow escape from total annihilation. Many have perished: many are but fragments; and chance, blind arbiter of the works of genius, has left us some, not of the highest value; which, however, have proved very useful, as a test to show the pedantry of those who adore antiquity not from true feeling, but from traditional prejudice.

We lost a great number of ancient authors by the conquest of Egypt by the Saracens, which deprived Europe of the use of the *papyrus*. They could find no substitute, and knew no other expedient but writing on parchment, which became every day more scarce and costly. Ignorance and barbarism unfortunately seized on Roman manuscripts, and industriously defaced pages once imagined to have been immortal! The most elegant compositions of classic Rome were converted into the psalms of a breviary, or the prayers of a missal. Livy and Tacitus "hide their diminished heads" to preserve the legend of a saint, and immortal truths were converted into clumsy fictions. It happened that the most voluminous authors were the greatest sufferers; these were preferred, because their volume being the greatest, most profitably repaid their destroying industry, and furnished ampler scope for future transcription. A Livy or a Diodorus was preferred to the smaller works of Cicero or Horace; and it is to this circumstance that Juvenal, Persius, and Martial have come down to us entire, rather probably than to these pious personages preferring their obscenities, as some have accused them. At Rome, a part of a book of Livy was found, between the lines of a parchment but half effaced, on which they had substituted a book of the Bible; and a recent discovery of Cicero *De Republicâ*, which lay concealed under some monkish writing, shows the fate of ancient manuscripts.[103]

That the Monks had not in high veneration the *profane* authors, appears by a facetious anecdote. To read the classics was considered as a very idle recreation, and some held them in great horror. To distinguish them from other books, they invented a disgraceful sign: when a monk asked for a pagan

---

103. This important political treatise was discovered in the year 1823, by Angelo Maii, in the library of the Vatican. A treatise on the Psalms covered it. This second treatise was written in the clear, minute character of the middle ages, but beneath it Maii saw distinct traces of the larger letters of the work of Cicero; and to the infinite joy of the learned succeeded in restoring to the world one of the most important works of the great orator.

author, after making the general sign they used in their manual and silent language when they wanted a book, he added a particular one, which consisted in scratching under his ear, as a dog, which feels an itching, scratches himself in that place with his paw—because, said they, an unbeliever is compared to a dog! In this manner they expressed an *itching* for those *dogs* Virgil or Horace![104]

There have been ages when, for the possession of a manuscript, some would transfer an estate, or leave in pawn for its loan hundreds of golden crowns; and when even the sale or loan of a manuscript was considered of such importance as to have been solemnly registered by public acts. Absolute as was Louis XI. he could not obtain the MS. of Rasis, an Arabian writer, from the library of the Faculty of Paris, to have a copy made, without pledging a hundred golden crowns; and the president of his treasury, charged with this commission, sold part of his plate to make the deposit. For the loan of a volume of Avicenna, a Baron offered a pledge of ten marks of silver, which was refused: because it was not considered equal to the risk incurred of losing a volume of Avicenna! These events occurred in 1471. One cannot but smile, at an anterior period, when a Countess of Anjou bought a favourite book of homilies for two hundred sheep, some skins of martins, and bushels of wheat and rye.

In those times, manuscripts were important articles of commerce; they were excessively scarce, and preserved with the utmost care. Usurers themselves considered them as precious objects for pawn. A student of Pavia, who was reduced, raised a new fortune by leaving in pawn a manuscript of a body of law; and a grammarian, who was ruined by a fire, rebuilt his house with two small volumes of Cicero.

At the restoration of letters, the researches of literary men were chiefly directed to this point; every part of Europe and Greece was ransacked; and, the glorious end considered, there was something sublime in this humble industry, which often recovered a lost author of antiquity, and gave one more classic to the world. This occupation was carried on with enthusiasm, and a kind of mania possessed many, who exhausted their fortunes in distant voyages and profuse prices. In reading the correspondence of the learned Italians of these times, their adventures of manuscript-hunting are very amusing; and their raptures, their congratulations, or at times their condolence, and even their censures, are all immoderate. The acquisition of a

---

104. "Many bishops and abbots began to consider learning as pernicious to true piety, and confounded illiberal ignorance with Christian simplicity," says Warton. The study of Pagan authors was declared to inculcate Paganism; the same sort of reasoning led others to say that the reading of the Scriptures would infallibly change the readers to Jews; it is amusing to look back on these vain efforts to stop the effect of the printing-press.

province would not have given so much satisfaction as the discovery of an author little known, or not known at all. "Oh, great gain! Oh, unexpected felicity! I intreat you, my Poggio, send me the manuscript as soon as possible, that I may see it before I die!" exclaims Aretino, in a letter overflowing with enthusiasm, on Poggio's discovery of a copy of Quintilian. Some of the half-witted, who joined in this great hunt, were often thrown out, and some paid high for manuscripts not authentic; the knave played on the bungling amateur of manuscripts, whose credulity exceeded his purse. But even among the learned, much ill-blood was inflamed; he who had been most successful in acquiring manuscripts was envied by the less fortunate, and the glory of possessing a manuscript of Cicero seemed to approximate to that of being its author. It is curious to observe that in these vast importations into Italy of manuscripts from Asia, John Aurispa, who brought many hundreds of Greek manuscripts, laments that he had chosen more profane than sacred writers; which circumstance he tells us was owing to the Greeks, who would not so easily part with theological works, but did not highly value profane writers!

These manuscripts were discovered in the obscurest recesses of monasteries; they were not always imprisoned in libraries, but rotting in dark unfrequented corners with rubbish. It required not less ingenuity to find out places where to grope in, than to understand the value of the acquisition. An universal ignorance then prevailed in the knowledge of ancient writers. A scholar of those times gave the first rank among the Latin writers to one Valerius, whether he meant Martial or Maximus is uncertain; he placed Plato and Tully among the poets, and imagined that Ennius and Statius were contemporaries. A library of six hundred volumes was then considered as an extraordinary collection.

Among those whose lives were devoted to this purpose, Poggio the Florentine stands distinguished; but he complains that his zeal was not assisted by the great. He found under a heap of rubbish in a decayed coffer, in a tower belonging to the monastery of St. Gallo, the work of Quintilian. He is indignant at its forlorn situation; at least, he cries, it should have been preserved in the library of the monks; but I found it *in teterrimo quodam et obscuro carcere*—and to his great joy drew it out of its grave! The monks have been complimented as the preservers of literature, but by facts, like the present, their real affection may be doubted.

The most valuable copy of Tacitus, of whom so much is wanting, was likewise discovered in a monastery of Westphalia. It is a curious circumstance in literary history, that we should owe Tacitus to this single copy; for the Roman emperor of that name had copies of the works of his illustrious ancestor placed in all the libraries of the empire, and every year had ten copies transcribed; but the Roman libraries seem to have been all destroyed, and the imperial protection availed nothing against the teeth of time.

The original manuscript of Justinian's Pandects was discovered by the

Pisans, when they took a city in Calabria; that vast code of laws had been in a manner unknown from the time of that emperor. This curious book was brought to Pisa; and when Pisa was taken by the Florentines, was transferred to Florence, where it is still preserved.

It sometimes happened that manuscripts were discovered in the last agonies of existence. Papirius Masson found, in the house of a bookbinder of Lyons, the works of Agobard; the mechanic was on the point of using the manuscripts to line the covers of his books.[105] A page of the second decade of Livy, it is said, was found by a man of letters in the parchment of his battledore, while he was amusing himself in the country. He hastened to the maker of the battledore—but arrived too late! The man had finished the last page of Livy—about a week before.

Many works have undoubtedly perished in this manuscript state. By a petition of Dr. Dee to Queen Mary, in the Cotton library, it appears that Cicero's treatise *De Republicâ* was once extant in this country. Huet observes that Petronius was probably entire in the days of John of Salisbury, who quotes fragments, not now to be found in the remains of the Roman bard. Raimond Soranzo, a lawyer in the papal court, possessed two books of Cicero "on Glory," which he presented to Petrarch, who lent them to a poor aged man of letters, formerly his preceptor. Urged by extreme want, the old man pawned them, and returning home died suddenly without having revealed where he had left them. They have never been recovered. Petrarch speaks of them with ecstasy, and tells us that he had studied them perpetually. Two centuries afterwards, this treatise on Glory by Cicero was mentioned in a catalogue of books bequeathed to a monastery of nuns, but when inquired after was missing. It was supposed that Petrus Alcyonius, physician to that household, purloined it, and after transcribing as much of it as he could into his own writings, had destroyed the original. Alcyonius, in his book *De Exilio*, the critics observed, had many splendid passages which stood isolated in his work, and were quite above his genius. The beggar, or in this case the thief, was detected by mending his rags with patches of purple and gold.

In this age of manuscript, there is reason to believe, that when a man of

---

105. Agobard was Archbishop of Lyons, and one of the most learned men of the ninth century. He was born in 779; raised to the prelacy in 816, from which he was expelled by Louis le Debonnaire for espousing the cause of his son Lothaire; he fled to Italy, but was restored to his see in 838, dying in 840, when the Church canonized him. He was a strenuous Churchman, but with enlightened views; and his style as an author is remarkable alike for its clearness and perfect simplicity. His works were unknown until discovered in the manner narrated above, and were published by the discoverer at Paris in 1603, the originals being bequeathed to the Royal Library at his death. On examination, several errors were found in this edition, and a new one was published in 1662, to which another treatise by Agobard was added.

letters accidentally obtained an unknown work, he did not make the fairest use of it, but cautiously concealed it from his contemporaries. Leonard Aretino, a distinguished scholar at the dawn of modern literature, having found a Greek manuscript of Procopius *De Bello Gothico*, translated it into Latin, and published the work; but concealing the author's name, it passed as his own, till another manuscript of the same work being dug out of its grave, the fraud of Aretino was apparent. Barbosa, a bishop of Ungento, in 1649, has printed among his works a treatise, obtained by one of his domestics bringing in a fish rolled in a leaf of written paper, which his curiosity led him to examine. He was sufficiently interested to run out and search the fish market, till he found the manuscript out of which it had been torn. He published it, under the title *De Officio Episcopi*. Machiavelli acted more adroitly in a similar case; a manuscript of the Apophthegms of the Ancients by Plutarch having fallen into his hands, he selected those which pleased him, and put them into the mouth of his hero Castrucio Castricani.

In more recent times, we might collect many curious anecdotes concerning manuscripts. Sir Robert Cotton one day at his tailor's discovered that the man was holding in his hand, ready to cut up for measures—an original Magna Charta, with all its appendages of seals and signatures. This anecdote is told by Colomiés, who long resided in this country; and an original Magna Charta is preserved in the Cottonian library exhibiting marks of dilapidation.

Cardinal Granvelle[106] left behind him several chests filled with a prodigious quantity of letters written in different languages, commented, noted, and underlined by his own hand. These curious manuscripts, after his death, were left in a garret to the mercy of the rain and the rats. Five or six of these chests the steward sold to the grocers. It was then that a discovery was made of this treasure. Several learned men occupied themselves in collecting sufficient of these literary relics to form eighty thick folios, consisting of original letters by all the crowned heads in Europe, with instructions for ambassadors, and other state-papers.

A valuable secret history by Sir George Mackenzie, the king's advocate in Scotland, was rescued from a mass of waste paper sold to a grocer, who had the good sense to discriminate it, and communicated this curious memorial to Dr. M'Crie. The original, in the handwriting of its author, has been deposited in the Advocate's Library. There is an hiatus, which contained the history of six years. This work excited inquiry after the rest of the MSS., which were found to be nothing more than the sweepings of an attorney's office.

Montaigne's Journal of his Travels into Italy has been but recently published. A prebendary of Perigord, travelling through this province to make researches relative to its history, arrived at the ancient *château* of Montaigne, in

---

106. The celebrated minister of Philip II.

possession of a descendant of this great man. He inquired for the archives, if there had been any. He was shown an old worm-eaten coffer, which had long held papers untouched by the incurious generations of Montaigne. Stifled in clouds of dust, he drew out the original manuscript of the travels of Montaigne. Two-thirds of the work are in the handwriting of Montaigne, and the rest is written by a servant, who always speaks of his master in the third person. But he must have written what Montaigne dictated, as the expressions and the egotisms are all Montaigne's. The bad writing and orthography made it almost unintelligible. They confirmed Montaigne's own observation, that he was very negligent in the correction of his works.

Our ancestors were great hiders of manuscripts: Dr. Dee's singular MSS. were found in the secret drawer of a chest, which had passed through many hands undiscovered; and that vast collection of state-papers of Thurloe's, the secretary of Cromwell, which formed about seventy volumes in the original manuscripts, accidentally fell out of the false ceiling of some chambers in Lincoln's-Inn.

A considerable portion of Lady Mary Wortley Montagu's Letters I discovered in the hands of an attorney: family-papers are often consigned to offices of lawyers, where many valuable manuscripts are buried. Posthumous publications of this kind are too frequently made from sordid motives: discernment and taste would only be detrimental to the views of bulky publishers.[107]

2. SOME NOTICES OF LOST WORKS
(*Curiosities*, vol. 1, pp. 58-60)

ALTHOUGH it is the opinion of some critics that our literary losses do not amount to the extent which others imagine, they are however much greater than they allow. Our severest losses are felt in the historical province, and particularly in the earliest records, which might not have been the least interesting to philosphical curiosity.

The history of Phœnicia by Sanchoniathon, supposed to be a contemporary with Solomon, now consists of only a few valuable fragments

---

107. One of the most curious modern discoveries was that of the Fairfax papers and correspondence by the late J. N. Hughes, of Winchester, who purchased at a sale at Leeds Castle, Kent, a box apparently filled with old coloured paving-tiles; on removing the upper layers he found a large mass of manuscripts of the time of the Civil wars, evidently thus packed for concealment; they have since been published, and add most valuable information to this interesting period of English history.

preserved by Eusebius. The same ill fortune attends Manetho's history of Egypt, and Berosus's history of Chaldea. The histories of these most ancient nations, however veiled in fables, would have presented to the philosopher singular objects of contemplation.

Of the history of Polybios, which once contained forty books, we have now only five; of the historical library of Diodorus Siculus fifteen books only remain out of forty; and half of the Roman antiquities of Dionysius Helicarnassensis has perished. Of the eighty books of the history of Dion Cassius, twenty-five only remain. The present opening book of Ammianus Marcellinus is entitled the fourteenth. Livy's history consisted of one hundred and forty books, and we only possess thirty-five of that pleasing historian. What a treasure has been lost in the thirty books of Tacitus! little more than four remain. Murphy elegantly observes, that "the reign of Titus, the delight of human kind, is totally lost, and Domitian has escaped the vengeance of the historian's pen." Yet Tacitus in fragments is still the colossal of history. Velleius Paterculas, of whom a fragment only has reached us, we owe to a single copy: no other having ever been discovered, and which has occasioned the text of this historian to remain incurably corrupt. Taste and criticism have certainly incurred an irreparable loss in that *Treatise on the Causes of the Corruption of Eloquence*, by Quintilian; which he has himself noticed with so much satisfaction in his "Institutes." Petrarch declares, that in his youth he had seen the works of Varro, and the second Decad of Livy; but all his endeavours to recover them were fruitless.

These are only some of the most known losses; but in reading contemporary writers we are perpetually discovering many important ones. We have lost two precious works in ancient biography: Varro wrote the lives of seven hundred illustrious Romans; and Atticus, the friend of Cicero, composed another, on the acts of the great men among the Romans. When we consider that these writers lived familiarly with the finest geniuses of their times, and were opulent, hospitable, and lovers of the fine arts, their biography and their portraits, which are said to have accompanied them, are felt as an irreparable loss to literature. I suspect likewise we have had great losses of which we are not always aware; for in that curious letter in which the younger Pliny describes in so interesting a manner the sublime industry, for it seems sublime by its magnitude, of his Uncle,[108] it appears that his Natural History, that vast register of the wisdom and the credulity of the ancients, was not his only great labour; for among his other works was a history in twenty books, which has entirely perished. We discover also the works of writers, which, by the accounts of them, appear to have equalled in genius those which have descended to us. Pliny has feelingly described a poet of whom he tells us,

---

108. Book III. Letter V. Melmoth's translation.

"his works are never out of my hands; and whether I sit down to write anything myself, or to revise what I have already wrote, or am in a disposition to amuse myself, I constantly take up this agreeable author; and as often as I do so, he is still new."[109] He had before compared this poet to Catullus; and in a critic of so fine a taste as Pliny, to have cherished so constant an intercourse with the writings of this author, indicates high powers. Instances of this kind frequently occur. Who does not regret the loss of the Anticato of Cæsar?

The losses which the poetical world has sustained are sufficiently known by those who are conversant with the few invaluable fragments of Menander, who might have interested us perhaps more than Homer: for he was evidently the domestic poet, and the lyre he touched was formed of the strings of the human heart. He was the painter of passions, and the historian of the manners. The opinion of Quintilian is confirmed by the golden fragments preserved for the English reader in the elegant versions of Cumberland. Even of Æschylus, Sophocles, and Euripides, who each wrote about one hundred dramas, seven only have been preserved of Æschylus and of Sophocles, and nineteen of Euripides. Of the one hundred and thirty comedies of Plautus, we only inherit twenty imperfect ones. The remainder of Ovid's Fasti has never been recovered.

I believe that a philosopher would consent to lose any poet to regain an historian; nor is this unjust, for some future poet may arise to supply the vacant place of a lost poet, but it is not so with the historian. Fancy may be supplied; but Truth once lost in the annals of mankind leaves a chasm never to be filled.

3. OF SUPPRESSORS AND DILAPIDATORS OF MANUSCRIPTS
(*Curiosities*, vol. 2, pp. 443-453)

MANUSCRIPTS are suppressed or destroyed from motives which require to be noticed. Plagiarists, at least, have the merit of preservation: they may blush at their artifices, and deserve the pillory, but their practices do not incur the capital crime of felony. Serassi, the writer of the curious Life of Tasso, was guilty of an extraordinary suppression in his zeal for the poet's memory. The story remains to be told, for it is but little known.

Galileo, in early life, was a lecturer at the university of Pisa: delighting in poetical studies, he was then more of a critic than a philosopher, and had Ariosto by heart. This great man caught the literary mania which broke out about his time, when the Cruscans so absurdly began their "Controversie Tassesche," and raised up two poetical factions, which infected the Italians

109. Book I. Letter XVI.

with a national fever. Tasso and Ariosto were perpetually weighed and outweighed against each other; Galileo wrote annotations on Tasso, stanza after stanza, and without reserve, treating the majestic bard with a severity which must have thrown the Tassoists into an agony. Our critic lent his manuscript to Jacopo Mazzoni, who, probably being a disguised Tassoist, by some accountable means contrived that the manuscript should be absolutely lost!—to the deep regret of the author and all the Ariostoists. The philosopher descended to his grave—not without occasional groans—nor without exulting reminiscences of Ariosto—and the rumour of such a work long floated on tradition! Two centuries had nearly elapsed, when Serassi, employed on his elaborate Life of Tasso, among his uninterrupted researches in the public libraries of Rome, discovered a miscellaneous volume, in which, on a cursory examination, he found deposited the lost manuscript of Galileo! It was a shock from which, perhaps, the zealous biographer of Tasso never fairly recovered; the awful name of Galileo sanctioned the asperity of critical decision, and more particularly the severe remarks on the language, a subject on which the Italians are so morbidly delicate, and so trivially grave. Serassi's conduct on this occasion was at once political, timorous, and cunning. Gladly would he have annihilated the original, but this was impossible! It was some consolation that the manuscript was totally unknown—for having got mixed with others, it had accidentally been passed over, and not entered into the catalogue; his own diligent eye only had detected its existence. "*Nessuno fin ora sa, fuori di me, se vi sia, nè dove sia, e così non potrà darsi alla luce,*" &c. But in the true spirit of a collector, avaricious of all things connected with his pursuits, Serassi cautiously, but completely, transcribed the precious manuscript, with an intention, according to his memorandum, to unravel all its sophistry. However, although the Abbate never wanted leisure, he persevered in his silence; yet he often trembled lest some future explorer of manuscripts might be found as sharpsighted as himself. He was so cautious as not even to venture to note down the library where the manuscript was to be found, and to this day no one appears to have fallen on the volume! On the death of Serassi, his papers came to the hands of the Duke of Ceri, a lover of literature; the transcript of the yet undiscovered original was then revealed! and this secret history of the manuscript was drawn from a note on the title-page written by Serassi himself. To satisfy the urgent curiosity of the literati, these annotations on Tasso by Galileo were published in 1793. Here is a work, which, from its earliest stage, much pains had been taken to suppress; but Serassi's collecting passion inducing him to preserve what he himself so much wished should never appear, finally occasioned its publication! It adds one evidence to the many which prove that such sinister practices have been frequently used by the historians of a party, poetic or politic.

Unquestionably this entire suppression of manuscripts has been too frequently practised. It is suspected that our historical antiquary, Speed, owed many obligations to the learned Hugh Broughton, for he possessed a vast number of his MSS. which he burnt. Why did he burn? If persons place themselves in suspicious situations, they must not complain if they be suspected. We have had historians who, whenever they met with information which has not suited their historical system, or their inveterate prejudices, have employed interpolations, castrations, and forgeries, and in some cases have annihilated the entire document. Leland's invaluable manuscripts were left at his death in the confused state in which the mind of the writer had sunk, overcome by his incessant labours, when this royal antiquary was employed by Henry the Eighth to write our national antiquities. His scattered manuscripts were long a common prey to many who never acknowledged their fountain head; among these suppressors and dilapidators pre-eminently stands the crafty Italian Polydore Vergil, who not only drew largely from this source, but, to cover the robbery, did not omit to depreciate the father of our antiquities—an act of a piece with the character of the man, who is said to have collected and burnt a greater number of historical MSS. than would have loaded a wagon, to prevent the detection of the numerous fabrications in his history of England, which was composed to gratify Mary and the Catholic cause.

The Harleian manuscript, 7379, is a collection of state-letters. This MS. has four leaves entirely torn out, and is accompanied by this extraordinary memorandum, signed by the principal librarian.

"Upon examination of this book, Nov. 12, 1764, these four last leaves were torn out.

"C. MORTON.
"Mem. Nov. 12, sent down to Mrs. Macaulay."

As no memorandum of the name of any student to whom a manuscript is delivered for his researches was ever made, before or since, or in the nature of things will ever be, this memorandum must involve our female historian in the obloquy of this dilapidation.[110] Such dishonest practices of party feeling,

---

110. It is now about thirty-seven years ago since I first published this anecdote; at the same time I received information that our female historian and dilapidator had acted in this manner more than once. At that distance of time this rumour, so notorious at the British Museum, it was impossible to authenticate. The Rev. William Graham, the surviving husband of Mrs. Macaulay, intemperately called on Dr. Morton, in a very advanced period of life, to declare that "it appeared to him that the note does not contain any evidence that the leaves were torn out by Mrs. Macaulay." It was more apparent to the unprejudiced that the doctor must have singularly lost the use of his memory, when he could not explain his own official note, which, perhaps, at the time he was compelled to insert. Dr. Morton was not unfriendly to Mrs. Macaulay's political party; he was the editor of Whitelocke's "Diary of his Embassy to

indeed, are not peculiar to any party. In Roscoe's "Illustrations" of his Life of Lorenzo de' Medici, we discover that Fabroni, whose character scarcely admits of suspicion, appears to have known of the existence of an unpublished letter of Sixtus IV., which involves that pontiff deeply in the assassination projected by the Pazzi; but he carefully suppressed its notice: yet, in his conscience, he could not avoid alluding to such documents, which he concealed by his silence. Roscoe has apologised for Fabroni overlooking this decisive evidence of the guilt of the hypocritical pontiff in the mass of manuscripts; a circumstance not likely to have occurred, however, to this laborious historical inquirer. All party feeling is the same active spirit with an opposite direction. We have a remarkable case, where a most interesting historical production has been silently annihilated by the consent of *both parties*. There once existed an important diary of a very extraordinary character, Sir George Saville, afterwards Marquis of Halifax. This master-spirit, for such I am inclined to consider the author of the little book of "Maxims and Reflections," with a philosophical indifference, appears to have held in equal contempt all the factions of his times, and consequently has often incurred their severe censures. Among other things, the Marquis of Halifax had noted down the conversation he had had with Charles the Second, and the great and busy characters of the age. Of this curious secret history there existed two copies, and the noble writer imagined that by this means he had carefully secured their existence; yet both copies were destroyed from opposite motives; the one at the instigation of Pope, who was alarmed at finding some of the catholic intrigues of the court developed; and the other at the suggestion of a noble friend, who was equally shocked at discovering that his party, the Revolutionists, had sometimes practised mean and dishonourable deceptions. It is in these legacies of honourable men, of whatever party they may be, that we expect to find truth and sincerity; but thus it happens that the last hope of posterity is frustrated by the artifices, or the malignity, of these party-passions. Pulteney, afterwards the Earl of Bath, had also prepared memoirs of his times, which he proposed to confide to Dr. Douglas, bishop of Salisbury, to be composed by the bishop; but his lordship's heir, the General, insisted on destroying these authentic documents, of the value of which we have a notion by one of those conversations which the earl was in the habit of indulging with Hooke, whom he at that time appears to have intended for his historian. The Earl of Anglesea's MS. History of the Troubles of Ireland, and also a Diary of his own Times, have been suppressed; a busy observer of his contemporaries, his tale would materially have assisted a later historian.

---

the Queen of Sweden," and has, I believe, largely castrated the work. The original lies at the British Museum.

The same hostility to manuscripts, as may be easily imagined, has occurred, perhaps more frequently, on the continent. I shall furnish one considerable fact. A French canon, Claude Joly, a bold and learned writer, had finished an ample life of Erasmus, which included a history of the restoration of literature at the close of the fifteenth and the beginning of the sixteenth century. Colomiés tells us, that the author had read over the works of Erasmus seven times; we have positive evidence that the MS. was finished for the press: the Cardinal de Noailles would examine the work himself; this important history was not only suppressed, but the hope entertained, of finding it among the cardinal's papers, was never realised.

These are instances of the annihilation of history; but there is a partial suppression, or castration of passages, equally fatal to the cause of truth; a practice too prevalent among the first editors of memoirs. By such deprivations of the text we have lost important truths, while, in some cases, by interpolations, we have been loaded with the fictions of a party. Original memoirs, when published, should now be deposited at that great institution, consecrated to our national history—the British Museum, to be verified at all times. In Lord Herbert's history of Henry the Eighth, I find, by a manuscript note, that several things were not permitted to be printed, and that the original MS. was supposed to be in Mr. Sheldon's custody, in 1687. Camden told Sir Robert Filmore that he was not suffered to print all his annals of Elizabeth; but he providently sent these expurgated passages to De Thou, who printed them faithfully; and it is remarkable that De Thou himself used the same precaution in the continuation of his own history. We like remote truths, but truths too near us never fail to alarm ourselves, our connexions, and our party. Milton, in composing his History of England, introduced, in the third book, a very remarkable digression, on the characters of the Long Parliament; a most animated description of a class of political adventurers with whom modern history has presented many parallels. From tenderness to a party then imagined to be subdued, it was struck out by command, nor do I find it restituted in Kennett's Collection of English Histories. This admirable and exquisite delineation has been preserved in a pamphlet printed in 1681, which has fortunately exhibited one of the warmest pictures in design and colouring by a master's hand. One of our most important volumes of secret history, "Whitelocke's Memorials," was published by Arthur, Earl of Anglesea, in 1682, who took considerable liberties with the manuscript; another edition appeared in 1732, which restored the many important passages through which the earl appears to have struck his castrating pen. The restitution of the castrated passages has not much increased the magnitude of this folio volume; for the omissions usually consisted of a characteristic stroke, or short critical opinion, which did not harmonise with the private feelings of the Earl of Anglesea. In consequence of the volume not being much enlarged to the eye, and being unaccompanied by a single line of preface to inform us of the value of this more complete edition, the booksellers imagine that there can be no material difference between the two editions, and wonder at the bibliopolical mystery that they can afford to sell the edition of 1682 at ten shillings, and have five guineas for the edition of 1732! Hume who, I have been told, wrote his history usually on a sofa, with the epicurean indolence of his fine genius, always refers to the old truncated and faithless edition of Whitelocke—so little in his day did the critical history of books enter into the studies of authors, or such was the carelessness of our historian! There is more philosophy in *editions* than some philosophers are aware of. Perhaps most "Memoirs" have been unfaithfully published, "curtailed of their fair proportions;" and not a few might be noticed which subsequent editors have restored to their original state, by uniting their dislocated limbs. Unquestionably Passion has sometimes annihilated manuscripts, and tamely revenged itself on the papers of hated writers! Louis the Fourteenth, with his own hands, after the death of Fénélon, burnt all the manuscripts which the Duke of Burgundy had preserved of his preceptor.

As an example of the suppressors and dilapidators of manuscripts, I shall give an extraordinary fact concerning Louis the Fourteenth, more in his favour. His character appears, like some other historical personages, equally disguised by adulation and calumny. That monarch was not the Nero which his revocation of the edict of Nantes made him seem to the French protestants. He was far from approving of the violent measures of his catholic clergy. This opinion of that sovereign was, however, carefully suppressed, when his "Instructions to the Dauphin" were first published. It is now ascertained that Louis the Fourteenth was for many years equally zealous and industrious; and, among other useful attempts, composed an elaborate "Discours" for the dauphin for his future conduct. The king gave his manuscript to Pelisson to revise; but after the revision our royal writer frequently inserted additional paragraphs. The work first appeared in an anonymous "Récueil d'Opuscules Littéraires, Amsterdam, 1767," which Barbier, in his "Anonymes," tells us was "rédigé par Pelisson; le tout publié par l'Abbé Olivet." When at length the printed work was collated with the manuscript original, several suppressions of the royal sentiments appeared; and the editors, too catholic, had, with more particular caution, thrown aside what clearly showed Louis the Fourteenth was far from approving of the violences used against the protestants. The following passage was entirely omitted: "It seems to me, my son, that those who employ extreme and violent remedies do not know the nature of the evil, occasioned in part by heated minds, which, left to themselves, would insensibly be extinguished, rather than rekindle them afresh by the force of contradiction; above all, when the corruption is not confined to a small number, but diffused through all parts of the state; besides, the Reformers said many true things! The best method to have reduced little by little the Huguenots of my kingdom, was not to have pursued them by any direct severity pointed at them."

Lady Mary Wortley Montague is a remarkable instance of an author nearly lost to the nation; she is only known to posterity by a chance publication; for such were her famous Turkish letters, the manuscript of which her family once purchased with an intention to suppress, but they were frustrated by a transcript. The more recent letters were reluctantly extracted out of the family trunks, and surrendered in exchange for certain family documents, which had fallen into the hands of a bookseller. Had it depended on her relatives, the name of Lady Mary had only reached us in the satires of Pope. The greater part of her epistolary correspondence was destroyed by her mother; and what that good and Gothic lady spared, was suppressed by the hereditary austerity of rank, of which her family was too susceptible. The entire correspondence of this admirable writer and studious woman (for once, in perusing some unpublished letters of Lady Mary's, I discovered that "she had been in the habit of reading seven hours a day for many years") would undoubtedly have exhibited a fine statue, instead of the torso we now possess; and we might have lived with her ladyship, as we do with Madame de Sévigné. This I have mentioned elsewhere; but I have since discovered that a considerable correspondence of Lady Mary's, for more than twenty years, with the widow of Colonel Forrester, who had retired to Rome, has been stifled in the birth. These letters, with other MSS. of Lady Mary's, were given by Mrs. Forrester to Philip Thicknesse, with a discretionary power to publish. They were held as a great acquisition by Thicknesse, and his bookseller; but when they had printed off the first thousand sheets, there were parts which they considered might give pain to some of the family. Thicknesse says, "Lady Mary had in many places been uncommonly severe upon her husband, for all her letters were loaded with a scrap or two of poetry at him."[111] A negotiation took place with an agent of Lord Bute's; after some time Miss Forrester put in her claims for the MSS.; and the whole terminated, as Thicknesse tells us, in her obtaining a pension, and Lord Bute all the MSS.

The late Duke of Bridgewater, I am informed, burnt many of the numerous family papers, and bricked up a quantity, which, when opened after his death, were found to have perished. It is said he declared that he did not choose that his ancestors should be traced back to a person of a mean trade, which it seems might possibly have been the case. The loss now cannot be appreciated; but unquestionably stores of history, and perhaps of literature,

---

111. There was one passage he recollected:—
Just left my bed
A lifeless trunk, and scarce a dreaming head!

were sacrificed. Milton's manuscript of Comus was published from the Bridgewater collection, for it had escaped the bricking up!

Manuscripts of great interest are frequently suppressed from the shameful indifference of the possessors.

Mr. Mathias, in his Essay on Gray, tells us, that "in addition to the valuable manuscripts of Mr. Gray, there is reason to think that there were some other papers, *folia Sibyllæ*, in the possession of Mr. Mason; but though a very diligent and anxious inquiry has been made after them, they cannot be discovered since his death. There was, however, one fragment, by Mr. Mason's own description of it, of very great value, namely, "The Plan of an intended Speech in Latin on his appointment as Professor of Modern History in the University of Cambridge." Mr. Mason says, "Immediately on his appointment, Mr. Gray sketched out an admirable plan for his inauguration speech; in which, after enumerating the preparatory and auxiliary studies requisite, such as ancient history, geography, chronology, &c., he descended to the authentic sources of the science, such as public treaties, state records, private correspondence of ambassadors, &c. He also wrote the exordium of this thesis, not, indeed, so correct as to be given by way of fragment, but so spirited in point of sentiment, as leaves it much to be regretted that he did not proceed to its conclusion." This fragment cannot now be found; and after so very interesting a description of its value and of its importance, it is difficult to conceive how Mr. Mason could prevail upon himself to withhold it. If there be a subject on which more, perhaps, than on any other, it would have been peculiarly desirable to know and to follow the train of the ideas of Gray, it is that of modern history, in which no man was more intimately, more accurately, or more extensively conversant than our poet. A sketch or plan from his hand, on the subjects of history, and on those which belonged to it, might have taught succeeding ages how to conduct these important researches with national advantage; and, like some wand of divination, it might have

Pointed to beds where sovereign gold doth grow.[112]

DRYDEN.

I suspect that I could point out the place in which these precious "folia Sibyllæ" of Gray's lie interred; they would no doubt be found among other Sibylline leaves of Mason, in two large boxes, which he left to the care of his executors. These gentlemen, as I am informed, are so extremely careful of them, as to have intrepidly resisted the importunity of some lovers of

---

112. I have seen a transcript, by the favour of a gentleman who sent it to me, of Gray's "Directions for Reading History." It had its merit, at a time when our best histories had not been published, but it is entirely superseded by the admirable "Méthode" of Lenglet du Fresnoy.

literature, whose curiosity has been aroused by the secreted treasures. It is a misfortune which has frequently attended this sort of bequests of literary men, that they have left their manuscripts, like their household furniture; and in several cases we find that many legatees conceive that all manuscripts are either to be burnt, like obsolete receipts, or to be nailed down in a box, that they may not stir a lawsuit!

In a manuscript note of the times, I find that Sir Richard Baker, the author of a chronicle, formerly the most popular one, died in the Fleet; and that his son-in-law, who had all his papers, burnt them for waste-paper; and he said that "he thought Sir Richard's life was among them!" An autobiography of those days which we should now highly prize.

Among these mutilators of manuscripts we cannot too strongly remonstrate with those who have the care of the works of others, and convert them into a vehicle for their own particular purposes, even when they run directly counter to the knowledge and opinions of the original writer. Hard was the fate of honest Anthony Wood, when Dr. Fell undertook to have his history of Oxford translated into Latin; the translator, a sullen, dogged fellow, when he observed that Wood was enraged at seeing the perpetual alterations of his copy made to please Dr. Fell, delighted to alter it the more; while the greater executioner supervising the printed sheets, by "correcting, altering, or dashing out what he pleased," compelled the writer publicly to disavow his own work! Such I have heard was the case of Bryan Edwards, who composed the first accounts of Mungo Park. Bryan Edwards, whose personal interests were opposed to the abolishment of the slave-trade, would not suffer any passage to stand in which the African traveller had expressed his conviction of its inhumanity. Park, among confidential friends, frequently complained that his work did not only not contain his opinions, but was even interpolated with many which he utterly disclaimed!

Suppressed books become as rare as manuscripts. In some researches relating to the history of the Mar-prelate faction, that ardent conspiracy against the established hierarchy, and of which the very name is but imperfectly to be traced in our history, I discovered that the books and manuscripts of the Mar-prelates have been too cautiously suppressed, or too completely destroyed; while those on the other side have been as carefully preserved. In our national collection, the British Museum, we find a great deal against Mar-prelate, but not Mar-prelate himself.

I have written the history of this conspiracy in the third volume of "Quarrels of Authors."

4. DESTRUCTION OF BOOKS
(*Curiosities*, vol. 1, pp. 47-57)

THE literary treasures of antiquity have suffered from the malice of Men as well as that of Time. It is remarkable that conquerors, in the moment of victory, or in the unsparing devastation of their rage, have not been satisfied with destroying *men*, but have even carried their vengeance to *books*.

The Persians, from hatred of the religion of the Phœnicians and the Egyptians, destroyed their books, of which Eusebius notices a great number. A Grecian library at Gnidus was burnt by the sect of Hippocrates, because the Gnidians refused to follow the doctrines of their master. If the followers of Hippocrates formed the majority, was it not very unorthodox in the Gnidians to prefer taking physic their own way? But Faction has often annihilated books.

The Romans burnt the books of the Jews, of the Christians, and the Philosophers; the Jews burnt the books of the Christians and the Pagans; and the Christians burnt the books of the Pagans and the Jews. The greater part of the books of Origen and other heretics were continually burnt by the orthodox party. Gibbon pathetically describes the empty library of Alexandria, after the Christians had destroyed it. "The valuable library of Alexandria was pillaged or destroyed; and near twenty years afterwards the appearance of the *empty shelves* excited the regret and indignation of every spectator, whose mind was not totally darkened by religious prejudice. The compositions of ancient genius, so many of which have irretrievably perished, might surely have been excepted from the wreck of idolatry, for the amusement and instruction of succeeding ages; and either the zeal or avarice of the archbishop might have been satiated with the richest spoils which were the rewards of his victory."

The pathetic narrative of Nicetas Choniates, of the ravages committed by the Christians of the thirteenth century in Constantinople, was fraudulently suppressed in the printed editions. It has been preserved by Dr. Clarke; who observes, that the Turks have committed fewer injuries to the works of art than the barbarous Christians of that age.

The reading of the Jewish Talmud has been forbidden by various edicts, of the Emperor Justinian, of many of the French and Spanish kings, and numbers of Popes. All the copies were ordered to be burnt: the intrepid perseverance of the Jews themselves preserved that work from annihilation. In 1569 twelve thousand copies were thrown into the flames at Cremona. John Reuchlin interfered to stop this universal destruction of Talmuds; for which he became hated by the monks, and condemned by the Elector of Mentz, but appealing to Rome, the prosecution was stopped; and the traditions of the Jews were considered as not necessary to be destroyed.

Conquerors at first destroy with the rashest zeal the national records of the conquered people; hence it is that the Irish people deplore the irreparable losses of their most ancient national memorials, which their invaders have been too successful in annihilating. The same event occurred in the conquest of Mexico; and the interesting history of the New World must ever remain imperfect, in consequence of the unfortunate success of the first missionaries. Clavigero, the most authentic historian of Mexico, continually laments this affecting loss. Everything in that country had been painted, and painters abounded there as scribes in Europe. The first missionaries, suspicious that superstition was mixed with all their paintings, attacked the chief school of these artists, and collecting, in the market-place, a little mountain of these precious records, they set fire to it, and buried in the ashes the memory of many interesting events. Afterwards, sensible of their error, they tried to collect information from the mouths of the Indians; but the Indians were indignantly silent: when they attempted to collect the remains of these painted histories, the patriotic Mexican usually buried in concealment the fragmentary records of his country.

The story of the Caliph Omar proclaiming throughout the kingdom, at the taking of Alexandria, that the Koran contained everything which was useful to believe and to know, and therefore he commanded that all the books in the Alexandrian library should be distributed to the masters of the baths, amounting to 4000, to be used in heating their stoves during a period of six months, modern paradox would attempt to deny. But the tale would not be singular even were it true: it perfectly suits the character of a bigot, a barbarian, and a blockhead. A similar event happened in Persia. When Abdoolah, who in the third century of the Mohammedan æra governed Khorassan, was presented at Nishapoor with a MS. which was shown as a literary curiosity, he asked the title of it—it was the tale of Wamick and Oozra, composed by the great poet Noshirwan. On this Abdoolah observed, that those of his country and faith had nothing to do with any other book than the Koran; and all Persian MSS. found within the circle of his government, as the works of idolaters, were to be burnt. Much of the most ancient poetry of the Persians perished by this fanatical edict.

When Buda was taken by the Turks, a Cardinal offered a vast sum to redeem the great library founded by Matthew Corvini, a literary monarch of Hungary: it was rich in Greek and Hebrew lore, and the classics of antiquity. Thirty amanuenses had been employed in copying MSS. and illuminating them by the finest art. The barbarians destroyed most of the books in tearing away their splendid covers and their silver bosses; an Hungarian soldier picked up a book as a prize: it proved to be the Ethiopics of Heliodorus, from which the first editiion was printed in 1534.

Cardinal Ximenes seems to have retaliated a little on the Saracens; for at the taking of Granada, he condemned to the flames five thousand Korans.

The following anecdote respecting a Spanish missal, called St. Isidore's, is not incurious; hard fighting saved it from destruction. In the Moorish wars, all these missals had been destroyed, excepting those in the city of Toledo. There, in six churches, the Christians were allowed the free exercise of their religion. When the Moors were expelled several centuries afterwards from Toledo, Alphonsus the Sixth ordered the Roman missal to be used in those churches; but the people of Toledo insisted on having their own, as revised by St. Isidore. It seemed to them that Alphonsus was more tyrannical than the Turks. The contest between the Roman and the Toletan missals came to that height, that at length it was determined to decide their fate by single combat; the champion of the Toletan missal felled by one blow the knight of the Roman missal. Alphonsus still considered this battle as merely the effect of the heavy arm of the doughty Toletan, and ordered a fast to be proclaimed, and a great fire to be prepared, into which, after his majesty and the people had joined in prayer for heavenly assistance in this ordeal, both the rivals (not the men, but the missals) were thrown into the flames—again St. Isidore's missal triumphed, and this iron book was then allowed to be orthodox by Alphonsus, and the good people of Toledo were allowed to say their prayers as they had long been used to do. However, the copies of this missal at length became very scarce; for now, when no one opposed the reading of St. Isidore's missal, none cared to use it. Cardinal Ximenes found it so difficult to obtain a copy, that he printed a large impression, and built a chapel, consecrated to St. Isidore, that this service might be daily chanted as it had been by the ancient Christians.

The works of the ancients were frequently destroyed at the instigation of the monks. They appear sometimes to have mutilated them, for passages have not come down to us, which once evidently existed; and occasionally their interpolations and other forgeries formed a destruction in a new shape, by additions to the originals. They were indefatigable in erasing the best works of the most eminent Greek and Latin authors, in order to transcribe their ridiculous lives of saints on the obliterated vellum. One of the books of Livy is in the Vatican most painfully defaced by some pious father for the purpose of writing on it some missal or psalter, and there have been recently others discovered in the same state. Inflamed with the blindest zeal against everything pagan, Pope Gregory VII. ordered that the library of the Palatine Apollo, a treasury of literature formed by successive emperors, should be committed to the flames! He issued this order under the notion of confining the attention of the clergy to the holy scriptures! From that time all ancient learning which was not sanctioned by the authority of the church, has been emphatically distinguished as *profane* in opposition to *sacred*. This pope is said to have burnt the works of Varro, the learned Roman, that Saint Austin should escape from the charge of plagiarism, being deeply indebted to Varro for much of his great work "the City of God."

The Jesuits, sent by the emperor Ferdinand to proscribe Lutheranism from Bohemia, converted that flourishing kingdom comparatively into a desert. Convinced that an enlightened people could never be long subservient to a tyrant, they struck one fatal blow at the national literature: every book they condemned was destroyed, even those of antiquity; the annals of the nation were forbidden to be read, and writers were not permitted even to compose on subjects of Bohemian literature. The mother-tongue was held out as a mark of vulgar obscurity, and domiciliary visits were made for the purpose of inspecting the libraries of the Bohemians. With their books and their language they lost their national character and their independence.

The destruction of libraries in the reign of Henry VIII. at the dissolution of the monasteries, is wept over by John Bale. Those who purchased the religious houses took the libraries as part of the booty, with which they scoured their furniture, or sold the books as waste paper, or sent them abroad in ship-loads to foreign bookbinders.[113]

The fear of destruction induced many to hide manuscripts under ground, and in old walls. At the Reformation popular rage exhausted itself on illuminated books, or MSS. that had red letters in the title page: any work that was decorated was sure to be thrown into the flames as a superstitious one. Red letters and embellished figures were sure marks of being papistical and diabolical. We still find such volumes mutilated of their gilt letters and elegant initials. Many have been found underground, having been forgotten; what escaped the flames were obliterated by the damp: such is the deplorable fate of books during a persecution!

The puritans burned everything they found which bore the vestige of popish origin. We have on record many curious accounts of their pious depredations, of their maiming images and erasing pictures. The heroic expeditions of one Dowsing are journalised by himself: a fanatical Quixote, to

---

113. Henry gave a commission to the famous antiquary, John Leland, to examine the libraries of the suppressed religious houses, and preserve such as concerned history. Though Leland, after his search, told the king he had "conserved many good authors, the which otherwyse had bene lyke to have peryshed, to the no smal incommodite of good letters," he owns to the ruthless destruction of all such as were connected with the "doctryne of a rowt of Romayne bysshopps." Strype consequently notes with great sorrow that many "ancient manuscripts and writings of learned British and Saxon authors were lost. Libraries were sold by mercenary men for anything they could get, in that confusion and devastation of religious houses. Bale, the antiquary, makes mention of a merchant that bought two noble libraries about these times for forty shillings; the books whereof served him for no other use but for waste paper; and that he had been ten years consuming them, and yet there remained still store enough for as many years more. Vast quantities and numbers of these books vanished with the monks and friars from their monasteries, were conveyed away and carried beyond seas to booksellers there, by whole ship ladings; and a great many more were used in shops and kitchens."

whose intrepid arm many of our noseless saints, sculptured on our Cathedrals, owe their misfortunes.

The following are some details from the diary of this redoubtable Goth, during his rage for reformation. His entries are expressed with a laconic conciseness, and it would seem with a little dry humour. "At *Sunbury*, we brake down ten mighty great angels in glass. At *Barham*, brake down the twelve apostles in the chancel, and six superstitious pictures more there; and eight in the church, one a lamb with a cross (+) on the back; and digged down the steps and took up four superstitious inscriptions in brass," &c. "*Lady Bruce's house*, the chapel, a picture of God the Father, of the Trinity, of Christ, the Holy Ghost, and the cloven tongues, which we gave orders to take down, and the lady promised to do it." At another place they "brake six hundred supersititous pictures, eight Holy Ghosts, and three of the Son." And in this manner he and his deputies scoured one hundred and fifty parishes! It has been humorously conjectured, that from this ruthless devastator originated the phrase to *give a Dowsing*. Bishop Hall saved the windows of his chapel at Norwich from destruction, by taking out the heads of the figures; and this accounts for the many faces in church windows which we see supplied by white glass.

In the various civil wars in our country, numerous libraries have suffered both in MSS. and printed books. "I dare maintain," says Fuller, "that the wars betwixt York and Lancaster, which lasted sixty years, were not so destructive as our modern wars in six years." He alludes to the parliamentary feuds in the reign of Charles I. "For during the former their differences agreed in the *same religion*, impressing them with reverence to all allowed muniments! whilst our *civil wars*, founded in *faction* and *variety* of pretended *religions*, exposed all naked church records a prey to armed violence; a sad vacuum, which will be sensible in our *English historie*."

When it was proposed to the great Gustavus of Sweden to destroy the palace of the Dukes of Bavaria, that hero nobly refused; observing, "Let us not copy the example of our unlettered ancestors, who, by waging war against every production of genius, have rendered the name of Goth universally proverbial of the rudest state of barbarity."

Even the civilisation of the eighteenth century could not preserve from the destructive fury of an infuriated mob, in the most polished city of Europe, the valuable MSS. of the great Earl of Mansfield, which were madly consigned to the flames during the riots of 1780; as those of Dr. Priestley were consumed by the mob at Birmingham.

In the year 1599, the Hall of the Stationers underwent as great a purgation as was carried on in Don Quixote's library. Warton gives a list of the best writers who were ordered for immediate conflagration by the prelates Whitgift and Bancroft, urged by the Puritanical and Calvinistic factions. Like thieves and outlaws, they were ordered *to be taken wheresoever they may be found.*—"It was also decreed that no satires or epigrams should be printed for the future. No plays were to be printed without the inspection and permission of the archbishop of Canterbury and the bishop of London; nor any *English historyes*, I suppose novels and romances, without the sanction of the privy council. Any pieces of this nature, unlicensed, or now at large and wandering abroad, were to be diligently sought, recalled, and delivered over to the ecclesiastical arm at London-house."

At a later period, and by an opposite party, among other extravagant motions made in parliament, one was to destroy the Records in the Tower, and to settle the nation on a new foundation! The very same principle was attempted to be acted on in the French Revolution by the "true sansculottes." With us Sir Matthew Hale showed the weakness of the project, and while he drew on his side "all sober persons, stopped even the mouths of the frantic people themselves."

To descend to the losses incurred by individuals, whose names ought to have served as an amulet to charm away the demons of literary destruction. One of the most interesting is the fate of Aristotle's library; he who by a Greek term was first saluted as a collector of books! His works have come down to us accidentally, but not without irreparable injuries, and with no slight suspicion respecting their authenticity. The story is told by Strabo, in his thirteenth book. The books of Aristotle came from his scholar Theophrastus to Neleus, whose posterity, an illiterate race, kept them locked up without using them, buried in the earth! Apellion, a curious collector, purchased them, but finding the MSS. injured by age and moisture, conjecturally supplied their deficiencies. It is impossible to know how far Apellion has corrupted and obscured the text. But the mischief did not end here; when Sylla at the taking of Athens brought them to Rome, he consigned them to the care of Tyrannio, a grammarian, who employed scribes to copy them; he suffered them to pass through his hands without correction, and took great freedoms with them; the words of Strabo are strong: "Ibique Tyrannionem grammaticum iis usum atque (ut fama est) *intercidisse*, aut *invertisse*." He gives it indeed as a report; but the fact seems confirmed by the state in which we find these works: Averroes declared that he read Aristotle forty times over before he succeeded in perfectly understanding him; he pretends he did at the one-and-fortieth time! And to prove this, has published five folios of commentary!

We have lost much valuable literature by the illiberal or malignant descendants of learned and ingenious persons. Many of Lady Mary Wortley Montague's letters have been destroyed, I am informed, by her daughter, who imagined that the family honours were lowered by the addition of those of literature: some of her best letters, recently published, were found buried in an old trunk. It would have mortified her ladyship's daughter to have heard, that her mother was the Sévigné of Britain.

At the death of the learned Peiresc, a chamber in his house filled with letters from the most eminent scholars of the age was discovered: the learned in Europe had addressed Peiresc in their difficulties, who was hence called "the attorney-general of the republic of letters." The niggardly niece, although repeatedly entreated to permit them to be published, preferred to use these learned epistles occasionally to light her fires![114]

The MSS. of Leonardo da Vinci have equally suffered from his relatives. When a curious collector discovered some, he generously brought them to a descendant of the great painter, who coldly observed, that "he had a great deal more in the garret, which had lain there for many years, if the rats had not destroyed them!" Nothing which this great artist wrote but showed an inventive genius.

Menage observes on a friend having had his library destroyed by fire, in which several valuable MSS. had perished, that such a loss is one of the greatest misfortunes that can happen to a man of letters. This gentleman afterwards consoled himself by composing a little treatise *De Bibliothecæ incendio*. It must have been sufficiently curious. Even in the present day men of letters are subject to similar misfortunes; for though the fire-offices will insure books, they will not allow *authors to value their own manuscripts*.

A fire in the Cottonian library shrivelled and destroyed many Anglo-Saxon MSS.—a loss now irreparable. The antiquary is doomed to spell hard and hardly at the baked fragments that crumble in his hand.[115]

Meninsky's famous Persian dictionary met with a sad fate. Its excessive rarity is owing to the siege of Vienna by the Turks: a bomb fell on the

---

114. One of the most disastrous of these losses to the admirers of the old drama occurred through the neglect of a collector—John Warburton, Somerset herald-at-arms (who died 1759), and who had many of these early plays in manuscript. They were left carelessly in a corner, and during his absence his cook used them for culinary purposes as waste paper. The list published of his losses is, however, not quite accurate, as one or more escaped, or were mislaid by this careless man; for Massinger's tragedy, *The Tyrant*, stated to have been so destroyed, was found among his books, and sold at his sale in 1759; another play by the same author, *Believe as You List*, was discovered among some papers from Garrick's library in 1844, and was printed by the Percy Society, 1849. It appears to be the very manuscript copy seen and described by Cibber and Chetwood.

115. One of these shrivelled volumes is preserved in a case in our British Museum. The leaves have been twisted and drawn almost into a solid ball by the action of fire. Some few of the charred manuscripts have been admirably restored of late years by judicious pressure, and inlaying the damaged leaves in solid margins. The fire occurred while the collection was temporarily placed in Ashburnham House, Little Dean's Yard, Westminster, in October, 1731. From the Report published by a Committee of the House of Commons soon after, it appears that the original number of volumes was 958—"of which are lost, burnt, or entirely spoiled, 114; and damaged so as to be defective, 98."

author's house, and consumed the principal part of his indefatigable labours. There are few sets of this high-priced work which do not bear evident proofs of the bomb; while many parts are stained with the water sent to quench the flames.

The sufferings of an author for the loss of his manuscripts strongly appear in the case of Anthony Urceus, a great scholar of the fifteenth century. The loss of his papers seems immediately to have been followed by madness. At Forli, he had an apartment in the palace, and had prepared an important work for publication. His room was dark, and he generally wrote by lamp-light. Having gone out, he left the lamp burning; the papers soon kindled, and his library was reduced to ashes. As soon as he heard the news, he ran furiously to the palace, and knocking his head violently against the gate, uttered this blasphemous language: "Jesus Christ, what great crime have I done! who of those who believed in you have I ever treated so cruelly? Hear what I am saying, for I am in earnest, and am resolved. If by chance I should be so weak as to address myself to you at the point of death, don't hear me, for I will not be with you, but prefer hell and its eternity of torments." To which, by the by, he gave little credit. Those who heard these ravings, vainly tried to console him. He quitted the town, and lived franticly, wandering about the woods!

Ben Jonson's *Execration on Vulcan* was composed on a like occasion; the fruits of twenty years' study were consumed in one short hour; our literature suffered, for among some works of imagination there were many philosophical collections, a commentary on the poetics, a complete critical grammar, a life of Henry V., his journey into Scotland, with all his adventures in that poetical pilgrimage, and a poem on the ladies of Great Britain. What a catalogue of losses!

Castelvetro, the Italian commentator on Aristotle, having heard that his house was on fire, ran through the streets exclaiming to the people, *alla Poetica! alla Poetica! To the Poetic! To the Poetic!* He was then writing his commentary on the Poetics of Aristotle.

Several men of letters have been known to have risen from their death-bed to destroy their MSS. So solicitous have they been not to venture their posthumous reputation in the hands of undiscerning friends. Colardeau, the elegant versifier of Pope's epistle of Eloisa to Abelard, had not yet destroyed what he had written of a translation of Tasso. At the approach of death, he recollected his unfinished labour; he knew that his friends would not have the courage to annihilate one of his works; this was reserved for him. Dying, he raised himself, and as if animated by an honourable action, he dragged himself along, and with trembling hands seized his papers, and consumed them in one sacrifice.—I recollect another instance of a man of letters, of our own country, who acted the same part. He had passed his life in constant study, and it was observed that he had written several folio volumes, which his modest fears would not permit him to expose to the eye even of his critical friends. He promised to leave his labours to posterity; and he seemed sometimes, with a glow on his countenance, to exult that they would not be unworthy of their acceptance. At his death his sensibility took the alarm; he had the folios brought to his bed; no one could open them, for they were closely locked. At the sight of his favourite and mysterious labours, he paused; he seemed disturbed in his mind, while he felt at every moment his strength decaying; suddenly he raised his feeble hands by an effort of firm resolve, burnt his papers, and smiled as the greedy Vulcan licked up every page. The task exhausted his remaining strength, and he soon afterwards expired. The late Mrs. Inchbald had written her life in several volumes; on her death-bed, from a motive perhaps of too much delicacy to admit of any argument, she requested a friend to cut them into pieces before her eyes—not having sufficient strength left herself to perform this funereal office. These are instances of what may be called the heroism of authors.

The republic of letters has suffered irreparable losses by shipwrecks. Guarino Veronese, one of those learned Italians who travelled through Greece for the recovery of MSS., had his perseverance repaid by the acquisition of many valuable works. On his return to Italy he was shipwrecked, and lost his treasures! So poignant was his grief on this occasion that, according to the relation of one of his countrymen, his hair turned suddenly white.

About the year 1700, Hudde, an opulent burgomaster of Middleburgh, animated solely by literary curiosity, went to China to instruct himself in the language, and in whatever was remarkable in this singular people. He acquired the skill of a mandarine in that difficult language; nor did the form of his Dutch face undeceive the physiognomists of China. He succeeded to the dignity of a mandarine; he travelled through the provinces under this character, and returned to Europe with a collection of observations, the cherished labour of thirty years, and all these were sunk in the bottomless sea.

The great Pinellian library, after the death of its illustrious possessor, filled three vessels to be conveyed to Naples. Pursued by corsairs, one of the vessels was taken; but the pirates finding nothing on board but books, they threw them all into the sea: such was the fate of a great portion of this famous library.[116] National libraries have often perished at sea, from the circumstance of conquerors transporting them into their own kingdoms.

---

116. Gianvincenzo Pinelli was descended from a noble Genoese family, and born at Naples in 1535. At the age of twenty-three he removed to Padua, then noted for its learning, and here he devoted his time and fortune to literary and scientific pursuits. There was scarcely a branch of knowledge that he did not cultivate; and at his death, in 1601, he left a noble library behind him. But the Senate of Venice, ever fearful that an undue knowledge of its proceedings should be made public, set their seal upon his collection of manuscripts, and took away more than two hundred volumes which related in some degree to its affairs. The rest of the books were packed to go to Naples, where his heirs resided. The printed books are stated to have filled one hundred and sixteen chests, and the manuscripts were contained in fourteen others. Three ships were freighted with them. One fell into the hands of corsairs, and the contents were destroyed, as stated in the text; some of the books, scattered on the beach at Fermo, were purchased by the Bishop there. The other shiploads were ultimately obtained by Cardinal Borromeo, and added to his library.

VI. PROPERTY AND POLITICS

1. THE CASE OF AUTHORS STATED
INCLUDING THE HISTORY OF LITERARY PROPERTY
(*Calamities*, vol. 5, pp. 15-21)

JOHNSON has dignified the booksellers as "the patrons of literature," which was generous in that great author, who had written well and lived but ill all his life on that patronage. Eminent booksellers, in their constant intercourse with the most enlightened class of the community, that is, with the best authors and the best readers, partake of the intelligence around them; their great capitals, too, are productive of good and evil in literature; useful when they carry on great works, and pernicious when they sanction indifferent ones. Yet are they but commercial men. A trader can never be deemed a patron, for it would be romantic to purchase what is not saleable; and where no favour is conferred, there is no patronage.

Authors continue poor, and booksellers become opulent; an extraordinary result! Booksellers are not agents for authors, but proprietors of their works; so that the perpetual revenues of literature are solely in the possession of the trade.

Is it then wonderful that even successful authors are indigent? They are heirs to fortunes, but by a strange singularity they are disinherited at their birth; for, on the publication of their works, these cease to be their own property. Let that natural property be secured, and a good book would be an inheritance, a leasehold or a freehold, as you choose it; it might at least last out a generation, and descend to the author's blood, were they permitted to live on their father's glory, as in all other property they do on his industry.[117]

---

117. The following facts will show the value of *literary property*"; immense profits and cheap purchases! The manuscript of "Robinson Crusoe" ran through the whole trade, and no one would print it; the bookseller who did purchase it, who, it is said, was not remarkable for his discernment, but for a speculative turn, got a thousand guineas by it. How many have the booksellers since accumulated? Burn's "Justice" was disposed of by its author for a trifle, as well as Buchan's "Domestic Medicine;" these works yield annual incomes. Goldsmith's "Vicar of Wakefield" was sold in the hour of distress, with little distinction from any other work in that class of composition; and "Evelina" produced five guineas from the niggardly trader. Dr. Johnson fixed the price of his "Biography of the Poets" at two hundred guineas; and Mr. Malone observes, the booksellers in the course of twenty-five years have probably got five thousand. I could add a great number of facts of this nature which relate to living writers; the profits of their own works for two or three years would rescue them from the horrors and humiliation of pauperism. It is, perhaps, useful to record, that, while

Something of this nature has been instituted in France, where the descendants of Corneille and Molière retain a claim on the theatres whenever the drama of their great ancestors are performed. In that country, literature has ever received peculiar honours—it was there decreed, in the affair of Crebillon, that literary productions are not seizable by creditors.[118]

The history of literary property in this country might form as ludicrous a narrative as Lucian's "true history." It was a long while doubtful whether any such thing existed, at the very time when booksellers were assigning over the perpetual copyrights of books, and making them the subject of family settlements for the provision of their wives and children! When Tonson, in 1739, obtained an injunction to restrain another bookseller from printing Milton's "Paradise Lost," he brought into court as a proof of his title an assignment of the original copyright, made over by the sublime poet in 1667, which was read. Milton received for this assignment the sum which we all know—Tonson and all his family and assignees rode in their carriages with the profits of the five-pound epic.[119]

The verbal and tasteless lawyers, not many years past, with legal metaphysics, wrangled like the schoolmen, inquiring of each other, "whether the *style* and *ideas* of an author were tangible things; or if these were a *property*, how is *possession* to be taken, or any act of *occupancy* made on mere intellectual *ideas*." Nothing, said they, can be an object of property but which has a

---

the compositions of genius are but slightly remunerated, though sometimes as productive as "the household stuff" of literature, the latter is rewarded with princely magnificence. At the sale of the Robinsons, the copyright of "Vyse's Spelling-book" was sold at the enormous price of 2200*l.*, with an *annuity* of fifty guineas to the author!

118. The circumstance, with the poet's dignified petition, and the King's honourable decree, are preserved in "Curiosities of Literature," vol. i. p. 406.

119. The elder Tonson's portrait represents him in his gown and cap, holding in his right hand a volume lettered "Paradise Lost"—such a favourite object was Milton and copyright! Jacob Tonson was the founder of a race who long honoured literature. His rise in life is curious. He was at first unable to pay twenty pounds for a play by Dryden, and joined with another bookseller to advance that sum; the play sold, and Tonson was afterwards enabled to purchase the succeeding ones. He and his nephew died worth two hundred thousand pounds.—Much old Tonson owed to his own industry; but he was a mere trader. He and Dryden had frequent bickerings; he insisted on receiving 10,000 verses for two hundred and sixty-eight pounds, and poor Dryden threw in the finest Ode in the language towards the number. He would pay in the base coin which was then current; which was a loss to the poet. Tonson once complained to Dryden, that he had only received 1446 lines of his translation of Ovid for his Miscellany for fifty guineas, when he had calculated at the rate of 1518 lines for forty guineas; he gives the poet a piece of critical reasoning, that he considered he had a better bargain with "Juvenal," which is reckoned "not so easy to translate as Ovid." In these times such a mere trader in literature has disappeared.

corporeal substance; the air and the light, to which they compared an author's ideas, are common to all; ideas in the MS. state were compared to birds in a cage; while the author confines them in his own dominion, none but he has a right to let them fly; but the moment he allows the bird to escape from his hand, it is no violation of property in any one to make it his own. And to prove that there existed no property after publication, they found an analogy in the gathering of acorns, or in seizing on a vacant piece of ground; and thus degrading that most refined piece of art formed in the highest state of society, a literary production, they brought us back to a state of nature; and seem to have concluded that literary property was purely ideal; a phantom which, as its author could neither grasp nor confine to himself, he must entirely depend on the public benevolence for his reward.[120]

The Ideas, that is, the work of an author, are "tangible things." "There are works," to quote the words of a near and dear relative, "which require great learning, great industry, great labour, and great capital, in their preparation. They assume a palpable form. You may fill warehouses with them, and freight ships; and the tenure by which they are held is superior to that of all other property, for it is original. It is tenure which does not exist in a doubtful title; which does not spring from any adventitious circumstances; it is not found—it is not purchased—it is not prescriptive—it is original; so it is the most natural of all titles, because it is the most simple and least artificial. It is paramount and sovereign, because it is a tenure by creation."[121]

There were indeed some more generous spirits and better philosophers fortunately found on the same bench; and the identity of a literary composition was resolved into its sentiments and language, besides what was more obviously valuable to some persons, the print and paper. On this slight principle was issued the profound award which accorded a certain term of years to any work, however immortal. They could not diminish the immortality of a book, but only its reward. In all the litigations respecting literary property, authors were little considered—except some honourable testimonies due to genius, from the sense of WILLES, and the eloquence of MANSFIELD. Literary property was still disputed, like the rights of a parish common. An honest printer, who could not always write grammar, had the shrewdness to make a bold effort in this scramble, and perceiving that even by this last favourable award all literary property would necessarily centre with the booksellers, now stood forward for his own body—the printers. This rough advocate observed that "a few persons who call themselves *booksellers*, about the number of *twenty-five*, have kept the *monopoly of books and copies* in their

---

120. Sir James Burrow's Reports on the question concerning Literary Property, 4to. London, 1773.

121. Mirror of Parliament, 3529.

hands, to the entire exclusion of all others, but more especially the *printers*, whom they have always held it a rule never to let become purchasers in *copy*." Not a word for the *authors!* As for them, they were doomed by both parties as the fat oblation: they indeed sent forth some meek bleatings; but what were AUTHORS, between judges, booksellers, and printers? the sacrificed among the sacrificers!

All this was reasoning in a circle. LITERARY PROPERTY in our nation arose from *a new state of society*. These lawyers could never develope its nature by wild analogies, nor discover it in any common-law right; for our common law, composed of immemorial customs, could never have had in its contemplation an object which could not have existed in barbarous periods. Literature, in its enlarged spirit, certainly never entered into the thoughts or attention of our rude ancestors. All their views were bounded by the necessaries of life; and as yet they had no conception of the impalpable, invisible, yet sovereign dominion of the human mind—enough for our rough heroes was that of the seas! Before the reign of Henry VIII. great authors composed occasionally a book in Latin, which none but other great authors cared for, and which the people could not read. In the reign of Elizabeth, ROGER ASCHAM appeared—one of those men of genius born to create a new era in the history of their nation. The first English author who may be regarded as the founder of our *prose style* was Roger Ascham, the venerable parent of our *native literature*. At a time when our scholars affected to contemn the vernacular idiom, and in their Latin works were losing their better fame, that of being understood by all their countrymen, Ascham boldly avowed the design of setting an example, in his own words, TO SPEAK AS THE COMMON PEOPLE, TO THINK AS WISE MEN. His pristine English is still forcible without pedantry, and still beautiful without ornament.[122] The illustrious BACON condescended to follow this new example in the most popular of his works. This change in our literature was like a revelation; these men taught us our language in books. We became a reading people; and then the demand for books naturally produced a new order of authors, who traded in literature. It was then, so early as in the Elizabethan age, that *literary property* may be said to derive its obscure origin in this nation. It was protected in an indirect manner by the *licensers* of the press; for although that was a mere political institution, only designed to prevent seditious and irreligious publications, yet, as no book could be printed without a licence, there was honour enough in the licensers not to allow other publishers to infringe on the privilege granted to the first claimant. In Queen Anne's time, when the office of licensers was extinguished, a more liberal genius was rising in the nation, and *literary property* received a more definite and a more powerful protection. A limited term was granted to every author to

---

122. See "Amenities of Literature" [pp. 359-367] for an account of this author.

reap the fruits of his labours; and Lord Hardwicke pronounced this statute "a universal patent for authors." Yet, subsequently, the subject of *literary property* involved discussion; even at so late a period as in 1769 it was still to be litigated. It was then granted that originally an author had at common law a property in his work, but that the act of Anne took away all copyright after the expiration of the terms it permitted.

As the matter now stands, let us address an arithmetical age—but my pen hesitates to bring down my subject to an argument fitted to "these coster-monger times."[123] On the present principle of literary property, it results that an author disposes of a leasehold property of twenty-eight years, often for less than the price of one year's purchase! How many living authors are the sad witnesses of this fact, who, like so many Esaus, have sold their inheritance for a meal! I leave the whole school of Adam Smith to calm their calculating emotions concerning "that unprosperous race of men" (sometimes this master-seer calls them "unproductive") "commonly called *men of letters*," who are pretty much in the situation which lawyers and physicians would be in, were these, as he tells us, in that state when "*a scholar* and *a beggar* seem to have been very nearly *synonymous terms*"—and this melancholy fact that man of genius discovered, without the feather of his pen brushing away a tear from his lid—without one spontaneous and indignant groan!

Authors may exclaim, "we ask for justice, not charity." They would not need to require any favour, nor claim any other than that protection which an enlightened government, in its wisdom and its justice, must bestow. They would leave to the public disposition the sole appreciation of their works; their book must make its own fortune; a bad work may be cried up, and a good work may be cried down; but Faction will soon lose its voice, and Truth acquire one. The cause we are pleading is not to calamities of indifferent writers, but of those whose utility or whose genius long survives that limited term which has been so hardly wrenched from the penurious hand of verbal lawyers. Every lover of literature, and every votary of humanity has long felt indignant at that sordid state and all those secret sorrows to which men of the finest genius, or of sublime industry, are reduced and degraded in society. Johnson himself, who rejected that perpetuity of literary property which some enthusiasts seemed to claim at the time the subject was undergoing the discussion of the judges, is, however, for extending the copyright to a *century*. Could authors secure this, their natural right, literature would acquire a permanent and a nobler reward; for great authors would then be distinguished by the very profits they would receive from that obscure multitude whose

---

123. A coster-monger, or Costard-monger, is a dealer in apples, which are so called because they are shaped like a *costard, i. e.,* a man's head. *Steevens.*—Johnson explains the phrase eloquently: "In these times when the prevalence of trade has produced that meanness, that rates the merit of everything by money."

common disgraces they frequently participate, notwithstanding the superiority of their own genius. Johnson himself will serve as a proof of the incompetent remuneration of literary property. He undertook and he performed an Herculean labour, which employed him so many years that the price he obtained was exhausted before the work was concluded—the wages did not even last as long as the labour! Where, then, is the author to look forward, when such works are undertaken, for a provision for his family, or for his future existence? It would naturally arise from the work itself, were authors not the most ill-treated and oppressed class of the community. The daughter of MILTON need not have craved the alms of the admirers of her father, if the right of authors had been better protected; his own "Paradise Lost" had then been her better portion and her most honourable inheritance. The children of BURNS [Burn] would have required no subscriptions; that annual tribute which the public pay to the genius of their parent was their due, and would have been their fortune.

Authors now submit to have a shorter life than their own celebrity. While the book markets of Europe are supplied with the writings of English authors, and they have a wider diffusion in America than at home, it seems a national ingratitude to limit the existence of works for their authors to a short number of years, and then to seize on their possession for ever.

2. LICENSERS OF THE PRESS
(*Curiosities*, vol. 2, pp. 216-228)

IN the history of literature, and perhaps in that of the human mind, the institution of the LICENSERS OF THE PRESS, and CENSORS OF BOOKS, was a bold invention, designed to counteract that of the Press itself; and even to convert this newly-discovered instrument of human freedom into one which might serve to perpetuate that system of passive obedience which had so long enabled modern Rome to dictate her laws to the universe. It was thought possible in the subtlety of Italian *astuzia* and Spanish monachism, to place a sentinel on the very thoughts as well as on the persons of authors; and in extreme cases, that books might be condemned to the flames as well as heretics.

Of this institution, the beginnings are obscure, for it originated in caution and fear; but as the work betrays the workman, and the national physiognomy the native, it is evident that so inquisitorial an act could only have originated in the Inquisition itself. Feeble or partial attempts might previously have existed, for we learn that the monks had a part of their libraries called the *inferno*, which was not the part which they least visited, for it contained, or hid, all the prohibited books which they could smuggle into it. But this inquisitorial power assumed its most formidable shape in the council of Trent, when some gloomy spirits from Rome and Madrid foresaw the revolution of this new age of books. The triple-crowned pontiff had in vain rolled the thunders of the Vatican, to strike out of the hands of all men the volumes of Wickliffe, of Huss, and of Luther, and even menaced their eager readers with death. At this council Pius IV. was presented with a catalogue of books of which they denounced that the perusal ought to be forbidden; his bull not only confirmed this list of the condemned, but added rules how books should be judged. Subsequent popes enlarged these catalogues, and added to the rules, as the monstrous novelties started up. Inquisitors of books were appointed; at Rome they consisted of certain cardinals and "the master of the holy palace;" and literary inquisitors were elected at Madrid, at Lisbon, at Naples, and for the Low Countries; they were watching the ubiquity of the human mind. These catalogues of prohibited books were called *Indexes;* and at Rome a body of these literary despots are still called "the Congregation of the Index." The simple *Index* is a list of condemned books which are never to be opened; but the *Expurgatory Index* indicates those only prohibited till they have undergone a purification. No book was allowed to be on any subject, or in any language, which contained a single position, an ambiguous sentence, even a word, which, in the most distant sense, could be construed opposite to the doctrines of the supreme authority of this council of Trent; where it seems to have been enacted, that all men, literate and illiterate, prince and peasant, the Italian, the Spaniard and the Netherlander, should take the mint-stamp of their thoughts from the council of Trent, and millions of souls be struck off at one blow, out of the same used mould.

The sages who compiled these Indexes, indeed, long had reason to imagine that passive obedience was attached to the human character: and therefore they considered, that the publications of their adversaries required no other notice than a convenient insertion in their indexes. But the heretics diligently reprinted them with ample prefaces and useful annotations; Dr. James, of Oxford, republished an Index with due animadversions. The parties made an opposite use of them: while the catholic crossed himself at every title, the heretic would purchase no book which had not been indexed. One of their portions exposed a list of those authors whose heads were condemned as well as their books: it was a catalogue of men of genius.

The results of these indexes were somewhat curious. As they were formed in different countries, the opinions were often diametrically opposite to each other. The learned Arias Montanus, who was a chief inquisitor in the Netherlands, and concerned in the Antwerp Index, lived to see his own works placed in the Roman Index; while the inquisitor of Naples was so displeased with the Spanish Index, that he persisted to assert that it had never been printed at Madrid! Men who began by insisting that all the world should not differ from their opinions, ended by not agreeing with themselves. A civil war raged among the Index-makers; and if one criminated, the other retaliated. If one discovered ten places necessary to be expurgated, another found thirty, and a third inclined to place the whole work in the condemned list. The inquisitors at length became so doubtful of their own opinions, that they sometimes expressed in their license for printing, that "they tolerated the reading, after the book had been corrected by themselves, till such time as the work should be considered worthy of some farther correction." The expurgatory Indexes excited louder complaints than those which simply condemned books; because the purgers and castrators, as they were termed, or as Milton calls them, "the executioners of books," by omitting, or interpolating passages, made an author say, or unsay, what the inquisitors chose; and their editions, after the death of the authors, were compared to the erasures or forgeries in records: for the books which an author leaves behind him, with his last corrections, are like his last will and testament, and the public are the legitimate heirs of an author's opinions.

The whole process of these expurgatory Indexes, that "rakes through the entrails of many an old good author, with a violation worse than any could be offered to his tomb," as Milton says, must inevitably draw off the life-blood, and leave an author a mere spectre! A book in Spain and Portugal passes through six or seven courts before it can be published, and is supposed to recommend itself by the information, that it is published with *all* the necessary privileges. They would sometimes keep works from publication till they had "properly qualified them, *interemse calificam*," which in one case is said to have occupied them during forty years. Authors of genius have taken fright at the gripe of "the master of the holy palace," or the lacerating scratches of the "corrector-general por su magestad." At Madrid and Lisbon, and even at Rome, this licensing of books has confined most of their authors to the body of the good fathers themselves.

The Commentaries on the Lusiad, by Faria de Souza, had occupied his zealous labours for twenty-five years, and were favourably received by the learned. But the commentator was brought before this tribunal of criticism and religion, as suspected of heretical opinions; when the accuser did not succeed before the inquisitors of Madrid, he carried the charge to that of Lisbon: an injunction was immediately issued to forbid the sale of the Commentaries, and it cost the commentator an elaborate defence, to demonstrate the catholicism of the poet and himself. The Commentaries finally were released from perpetual imprisonment.

This system has prospered to admiration, in keeping public opinion down to a certain meanness of spirit, and happily preserved stationary the childish stupidity through the nation, on which so much depended.

Nani's History of Venice is allowed to be printed, because it contained *nothing against princes*. Princes then were either immaculate or historians false. The History of Guicciardini is still scarred with the merciless wound of the papistic censor; and a curious account of the origin and increase of papal power was long wanting in the third and fourth book of his history. Velly's History of France would have been an admirable work had it not been printed at Paris!

When the insertions in the Index were found of no other use than to bring the peccant volumes under the eyes of the curious, they employed the secular arm in burning them in public places. The history of these literary conflagrations has often been traced by writers of opposite parties; for the truth is, that both used them: zealots seem all formed of one material, whatever be their party. They had yet to learn, that burning was not confuting, and that these public fires were an advertisement by proclamation. The publisher of Erasmus's Colloquies intrigued to procure the burning of his book, which raised the sale to twenty-four thousand!

A curious literary anecdote has reached us of the times of Henry VIII. Tonstall, Bishop of London, accused at that day for his moderation in preferring the burning of books to that of authors, which was then getting into practice, to testify his abhorrence of Tindal's principles, who had printed a translation of the New Testament, a sealed book for the multitude, thought of purchasing all the copies of Tindal's translation, and annihilating them in the common flame. This occurred to him when passing through Antwerp in 1529, then a place of refuge for the Tindalists. He employed an English merchant there for this business, who happened to be a secret follower of Tindal, and acquainted him with the bishop's intention. Tindal was extremely glad to hear of the project, for he was desirous of printing a more correct edition of his version; the first impression still hung on his hands, and he was too poor to make a new one; he gladly furnished the English merchant with all his unsold copies, which the bishop as eagerly bought, and had them all publicly burnt in Cheapside. The people not only declared this was a "burning of the word of God," but it inflamed the desire of reading that volume; and the second edition was sought after at any price. When one of the Tindalists, who was sent here to sell them, was promised by the lord chancellor, in a private examination, that he should not suffer if he would reveal who encouraged and supported his party at Antwerp, the Tindalist immediately accepted the offer, and assured the lord chancellor that the greatest encouragement they had was from Tonstall, the Bishop of London, who had bought up half the impression, and enabled them to produce a second!

In the reign of Henry VIII. We seem to have burnt books on both sides; it was an age of unsettled opinions; in Edward's, the Catholic works were burnt; and Mary had her pyramids of Protestant volumes; in Elizabeth's, political pamphlets fed the flames; and libels in the reign of James I. and his sons.

Such was this black dwarf of literature, generated by Italian craft and Spanish monkery, which, however, was fondly adopted as it crept in among all the nations of Europe. France cannot exactly fix on the era of her *Censeurs de Livres;* and we ourselves, who gave it its death-blow, found the custom prevail without any authority from our statutes. The practice of licensing books was unquestionably derived from the Inquisition, and was applied here first to books of religion. Britain long groaned under the leaden stamp of an *Imprimatur.* Oxford and Cambridge still grasp at this shadow of departed literary despotism; they have their licensers and their Imprimaturs. Long, even in our land, men of genius were either suffering the vigorous limbs of their productions to be shamefully mutilated in public, or voluntarily committed a literary suicide in their own manuscripts. Camden declared that he was not suffered to print all his Elizabeth, and sent those passages over to De Thou, the French historian, who printed his history faithfully two years after Camden's first edition, 1615. The same happened to Lord Herbert's History of Henry VIII. which has never been given according to the original, which is still in existence. In the poems of Lord Brooke, we find a lacuna of the first twenty pages; it was a poem on Religion, cancelled by the order of Archbishop Laud. The great Sir Matthew Hale ordered that none of his works should be printed after his death; as he apprehended that, in the licensing of them, some things might be struck out or altered, which he had observed, not without some indignation, had been done to those of a learned friend; and he preferred bequeathing his uncorrupted MSS. to the Society of Lincoln's Inn, as their only guardians, hoping that they were a treasure worth keeping. Contemporary authors have frequent allusions to such books, imperfect and mutilated at the caprice or the violence of a licenser.

The laws of England have never violated the freedom and the dignity of its press. "There is no law to prevent the printing of any book in England, only a decree in the Star-chamber," said the learned Selden.[124] Proclamations were occasionally issued against authors and books; and foreign works were, at times, prohibited. The freedom of the press was rather circumvented, than openly attacked, in the reign of Elizabeth, who dreaded the Roman Catholics, who were at once disputing her right to the throne, and the religion of the state. Foreign publications, or "books from any parts beyond the seas," were therefore prohibited.[125] The press, however, was not free under the reign of a

---

124. Sir Thomas Crew's Collection of the Proceedings of the Parliament, 1628, p. 71.

125. The consequence of this prohibition was, that our own men of learning were at a loss to know what arms the enemies of England, and of her religion, were fabricating against us. This knowledge was absolutely necessary, as appears by a curious fact in Strype's Life of Whitgift. A license for the importation of foreign books was granted to an Italian merchant, with orders to collect abroad this sort of libels; but he was to deposit them with the archbishop and the privy council. A few, no doubt, were obtained by the curious, Catholic or Protestant.—Strype's "Life of Whitgift," p. 268.

sovereign, whose high-toned feelings, and the exigencies of the times, rendered as despotic in *deeds*, as the pacific James was in *words*. Although the press had then no restrictions, an author was always at the mercy of the government. Elizabeth too had a keen scent after what she called treason, which she allowed to take in a large compass. She condemned one author (with his publisher) to have the hand cut off which wrote his book; and she hanged another.[126] It was Sir Francis Bacon, or his father, who once pleasantly turned aside the keen edge of her regal vindictiveness; for when Elizabeth was inquiring whether an author, whose book she had given him to examine, was not guilty of treason, he replied, "Not of treason, madam, but of robbery, if you please; for he has taken all that is worth noticing in him from Tacitus and Sallust." With the fear of Elizabeth before his eyes, Holinshed castrated the volumes of his History. When Giles Fletcher, after his Russian embassy, congratulated himself with having escaped with his head, and on his return wrote a book called "The Russian Commonwealth," describing its tyranny, Elizabeth forbad the publishing of the work. Our Russian merchants were frightened, for they petitioned the queen to suppress the work; the original petition, with the offensive passages, exists among the Lansdowne manuscripts. It is curious to contrast this fact with another better known, under the reign of William the Third; then the press had obtained its perfect freedom, and even the shadow of the sovereign could not pass between an author and his work. When the Danish ambassador complained to the king of the freedom which Lord Molesworth had exercised on his master's government, in his Account of Denmark, and hinted that, if a Dane had done the same with a King of England, he would, on complaint, have taken the author's head off—"That I cannot do," replied the sovereign of a free people;

---

126. The author, with his publisher, who had their right hands cut off, was John Stubbs of Lincoln's lnn, a hot-headed Puritan, whose sister was married to Thomas Cartwright, the head of that faction. This execution took place upon a scaffold, in the market-place at Westminster. After Stubbs had his right hand cut off; with his left he pulled off his hat, and cried with a loud voice, "God save the Queen!" the multitude standing deeply silent, either out of horror at this new and unwonted kind of punishment, or else out of commiseration of the undaunted man, whose character was unblemished. Camden, a witness to this transaction, has related it. The author, and the printer, and the publisher were condemned to this barbarous punishment, on an act of Philip and Mary, *against the authors and publishers of seditious writings*. Some lawyers were honest enough to assert that the sentence was erroneous, for that act was only a temporary one, and died with Queen Mary; but, of these honest lawyers, one was sent to the Tower, and another was so sharply reprimanded, that he resigned his place as a judge in the Common Pleas. Other lawyers, as the lord chief justice, who fawned on the prerogative far more then than afterwards in the Stuart reigns, asserted that Queen Mary was a king; and that an act made by any king, unless repealed, must always exist, because the King of England never dies!

"but if you please, I will tell him what you say, and he shall put it into the next edition of his book." What an immense interval between the feelings of Elizabeth and William, with hardly a century betwixt them!

James the First proclaimed Buchanan's history, and a political tract of his, at "the Mercat Cross;" and every one was to bring his copy "to be perusit and purgit of the offensive and extraordinare materis," under a heavy penalty. Knox, whom Milton calls "the Reformer of a Kingdom," was also curtailed; and "the sense of that great man shall, to all posterity, be lost for the fearfulness or the presumptuous rashness of a perfunctory licenser."

The regular establishment of licensers of the press appeared under Charles the First. It must be placed among the projects of Laud, and the king, I suspect, inclined to it; for by a passage in a manuscript letter of the times, I find, that when Charles printed his speech on the dissolution of the parliament, which excited such general discontent, some one printed Queen Elizabeth's last speech as a companion-piece. This was presented to the king by his own printer, John Bill, not from a political motive, but merely by way of complaint that another had printed, without leave or license, that which, as the king's printer, he asserted was his own copyright. Charles does not seem to have been pleased with the gift, and observed, "You printers print anything." Three gentlemen of the bed-chamber, continues the writer, standing by, commended Mr. Bill very much, and prayed him to come oftener with such rarities to the king, because they might do some good.[127]

One of the consequences of this persecution of the press was, the raising up of a new class of publishers, under the government of Charles I., those who became noted for what was then called "unlawful and unlicensed books." Sparkes, the publisher of Prynne's "Histriomastix," was of this class. I have elsewhere entered more particularly into this subject.[128] The Presbyterian party in parliament, who thus found the press closed on them, vehemently cried out for its freedom: and it was imagined, that when they had ascended into power, the odious office of a licenser of the press would have been abolished; but these pretended friends of freedom, on the contrary, discovered themselves as tenderly alive to the office as the old government, and maintained it with the extremest vigour. Such is the political history of mankind.

The literary fate of Milton was remarkable: his genius was castrated alike by the monarchical and the republican government. The royal licenser expunged several passages from Milton's history, in which Milton had painted the superstition, the pride, and the cunning of the Saxon monks, which the sagacious licenser applied to Charles II. and the bishops; but Milton had before suffered as merciless a mutilation from his old friends the republicans;

---

127. A letter from J. Mead to Sir M. Stuteville, July 19, 1628. Sloane MSS. 4178.
128. See "Calamities of Authors," vol. ii. p. 116.

who suppressed a bold picture, taken from life, which he had introduced into his History of the Long Parliament and Assembly of Divines. Milton gave the unlicensed passages to the Earl of Anglesea, a literary nobleman, the editor of Whitelocke's Memorials; and the castrated passage, which could not be licensed in 1670, was received with peculiar interest when separately published in 1681.[129] "If there be found in an author's book one sentence of a venturous edge, uttered in the height of zeal, and who knows whether it might not be the dictate of a divine spirit, yet not suiting every low decrepit humour of their own, they will not pardon him their dash."

This office seems to have lain dormant a short time under Cromwell, from the scruples of a conscientious licenser, who desired the council of state, in 1649, for reasons given, to be discharged from that employment. This Mabot, the licenser, was evidently deeply touched by Milton's address for "The Liberty of Unlicensed Printing." The office was, however, revived on the restoration of Charles II.; and through the reign of James II. the abuses of licensers were unquestionably not discouraged: their castrations of books reprinted appear to have been very artful; for in reprinting Gage's "Survey of the West Indies," which originally consisted of twenty-two chapters, in 1648 and 1657, with a dedication to Sir Thomas Fairfax,—in 1677, after expunging the passages in honour of Fairfax, the dedication is dexterously turned into a preface; and the twenty-second chapter being obnoxious for containing particulars of the artifices of "the papalins," as Milton calls the Papists, in converting the author, was entirely chopped away by the licenser's hatchet. The castrated chapter, as usual, was preserved afterwards separately. Literary despotism at least is short-sighted in its views, for the expedients it employs are certain of overturning themselves.

On this subject we must not omit noticing one of the noblest and most eloquent prose compositions of Milton; "the Areopagitica; a Speech for the Liberty of Unlicensed Printing." It is a work of love and inspiration, and breathing the most enlarged spirit of literature; separating, at an awful distance from the multitude, that character "who was born to study and to love learning for itself, not for lucre, or any other end, but, perhaps, for that lasting fame and perpetuity of praise, which God and good men have consented shall

---

129. It is a quarto tract, entitled "Mr. John Milton's Character of the Long Parliament and Assembly of Divines in 1641; omitted in his other works, and never before printed, and very seasonable for these times.1681." It is inserted in the uncastrated edition of Milton's prose works in 1738. It is a retort on the *Presbyterian* Clement Walker's History of the *Independents;* and Warburton, in his admirable characters of the historians of this period, alluding to Clement Walker, says—"Milton was even with him in the fine and severe character he draws of the Presbyterian administration."

be the reward of those whose published labours advance the good of mankind."

One part of this unparalleled effusion turns on "the quality which ought to be in every licenser." It will suit our new licenser of public opinion, a laborious corps well known, who constitute themselves without an act of Star-chamber. I shall pick out but a few sentences, that I may add some little facts, casually preserved, of the ineptitude of such an officer.

"He who is made judge to sit upon the birth or death of books, whether they may be wafted into this world or not, had need to be a man above the common measure, both studious, learned, and judicious; there may be else no mean mistakes in his censure. If he be of such worth as behoves him, there cannot be a more tedious and unpleasing journey-work, a greater loss of time levied upon his head, than to be made the perpetual reader of unchosen books and pamphlets. There is no book acceptable, unless at certain seasons; but to be enjoyned the reading of that at all times, whereof three pages would not down at any time, is an imposition which I cannot believe how he that values time and his own studies, or is but of a sensible nostril, should be able to endure.—What advantage is it to be a man over it is to be a boy at school, if we have only 'scaped the ferula to come under the fescue of an *Imprimatur?*—if serious and elaborate writings, as if they were no more than the theme of a grammar lad under his pedagogue, must not be uttered without the cursory eyes of a temporising licenser? When a man writes to the world, he summons up all his reason and deliberation to assist him; he searches, meditates, is industrious, and likely consults and confers with his judicious friends, as well as any that writ before him; if in this, the most consummate act of his fidelity and ripeness, no years, no industry, no former proof of his abilities can bring him to that state of maturity as not to be still mistrusted and suspected, unless he carry all his considerate diligence, all his midnight watching, and expense of Palladian oil, to the hasty view of an unleisured licenser, perhaps one who never knew the labour of book writing; and if he be not repulsed or slighted, must appear in print like a Punie with his guardian, and his censor's hand on the back of his title to be his bail and surety that he is no idiot or seducer, it cannot be but a dishonour and derogation to the author, to the book, to the privilege and dignity of learning."

The reader may now follow the stream in the great original; I must, however, preserve one image of exquisite sarcasm.

"Debtors and delinquents walk about without a keeper; but inoffensive books must not stir forth without a visible jailor in their title; nor is it to the common people less than a reproach; for if we dare not trust them with an

English pamphlet, what do we but censure them for a giddy, vitious, and ungrounded people, in such a sick and weak state of faith and discretion, as to be able to take nothing but thro' the glister-pipe of a licenser!"

The ignorance and stupidity of these censors were often, indeed, as remarkable as their exterminating spirit. The noble simile of Milton, of Satan with the rising sun, in the first book of the Paradise Lost, had nearly occasioned the suppression of our national epic: it was supposed to contain a treasonable allusion. The tragedy of Arminius, by one Paterson, who was an amanuensis of the poet Thomson, was intended for representation, but the dramatic censor refused a license: as Edward and Eleanora was not permitted to be performed, being considered a party work, our sagacious state-critic imagined that Paterson's *own* play was in the same predicament by being in the same hand-writing! Malebranche said, that he could never obtain an approbation for his "Research after Truth," because it was unintelligible to his censors; at length Mezeray, the historian, approved of it as a book of geometry. Latterly, in France, it is said that the greatest geniuses were obliged to submit their works to the critical understanding of persons who had formerly been low dependents on some man of quality, and who appear to have brought the same servility of mind to the examination of works of genius. There is something, which, on the principle of incongruity and contrast, becomes exquisitely ludicrous, in observing the works of men of genius allowed to be printed, and even commended, by certain persons who have never printed their names but to their licenses. One of these gentlemen suppressed a work, because it contained principles of government which appeared to him not conformable to the laws of Moses. Another said to a geometrician—"I cannot permit the publication of your book: you dare to say, that, between two given points, the shortest line is the straight line. Do you think me such an idiot as not to perceive your allusion? If your work appeared, I should make enemies of all those who find, by crooked ways, an easier admittance into court, than by a straight line. Consider their number!" This seems, however, to be an excellent joke. At this moment the censors in Austria appear singularly inept; for, not long ago, they condemned as heretical, two books; one of which, entitled "*Principes de la Trigonométrie*," the censor would not allow to be printed, because the *Trinity*, which he imagined to be included in trigonometry, was not permitted to be discussed: and the other, on the "Destruction of Insects," he insisted had a covert allusion to the *Jesuits*, who, he conceived, were thus malignantly designated.

A curious literary anecdote has been recorded of the learned Richard Simon. Compelled to insert in one of his works the qualifying opinions of the censor of the Sorbonne, he inserted them within crotchets. But a strange misfortune attended this contrivance. The printer, who was not let into the secret, printed the work without these essential marks: by which means the enraged author saw his own peculiar opinions overturned in the very work written to maintain them!

These appear trifling minutiæ; and yet, like a hair in a watch, which utterly destroys its progress, these little ineptiæ obliged writers to have recourse to foreign presses; compelled a Montesquieu to write with concealed ambiguity, and many to sign a recantation of principles which they could never change. The recantation of Selden, extorted from his hand on his suppressed "Historie of Tithes," humiliated a great mind; but it could not remove a particle from the masses of his learning, nor darken the luminous conviction of his reasoning; nor did it diminish the number of those who assented and now assent to his principles. Recantations usually prove the force of authority rather than the change of opinion. When a Dr. Pocklington was condemned to make a recantation, he hit the etymology of the word, while he caught at the spirit—he began thus: "If *canto* be to sing, *recanto* is to sing again." So that he rechanted his offending opinions, by repeating them in his *recantation*.

At the Revolution in England, licenses for the press ceased; but its liberty did not commence till 1694, when every restraint was taken off by the firm and decisive tone of the Commons. It was granted, says our philosophic Hume, "to the great displeasure of the king and his ministers, who, seeing nowhere in any government, during present or past ages, any example of such unlimited freedom, doubted much of its salutary effects; and probably thought that no books or writings would ever so much improve the general understanding of men, as to render it safe to entrust them with an indulgence so easily abused."

And the present moment verifies the prescient conjecture of the philosopher. Such is the licentiousness of our press, that some, not perhaps the most hostile to the cause of freedom, would not be averse to manacle authors once more with an IMPRIMATUR. It will not be denied that Erasmus was a friend to the freedom of the press; yet he was so shocked at the licentiousness of Luther's pen, that there was a time when he considered it necessary to restrain its liberty. It was then as now. Erasmus had, indeed, been miserably calumniated, and expected future libels. I am glad, however, to observe, that he afterwards, on a more impartial investigation, confessed that such a remedy was much more dangerous than the disease. To restrain the liberty of the press, can only be the interest of the individual, never that of the public; one must be a patriot here: we must stand in the field with an unshielded breast, since the safety of the people is the supreme law. There were, in Milton's days, some who said of this institution, that, although the inventors were bad, the thing, for all that, might be good. "This may be so," replies the vehement advocate for "unlicensed printing." But as the commonwealths have existed through all ages, and have forborne to use it, he sees no necessity for the invention; and held it as a dangerous and suspicious fruit from the tree which bore it. The ages of the wisest commomwealths,

Milton seems not to have recollected, were not diseased with the popular infection of publications, issuing at all hours, and propagated with a celerity on which the ancients could not calculate. The learned Dr. *James*, who has denounced the invention of the *Indexes*, confesses, however, that it was not unuseful when it restrained the publications of atheistic and immoral works. But it is our lot to bear with all the consequent evils, that we may preserve the good inviolate; since, as the profound Hume has declared, "THE LIBERTY OF BRITAIN IS GONE FOR EVER, when such attempts shall succeed."

A constitutional sovereign will consider the freedom of the press as the sole organ of the feelings of the people. Calumniators he will leave to the fate of calumny; a fate similar to those who, having overcharged their arms with the fellest intentions, find that the death which they intended for others, in bursting, only annihilates themselves.

3. THE WAR AGAINST BOOKS
(*Amenities*, pp. 738-756)

THE history of our literature, at the early era of printing, till the first indications appear of what is termed "copyright," forms a chapter in the history of our civilization which has not been opened to us.

This history includes two important incidents in our literary annals; the one, an exposition of the complicate arts practised by an alarmed government to possess an absolute control over the printers, which annihilated the freedom of the press; and the other, the contests of those printers and booksellers who had grants and licenses, and other privileges of a monopoly, with the rest of the brotherhood, who maintained an equal right of publication, and contended for the freedom of the trade.

Although Caxton, our first printer, bore the title of *Regius Impressor,* printed books were still so rare in this country under Richard the Third, that an act of parliament in 1483 contains a proviso in favour of aliens to encourage the importation of books. During a period of forty years, books were supplied by foreign printers, some of whom appear to have accompanied their merchandise, and to have settled themselves here. It became necessary to repeal this privilege conceded to foreign presses, when under Henry the Eighth the art of printing was skilfully exercised by the King's natural subjects, and to protect the English printers lest their art should decline from a failure of encouragement.

Our earliest printers were the vendors and the binders of their own books, and their domicile on their title-pages directed the curious to their abodes. Few in number, their limited editions, it is conjectured, did not exceed from two to four hundred copies. The first printers were generally men of competent wealth; and every book was the sole property of its single printer.

The separate departments of author, bookseller, and bookbinder, were not yet required, for as yet there was no "reading public." Some of our ancient printers combined all these characters in themselves. The commerce of literature had not yet opened in the speculative vendors of books, and that race of writers who have been designated in the modern phrase as "authors by profession." The very nature of literary property could only originate in a more advanced and intellectual state of society, when unsettled opinions and contending principles would create a growing demand for books which no one yet contemplated, and a property, of a novel and peculiar nature, in the very thoughts and words of a writer.

The art of printing, confined within a few hands, was usually practised under the patronage of the King, or the Archbishop, or some nobleman. There existed not the remotest suspicion, that the simple machinery of the printer's press, could ever be converted into an engine of torture to try the strength, or the truth, of the church and the state. Sedition, or any allusion to public affairs, never entered the brains of the ingenious mechanics, solely occupied in lowering the prices of the text-writers in the manuscript market, by their own novel and wondrous transcript. Their first wares had consisted of romances which were consulted as authentic histories; "dictes, or sayings," of ancient sages which no one cared to contradict; and homilies and allegories whose voluminousness had no tediousness. Neither did the higher powers ever imagine that any control seemed needful over the printer's press. They only lent the sanction of their names, or the shelter of their abode, at the Abbey of Westminster or the monastery of St. Albans, to encourage the manufacture of a novel curiosity, for its beautiful toy, a printed book—and the press at first was at once free and innocent.

But the day of portents was not slow in its approach—a stirring age pressed on, an age for books. Under Henry the Eighth, books became the organs of the passions of mankind, and were not only printed, but spread about; for if the presses of England dared not disclose the hazardous secrets of the writers, the people were surreptitiously furnished with English books from foreign presses. It was then that the jealousy of the state opened its hundred eyes on the awful track of the strange omnipotence of the press. Then first began that WAR AGAINST BOOKS which has not ceased in our time.

Perhaps he who first, with a statesman's prescient view, had contemplated on this novel and unknown power, and, as we shall see, had detected its insidious steps stealing into the cabinet of the sovereign, was the great minister of this great monarch. It has been surmised that the cardinal aimed to crush the head of the serpent, by stopping the printing press in the monastery at St. Albans, of which he was the abbot; for that press remained silent for half a century. In a convocation the cardinal expressed his hostility against printing; assuring the simple clergy that, if they did not in time suppress printing, printing would suppress them.[130] This great statesman, at this early period, had taken into view its remote consequences. Lord Herbert has curiously assigned to the cardinal his ideas as addressed to the pope:—"This new invention of printing has produced various effects of which your Holiness cannot be ignorant. If it has restored books and learning, it has also been the occasion of those sects and schisms which daily appear. Men begin to call in question the present faith and tenets of the church; and the laity read the Scriptures; and pray in their vulgar tongue. Were this suffered, the common people might come to believe that there was not so much use of the clergy. If men were persuaded that they could make their own way to God, and in their ordinary language as well as Latin, the authority of the mass would fall, which would be very prejudicious to our ecclesiastical orders. The mysteries of religion must be kept in the hands of priests—the secret and arcanum of church government. Nothing remains more to be done than to prevent further apostacy. For this purpose, since printing could not be put down, it were best to set up learning against learning; and, by introducing able persons to dispute, to suspend the laity between fears and controversies. Since printing cannot be put down, it may still be made useful." Thus, the statesman, who could not by a single blow annihilate this monster of all schism, would have wrestled with it with a statesman's policy.

The cardinal at length was shaken by terrors he had never before felt from the hated press. This minister had writhed under the printed personalities of the rabid SKELTON and the merciless ROY; but a pamphlet in the form of *"The Supplication of Beggars"* is a famed invective, which served as a prelude to the fall of the minister. The author, SIMON FISH, had been a student of Gray's Inn, where, in an Aristophanic interlude, he had enacted his grace the cardinal to the life, and deemed himself fortunate to escape from his native shores to elude the gripe of Wolsey. In this pamphlet all the poverty of the nation,—for our national poverty at all times is the cry of "The Beggars,"—the taxation, and the grievances, are all laid to the oppression of the whole motley prelacy. These were the thieves and the freebooters, the cormorants and the wolves of the state, and the king had nothing more to do than to put them to the cart's tail, and end all the beggary of England by appropriating the monastic lands.

On a day of a procession at Westminster this seditious tract, aiming at the annihilation of the whole revenues of churchmen, was found scattered in the streets. Wolsey had the copies carefully gathered and delivered to him, to prevent any from reaching the king's eyes. Merchants, at that day, were often itinerants in their way of trade with their foreign correspondents, and frequently conveyed to England these writings of our fugitive reformers. Two

---

130. See a curious note of Hearne's in his Glossary to "Peter Langtoft's Chronicle," p. 685. Also Herbert's "Typog. Antiq." p. 1435.

of these merchants, by the favour of Anne Bullen, had a secret interview with the king. They offered to recite to the royal ear the substance of the suppressed libel. "I dare say you have it all by heart," the king shrewdly observed, and listened. After a pause, Henry let fall this remarkable observation—"If a man should pull down an old stone wall, and begin at the lower part, the upper might chance to fall on his head." What at that moment was passing in the sagacious mind of the future regal reformer, is now more evident than probably it was to its first hearers. Wolsey, suspicious and troubled, came to warn the king of "a pestilent heretical libel being abroad." Henry, suddenly drawing the very libel out of his bosom, presented a portentous copy to the startled and falling minister. The book became a court-book; and "the witty atheistical author," as the Roman Catholic historian designated him, was invited back to England under the safeguard of the royal protection.

But the secret, and, perhaps, the yet obscure influence of the press, must often have been apparent to Henry the Eighth, when the king sat in council. There he marked the alarms of Wolsey, and the terrified remonstrances of the entire body of "the Papelins;" and when the day came that their ejectors filled their seats, the king discovered, that though the objects were changed, the same dread of the press continued. The war against books commenced; an expurgatory index, or a catalogue of prohibited books, chiefly English, was sent forth before Henry had broken with the papal power; subsequently, the fresher proclamation declared the books of the Papelins to be "seditious," as the use of "the new learning" had been anathematized as "heretical."

In these rapid events, dates become as essential as arguments. In 1526, anti-popery books, with their dispersers, were condemned as heretical. In 1535, all books favouring popery were decreed to be "seditious books." There were books on the king's supremacy, for or against, which cost some of their writers their heads; and there were "injunctions against English books," frequently renewed as "pestilent and infectious learnings."[131] All these show that now the press had obtained activity, and betray the uneasy condition of the ruling powers, who were startled by a supernatural voice which they had never before heard.

When the first persecution of "the new religion" occurred, it did not abate the secret importations of Lutheran books.[132] These with the merchant had become an article of commerce; and with the zealous dispensers, an article of faith: both alike ventured their lives in conveying them to London, and other places, and even smuggled them into the universities. They landed their

131. Strype's "Memorials," i. 344 and 218.
132. A curious and a copious catalogue of these books, "though the books themselves are almost perished," may be seen in Strype's "Ecclesiastical Memorials," i. 165.

prohibited goods in the most distant places, at Colchester, or in Norfolk. One of these chapmen in this hazardous commodity of free-thinking was at last caught at his bookbinder's. He suffered at the flaming stake, and others met his fate.

It was now apparent that the secrecy and velocity of conveying the novel projects of reform, which could not otherwise have been communicated to the great body of the people, till this awful instrument had been set to work; the unity of opinion which it might create among the confused multitude; and the passions which a party either in terror, or in triumph, could artfully rouse in the sympathies of men; were felt and acknowledged by the monarch, who had himself staked the possession of his independent dominion on the energy and the eloquence of a single book,[133] to prepare his people for his meditated emancipation from the Tiara; and were any other proof wanting, we discover the terror of the Bishop of Durham, on the appearance of "a little book printed in English, issuing from Newcastle." His lordship writes in great trepidation to the minister Cromwell, of this portentous little book, "like to do great harm among the people," and advising that "letters be directed to all havens, towns, and other places, to forbid the book to be sold." All the ports to be closed against "a little book brought by some folks from Newcastle!" These incidents were certain demonstrations of the political influence of this new sovereignty of the printing-press.

In the simplicity of this early era of printing, the same bishop had all the copies of Tindal's Testament bought up at Antwerp, and burned. The English merchant employed on this occasion was a secret follower of the modern apostle, who, on his part, gladly furnished all the unsold copies which had hung on hand, anxious to correct a new edition which he was too poor to publish. When one of the Tindalites was promised his pardon if he would reveal the name of the person who had encouraged this new edition, he accepted the grace; and he assured the Lord Chancellor that the greatest encourager and supporter of his Antwerp friends had been the bishop himself, who, by buying up half the unsold impression, had enabled them to produce a second. This was the first lesson which taught that it is easier to burn authors than books.

There were two methods by which governments could counteract the inconveniences of the press: the one, by clipping its wings, and contracting the sphere of its action, which we shall see was early attempted; and the other, by adroitly turning its vehemence into an opposite direction, making the press contend with the press, and by division weaken its dominion.

---

133. The book, "De Verâ Differentiâ inter Regiam Potestatem et Ecclesiasticam," was called "The King's Book." It seems that the scholastic monarch gave some finishing strokes to what had probably passed through the hands of his most expert casuists.

Henry the Eighth left the age he had himself created, with its awakened spirit. The three succeeding reigns, acting in direct opposition to each other, disturbed the minds of the people; controversies raged, and books multiplied. The sphere of publication widened, in this vertiginous era, printers greatly increased in the reign of Edward the Sixth. But the craft did not flourish, when the craftmen had become numerous. We have the contemporary authority of one of the most eminent printers, that the practice of the art, and the cost of the materials, had become so exceedingly chargeable, that the printers were driven by necessity to throw themselves into the hands of "the Stationers," or booksellers, for "small gains."[134] It is probable that at this period, the printers perceived that vending their books at the printing-office was not a mode which made them sufficiently public. This is the first indication that the printing, and the publication or the sale of books, were becoming separate trades.

In this history of the progress of the press in our country, the Stationers' Company now appears. This institution becomes an important branch of our investigation, for its influence over our literature, for its monopoly, opposed to the interests of other publishers, and above all, for the practice of the government in converting this company into a ready instrument to restrain the freedom of the press.

Anterior to the invention of printing, there flourished a craft or trade who were denominated *Stationers;* they were scribes and limners, and dealers in manuscript copies, and in parchment and paper, and other literary wares. It is believed by our antiquaries that they derived their denomination from their fixed locality, or *station in a street,* either by a shop or shed, and probably when their former occupation had gone, still retained their dealings in literature, and turned to booksellers.[135] This denomination of *stationers,* indicating their stationary residence, would also distinguish them from the itinerant vendors, who in a more subordinate capacity at a later period, appear to have hawked about the town and the country pamphlets and other portable books.

In the reign of Philip and Mary "the Stationers" were granted a charter of incorporation, and were invested with the most inquisitorial powers.

The favours of a tyrant are usually favours to individuals who profit at the cost of the community, and who themselves overlooking every principle of justice, bind up their own selfish monopoly with the prosperity of criminal

---

134. "Archæologia," vol. xxv. 104.

135. Pegge, in his "Anecdotes of the English Language," has somewhat crudely remarked that "the term *Stationers* was appropriated to *Booksellers* in the year 1622;" but it was so long before. It is extraordinary that Mr. Todd, well read in our literary history, admits this imperfect disclosure of Pegge into the "Dictionary of the English Language." The term *Stationer* and *Bookseller* were synonymous and in common use in the reign of Elizabeth, and may be found in Baret's "Alvearie," 1573.

power. This we discover in the Company of Stationers, who were the willing dupes of that absolute power in the State which had created the corporation to do its watchful work, to carry on the war against books, and by their passive obedience they secured to themselves those privileges, and licenses, and other monopolies, which they now amply enjoyed.

By this charter of the Stationers, it was specified that no one was to exercise the art of printing, unless he was one of the society; and the corporation, with their extraordinary but lawful authority, were to search as often as they pleased any house or chamber, &c., of any stamper or printer, or binder, or seller, of any manner of books, which they deemed obnoxious to the State, or their own interest!—to seize, burn, take away, or destroy, or convert to their own use.[136] The Stationers were, in fact, a Spanish inquisition for the cabinet of Philip and Mary, and whom the queen consulted on critical occasions, for her majesty once sent for the warden to inquire whether they had seen or heard of a sort of books sent from Zurich? The war against books was never pushed to such extremities as in a proclamation of Philip and Mary, which Strype calls, "a short but terrible proclamation." Here we learn that "whoever finds books of heresy, sedition, and treason, and does not forthwith burn the same without showing or reading them to any other person, shall be *executed for a rebel!*"[137] It is evident, that the grant of this incorporation was designed to make the interests of the company subservient to those of the court; for by the intermediate aid of the vigilant Stationers, every printer would be controlled, since none were allowed to be printers who were not members of this corporation, and therefore amenable to its laws.

In the succeeding reign of Elizabeth everything changed except these state-proclamations in the war against books. The object had altered, but not the objection, for though the books were different the Elizabethan style is identical with the Marian. The same plenary powers of the Stationers were strengthened by an additional injunction, by which the government held the whole brotherhood with a closer grasp. The company were commissioned not only "to search into bookbinders' shops, as well as printing-offices, for unlawful and heretical books," but they were responsible for "any unruly printer who might endanger the church and state," and "who for covetousness regard not what they print, whereby ariseth great disorder by publication of unfruitful, vain, and infamous books and papers. None shall print any manner of book except the same be first *licensed by her majesty by express words in writing,* or by *six of her privy council.*"[138]

---

136. The Charter may be found in Herbert's "Typographical Antiquities," p. 1584.
137. Strype's "Memorials," iii. part 2nd. p. 130.
138. In the Lansdowne Manuscripts, 43, fol. 76, will be found "an act to restrain the licentious printing of unprofitable and hurtful books," 1580. After declaring that the art of printing is "a most happy and profitable invention," it is pointed at those

When we recollect that the Stationers' Company under Mary, were composed of the very same individuals who two years after under Elizabeth, were busily ornamenting their shelves with all their late "seditious and heretical" books, and in removing out of sight all their late lawful and loyal ware, this transition of the feelings must have placed them in a position painful as it was ridiculous. But the true genius of a commercial body is of no party, save the predominant; pliant with their interests, a corporation, like a republic, in their zealous union can do that with public propriety which, in the individuals it is composed of, would be incongruous and absurd.

The rage of government in this war against books was still sharper at a later period, provoked by the spread of the Mar-prelate pamphlets. A decree of the Star-chamber in 1586, among other orders, allows no printer to have an additional press without license; awards that there shall be no printing in any obscure part of a house; nor any printer out of the city of London, excepting at the two Universities; and till "the excessive multitude of printers be abated, diminished, or by death given over," no one shall resume that trade; and that the wardens of the Stationers' Company, with assistants, shall enter at all times warehouses, shops, &c., to seize all "letter-presses, and other printing instruments, to be defaced, melted, sawed in pieces, broken or battered at the smith's forge."[139] Amid all this book-phobia, a curious circumstance occurred. The learned could not prosecute their studies for the prohibition against many excellent works, written by those who were "addicted to the errors of Popery in foreign parts," and which also contained "matters against the state of this land." In this dilemma, a singular expedient was adopted. The archbishop allowed "Ascanius de Renialme, a merchant bookseller", to bring into this realm *some few copies* of every such sort of books, upon this condition only, that they be first brought to me, and so delivered only to such persons whom we deem most meet men to have the reading of them." At this time it must have been an affair of considerable delicacy and difficulty to obtain a quotation, without first hastening to Lambeth Palace, there to be questioned!

Printing and literature, during the long reign of Elizabeth, in spite of all these Star-chamber edicts, amazingly increased; there seemed to be a swell from all the presses. Of 175 stationers, 140 had taken their freedom since this queen's accession. "So much had printing and learning come in request under

---

"who pen or translate in the English tongue poesies, ditties, and songs, serving for a great part of them to none other end, what titles soever they bear, but to set up an art of making lascivious and ungodly love, to the intolerable corruption of life and manners—*and to the no small or sufferable waste of the treasure of this realm, which is thereby consumed in paper, a forren and chargeable commoditie,"* The first paper made in England was at Dartford, in 1588, by a German, who was knighted by the queen.

139. This decree of the Star-chamber is printed in Herbert's "Typographical Antiquities," p. 1668.

the Reformation," observes our historical antiquary Strype. And such was the proud exultation of the great printer John Day, that when he compared the darkness of the preceding period with what this publisher of Fox's mighty tomes of Martyrology deemed its purer enlightenment, he never printed his name without this pithy insinuation to the reader, "Arise, for it is DAY!" Books not only multiplied, but unquestionably it was at this period that first appeared the art of aiding these ephemeral productions of the press which supplied the wants of numerous readers. The rights of authors had hitherto derived a partial existence in privilege conceded by the royal patron, but it was now that they first gathered the fuller harvests of public favour. We shall shortly find a notice among the book-trade of what is termed "copyright."[140]

If the freedom of the press had been wholly wrested from the printers, it was not the sole grievance in the present state of our literature, for another custom had been assumed which hung on the royal prerogative—that of granting letters patent, or privileged licenses, under the broad seal to individuals, to deal in a specific class of books, to the exclusion of every other publisher. Possibly the same secret motive which had contrived the absolute control of the press, suggested the grants of these privileges. One enjoyed the privilege of printing Bibles; another all law-books; another grammars; another "almanacks and prognostications;" and another, ballads and books in prose and metre. These privileges assuredly increased the patronage of the great, and the dispensations of these favours were doubtless often abused. A singing man had the license for printing music-books, which he extended to that of being the sole vendor of all ruled paper, on the plea that where there were ruled lines, musical notes might be pricked down; and a private gentleman, who was neither printer nor stationer, had the privilege of printing grammars and other things, which he farmed out for a considerable annual revenue, by which means these books were necessarily enhanced in price.

Such monopolies, which entered into the erroneous policy of that age, and the corrupt practices of patronage, long continued a source of discontent among the generality. This was now a period when the spirit of the times raised up men who would urge their independent rights. A struggle ensued between the monopolists and the excluded, who clamoured for the freedom of the trade. "Unruly printers" not only resisted when their own houses were besieged by "the searchers" of the stationers, but openly persisted in printing any "lawful books" they chose, in defiance of any royal privilege. A busy lawyer had been feed, who questioned this stretch of the prerogative. But the

---

140. The privilege of a royal grant to the author was the only protection the author had for any profits of his work. Henry the Eighth granted Palsgrave his exclusive right for the printing of his book for seven years. Bishop Cooper obtained a privilege for the sale of his "Thesaurus" for twelve years; and a translator of Tacitus, for his version, during his natural life.

patriotism or the despair of these "unruly printers" led to the Clink or to Ludgate—to imprisonment or to bankruptcy! The day had not yet arrived when civil freedom, though youthful and bold, with impunity could "kick against the pricks" of the prerogative. It is curious here to discover that the aggrieved had even formed "a trade-union" for contributions to defend suits at law against the privileged; and when they were reminded that this mode only aggravated their troubles, and were asked by the sleek monopolists what they would gain if all were in common, which, as the privileged assumed, "would make havoc for one man to undo another," that is, those who were patentless would undo the patentees—these Cains, in the bitterness of their hearts, fiercely replied to their more favoured brothers, "We should make you beggars like ourselves!"[141]

Amid these clamours in the commonwealth of literature, the patentees became alarmed at the danger of having their patents revoked. The booksellers had become the more prosperous race, and some of these, combining with the Stationers' Company, opposed the privileged few. The advocates for the freedom of the trade advanced a proposition too tender to be handled by the Doctor of Civil Law, who was chosen for the arbitrator. At once these boldly impugned the prerogative royal itself in its exercise of granting privileges to printers, which they declared, was against law; and however they might more successfully urge, that the better policy for the public was to admit of competition, and moderating of prices by this freedom of publication, they add, "So, too, let every man print what 'lawful book' he choose, without any exceptions, even 'any book of which the copies thereof had been *bought of the authors* for their money.'" Here we find the first notice of "copyright," and the very inadequate notions yet entertained of its nature.

The plea of the patentees more skilfully addressed the Doctor of Civil Law by their assumption of the irrefragable rights of the royal prerogative. Their own privileges they maintained by the custom, as they showed that "all princes in Christendom had granted privileges for printing, sometimes for a term of years, or for life; that ancient books bore this inscription, *Cum privilegio ad imprimendum solum;* that the queen's progenitors had exercised this right, and would any dare to lessen her majesty's prerogative?" All infringers had ever been punished. They further urged, that the good of the commonwealth required that printing should be in the hands of known men, being an art most dangerous and pernicious if it were not straitened and restrained by politic order of the prince or magistrates. With truer arguments they alleged that many useful books were now published unprofitable to the patentees, who had no other means of repaying themselves but by the sale of other books restricted to them by the protection of their privileges; and finally, they

---

141. "Archæologia," xxv. 112.

declared that the public were incurring some danger that good books might not be printed at all if privileges were revoked, for *the first printer was at charge for the author's pains and other extraordinary cost;* but should any succeeding printer who had *"the copy gratis"* sell cheaper on better paper, and with notes and additions, it would put an end to the sale of the original edition; and they pithily conclude with the old wisdom, that "It is easier to amend than to invent." Here again we see specified the cost of "copyright" in the publication of a new book.

This attempt to open the freedom of the trade, which occurred about 1583, the twenty-fifth year of the reign of Elizabeth, at length was not wholly unsuccessful; the monopolists conceded certain advantages,[142] and about twenty years subsequently, towards the end of that queen's reign, when the craft of authorship, adapting its wares to the fashion of the day, was practised by a whole race of popular writers, the booksellers became almost the sole publishers of books, employing the printers in their single capacity.[143]

In this war against books, the severe decree of the Star Chamber, 1586, was renewed with stricter prohibitions, and more penal severity by a decree of the Star Chamber, under Charles the First, in 1637. Printing and printers were now placed under the supervision of the great officers of state; law-books were to be judiciously approved by the lord chief-justice; historical works were to be submitted to the secretaries of state; heraldry was left to the lord marshal; divinity, physic, philosophy, and poetry, were to be sanctioned by the Archbishop of Canterbury or the Bishop of London. Two copies of every work were to be preserved in custody, to prevent any alterations being made in the published volumes, which would be detected on their comparison. Admirable preparatory and preventive measures! Here would ensue a general purgation of every atom in the human system, occasioning obstructions to the doctrines and discipline of the Church of England, and the state of government. The aim of all these decrees and proclamations was to abridge the number of printers, and to invigorate the absolute power conferred on the Stationers' Company, who had long delivered themselves, bound hand and foot, to the government, for the servile possession of their privileges. Printers were still limited to twenty, as in the reign of Elizabeth, and only four letter-founders allowed. Every printed book on paper was to bear the impress of the printer's name, on pain of corporal punishment. They held books in such terror, that even those which had formerly been licensed, were not allowed to

---

142. Nichols on the Stationers' Company.—"Lit. Anecdotes," iii.

We have a list "of books yielded by the richer printers who had licenses from the queen;" but whether they were only copies bestowed in charity for the poorer "stationers," or given up by the monopolist, I do not understand.—Herbert's "Typographical Antiq." p. 1672.

143. Herbert's "Typographical Antiq."—preface.

be reprinted, without being "reviewed," as they express it, and re-watched by placing on guard this double sentinel. There are some extraordinary clauses which betray the feeble infancy of the rude policy of that day. The decree tells us that "printing in corners without license had been usually done by journeymen out of work," and to provide against this source of inquietude, it compels the printers to employ all journeymen out of employ, "though the printer should be able to do his own work without these journeymen;" and in the same spirit of compulsion, it ordains that all such unemployed shall be obliged to work whenever called on.[144] Masters and men were equally amenable to fines impossible to be paid, and penal pains almost too horrible to endure, short of life, but not of ruin: a dark, a merciless, a mocking tribunal where the judges sate the prosecutors, and whose unwritten laws hung on their own lips; and where to discharge any accused person as innocent was looked on as a reproach of their negligence, or an imputation of their sagacity.

Did the severity of these decrees produce the evils they encountered, or was it the existence of the evils which provoked the issue of these edicts? Did the terrific executions eradicate the political mischief? There was no free press in Elizabeth's reign, and yet libels abounded! The government compulsively contracted the press by their twenty stationary printers; and behold! moveable presses, whose ubiquity was astonishing as their ceaseless working. An invisible printer mysteriously scattered his publications here and there, during the contest of the Mar-prelate faction with the bishops; and the libels of the Jesuit Parsons, and others of the Roman party, were as rife against her majesty and her minister. The same occurred when the Star-chamber was guided by the genius of Laud; the altar was raised, and the sacerdotal knife struck! but the groans of the immolated victims were a shout of triumph. A clear demonstration that nothing is really gained by the temporary suppressions which power may enforce; the sealed book circulates till it is hoarded, and the author pilloried, mutilated, or hanged, obtains a popularity, which often his own genius afforded him no chance to acquire.

The secret design of all these entangling edicts was to hold the printers in passive obedience to the government, whatever that government might be; for each separate government, though acting on opposite principles, manifested a remarkable uniformity in their proceedings with the press. In the arbitrary days of Charles the Second, an extraordinary, if not an audacious, attempt was made to wrest the art of printing out of the hands of its professors, and to place the press wholly at the disposal of the sovereign. This usurping doctrine was founded on a startling plea. As our monarchs had granted privileges to

---

144. This remarkable "Decree of Starr-chamber concerning Printing" was in the possession of Thomas Hollis, and is printed in the Appendix to his curious Memoirs, p. 641.

the earliest printers, and, from the introduction of the art into England, had never ceased their patronage or their control, it was inferred, that our kings had never yielded *the royal prerogative of printing* any more than they had that of *coining*. The "mystery" of printing, in the style of the lawyers, was "a flower of the crown!"—the exercise of the prerogative; and therefore every printer in England must be a sworn servant of the crown. At such a period we are not surprised to find an express treatise put forth to demonstrate to his sacred majesty, that "printing belonged to him, in his public and private capacity, as supreme *magistrate* and as *proprietor;*" in reality there was to be but one printer for all England, and that printer the king! This was giving at once the most elevated and the most degraded notions of "the divine art," which this servile assumer describes can "not only bereave the king of his good name, but of the very hearts of his people."[145]

We observe the lamentations of these advocates of arbitrary power over the freedom of the press, or, as such maintained, the confusion produced "by the exorbitant and unlawful exercise of printing in modern times." They appeal to the miseries and calamities not only recently witnessed in our own country, but in Germany, France, the Netherlands, and Switzerland. Wherever they track a footstep of the liberty of the press, they pause to discover its accompanying calamity. One of these writers, to convey an adequate notion of the spread and political influence of the press, has thrown out a very excitable remark:—"Had this art been known in the time of the grand profession of the Donatist and Arian heresy, it would have drowned the world in a second deluge of blood and confusion, to its utter destruction long time since." A stroke of church history which might suggest a whole volume!

The interests of the printers had coincided with the designs of government, in limiting the number of presses; for the policy of their narrow confederacy was, the fewer printers the more printing! But the interests of the booksellers were quite opposite; they were for encouraging supernumerary printers, and overstocking the printing-offices with journeymen, and by this means they succeeded in bringing the printers down to their price or their purpose; and it is insinuated, on the Machiavelian principle, that the number being greater than could live honestly by the trade, one-half must be knaves, or starve. And it seems that "knaves" were in greater requisition by the publishers of "the unlawful," or, as these were afterwards called on the

---

145. "The Original and Growth of Printing, collected out of History and the Records of this Kingdom," &c., by Richard Atkyns, Esq., 1664. In this rare tract first appeared a narrative of the introduction of printing into Oxford, *before Caxton,* by the printer Francis Corsellis, to prove that printing was brought into England by Henry the Sixth.

establishment of a licenser of the press, "the unlicensed books," who revelled in their seductive profits.[146]

Among the effusions of the political Literature of the egregious Sir ROGER L'ESTRANGE, versed in the arcana of the publishing system of his day, I discover a project which terminated in renewing the office of the Licenser of Books, in his own person; the only pitiful preferment the Restoration brought the clamorous Loyalist. Our literary knight addressed Charles the Second, to impress on his Majesty the urgency of an immediate regulation of the press; "this great business of the press being now engrossed by Oliver's creatures, and the *honest* printers being impoverished by the late times."

This project to regulate the press by L'Estrange, chiefly turned on the dexterous management of the printers. He calculated, for four thousand pounds, to buy up the presses of the poor printers, who were willing to be reimbursed, and look to better trades. The bolder project was to emancipate the printers from the tyranny of the booksellers, by which means they would no longer be necessitated to print whatever their masters ordered. The printers at this moment had menaced to separate themselves from the stationers, with a view of their own.

The printers had been gradually deprived of any shares in new publications; they had been thrown out of all copyright, and probably had grown somewhat jealous of their prosperous masters; the printers complained that they were nothing else than slaves to the booksellers. They called for an independent company of "the mystery," and reverting to the custom of the early printers, they desired to have their own presses under their own management, and to print only the copies of which they themselves were the proprietors.

The future licenser of the press, who was throwing his net to haul in all these fish at a cast, took advantage of this project, which at once was levelled at the freedom of the trade, and the freedom of the press. Printers solely working on their own copies, would indeed check "the ungovernable ambition of the booksellers," by diminishing their copyrights; while those "unhappy printers" would be relieved, who at present have no other work than what "the great dealers in treasonous or seditious books" furnished them. All these were but the ostensible motives, for the real object designed was that the printers should become the creatures of the patronage of government, and, by the diminution of their number, the contracted circle would be the more easily managed.

---

146. For "unlicensed books" the printer charged twenty-five per cent. extra, but the booksellers sold them for double and treble the cost of other books.

"Considerations and Proposals in order to the Regulation of the Press, together with diverse instances of Treasonous and Seditious Pamphlets, proving the necessity thereof," 1663.

Such were the systematic struggles of our governments in the revival of the severe acts for the regulation of printing at various periods. It was long assumed that printing was not a free trade, but always to remain under regulation.

When Dr. Johnson, labouring under the pressure of his ancient notions, contending with the clear perception of his sceptical sagacity, once stood awed before the sublime effusion of Milton's "Areopagitica," he hazarded this opinion, for by balancing his notions it cannot be accepted as a decision: "The danger of such unbounded liberty, and the danger of bounding it, have produced a problem in the science of government which human understanding seems unable to solve."

And whatever either the advocates or the adversaries of the freedom of the press may allege, this problem in the science of government remains as insoluble at this day as at any former period—a truth demonstrated by a circumstance which has repeatedly occurred in our own political history. The noble treatise of Milton for a free press had not the slightest influence on that very parliament whose members had long suffered from its oppression. The Catholics clamoured for a free press under Charles the Second, but the same act operating against them under James the Second, from the use of the press by the Protestant party—the liberty of the press was then condemned as exorbitant and intolerable. The advocates of a free press thus become its adversaries whenever they themselves form the ruling power. Orators for the freedom of the press suddenly send forth outcries against its abuses; but as those, whoever the party may be, who are in place, are called the government, it always happens that the opposition, whatever may be their principles, must submit to the risk, of being deemed seditious libellers.

VII. LIBRARIES

1. LIBRARIES
(Curiosities, vol. 1, pp. 1-8)

THE passion for forming vast collections of books has necessarily existed in all periods of human curiosity; but long it required regal munificence to found a national library. It is only since the art of multiplying the productions of the mind has been discovered, that men of letters themselves have been enabled to rival this imperial and patriotic honour. The taste for books, so rare before the fifteenth century, has gradually become general only within these four hundred years: in that small space of time the public mind of Europe has been created.

Of LIBRARIES, the following anecdotes seem most interesting, as they mark either the affection, or the veneration, which civilised men have ever felt for these perennial repositories of their minds. The first national library founded in Egypt seemed to have been placed under the protection of the divinities, for their statues magnificently adorned this temple, dedicated at once to religion and to literature. It was still further embellished by a well-known inscription, for ever grateful to the votary of literature; on the front was engraven,—"The nourishment of the soul;" or, according to Diodorus, "The medicine of the mind."

The Egyptian Ptolemies founded the vast library of Alexandria, which was afterwards the emulative labour of rival monarchs; the founder infused a soul into the vast body he was creating, by his choice of the librarian, Demetrius Phalereus, whose skilful industry amassed from all nations their choicest productions. Without such a librarian, a national library would be little more than a literary chaos; his well exercised memory and critical judgment are its best catalogue. One of the Ptolemies refused supplying the famished Athenians with wheat, until they presented him with the original manuscripts of Æschylus, Sophocles, and Euripides; and in returning copies of these autographs, he allowed them to retain the fifteen talents which he had pledged with them as a princely security.

When tyrants, or usurpers, have possessed sense as well as courage, they have proved the most ardent patrons of literature; they know it is their interest to turn aside the public mind from political speculations, and to afford their subjects the inexhaustible occupations of curiosity, and the consoling pleasures of the imagination. Thus Pisistratus is said to have been among the earliest of the Greeks, who projected an immense collection of the works of the learned, and is supposed to have been the collector of the scattered works, which passed under the name of Homer.

The Romans, after six centuries of gradual dominion, must have possessed the vast and diversified collections of the writings of the nations they conquered: among the most valued spoils of their victories, we know that manuscripts were considered as more precious than vases of gold. Paulus Emilius, after the defeat of Perseus, king of Macedon, brought to Rome a great number which he had amassed in Greece, and which he now distributed among his sons, or presented to the Roman people. Sylla followed his example. After the siege of Athens he discovered an entire library in the temple of Apollo, which having carried to Rome, he appears to have been the founder of the first Roman public library. After the taking of Carthage, the Roman senate rewarded the family of Regulus with the books found in that city. A library was a national gift, and the most honourable they could bestow. From the intercourse of the Romans with the Greeks, the passion for forming libraries rapidly increased, and individuals began to pride themselves on their private collections.

Of many illustrious Romans, their magnificent taste in their *libraries* has been recorded. Asinius Pollio, Crassus, Cæsar, and Cicero, have, among others, been celebrated for their literary splendor. Lucullus, whose incredible opulence exhausted itself on more than imperial luxuries, more honourably distinguished himself by his vast collections of books, and the happy use he made of them by the liberal access he allowed the learned. "It was a library," says Plutarch, "whose walks, galleries, and cabinets, were open to all visitors; and the ingenious Greeks, when at leisure, resorted to this abode of the Muses to hold literary conversations, in which Lucullus himself loved to join." This library enlarged by others, Julius Cæsar once proposed to open for the public, having chosen the erudite Varro for its librarian; but the daggers of Brutus and his party prevented the meditated projects of Cæsar. In this museum, Cicero frequently pursued his studies, during the time his friend Faustus had the charge of it; which he describes to Atticus in his 4th Book, Epist. 9. Amidst his public occupations and his private studies, either of them sufficient to have immortalised one man, we are astonished at the minute attention Cicero paid to the formation of his libraries and his cabinets of antiquities.

The emperors were ambitious, at length, to give *their names* to the *libraries* they founded; they did not consider the purple as their chief ornament. Augustus was himself an author; and to one of those sumptuous buildings, called *Thermæ*, ornamented with porticos, galleries, and statues, with shady walks, and refreshing baths, testified his love of literature by adding a magnificent library. One of these libraries he fondly called by the name of his sister Octavia; and the other, the temple of Apollo, became the haunt of the poets, as Horace, Juvenal, and Persius have commemorated. The successors of Augustus imitated his example, and even Tiberius had an imperial library, chiefly consisting of works concerning the empire and the acts of its sovereigns. These Trajan augmented by the Ulpian library, denominated from his family name. In a word, we have accounts of the rich ornaments the ancients bestowed on their libraries; of their floors paved with marble, their walls covered with glass and ivory, and their shelves and desks of ebony and cedar.

The first *public library* in Italy was founded by a person of no considerable fortune: his credit, his frugality, and fortitude, were indeed equal to a treasury. Nicholas Niccoli, the son of a merchant, after the death of his father relinquished the beaten roads of gain, and devoted his soul to study, and his fortune to assist students. At his death, he left his library to the public, but his debts exceeding his effects, the princely generosity of Cosmo [*sic*] de' Medici realised the intention of its former possessor, and afterwards enriched it by the addition of an apartment, in which he placed the Greek, Hebrew, Arabic, Chaldaic, and Indian MSS. The intrepid spirit of Nicholas V. laid the foundations of the Vatican; the affection of Cardinal Bessarion for his country first gave Venice the rudiments of a public library; and to Sir 'I'. Bodley we owe the invaluable one of Oxford. Sir Robert Cotton, Sir Hans Sloane, Dr. Birch, Mr. Cracherode, Mr. Douce, and others of this race of lovers of books, have all contributed to form these literary treasures, which our nation owe to the enthusiasm of individuals, who have consecrated their fortunes and their days to this great public object; or, which in the result produces the same public good, the collections of such men have been frequently purchased on their deaths, by government, and thus have been preserved entire in our national collections.[147]

LITERATURE, like virtue, is often its own reward, and the enthusiasm some experience in the permanent enjoyments of a vast library has far outweighed the neglect or the calumny of the world, which some of its votaries have received. From the time that Cicero poured forth his feelings in his oration for the poet Archias, innumerable are the testimonies of men of letters of the pleasurable delirium of their researches. Richard de Bury, Bishop of Durham, and Chancellor of England so early as 1341, perhaps raised the first private library in our country. He purchased thirty or forty volumes of the Abbot of

---

147. The Cottonian collection is the richest English historic library we possess, and is now located in the British Museum, having been purchased for the use of the nation by Parliament in 1707, at a cost of 4500 *l*. The collection of Sir Hans Sloane was added thereto in 1753, for the sum of 20,000 *l*. Dr. Birch and Mr. Cracherode bequeathed their most valuable collections to the British Museum. Mr. Douce is the only collector in the list above who bequeathed his curious gatherings elsewhere. He was an officer of the Museum for many years, but preferred to leave his treasures to the Bodleian Library, where they are preserved intact, according to his earnest wish, a wish he feared might not be gratified in the national building. It is to this scholar and friend, the author of these volumes has dedicated them, as a lasting memorial of an esteem which endured during the life of each.

St. Albans for fifty pounds' weight of silver. He was so enamoured of his large collection, that he expressly composed a treatise on his love of books, under the title of *Philobiblion;* and which has been recently translated.[148]

He who passes much of his time amid such vast resources, and does not aspire to make some small addition to his library, were it only by a critical catalogue, must indeed be not more animated than a leaden Mercury. He must be as indolent as that animal called the Sloth, who perishes on the tree he climbs, after he has eaten all its leaves.

Rantzau, the founder of the great library at Copenhagen, whose days were dissolved in the pleasures of reading, discovers his taste and ardour in the following elegant effusion:—

> Salvete aureoli mei libelli,
> Meæ deliciæ, mei lepores!
> Quam vos sæpe oculis juvat videre,
> Et tritos manibus tenere nostris!
> Tot vos eximii, tot eruditi,
> Prisci lumina sæculi et recentis,
> Confecere viri, suasque vobis
> Ausi credere lucubrationes:
> Et sperare decus perenne scriptis;
> Neque hæc irrita spes fefellit illos.

> IMITATED.

> Golden volumes! richest treasures!
> Objects of delicious pleasures!
> You my eyes rejoicing please,
> You my hands in rapture seize!
> Brilliant wits, and musing sages,
> Lights who beamed through many ages,
> Left to your conscious leaves their story,
> And dared to trust you with their glory;
> And now their hope of fame achieved,
> Dear volumes! you have not deceived!

This passion for the enjoyment of *books* has occasioned their lovers

---

148. By Mr. Inglis, in 1832. This famous bishop is said to have possessed more books than all the others in England put together. Like Magliabechi, he lived among them, and those who visited him had to dispense with ceremony and step over the volumes that always strewed his floor.

embellishing their outsides with costly ornaments;[149] a fancy which ostentation may have abused; but when these volumes belong to the real man of letters, the most fanciful bindings are often the emblems of his taste and feelings. The great Thuanus procured the finest copies for his library, and his volumes are still eagerly purchased, bearing his autograph on the last page. A celebrated amateur was Grollier; the Muses themselves could not more ingeniously have ornamented their favourite works. I have seen several in the libraries of curious collectors. They are gilded and stamped with peculiar neatness; the compartments on the binding are drawn, and painted, with subjects analogous to the works themselves; and they are further adorned by that amiable inscription, *Jo. Grollierii et amicorum!*—purporting that these literary treasures were collected for himself and for his friends.

The family of the Fuggers had long felt an hereditary passion for the accumulation of literary treasures: and their portraits, with others in their picture gallery, form a curious quarto volume of 127 portraits, rare even in Germany, entitled "Fuggerorum Pinacotheca."[150] Wolfius, who daily haunted

---

149. The earliest decorated books were the Consular Diptycha, ivory book-covers richly sculptured in relief, and destined to contain upon their tablets the Fasti Consulares, the list ending with the name of the new consul, whose property they happened to be. Such as have descended to our own times appear to be works of the lower empire. They were generally decorated with full length figures of the consul and attendants, superintending the sports of the circus, or conjoined with portraits of the reigning prince and emblematic figures. The Greek Church adopted the style for the covers of the sacred volume, and ancient clerical libraries formerly possessed many such specimens of early bookbinding; the covers being richly sculptured in ivory, with bas-reliefs designed from Scripture history. Such ivories were sometimes placed in the centre of the covers; and framed in an ornamental metal-work studded with precious stones and engraved cameos. The barbaric magnificence of these volumes has never been surpassed; the era of Charlemagne was the culmination of their glory. One such volume, presented by that sovereign to the Cathedral at Treves, is enriched with Roman ivories and decorative gems. The value of manuscripts in the middle ages, suggested costly bindings for books that consumed the labour of lives to copy, and decorate with ornamental letters, or illustrative paintings. In the fifteenth century covers of leather embossed with storied ornament were in use; ladies also frequently employed their needles to construct, with threads of gold and silver, on grounds of coloured silk, the cover of a favourite volume. In the British Museum one is preserved of a later date—the work of our Queen Elizabeth. In the sixteenth century small ornaments, capable of being conjoined into a variety of elaborate patterns, were first used for stamping the covers with gilding; the leather was stained of various tints, and a beauty imparted to volumes which has not been surpassed by the most skilful modern workmen.

150. The Fuggers were a rich family of merchants, residing at Augsburg, carrying on trade with both the Indies, and from thence over Europe. They were ennobled by the Emperor Maximilian I. Their wealth often maintained the armies of Charles V.;

their celebrated library, pours out his gratitude in some Greek verses, and describes this bibliothèque as a literary heaven, furnished with as many books as there were stars in the firmament; or as a literary garden, in which he passed entire days in gathering fruit and flowers, delighting and instructing himself by perpetual occupation.

In 1364, the royal library of France did not exceed twenty volumes. Shortly after, Charles V. increased it to 900, which, by the fate of war, as much at least as by that of money, the Duke of Bedford afterwards purchased and transported to London, where libraries were smaller than on the continent, about 1440. It is a circumstance worthy observation, that the French sovereign, Charles V. surnamed the Wise, ordered that thirty portable lights, with a silver lamp suspended from the centre, should be illuminated at night, that students might not find their pursuits interrupted at any hour. Many among us, at this moment, whose professional avocations admit not of morning studies, find that the resources of a public library are not accessible to them, from the omission of the regulation of the zealous Charles V. of France. An objection to night-studies in public libraries is the danger of fire, and in our own British Museum not a light is permitted to be carried about on any pretence whatever. The history of the "Bibliothèque du Roi" is a curious incident in literature; and the progress of the human mind and public opinion might be traced by its gradual accessions, noting the changeable qualities of its literary stores chiefly from theology, law, and medicine, to philosophy and elegant literature. It was first under Louis XIV. that the productions of the art of engraving were there collected and arranged; the great minister Colbert purchased the extensive collections of the Abbé de Marolles, who may be ranked among the fathers of our print-collectors. Two hundred and sixty-four ample portfolios laid the foundations, and the very catalogues of his collections, printed by Marolles himself, are rare and high-priced. Our own national print gallery is growing from its infant establishment.

Mr. Hallam has observed, that in 1440, England had made comparatively but little progress in learning—and Germany was probably still less advanced. However, in Germany, Trithemius, the celebrated abbot of Spanheim [Sponheim], who died in 1516, had amassed about two thousand manuscripts; a literary treasure which excited such general attention, that princes and eminent men travelled to visit Trithemius and his library. About this time, six or eight hundred volumes formed a royal collection, and their cost could only be furnished by a prince. This was indeed a great advancement in libraries, for at the beginning of the fourteenth century the library of Louis IX. contained

---

and when Anthony Fugger received that sovereign at his house at Augsburg he is said, as a part of the entertainment, to have consumed in a fire of fragrant woods the bond of the emperor who condescended to become his guest.

only four classical authors; and that of Oxford, in 1300, consisted of "a few tracts kept in chests."

The pleasures of study are classed by Burton among those exercises or recreations of the mind which pass *within doors*. Looking about this "world of books," he exclaims, "I could even live and die with such meditations, and take more delight and true content of mind in them, than in all thy wealth and sport! There is a sweetness, which, as Circe's cup, bewitcheth a student: he cannot leave off, as well may witness those many laborious hours, days, and nights, spent in their voluminous treatises. So sweet is the delight of study. The last day is *prioris discipulus*. Heinsius was mewed up in the library of Leyden all the year long, and that which, to my thinking, should have bred a loathing, caused in him a greater liking. 'I no sooner,' saith he, 'come into the library, but I bolt the door to me, excluding Lust, Ambition, Avarice, and all such vices, whose nurse is Idleness, the mother of Ignorance and Melancholy. In the very lap of eternity, amongst so many divine souls, I take my seat with so lofty a spirit, and sweet content, that I pity all our great ones and rich men, that know not this happiness.'" Such is the incense of a votary who scatters it on the altar less for the ceremony than from the devotion.[146]

There is, however, an intemperance in study, incompatible often with our social or more active duties. The illustrious Grotius exposed himself to the reproaches of some of his contemporaries for having too warmly pursued his studies, to the detriment of his public station. It was the boast of Cicero that his philosophical studies had never interfered with the services he owed the republic, and that he had only dedicated to them the hours which others give to their walks, their repasts, and their pleasures. Looking on his voluminous labours, we are surprised at this observation;—how honourable is it to him, that his various philosophical works bear the titles of the different villas he possessed, which indicates that they were composed in these respective retirements! Cicero must have been an early riser; and practised that magic art in the employment of time, which multiplies our days.

2. EARLY LIBRARIES
(*Amenities*, pp. 221-227)

THERE probably was a time when there existed no private libraries in the

---

146. A living poet thus enthusiastically describes the charms of a student's life among his books—"he has his Rome, his Florence, his whole glowing Italy, within the four walls of his library. He has in his books the ruins of an antique world, and the glories of a modern one."—Longfellow's *Hyperion*.

kingdom, nor any save the monastic; that of Oxford, at the close of the thirteenth century, consisted of "a few tracts kept in chests." In that primeval age of book-collecting, shelves were not yet required. Royalty itself seems to have been destitute of a royal library. It appears, by one of our recently published records, that King John borrowed a volume from a rich abbey, and the king gave a receipt to Simon his Chancellor for "the book called Pliny," which had been in the custody of the Abbot and Convent of Reading. "The Romance of the History of England," with other volumes, have also royal receipts. The king had either deposited these volumes for security with the Abbot, or, what seems not improbable, had no established collection which could be deemed a library, and, as leisure or curiosity stimulated, commanded the loan of a volume.

The borrowing of a volume was a serious concern in those days, and heavy was the pledge or the bond required for the loan. One of the regulations of the library of the Abbey of Croyland, Ingulphus has given. It regards "the lending of their books, as well the smaller without pictures as the larger with pictures;" any loan is forbidden under no less a penalty than that of excommunication, which might possibly be a severer punishment than the gallows.

Long after this period, our English libraries are said to have been smaller than those on the Continent; and yet, one century and a half subsequently to the reign of John, the royal library of France, belonging to a monarch who loved literature, Jean le Bon, did not exceed ten volumes. In those days they had no idea of establishing a library; the few volumes which each monarch collected, at great cost, were always dispersed by gifts or bequests at their death; nothing passed to their successor but the missals, the *heures,* and the *offices* of their chapels. These monarchs of the thirteenth and fourteenth centuries, amid the prevailing ignorance of the age, had not advanced in their comprehension of the uses of a permanent library beyond their great predecessor of the ninth, for Charlemagne had ordered his books to be sold after his death, and the money given to the poor.

Yet among these early French kings there were several who were lovers of books, and were not insensible of the value of a studious intercourse, anxious to procure transcribers and translators. A curious fact has been recorded of St. Louis, that, during his crusade in the East, having learned that a Saracen prince employed scribes to copy the best writings of philosophy for the use of students, on his return to France he adopted the same practice, and caused the Scriptures und the works of the Fathers to be transcribed from copies found in different abbeys. These volumes were deposited in a secure apartment, to which the learned might have access; and he himself passed much of his time there, occupied in his favourite study, the writings of the Fathers.[147]

Charles le Sage, in 1373, had a considerable library, amounting to nine hundred volumes. He placed this collection in one the towers of the Louvre, hence denominated the "Tour de la Librarie," and entrusted it to the custody of his valet-de-chambre, Gilles Malet, constituting him his librarian.[148] He was no common personage, for great as was the care and ingenuity required, he drew up an inventory with his own hand of this royal library. In that early age of book-collecting, volumes had not always titles to denote their subjects, or they contained several in one volume,[149] hence they are described by their outsides, their size, and their shape, their coverings and their clasps. This library of Charles the Fifth shines in extreme splendour, with its many-coloured silks and velvets, azure and vermeil, green and yellow, and its cloths of silver and of gold, each volume being distinctly described by the colour and the material of its covering. This curious document of the fourteenth century still exists.[150]

This library passed through strange vicissitudes. The volumes in the succeeding reigns were seized on, or purchased at a conqueror's price, by the Duke of Bedford, Regent of France. Some he gave to his brother Humphrey, the Duke of Gloucester, and they formed a part of the rich collection which that prince presented to Oxford, there finally to be destroyed by a fanatical English mob; others of the volumes found their way back to the Louvre, repurchased by the French at London. The glorious missal that bears the Regent's name remains yet in this country, the property of a wealthy individual.

Accident has preserved a few catalogues of libraries of noblemen in the fourteenth and fifteenth century, more pleasant than erudite. In the

147. "Essai Historique sur la Bibliothèque du Roi," par M. Le Prince.

148. This Gilles Malet, who was also the king's reader, had great strength of character; he is thus described by Christine de Pise.—"Souverainement bien lisoit, et bien penttoit, et entendens homs estoit;" "he read sovereignly well, with good punctuation, and was an understanding man." She has recorded a personal anecdote of him. One day a fatal accident happened to his child, but such was the discipline of official duties, that he did not interrupt his attendance on the king at the usual hour of reading. The king having afterwards heard of the accident which had bereaved the father of his child, observed, "If the intrepidity of this man had not exceeded that which nature bestows upon ordinary men, his paternal emotion would not have allowed him to conceal his misfortune."

149. The reader may form some idea of the discordant arrangement of a volume of manuscripts by the following entries:—"Un Livre qui commence de Genesis, et aussi traite des fais Julius Cesar, appelle Suetoine." "Un Livre en François, en un volume, qui ce commence de Genesis, et traite du fait des Romains, de la vie des SS. Peres Hermites, et de Merlin."

150. "Hist. de l' Académie Royale des Inscriptions," tome i. 421, 12mo.

fourteenth century, the volumes consisted for the greater part of those romances of chivalry, which so long formed the favourite reading of the noble, the dame and the damoiselle, and all the lounging damoiseaux in the baronial castle.[151]

The private libraries of the fifteenth century were restricted to some French tomes of chivalry, or to "a merrie tale in Boccace;" and their science advanced not beyond "The Shepherd's Calendar," or "The Secrets of Albert the Great." There was an intermixture of legendary lives of saints, and apocryphal adventures of "Notre Seigneur" in Egypt; with a volume or two of physic and surgery and astrology.

A few catalogues of our monastic libraries still remain, and these reflect an image of the studies of the middle ages. We find versions of the Scriptures in English and Latin—a Greek or Hebrew manuscript is not noted down; a commentator, a father, and some schoolmen; and a writer on the canon law, and the mediæval Christian poets who composed in Latin verse. A romance, an accidental classic, a chronicle and legends—such are the usual contents of these monastic catalogues. But though the subjects seem various, the number of volumes were exceedingly few. Some monasteries had not more than twenty books. In such little esteem were any writings in the vernacular idiom held, that the library of Glastonbury Abbey, probably the most extensive in England, in 1248, possessed no more than four books in English,[152] on religious topics; and in the later days of Henry the Eighth, when Leland rummaged the monasteries, he did not find a greater number. The library of the monastery of Bretton, which, owing to its isolated site, was among the last dissolved, and which may have enlarged its stores with the spoils of other collections which the times offered, when it was dissolved in 1558, could only boast of having possessed one hundred and fifty distinct works.[153]

In this primitive state of book-collecting, a singular evidence of their bibliographical passion was sometimes apparent in the monastic libraries. Not deeming a written catalogue, which might not often be opened, sufficiently attractive to remind them of their lettered stores, they inscribed verses on their windows to indicate the books they possessed, and over these inscriptions they placed the portraits of the authors. Thus they could not look through their windows without being reminded of their volumes; and the very portraits of authors, illuminated by the light of heaven, might rouse the

---

151. *Dame* was the lady of the knight; the *Damoiselle*, the wife of an esquire; *Dameisel*, or *Damoiseau*, was a youth of noble extraction, but who had not yet attained to knighthood.—Rocquefort, "Glossaire de la Langue Romane."

152. Ritson's "Dissertation on Romance and Minstrelsy," lxxxi.

153. See an "Essay on English Monastic Libraries," by that learned and ingenious antiquary, the Rev. Joseph Hunter.

curiosity which many a barren title would repel.[154]

To us accustomed to reckon libraries by thousands, these scanty catalogues will appear a sad contraction of human knowledge. The monastic studies could not in any degree have advanced the national character; they could only have kept it stationary; and, excepting some scholastic logomachies, in which the people could have no concern, one monkish writer could hardly ever have differed from another.

The monastic libraries have been declared to have afforded the last asylums of literature in a barbarous era; and the preservation of ancient literature has been ascribed to the monks: but we must not accept a fortuitous occurrence as any evidence of their solicitude or their taste. In the dull scriptorium of the monk, if the ancient authors always obtained so secure a place, they slept in comparative safety, for they were not often disturbed by their first Gothic owners, who hardly ever allude to them. If ancient literature found a refuge in the monastic establishments, the polytheistical guests were not slightly contemned by their hosts, who cherished with a different taste a bastardised race of the Romans. The purer writers were not in request; for the later Latin versemakers being Christians, the piety of the monks proved to be infinitely superior to their taste. Boethius was their great classic; while Prudentius, Sedulius, and Fortunius, carried the votes against Virgil, Horace, and even Ovid; though Ovid was in some favour for his marvellous Romance. The polytheism of the classical poets was looked on with horror, so literally did they construe the allegorical fables of the Latin muse. Even till a later day, when monkery itself was abolished, the same Gothic taste lingered among us in its aversion to the classical poets of antiquity, as the works of idolaters!

Had we not obtained our knowledge of the great ancients by other circumstances than by their accidental preservation by the monks, we should have lost a whole antiquity. The vellum was considered more precious than the genius of the author; and it has been acutely conjectured that the real cause of the minor writers of antiquity having come down to us entire, while we have to lament for ever the lacerations of the greater, has been owing to the scantiness of the parchment of a diminutive volume. They coveted the more voluminous authors to erase some immortal page of the lost decades of Livy, or the annals of Tacitus, to inscribe on it some dull homily or saintly legend. That the ancients were neglected by these guardians appears by the dungeon-darkness from which the Italian Poggio disinterred many of our ancient classics; and Leland, in his literary journey to survey the monastic libraries of England, often shook from the unknown author a whole century

---

154. Some of these extraordinary window-catalogues of the monastic library of St. Albans were found in the cloisters and presbytery of that monastery, and are preserved in the "Monasticon Anglicanum."

of dust and cobwebs. When libraries became one source of the pleasures of life, the lovers of books appear to have been curious in selecting their site for perfect seclusion and silence amid their noble residences, and also in their contrivances to arrange their volumes, so as to have them at instant command. One of these Gothic libraries, in an old castle belonging to the Percys, has been described by Leland with congenial delight. I shall transcribe his words, accommodating the reader with our modern orthography.

"One thing I liked extremely in one of the towers; that was a STUDY called PARADISE; where was a closet in the middle of eight squares latticed 'abrate;' and at the top of every square was a desk ledged to set books on, on coffers within them, and these seemed as joined hard to the top of the closet; and yet by pulling, one or all would come down breast-high in rabbets (or grooves), and serve for desks to lay books on."

However clumsy this invention in "Paradise" may seem to us, it was not more so than the custom of chaining their books to the shelves, allowing a sufficient length of chain to reach the reading-desk—a mode which long prevailed when printing multiplied the cares of the librarian.

All these libraries, consisting of manuscripts, were necessarily limited in their numbers; their collectors had no choice, but gladly received what occurred to their hands; it was when books were multiplied by the press, that the minds of owners of libraries shaped them to their own fancies, and stamped their characters on these companions of their solitude.

We have a catalogue of the library of Mary Queen of Scots, as delivered up to her son James the Sixth, in 1578,[155] very characteristic of her elegant studies; the volumes chiefly consist of French authors and French translations, a variety of chronicles, several romances, a few Italian writers, Petrarch, Boccaccio, and Ariosto, and her favourite poets, Alain Chartier, Ronsard, and Marot. This library forms a striking contrast with that of Elizabeth of England, which was visited in 1598 by Hentzner, the German traveller. The shelves at Whitehall displayed a more classical array; the collection consisted of Greek, Latin, as well as Italian and French books.

The dearness of parchment, and the slowness of the scribes, made manuscripts things only purchasable by princely munificence. It was the discovery of paper from rags, and the novel art of taking copies without penmen, which made books mere objects of commerce, and dispersed the treasures of the human mind free as air, and cheap as bread.

---

155. Dibdin's "Bibliographical Decameron," iii. 245.

3. THE FIRST FOUNDER OF A PUBLIC LIBRARY
(*Amenities*, pp. 661-669)

THE first marked advancement in the progress of the national understanding was made by a new race of public benefactors, who, in their munificence, no longer endowing obsolete superstitions, and inefficient or misplaced charities, erected libraries and opened academies; founders of those habitations of knowledge whose doors open to the bidding of all comers.

To the privacy and the silent labours of some men of letters and some lovers of the arts, usually classed under the general designation of COLLECTORS, literary Europe, for the great part, owes its public museums and its public libraries. It was their ripe knowledge only which could have created them, their opulence only which could render them worthy of a nation's purchase, or of its acceptance, when in their generous enthusiasm they consecrated the intellectual gift for their countrymen.

These collections could only have acquired their strength by their growth, for gradual were their acquisitions and innumerable were their details; they claimed the sleepless vigilance of a whole life, the devotion of a whole fortune, and often that moral intrepidity which wrestled with insurmountable difficulties. We may admire the generous enthusiasm whose opulence was solely directed to enrich what hereafter was to be consecrated as public property; but it has not always received the notice and the eulogy so largely its due. It is but bare justice to distinguish these men from their numerous brothers whose collections have terminated with themselves, known only to posterity by their posthumous catalogues—the sole record that these collectors were great buyers and more famous sellers. Of many of the FOUNDERS of public collections the names are not familiar to the reader, though some have sometimes been identified with their more celebrated collections, from the gratitude of a succeeding age.

A collection formed by a single mind, skilled in its favourite pursuit, becomes the tangible depository of the thoughts of its owner; there is a unity in this labour of love, and a secret connexion through its dependent parts. Thus we are told that Cecil's library was the best for history; Walsingham's, for policy; Arundel's, for heraldry; Cotton's, for antiquity; and Usher's, for divinity. The completion of such a collection reflects the perfect image of the mind of the philosopher, the philologist, the antiquary, the naturalist, the scientific or the legal character, who into one locality has gathered together und arranged this furniture of the human intellect.

To disperse their collections would be, to these elect spirits, to resolve them back into their first elements—to scatter them in the air, or to mingle them with the dust.[156] Happily for mankind, these have been men to whom the perpetuity of their intellectual associations was a future existence. Conscious that their hands had fastened links in the unbroken chain of human inquiry, they left the legacy to the world. The creators of these collections have often betrayed their anxiety to preserve them distinct and entire. Confident I am that such was the real feeling of a recent celebrated collector. The rich and peculiar collection of manuscripts, and of rare and chosen volumes, of FRANCIS DOUCE, from his earliest days had been the objects of his incessant cares. With means extremely restricted, but with a mind which no obstructions could swerve from its direct course, through many years he accomplished a glorious design. Our modest antiquary startled the most curious, not only of his countrymen but of foreigners, by his knowledge, diversified as his own unrivalled collections, in the recondite literature of the middle ages, and whatever exhibited the manners, the customs, and the arts of every people and of every age. Late in life he accidentally became the possessor of a considerable fortune, and having decided that this work of his life should be a public inheritance, he seemed at a loss where it might at once rest in security, and lie patent for the world. The idea of its dispersion was very painful, for he was aware that the singleness of design which had assembled such various matters together could never be resumed by another. He often regretted that in the great national repository of literature the collection would merge into the universal mass. It was about this time that we visited together the great library of Oxford. Douce contemplated in the Bodleian that arch over which is placed the portrait of SELDEN, and the library of Selden preserved entire; the antiquary's closet which holds the great topographical collections of Gough; and the distinct shelves dedicated to the small Shakespearian library of MALONE. He observed that the collections of Rawlinson, of Tanner, and of others, had preserved their identity by their separation. This was the subject of our conversation. At this moment Douce must have decided on the locality where his precious collection was to find a perpetual abode; for it was immediately on his return home that our literary antiquary bequeathed his collection to the Bodleian Library, where it now occupies more than one apartment.

To the anxious cares of such founders of public collections, England, as well as Italy and France, owes a national debt; nor can we pass over in silence

---

156. Sir Simonds d'Ewes feelingly describes in his will his "precious library." "It is my inviolable injunction that it be kept entire, and not sold, divided, or dissipated." It was not, however, to be locked up from the public good. Such was the feeling of an eminent antiquary.

A later Sir Simonds d'Ewes was an extravagant man, and seems to have sold everything about 1716, when the collection passed into the possession of the Earl of Oxford.

the man to whom first occurred the happy idea of instituting a library which should have for its owners his own fellow-citizens. A Florentine merchant, emancipated from the thraldom of traffic, vowed himself to the pursuits of literature, and, just before the art of printing was practised, to the preservation of manuscripts, which he not only multiplied by his unwearied hand, but was the first of that race of critics who amended the texts of the early copyists. What he could not purchase, his pure zeal was not the less solicitous to preserve. Boccaccio had bequeathed his own library to a convent in Florence, and its sight produced that effect on him which the library of Shakespeare, had it been preserved, might have had on an Englishman; and since he could not possess it, he built an apartment solely to preserve it distinct from any other collection.

At a period when the owners of manuscripts were so avaricious of their possessions that they refused their loan, and were frugal even in allowing a sight of their leaves, the hardy generosity of this Florentine merchant conceived one of the most important designs for the interests of learning;—to invite readers, he bequeathed his own as A PUBLIC LIBRARY.[157] He who occupied but a private station, first offered Europe a model of patriotic greatness which princes and nobles in their magnificence would emulate. It has been said that the founder *of* this public library at Florence had only revived the noble design of the ancients, who had displayed their affection for literature by even bestowing their own names on public libraries; but this must not detract from the true glory of the merchant of Florence; it was at least an idea which had wholly escaped the less liberal of his learned contemporaries.

Sir THOMAS BODLEY may be considered as the first founder of a public library in this country, raised by the hand of an individual. A picture of the obstructions, the anxieties, the hopes, and the disappointments of the founder of the Bodleian, exhibits a person of rank and opulence submitting even to minute drudgery, and to the most humiliating solicitations, and busily occupied by a foreign as well as a domestic correspondence, to accomplish what he long despaired of—a library adequate to the wants of every English student.

BODLEY, in the sketch of his own life, betrays that early book-love which subsequently broke out into that noble passion for "his reverend mother, the University of Oxford." Sir Thomas Bodley had ably served in some of the highest state-employments; but, at length, discovered the secret pathway to escape from "court contentions;" and this he found when busying himself with a vast ideal library—the future Bodleian! Long, indeed, it was but ideal; the labour of his day, the dream of his night, so slowly rose the reality of the fabric. It was difficult to determine on the class or the worth of

---

157. Tiraboschi, VI. pt. i. 131.

authors—often rejecting, always augmenting, still consulting, now advising, or being advised; sometimes irresolute, and at others decisive; now exulting, and now despondent. However fervid was his noble enthusiasm for literature, and for his library, not less remarkable was that provident sagacity which he combined with it, and by which only he could carry on the vast design.

What were the emotions of Bodley through this long period, what his first intentions, and what his immutable decision, have fortunately been laid open to us in a close correspondence with his first librarian. Our parent-founder of a public library, with the forcible simplicity of the natural colloquial style of that day, has developed his own character. "Examining exactly for the rest of my life what course I might take, and having sought, as I thought, all the ways to the wood, to select the most proper, I concluded, at the last, to set up my staff at the library door in Oxon; being thoroughly persuaded, that in my solitude and surcease from the commonwealth affairs, I could not busy myself to better purpose." He early discovered that the formation of his library required the cooperation of many favourable circumstances: "some kind of knowledge, some purse-ability, great store of honourable friends; else it would prove a vain attempt and inconsiderate." After many perplexities, the great resolve seemed to sanction the act, and he exclaims—"The project is cast, and whether I live or die, to such ends altogether I address my thoughts and deeds!" Such was the solemn pledge, and such the deed of gift, which Bodley, in the greatness of his mind, contracted with posterity.

But the minor cares and the minuter anxieties were to open on him; and it must be confessed that he tried the patient duties of the learned Dr. James, whom he had judiciously elected for the first librarian, but who often vents a groan on his interminable labours. Sir Thomas gently reproaches him: "I am toiled exceedingly, no less than yourself, with writing, buying, binding, disposing, &c.; but I am fed with pleasure of seeing the end." Bodley had not only to form a universal library, but to build one on the desolate ruins of that founded by Duke Humphrey, whose royal name could not save his books and manuscripts, which had all been purloined and wasted. The pledges left for their loan not being worth half the value of the books, the volumes were never returned; and those which remained in the reign of Edward the Sixth were burned as "superstitious," for their rubrics and illuminations. The history of this library might have deterred our new founder, by reminding him of the fate which may await even on public libraries. At all events, for many years it required all his fortitude to encounter a rabble of master-carpenters, joiners, carvers, glaziers, builders, claspers, and stringers, and the chain-smiths; for at that day books were chained to their shelves, with chains long enough to reach the desk. A book was tethered, and could never stray from its paddock. Then came the classification and the arrangements! discussions not easily to be adjusted with his librarian, whether a book should be classed as a work of theology or of politics? Sir Thomas found an incessant business at

London in packing up "dry fats," or vats of books, barging them for Oxford; he was receiving fresh supplies from Italy, from Spain, from Turkey, and designed to send a scholar to travel in the East, to collect Arabic and Persian books, on which he sagaciously observed, that "in process of time, by the extraordinary diligence of some one student, these Eastern languages may be readily understood." Bodley anticipated our Society for Oriental Literature.

But not merely solicitous to erect a vast library, Bodley was equally anxious to consecrate the spot to study itself. He is uneasy at too public an admission, lest idlers should mix among the students, and, as he plainly tells, "be daily pestering the room with their gazing and babbling, and trampling up and down, disturbing the real studious." With what fervour he rejoices when, at length, he lived to witness the day of the opening of the library, and found that "all proceeded orderly, and with such silence!" But although he had bestowed all his cares and his fortune on this institution, it still was but an infant, and he had to look towards spirits as enlarged as his own, to protect the orphan of the public. It met with some who adopted it, and Bodley had their names inscribed in the register of this public library; but he was as cautious as he was courteous—the vain were not to be gratified for penurious gifts. Books, and not names, were wanted. At first, impatiently zealous, he murmurs of "promises received for performances." But latterly, he had occasion to exhort the university to mark by their particular acknowledgments, the donations in volumes or in money. The honourable roll on which the names are inscribed, includes not only those of the most eminent of our country, but also of several ladies, who rivalled those heroes and statesmen who had the honour of laying the foundation of the Bodleian Library.[158]

In Sir Thomas Bodley's character we view the conscious dignity of a great design, yet combined with the sedate reflection of a man practised in the world. There were certain traits of vanity, which may give a colour to the insinuations of some—who might consider they had been deprived of legacies—that it was his enormous vanity which raised this edifice of learning. It is amusing to discover, that when the Bishop of Exeter proposed to visit the library, a letter of Sir Thomas immediately precedes his visitor. "I pray you, observe his speeches, and liking or disliking, and in your next let me know it," When James the First was preparing to visit the library, he furnished hints to the librarian for his speech to the literary monarch: "It must not carry greater length than for half a quarter of an hour's utterance. It must be short and sweet, and full of stuff." The librarian was desirous to hide Buchanan when the king came down to Oxford; but Bodley, probably not approving the

158. See Gutch's edition of Wood's "Annals of the University of Oxford," vol. I. pt. ii. p. 928.

concealment of any of his literary stores, observed, "It will not avail to conceal him in his desk since he is in the catalogue, nor have we any reason to take any notice of the king's dislike; but," he warily adds, "should it excite his Majesty's notice, we must allege that the books were put there in the Queen's time." But nothing save the most delicate attention towards an author could have prompted his order concerning Coryat the traveller, who had presented his book to the library. On the author's coming to Oxford, Sir Thomas desired that "it should be placed in such a manner, that when the author came down, it may seem to magnify the author and the book." In his ardour for the general interests of his library, Bodley absolutely insisted that his librarian should persevere in his forlorn fellowship, for "marriage," opined the founder of the Bodleian Library, "is too full of domestic impeachments to afford him so much time from his private affairs." The doctor decided against the celibacy of a librarian, and was gravely admonished on the absurdity of such conduct in one who had the care of a public library! for "it was opening a gap to disorder hereafter." With a happier prescience, Bodley foresaw that race of generous spirits who, long after, and at distant intervals, have carried on his great views. Listen to the simplicity and force of the venerable style of our first founder of a PUBLIC LIBRARY.

"We cannot but presume that, casting (counting) what number of noble benefactors have already concurred in a FERVOUR OF AFFECTION to that PUBLIC PLACE OF STUDY, we shall be sure in TIME TO COME to find same OTHERS OF THE LIKE DISPOSITION to the advancement of learning."[159]

With such a hallowed purpose ever before him, can we conceive the agonies of the founder of a public library, on being for ever denied an entrance into it? and yet such was the fate of one of the most illustrious of this race. The mournful history of the founder of the Cottonian Library will ever excite the regrets of a grateful posterity, and its catastrophe will witness how far above life he loved and valued his collected lore! It happened that among the many rare manuscripts collected by Sir ROBERT COTTON, one reached his hands, which struck him by the singularity of the subject; it was a political theory to show the kings of England "how to bridle the impertinency of Parliaments." An unfaithful amanuensis, the son of the Dr. James whom we have just noticed, took copies and sold them to the curious. When the original was at length traced to the Cottonian collection, Sir Robert was sued in the Star-chamber, and considered as the author of a work whose tendency

---

159. The vigilant curiosity of Tom Hearne, the antiquary, collected the singular correspondence of the Founder of the Bodleian Library with Dr. James, the first librarian, and published it under the title of "Reliquiæ Bodleianæ, or Some Genuine Remains of Sir Thomas Bodley," 1703, 8vo. The curious reader will find in Gutch's edition of Wood's "Annals of the University of Oxford" many letters by Bodley, and his liberal endowments to provide a fixed revenue after his decease.

was to enslave the nation. It was lang afterwards discovered that this manuscript had been originally written by Sir Robert Dudley, when in exile at Florence. Cotton was now denied all access to his library; his spirits sunk in the blackest melancholy; and he declared to an intimate friend, that "those who had locked up his library from him had broken his heart." Now deprived of that learned crowd who once were flowing into his house, consulting and arranging his precious manuscripts; torn away from the delightful business of his life, and in torment at the doubtful fate of that manuscript collection, which had consumed forty years at every personal sacrifice to form it for the "use and service of posterity," he sunk at the sudden stroke. In the course of a few weeks, he was so worn by injured feelings, that from a ruddy-complexioned man, "his face was wholly changed into a grim blackish paleness, near to the resemblance and hue of a dead visage." Such is the expression of one who knew him well. Before he died, Sir Robert requested the learned Spelman to acquaint the Privy Council that "their so long detaining his books from him had been the cause of his mortal malady." "On this message," says the writer of a manuscript letter of the day, "the Lord Privy Seal came to Sir Robert, when it was too late to comfort him, from the King, from whom also the Earl of Dorset came within half an hour of Sir Robert's death, to condole with Sir Thomas Cotton, his son, for his father's death; and with an assurance that as his Majesty loved his father, so he would continue his love to him: Sir Robert hath intailed his library of books as sure as he can make it upon his son and his posterity. If Sir Robert's heart could be ripped up, his library would appear in it, as Calais in Queen Mary's." Such is the affecting fate of the founder of the Cottonian Library, that great individual whose sole labour silently formed our national antiquities, and endowed his country with this wealth of manuscripts.

DIRECTORY OF PERSONAL NAMES

Aaron, biblical figure 72

Abdoolah (fl. c. 9th cent.), ruler of Khorassan 182

Abelard, Peter (1079-1142), French philosopher and theologian 68, 188

Abraham, biblical figure 94, 98

Achilles, Greek mythological figure 118

Addison, Joseph (1672-1719), essayist and poet 24, 31, 86, 163

Ælian (Claudius Alienus) (170-235), Roman author 19

Æschines (389-324 BC), Athenian orator 73

Æschylus (525?-456 BC), Greek tragedian 172, 222

Agobard (779-840), French prelate and author 168

Ajax, Greek mythological figure 122

Akenside, Mark (1721-1770), poet and physician 34, 95

Alaric I (c. 370-410), king of the Visigoths 83

Albinus (Aulus Albinus) (fl. 2nd cent. BC), Roman consul and historian 83

Alcides (also Hercules), Greek and Roman mythological figure 92

Alcyonius, Peter (Alcioni, Pietro) (1487-1527), Italian poet 168

Aldus Manutius (Manuzio, Aldo) (1449-1515), Venetian scholar and printer
  51, 52, 53, 82

Alexander ab Alexandro (Alessandri, Alessandro di) (1461-1523), Italian jurist
  and man of letters 88

Alexander the Great (356-323 BC), king of Macedonia 83,

Alexander VI (Borgia, Rodrigo) (1431-1503), pope 159

Alfred (849-901), king of the West Saxons 104

Alison, Archibald (1757-1839), Scottish minister and aesthetician 134

Allatius, Leo (1586-1669), Greek author and librarian 75

Alphonsus (Alfonso) VI (1065-1109), king of León and Castile 183

Alphonsus (Alfonso) X (1221-1284), king of León and Castile 20

Amberback (Amerbach), Johann (1430-1514), German printer 145

Amelot de la Houssaye, Abraham Nicolas (1634-1706), French historian 83,
  144

Amhurst, Nicholas (1697-1742), poet and political writer 109

Ammianus Marcellinus (c. 330-390), Roman historian 171

Ancillon, David (1617-1692), French bibliophile 35, 118, 119

Anglesea, earl of (Annesley, Arthur) (1614-1686), statesman and author 175,
  176, 203

Anglus (White), Thomas (1593-1676), philosopher and controversialist 142

Anjou, countess of (fl. before 1471) 166

Anne (1665-1714), queen of Great Britain and Ireland 13, 18, 19, 26, 194, 195

Annius of Viterbo (Annio, Tito, also Nanni, Giovanni) (1432-1502),
  Dominican friar and scholar 148, 149, 159

Anthony, Saint (251-356), Egyptian anchorite 51

Elphinston, James (1721-1809), educationalist 13
Emilius (Aemilius) Paulus, Lucius (d. 216 BC), Roman consul 223
Ennius, Quintus (c. 239-169 BC), Roman poet 119, 167
Epicurus (341-270 BC), Greek philosopher 88
Erasmus, Desiderius (1466-1536), Dutch humanist 139, 176, 199, 206
Esau, biblical figure 195
Euclid (fl. 300 BC), Greek mathematician 25
Euripides (484 or 480-406 BC), Greek tragedian 172, 222
Eusebius of Caesarea (c. 264-340), Palestinian theologian and historian 149,
    171, 181
Eve, biblical figure 95
Evelyn, John (1620-1706), diarist and author 34, 131
Ezekiel, biblical figure 158
Fabroni, Angelo (1732-1803), Italian biographer and humanist 175
Fabian (Fabyan), Robert (d. 1513), chronicler 55
Fairfax, Edward (d. 1635), translator 105
Fairfax, Thomas (1612-1671), parliamentary soldier 170, 203
Faria de Souza, Emmanuel (1590-1649), Portuguese historian and poet 198
Father Paul, see Barri, Paolo
Fatima (fl. 7th cent.), youngest daughter of Mohammed 160
Faust, see Fust
Faustus, Johann (fl. 16th cent.), German astrologer and alchemist 51
Faustus, see Fust
Faustus, Caius Flavius (d. 42 BC), Roman friend of Cicero 223
Fell, John (1625-1686), dean of Christ Church and bishop of Oxford 180
Fénelon, François de Salignac de la Mothe (1671-1715), French author 16, 32,
    177
Fenn, John (1739-1794), antiquary 7
Ferdinand II (1578-1637), Holy Roman emperor 183
Fernel, Jean François (1500-1558), physician to Henry II of France 39
Fèvre (Le Fèvre), Raoul (fl. 1460-1467), French clergyman and author 51, 54
Fielding, Henry (1707-1754), novelist 110, 140, 162
Filmore (Filmer), Robert (d. 1653), political writer 176
Finiguerra, Tommaso (1426-1464), Italian engraver 43, 44
Fish, Simon (d. 1531), theologian and pamphleteer 75, 209
Flavigny, Valerien de (d. 1674), French Hebraist 94
Fléchier, Esprit (1632-1710), bishop of Nîmes and biographer 141
Fletcher, Giles (1549?-1611), ambassador and poet 201
Florus, Lucius Annaeus (fl. 2nd cent.), Roman historian 159
Fontana, Felice (1730-1805), Italian microscopist and neurologist 44
Fontanini, Giusto (1666-1736), Italian scholar 123
Fontenelle, Bernard le Bouyer de (1657-1757), French author 82, 142
Formey, Jean Henri Samuel (1711-1797), French theologian 39

Raleigh, Walter (1552?-1618), courtier, poet, and author 99
Ranaud, Théophile (1583-1663), French Jesuit and theologian 61, 68, 69, 70
Rangouze (Rangouse), N ... (ment. 1640), French letter-writer 76
Rantzau, Henrik (1526-1598), Danish bibliophile 225
Rapin, Paul de (1661-1725), French historian 60
Rasis (Rhazes) (852-932), Arabian physician 166
Rawlinson, Richard (1690-1755), antiquary and bibliophile 143, 235
Raynaud and Raynaudus, see Ranaud
Réaumur, René Antoine Ferchault de (1683-1757), French physicist 124
Reed, Isaac (1742-1807), editor of Shakespeare 91
Regnault, François (or Reynold, Francis) (d. c. 1541), French printer 55
Regulus, Roman family 223
Regulus, Rosius (fl. 1st cent.), Roman consul 77
Reuchlin, Johann (1455-1522), German humanist and Hebraist 181
Richard III (1452-1485), king of England 207
Richelieu, Armand Jean Duplessis (1585-1642), French prelate and statesman
     39, 74, 78, 79, 136
Richesource (Soudier de Richesource), Jean (d. c. 1696), French pedagogue
     140, 141
Ritson, Joseph (1752-1803), antiquary 121, 231
Rive, Jean Joseph (1730-1791), French bibliographer 121, 122, 123
Robertson, William (1721-1793), Scottish historian 21, 80, 84, 88, 116, 124,
     133
Robinsons (Robinson), G. & J. (fl. 18-19th cent.), publishers 192
Rocquefort (Roquefort), Jean Baptiste Bonaventure de (1777-1834), French
     philologist and lexicographer 231
Rogers, Samuel (1763-1855), poet 17
Ronsard, Pierre de (1524-1585), French poet 233
Roscoe, William (1753-1831), historian 175
Rowley, William (1585?-1642?), dramatist 159
Roxburgh, duke of (Ker, John) (1740-1804), book collector 126
Roy, William (fl. 1527-1531), friar and pamphleteer 209
Rubens, Peter Paul (1577-1640), Flemish painter 126
Rutilius, Publius Rufus (fl. 2nd cent. BC), Roman consul 40
Sachs (Sachse) von Löwenheim, Philipp Jakob (1627-1672), German
     physician 75
Sackville, Thomas (1536-1608), dramatist 100
Sade, Laura de (fl. 14th cent.), purported Petrarch model 151
Sallust (Caius Sallustius Crispus) (86-34 BC), Roman historian and politician
     139, 201
Samson, biblical figure 120
Sanchoniathon (Sanchuniathon) (c. 14-13th cent. BC), Phoenecian author
     149, 170